The Specter of Skepticism in the Age of Enlightenment

The Specter of Skepticism in the Age of Enlightenment

ANTON M. MATYTSIN

Johns Hopkins University Press

Baltimore

Johns Hopkins University Press
2715 North Charles Street
Baltimore, Maryland 21218-4363
www.press.jhu.edu

Library of Congress Cataloging-in-Publication Data

Names: Matytsin, Anton M., 1985– author.
Title: The specter of skepticism in the age of Enlightenment /
Anton M. Matytsin.
Description: Baltimore : Johns Hopkins University Press, 2016. | Includes
bibliographical references and index.
Identifiers: LCCN 2015047646 | ISBN 9781421420523 (hardcover : alk. paper) |
ISBN 9781421420530 (electronic) | ISBN 142142052X (hardcover : alk. paper) |
ISBN 1421420538 (electronic)
Subjects: LCSH: Enlightenment. | Skepticism—History—18th century. |
Rationalism.
Classification: LCC B802 .M38 2016 | DDC 190.9/0336—dc23
LC record available at https://lccn.loc.gov/2015047646

A catalog record for this book is available from the British Library.

Special discounts are available for bulk purchases of this book.
For more information, please contact Special Sales at 410-516-6936 or
specialsales@press.jhu.edu.

Johns Hopkins University Press uses environmentally friendly book materials,
including recycled text paper that is composed of at least 30 percent
post-consumer waste, whenever possible.

*To my late grandfather Pavel Vasil'evich Volobuev,
a historian of great integrity whose beautiful
stories taught me to love the past*

CONTENTS

An undertaking of this magnitude is a lonely affair, much like a marathon, but it is also impossible to accomplish without the assistance and moral support of countless individuals. This book owes its inception and its completion to the help of brilliant colleagues, generous organizations, loving friends, and supportive relatives.

Above all others, I must thank Alan Charles Kors, my close friend and former dissertation supervisor at the University of Pennsylvania. This project would never have gotten off the ground without Alan, and it would most certainly not have been finished without his invaluable input. Alan spent countless hours discussing this book with me in its various stages and incarnations, and he read through all the parts of the work with great attention and a critical eye. Most importantly, Alan has taught me how to write, how to think like an intellectual historian, and how to bring the learned world of the eighteenth century to life.

Since this book was completed during my time as Andrew W. Mellon Fellow in the Humanities at Stanford University, I must express my deep gratitude to the Mellon Foundation for its generous funding and to Caroline Winterer and the Stanford Humanities Center for their continued hospitality. Dan Edelstein not only offered me a home in the Department of French and Italian but continuously helped me to reshape my project and to formulate my ideas in the most coherent possible way. He has been a terrific mentor who helped me mature as a scholar during my two years at Stanford. R. Lanier Anderson and J. P. Daughton, the outstanding directors of the Mellon Fellowship, provided me with excellent opportunities to present my research and made important comments on my manuscript. Keith Baker's input helped me to think about incorporating John Locke more fully into my story about the reception of philosophical skepticism. Frederic Clark, whose Mellon Fellowship coincided with mine, spent numerous hours discussing the larger themes of my work and provided extremely useful comments on several chapters of this book. He is also responsible for the more creative chapter names. I am grateful to Thomas Wallnig for his important comments on my last chapter. I would also like to thank Joe Boone and Chloe Edmondson Summers for taking the time to proofread parts of my text at the eleventh hour. I cannot enumerate all the colleagues who offered great ideas over the two years I spent at Stanford, but I must thank Alvan Ikoku, Jessica Riskin, Paula Findlen, Derek Vanderpool, Katie McDonough, Joël Castonguay-Bélanger, Jessica Merrill, Audrey Truschke, and Anne Austin for their input.

I would also like to thank my other mentors at the University of Pennsylvania, where the project originally began as a doctoral dissertation. Ann Moyer—who, like Alan, has known me for the last twelve years and oversaw a number of papers that eventually led me to compose my dissertation—provided excellent comments and critiques throughout the process of writing this book. Peter Holquist, also with this project from its nascent stages, gave me excellent feedback that helped me to revise the text.

Jeffrey D. Burson likewise deserves my deep gratitude for agreeing to serve as an outside member of my dissertation committee and for providing invaluable comments that helped me to revise this work. I must also thank Sébastien Charles, who encouraged me to work on skepticism and anti-skepticism early in my graduate career. The numerous conferences and panels that he organized made essential intellectual contributions to this project and shaped the way I think about skepticism in the eighteenth century. During my time in Paris, Ann Thomson was a most terrific colleague and supervisor. She helped me to obtain the prestigious Chateaubriand Fellowship and introduced me to many *dix-huitièmistes* in France. Her methodological approach to intellectual history and her understanding of eighteenth-century thought have guided my own research. John Christian Laursen also offered tremendously useful and encouraging comments on the nearly completed manuscript, while Darrin M. McMahon helped me to think about the Counter-Enlightenment and its relationship to anti-skeptical thought.

Ideas are often formed most clearly in informal conversations with other scholars. I must therefore thank Robert Ingram and Bill Bulman for organizing the exceptional conference "God in the Enlightenment" at Ohio University, which helped me to formulate important conclusions and clarify the implications of my thesis for understanding the learned world of the eighteenth century. Similarly, I want to express my gratitude to Brad Gregory, Jonathan

Clark, and Jonathan Israel for very fruitful conversations about the meanings of *the Enlightenment* and the relationship between reason and religion in the eighteenth century. I am also grateful to Gianni Paganini, Dario Perinetti, Todd Ryan, Michael Hickson, Rodrigo Brandão, Stephane Pujol, Luiz Eva, and Plínio Junqueira Smith for their ideas about the role of skepticism in eighteenth-century thought.

I could not have done the work that went into this book without the extremely generous assistance of the Lynde and Harry Bradley Foundation, which funded my research for most of my graduate career. The foundation's fellowships allowed me to travel for research and to make presentations at several major international conferences. Likewise, I am indebted to the Institute for Humane Studies for continued and generous funding and mentorship. The IHS's Steve Davies and Phil Magness were wonderful colleagues and mentors, helping me to develop professionally throughout my years as a graduate student. I would also like to express my gratitude to the French Embassy in the United States for generously awarding me the Chateaubriand Fellowship for the 2011–12 academic year. The fellowship allowed me to have access to crucial sources in France, and it opened the door to the world of Parisian academic life.

Finally, I would like to thank my family and friends for their continued support. My mother, Anna Åslund, my stepfather, Anders Åslund, my father, Mikhail Matytsin, and my stepmother, Natalia Mandrova, have all continued to believe in me despite their skepticism about the prospects of pursuing the study of intellectual history professionally. My friends Aziz Lalljee, Neal Nagarajan, Mayra Lujan, Erika Kors, Matthew Gaetano, Andrew Berns, Dan Cheely, Ronan Crepin, Solène Houlle-Crepin, Jean-Luc Leblond, Sári Falus, David Simmons III, Raymond Koytcheff, Deirdre Norris, Allison Pickens, Jessica Scheppmann, Lamar Stevens, João Vitor Fernandes Serra, Sandrine Roux, Lucy Alford, Claude Willan, Fred Donner, Alexander Statman, Lucian Petrescu, and Robby Wilson all provided intellectual and moral support at various stages of this project. During the more difficult parts of this undertaking, I found great encouragement in being surrounded by wonderful people, all of whom continued to have confidence in me even when I did not think I would be able to cross the finish line.

I dedicate this book to my late grandfather. In his integrity as a historian, his moral purity, his persistence in professional and personal matters, and his unwavering adoration he embodied what all scholars and human beings should aspire to be. I regret deeply that he passed away before we could speak as colleagues.

The Specter of Skepticism in the
Age of Enlightenment

Introduction

Pyrrhonism has always grown hand in hand with the revival of letters, and it seems to be at it its highest point today, because philosophy has been brought to more precise demonstrations than ever before by paths that are more enlightened and more certain than the ones followed by our ancestors. It is thus particularly important to attack and destroy [Pyrrhonism] immediately.

—*Histoire des ouvrages des savans* (1697)

The "Age of Reason" and the Specter of Skepticism

A specter was haunting Europe in the early eighteenth century—the specter of skepticism. The revival of this ancient Greek philosophy after the Reformation and its spread across a wide spectrum of disciplines in the 1600s laid the foundations of a true crisis of confidence in the powers of human understanding, casting a long shadow over the European learned world. The call for a total suspension of judgment in all philosophical questions—first advocated by Pyrrho of Elis (360–270 BCE) and recorded in the texts of Sextus Empiricus (160–210 CE)—was based on the assumption that the mind was incapable of obtaining true and certain knowledge of the surrounding world and of its own operations. The rediscovery and appropriation of skeptical arguments by various philosophical schools in the late Renaissance would have a dramatic impact on European intellectual culture. The early modern skeptics were more dogmatic than their ancient forerunners. They expressed doubt concerning the existence of any objective reality that was independent of human perception, questioned long-standing philosophical assumptions, and at times undermined the foundations of political, moral, and religious authorities. Philosophical skepticism—or Pyrrhonism, as it was commonly referred to by contemporaries—was a coherent yet diverse philosophical (or anti-philosophical) movement that became increasingly popular among European savants over the course of the seventeenth century, reaching its apex of popularity at the dawn of the so-called Age of Enlightenment. Although historians frequently associate the Enlightenment with a growing confidence in the powers of human understanding, many overlook the fact that thinkers of this period continued to grapple with the deep challenge of philosophical skepticism. In fact, it was precisely through a set of complex and prolonged engagements with the claims of Pyrrhonism that eighteenth-century thinkers came to redefine the powers and demarcate the limits of human reason.

This book describes the making of a new conception of rationality that emerged during the eighteenth century out of a crucible of debates surrounding philosophical skepticism. It explores the remarkable transition from the "Pyrrhonian crisis" of the early 1700s to a period that is generally associated with a widespread confidence in the ability of the human mind to understand the external world and to use that knowledge with unprecedented audacity.[1] By casting doubt over all received knowledge and questioning accepted methods for gathering true and certain information about the surrounding world, Pyrrhonian claims forced philosophers to formulate the principles and assumptions that they considered to be certain or, at the very least, highly probable. In attempting to answer the deep challenge of philosophical skepticism, these thinkers explicitly articulated the rules of attaining true and certain knowledge and defined the boundaries beyond which human understanding could not venture. Scholars often credit the early modern skeptics with ushering in modernity by providing effective critiques of traditional intellectual authorities. However, their opponents played an equal if not more important role in formulating new criteria of doubt and certainty. While many of the thinkers who undertook refutations of philosophical skepticism did so in order to defend the rational basis of religious belief, they ended up devising the essential intellectual groundwork of the "Age of Reason" that is so frequently associated with critiques of organized religion. By examining the ways in which eighteenth-century thinkers tried either to preserve or to reconstruct the foundations of their world-views and systems of thought, this book explains how these orthodox authors became, ironically, agents of intellectual change.

The debates between the skeptics and their numerous opponents are at the heart of the origin story of modern conceptions of reason, and they help to explain how and why certain forms of rationality came to be privileged over others. The contests over the powers and limits of rational understanding shed light on the fundamental changes in eighteenth-century intellectual culture. These disputes transformed both philosophical skepticism, mitigating its claims, and the various competing theories of knowledge, leading thinkers to regard probability and verisimilitude as acceptable alternatives to metaphysical certainty. The reformulation of assumptions about the extent and limits of rational understanding produced what Keith Baker has termed an "epistemological middle-ground" that emerged "between absolute certainty and absolute doubt."[2] Far from having extreme confidence in the powers of human reason, the most vocal opponents of the established intellectual, religious, and political authorities (including the editors of the audacious *Encyclopédie* project) remained deeply aware of the limits of rational inquiry and the weakness of human understanding. Many eighteenth-century thinkers chose *practicable* reason, concerned with concrete empirical observations of phenomena that affected matters deemed practical and useful, over *speculative* reason, which dealt with abstract metaphysical notions. They accepted probable knowledge as sufficient in most cases, and they focused on questions that could be resolved with recourse to empirically verifiable evidence.

The Age of Skepticism: The *Crise pyrrhonienne* of the Early Eighteenth Century

When I first applied myself to the study of philosophy in my youth, I was very much disturbed by those perpetual disputes of philosophers about all kinds of subjects; and while expecting the great advantages of philosophy, which were so much boasted of, [such as] the knowledge of truth and the tranquility of mind, I was much surprised to find myself plunged into the thick darkness of invincible ignorance and into debates to which I could see no end.

—Pierre-Daniel Huet (1723)[3]

The spirit of dispute was no less prevalent in the Christian schools than in ancient Greek ones. . . . It was thus natural to doubt everything when one found in the systems of the schools, both philosophical and theological, nothing but shadows from beginning to end; matters of dispute in each article, empty/meaningless verbiage in objections, empty/meaningless verbiage in responses.

—Jean-Pierre de Crousaz (1733)[4]

Philosophical skepticism was a rich and variegated intellectual tradition that extended back to antiquity. The ancient Pyrrhonians, who represented one of the branches of skepticism, had enumerated several reasons why they questioned the certainty of the entire spectrum of human knowledge: the inconsistency in sense perceptions and opinions in individuals; the variability of sense experiences among individuals; the consequent plurality of opposing and differing opinions among humankind; the indeterminate relationship between the external world and the way it is represented to the mind; and the lack of a clear criterion of certainty on which one could rely to resolve these various differences.[5] The ancient Pyrrhonians had opposed various dogmatic sects, each of which had claimed to have discovered absolute and definitive truths about the surrounding world. Furthermore, they had asserted that the ultimate conclusion of skepticism was itself inconclusive: the mind could not know anything with certainty, including the veracity of the proposition that the mind could not know anything with certainty.[6]

The rediscovery of Sextus Empiricus's *Outlines of Pyrrhonism* in the late Renaissance and the popularization of Pyrrhonian skepticism in the sixteenth and seventeenth centuries—a process that will be detailed more fully in chapter 1—presented new challenges for European intellectuals. Ancient skepticism found a natural place in a learned culture that was simultaneously grappling with an expanding diversity of ancient philosophies, unsettling encounters with new cultures, and intense religious conflicts following the Reformation. Disputes over the powers and limitations of human reason became ever more complex and variegated when early modern thinkers, beginning with Michel de Montaigne (1533–92), began to apply skepticism to questions of abstract philosophy and to the methodologies of different disciplines. Thinkers from rival philosophical camps often used skeptical arguments merely to undermine opposing positions, without intending to embrace the full conclusions of Pyrrhonism. Through such tactical deployments of skeptical propositions, philosophers could both challenge competing premises and assumptions about the created world and highlight the potential dangers that followed from their opponents' claims.

Skepticism of the late seventeenth century comprised a diverse set of arguments that challenged the truth claims of philosophers, theologians, and historians.[7] Skeptical philosophers disputed the reliability of contemporaneous theories of knowledge, suggesting that there was little reason to assume that sense perceptions corresponded to an objective reality outside the mind. They contended that the variability of sensations, both among individuals and within the same person, served as evidence against the possibility of accurately establishing the nature of the external world or of the mind's operations. Some questioned the new theories of natural philosophy, suggesting that they relied on dubious assumptions and presented systems that were no more reliable or accurate than those of previous centuries. Other skeptics, frequently characterized as impious and generally known as the *libertins érudits*, challenged what they saw as the arbitrary religious and moral orders of their societies and questioned the legitimacy of all ecclesiastical authority. Some distrusted the veracity of their received historical traditions, pointing to apparent forgeries and conspiracies. Still other skeptics, generally identified as fideists, suggested that the inherent weakness of reason rendered faith in the Christian revelation as the only source of certainty.

In addition to comprising a set of philosophical—or anti-philosophical—views, Pyrrhonian skepticism was also perceived as a dangerous threat to the intellectual, religious, and moral fabric of European culture. As we will see in chapter 1, philosophers frequently conjured up the specter of Pyrrhonism and voiced anxiety about the implications that followed from extreme skeptical doubt. Whether it was real or partially imagined and exaggerated, Pyrrhonism preoccupied the minds of numerous seventeenth- and eighteenth-century thinkers. Many of them sought to formulate arguments that would be able to overcome the potential or actual claims of philosophical skepticism. Indeed, numerous thinkers of rival philosophical and theological persuasions shared in the perception of a crisis of philosophical confidence that seemed to hover over their world.

The editors of the Protestant learned periodical *Histoire des ouvrages des savans*—quoted in the epigraph that opens this introduction—noted a peculiar paradox in their review of Pierre de Villemandy's (c. 1636–1703) *Scepticismus debellatus* (1697). Villemandy and his reviewers observed that Pyrrhonism appeared to grow in strength alongside progressive improvements in all aspects of human learning. The Huguenot Villemandy, who had been a professor of philosophy at the Academy of Saumur and director of the Walloon collège in Leiden after the revocation of the Edict of Nantes, attempted to show the moral and intellectual dangers of skepticism and to offer a definitive refutation of this ancient philosophy. Describing Pyrrhonism as a "sect" that was "dangerous and harmful to humankind," he insisted on the necessity and urgency of "stomping it out."[8] Such dramatic calls to arms against philosophical skepticism were quite common in this period, as we will see. Opponents often saw Pyrrhonism as a kind of gateway philosophy that invariably led its disciples toward atheism and moral relativism.

Despite their fundamental disagreements in matters of religion and philosophy, the bishop of Avranches, Pierre-Daniel Huet (1630–1721), and the Swiss Huguenot logician Jean-Pierre de Crousaz (1633–1750) voiced concerns about the apparent crisis of philosophical confidence. They made similar observations about the argumentative nature of their contemporaries. Both believed that endless philosophical and theological debates had resulted in the growing popularity of Pyrrhonism. Huet revealed his commitment to philosophical skepticism in his posthumously published *Traité philosophique de la foiblesse de l'esprit humain* (1723). Crousaz, on the other hand, was a staunch opponent of this philosophical school, and he dedicated much of his scholarly career to attempting to refute its tenets. Nevertheless, both thinkers diagnosed it as a symptom that affected the contentious landscape of their intellectual culture.

The quotation from Huet's *Traité* at the beginning of this section is part of a longer explanation of his educational journey and his eventual embrace of skepticism. His account describes the consequences of the intellectual itinerary of a student who received a traditional education in Aristotelian philosophy, who was attracted by the novelty and apparent simplicity of René Descartes's (1596–1650) metaphysics, who explored the materialist theories of Pierre Gassendi (1592–1655), and who ultimately embraced skepticism because of his thorough disillusionment with all "dogmatic" philosophical systems. The apparent equivalence among the various "sects" of philosophy and the audacity with which each claimed to represent the absolute truth led Huet to doubt the veracity of all philosophical systems and to question the ability of the human mind to obtain any true and certain knowledge of the surrounding world or of its own operations. In a similar manner, Crousaz, who vehemently opposed Pyrrhonism, nevertheless understood that the intense philosophical and theological disputes had led many of his contemporaries to doubt the possibility of ever resolving the most essential questions.

The diversity of the philosophical landscape of the late seventeenth and early eighteenth centuries is truly striking and helps to explain the confusion felt by a scholar such as Huet. Students of philosophy could choose from among Aristotelian Scholasticism, different forms of Neoplatonism, Epicureanism and other forms of atomism, various branches of Cartesian and Malebranchist rationalism, Lockean empiricism, Spinozist monism, Leibnizianism, and other schools of thought. The advocates of these philosophical systems sought to provide complex theories of knowledge, to expound on the nature of the human soul, and to account for the interaction between mind and body. They also endeavored to explain the nature of the physical universe and its creator. Loyal adherents to each school claimed to provide truthful and accurate descriptions of the world and to offer the best possible methods of learning about it. Students and scholars attempted to navigate the minefield of theologically loaded questions and to choose among a variety of competing philosophical explanations. Thinkers often combined elements of multiple competing philosophical systems, thereby adding further confusion and complexity to the intellectual flux that characterized this period.

The ferocious contest between rival schools of philosophy in the late seventeenth and early eighteenth centuries gradually reshaped the fundamental assumptions concerning what the human mind could know about the surrounding world and about its own operations. In seeking to attract followers, proponents of the new systems not only attacked established intellectual authorities, creating what the historian Paul Hazard termed the "crisis of the European mind" (*crise de la conscience européenne*). The intense rivalry among these philosophical schools produced a growing polarization and a mutual destruction of existing systems, leading to an increasing sense of uncertainty. The learned world of the early eighteenth century did indeed experience a "crisis," but it was not, as Hazard famously presented it, a clash between reason and religion, between philosophy and theology. Instead, it was a battle between competing claims to truth— no less intense than the one Hazard imagined—among various schools and sects, and it was waged in multiple areas of human knowledge, including natural philosophy, metaphysics, theology, and history. The defenders of each particular interpretation declared themselves to be *the* most rational and *the* most accurate. Consequently, doubt about religious matters arose not from secular champions of "reason" who dared to attack received theological assumptions but precisely from among those whom Hazard dubbed as *religionnaires*.[9] In seeking to strengthen the rational foundations of religion and to provide the best possible demonstrations of the truth of Christianity, the disciples and representatives of different theological and philosophical schools attacked one another and unintentionally undermined all such rational foundations of belief.[10] Heated debates among adherents of rival philosophical systems had striking theological implications that could easily lead thinkers to abandon the quest for a true understanding of the natural world and to embrace Pyrrhonism. Philosophical skepticism offered an intellectual refuge for those who became weary of the endless philosophical and theological disputes. Skeptical philosophers also used the ongoing debates among the rival philosophical schools as the clearest evidence both of the inability of human reason to obtain certainty and of the mind's tendency to fashion labyrinths from which it could not find a way out.

The growing assault of philosophical skepticism within a variety of disciplines during this intellectually turbulent period prompted an increasing theological and philosophical unease about the perceived negative implications of Pyrrhonism. Intellectuals responded in a variety of ways to the dangers posed by the specter of skepticism. While the French philosophes invoked the superiority of rational inquiry against what they viewed as religious superstition and blind deference to established intellectual authorities, their religious opponents claimed to defend both reason and faith against the irrational attacks of philosophical and religious skeptics. Some launched *ad hominem* attacks against the putative irreverence and irreligion of their skeptical opponents, but they also sought to formulate new methods of proving the existence of God against what they saw as assaults by militant atheists. Others chose to refute the epistemological claims of skepticism by proposing novel foundations for acquiring true and certain knowledge. Still others attempted to articulate new ways of evaluating historical evidence in order to establish a more accurate and solid understanding of the past. The emerging debates over the implications of philosophical skepticism thus had a profound role in shaping the intellectual foundations of the so-called Age of Reason. The relative confidence of Enlightenment thinkers in the powers of human reason did not arise from a radical break with preceding intellectual and scholarly traditions. It developed gradually out of intense contests over the nature and extent of the powers of understanding.

Doubt and Certainty in the Age of Reason

> Today one sees those who carry blindness and insolence to such a degree that they consider themselves superior minds and believe themselves to be more enlightened than other men, even though they dare to prefer the shadows of irreligion to the purest lights of reason and to the brightness of Divine revelation.
> —Jean-Pierre de Crousaz (1733)[11]

> Others, in whom the freedom of thinking serves as reasoning, see themselves as the only true philosophes, because they dared to overthrow the sacred limits posed by religion, and they broke the shackles that faith placed over their reason. . . . Reason is to the philosopher what grace is to the Christian. Grace moves the Christian to act, reason moves the philosophe. Other men are carried away by their passions, their actions not being preceded by reflection: these are the men who walk in darkness; the philosophe, on the other hand, even in his passions acts only upon reflection; he walks in the night, but he is led by a torch. . . . Truth is not for the philosophe a mistress who corrupts his imagination . . . ; he is satisfied to be able to bring

it to light when he is able to perceive it. He certainly does not confuse it with probability; he takes as true that which is true, as false that which is false, as doubtful that which is doubtful, and as probable that which is only probable. He goes further—and here is a great perfection of the philosophe—when he has no proper motive for judging, he remains undecided.

—"Philosophe,"

in the *Encyclopédie* (1765)[12]

Many scholars of the Age of Enlightenment, no matter how differently they may describe the period and the phenomena associated with it, generally identify it with a set of ideas and practices centered on a growing confidence in the powers of human reason. Immanuel Kant's (1724–1804) dictum that enlightenment consisted in the autonomous "use of one's own understanding" is taken as axiomatic, often without consideration of the variety of ways in which thinkers of this period actually defined concepts such as reason and understanding.[13] With the notable exceptions of Keith Baker's work on Condorcet (1743–94), Lorraine Daston's study of the emergence of probability, and Giorgio Tonelli's essays on French and German philosophy, few scholars have emphasized the extent to which Enlightenment thinkers remained concerned about the limits of rational understanding.[14] The eighteenth century, particularly the latter part, is still presented in historical accounts as an "Age of Reason," an "Age of Philosophy," an era of "confidence in the power of human reason," a "dramatic step towards secularization and rationalization," a time of the "adoption of philosophical (mathematical-historical) reason as the only and exclusive criterion of what is true," and a quest "for an exclusively rationalist utopia."[15] Without a doubt, autonomous reason was invoked by numerous thinkers in the long eighteenth century. Some of the most radical participants in the French Revolution went so far as to rename the Notre Dame de Paris and other major cathedrals Temples of Reason (*Temples de la Raison*), thereby adding a material dimension to a reified term. However, the majority of historical accounts overlook the lasting influence of the skeptical critiques of reason that had complex philosophical, religious, and moral implications for European learned culture in the late seventeenth and early eighteenth centuries.

The Enlightenment continues to be so closely associated with the unrestrained rule of reason precisely because during the course of the eighteenth century a particular form of rationality became the commonly accepted, indeed the sole, criterion of truth. Eighteenth-century thinkers frequently invoked reason as the guide to true and certain knowledge of the world, contrasting it with prejudice and the presumptive authority of the past. The propensity to appeal to this new normative authority of reason—one that seems so natural to modern readers—emerged out of a process of contestations over the legitimate sources of certainty. This transformation did not happen overnight, as Hazard implied, but was a result of protracted debates concerning the proper means of procuring true and certain knowledge. It was through the disputes about the proper criteria of truth and the legitimate sources of intellectual authority that a significant number of eighteenth-century thinkers came to embrace a new shared conception of reason, one that was defined by its limits as much as by its ambitions.[16]

The historical process of determining new criteria of truth and certainty is closely bound up with the heroic narratives that were formulated by Enlightenment thinkers and that remain at the heart of the founding myths of modernity. Like the Renaissance humanists, who etched the notion of the "Dark Ages" deep into the minds of posterity, many eighteenth-century intellectuals, above all the French philosophes, formulated influential accounts about their own place in history. Seeking to break with the past, they claimed to live in an enlightened age, one in which the progress of modern science fused with a methodological application of the *esprit philosophique* to bring mankind to an unprecedented apex of intellectual achievement.[17] Overcoming centuries of ignorance, they believed, humanity had finally freed itself from the shackles of political despotism and religious superstition. French revolutionaries such as Maximilien Robespierre (1758–94) and Jean-Paul Marat (1743–93) and critics of the Revolution such as the abbé Augustin Barruel (1741–1820), Edmund Burke (1729–97), and Germaine de Staël (1766–1817) helped to solidify and perpetuate this progressive narrative. The critics portrayed the political upheavals of the 1790s as the inevitable outcomes of a conspiratorial plot of radical philosophes who sought to overthrow the political, social, and religious fabric of the *ancien régime*.[18] *Philosophe* was thus not a superimposed historical description but a term applied to the group by its own members and by its various opponents. As a result, modern scholars face the problem of distinguishing actual historical reality from the myth constructed by those who perceived themselves to be either a part of or diametrically opposed to a distinct group and who had a stake in defining its essence, origins, and mission.

Because the Enlightenment is at the heart of the founding myth of modernity, the term *Enlightenment* remains a deeply contested one among contemporary scholars.[19] Twentieth-century scholars such as Ernst Cassirer and Peter Gay have insisted on the existence of a philosophical essence that united thinkers of "the Enlightenment." Cassirer pointed to "the unity of [the Enlightenment's] conceptual origin and of its underlying principle," characterized most explicitly by "philosophic thought" and a "universal method of reason."[20] Gay, in turn, defined the Enlightenment as the *"philosophes'* rebellion against their Christian world" and identified a concrete "program of the *philosophes"* with a connecting "method and goal."[21] For Gay, the Enlightenment was based primarily in France and encompassed a project of liberal reform aimed at the temporal progress of humanity. Such teleological narratives have reached into the past to identify the roots of modern secular liberalism. These interpretations also took the philosophes' rhetoric at face value. They failed to recognize, as Tonelli has remarked, that "Enlightenment intellectuals, while pretending to substitute the rule of Reason for tradition and authority, were simply substituting for other traditions and authorities some traditions and some authorities which they considered as the true ones."[22]

Indeed, a number of scholars have begun to poke rather large holes in these triumphalist and teleological depictions of the Enlightenment. In critiquing Whiggish accounts that fundamentally overlooked the diversity and plurality of ideas, beliefs, and assumptions of European intellectuals in the long eighteenth century, historians have begun to question the possibility of speaking about a single and uniform "Enlightenment." By decentering France and the philosophes from this narrative and considering more isolated contexts, J. G. A. Pocock insisted on using the plural term *Enlightenments* and on discussing "species of Enlightenment" and talking about "a family of phenomena" in order to avoid latent modernist assumptions.[23] The recent trend in historical literature has involved descriptions of various "micro-Enlightenments."[24] Some scholars have tended to emphasize the national peculiarities of the different Enlightenments, drawing contrasts between, for example, the French Enlightenment and the Scottish, English, and German versions.[25] Others have attempted to construct a scale on which to evaluate the relative standing of Enlightenment ideas, creating distinctions among the "Radical Enlightenment," the "Moderate Enlightenment," and the "Counter-Enlightenment."[26]

Still others have even described the scholarly practices of thinkers who belonged to various religious orders, giving us terms such as *Catholic Enlightenment*[27] or *Theological Enlightenment,*[28] thereby challenging the alleged opposition between the Enlightenment and religion.[29] Dale Van Kley, James Bradley, David Sorkin, S. J. Barnett, Jonathan Sheehan, Jeffrey D. Burson, and Ulrich L. Lehner, among others, have clearly demonstrated that Gay's presentation of a clash between reason and religion and the Whiggish secularization thesis do not accurately reflect the intellectual culture of the eighteenth century.[30] The opposition between faith and reason is a false dichotomy, since the tensions between fideistic mysticism and rationalist accounts were part of intra-Christian debates long before the 1700s.

The fundamental problem with attempts to define objectively some essential feature of the Enlightenment—one that not only is common to various geographical regions but also helps to encompass the wide variety of diverse and often opposing intellectual currents—is that they all inevitably apply a form of ex post facto reasoning. By investing the term *Enlightenment* with certain meanings, most of these interpretations attempt to explain some aspect of the present world by seeking its origins in the past. While the task of determining the genesis of our present world is by no means an unimportant endeavor, our interpretations of the Enlightenment end up revealing more about ourselves and our concerns than they do about the eighteenth century.[31]

The ironic and often unintended outcome of the various "micro-Enlightenment" accounts has been the expansion of the phrase *the Enlightenment* to the point that it can be used to describe almost any aspect of intellectual culture in the long eighteenth century. Indeed, the phrase has been stretched beyond its conceptual utility to such a point that it has lost most of its original meaning. Just as in the case of debates about the Renaissance, the conceptual explosion of the term *Enlightenment* has led historians to use it as a shorthand for "eighteenth-century intellectual culture." *The Enlightenment* has been defined so broadly and extended to so many subgroups, ideas, and practices that it is hardly possible to determine what the Enlightenment was and was not. Everyone, from Benedictine monks engaged in a philological analysis of Scripture, to the members of the nobility discussing materialism in Parisian salons, to Scottish Presbyterians writing historical accounts, was, consciously or not, engaged in the so-called Enlightenment project.[32] As S. J. Barnett recently suggested, "The dividing line between the enlightened and non-enlightened is, at best, often vague."[33] After all, if *the Enlightenment* is merely a placeholder for "eighteenth-century intellectual culture," then the claim that a given thinker or group of intellectuals from the eighteenth century was part of the Enlightenment is both self-evident and redundant.

In some ways, this might be a welcome de-fetishization of an anachronistic name that, at least in its English formulation, was not used until the mid-nineteenth century and was deployed with a specific agenda. Jonathan Clark recently went so far as to claim that the term did not "correspond to any clearly demarcated eighteenth-century phenomena, and could be made to mean whatever its nineteenth- and twentieth-century users wished."[34] However, as much as our understanding of the eighteenth century has been distorted by various modern accounts, it might be worth considering whether we can preserve the notion of the Enlightenment as a distinct historical phenomenon and not merely a construct created by later generations.

One way to address this conceptual failure, brought about as much by anachronistic and ahistorical descriptions that have been imposed on the supposed phenomenon by posterity as by attempts to correct those original misconceptions, is to talk about the Age of Enlightenment as a purely chronological designation. By divesting the term of its philosophical and cultural essences, historians might be able to discuss more productively the sheer variety of intellectual trends, cultural shifts, and social transformations that occurred over the course of the long eighteenth century. This is largely the approach that I adopt in this book in order to avoid the perilous debate about separating the enlightened from the less enlightened, the unenlightened, and those categorically opposed to the Enlightenment project.

Yet another way to solve the problem posed by existing terminology is to examine how thinkers in this period reflected on their own activities. Indeed, if any intellectual or cultural phenomena that could be broadly described as the Enlightenment did indeed occur in eighteenth-century Europe, we might be able determine their existence by investigating if and how participants in the learned culture of that period viewed the nature and goals of their scholarly projects. Dan Edelstein fruitfully pursues this methodology in his interpretive essay on the genealogy of the Enlightenment, in which he analyzes how the participants in the vibrant debates of the eighteenth century understood their own place in the process of historical development and how they perceived their intellectual culture as being distinct from the past.[35] Historians may point to the infinite diversity of various "Enlightenments" and question the essential differences between those included in the Enlightenment canon and those excluded from it. Nevertheless, it remains an undisputed fact that there were groups in France, in the German principalities, and in Scotland, among other places, who perceived themselves as participating in a concrete philosophical project. What united them was not necessarily a more rational attitude toward knowledge. Rather, it was the act of self-reflection about their activities that, in the minds of these groups, made them "enlightened." The "idea of the Enlightenment," expressed as the "awareness . . . that a particular action belonged to a set of practices considered 'enlightened,'" was a meta-reflection, or a "second-order observation," that provided coherence to various intellectual and cultural developments.[36]

This self-identification was by no means uncontested. As Sylviane Albertan-Coppola, Didier Masseau, and Darrin McMahon have demonstrated, religious apologists and the defenders of the established order quickly adopted the rhetoric of their philosophe opponents.[37] Each faction declared itself to be defending light against darkness and to be representing reason against fanaticism and ignorance.[38] In most cases, the question that was most divisive for the parties claiming to fight in favor of light, at least in the French-speaking world, concerned the appropriate role of organized religion in the maintenance of society and in the quest for knowledge about the natural world. Among other things, the philosophes explicitly denounced the privileged role of the Catholic clergy, the superstition and irrationality of faith-based claims, religious intolerance and enthusiasm, and the arbitrary power of the Crown and the nobility. The religious apologists, in turn, not only articulated a priori and a posteriori proofs of the existence of God but also made utilitarian and temporal arguments against the potential chaos and disorder that would result from the abandonment of religious belief in general and of the Christian belief in the immortality of the soul in particular. As illustrated by the words of the Swiss Huguenot logician Jean-Pierre de Crousaz cited at the beginning of this section, however, those who defended religion certainly perceived themselves to be championing reason and promoting enlightenment as much as the philosophes.

The question of self-definition is a crucial one. As each new generation of scholars composes its own history of the Enlightenment, attempting to define it according to a set of objective criteria, eighteenth-century narratives continue to shape modern views of the period on a subconscious level. Numerous scholars do not see a clear opposition between reason and religion during the eighteenth century and wish to argue for the plurality of "Enlightenments" precisely because a vast majority of claims, whether they were articulated by the philosophes or by their opponents, evoked reason and *évidence* as the criteria of truth. If one looks at eighteenth-century discourses, one easily identifies a great number of claims that establish their own validity by an appeal to autonomous reason. However, few scholars have analyzed the various equivocal uses of the term *reason* or questioned the self-referential status of such claims in the Enlightenment. This relative neglect leaves us in the dark about the very nature of what scholars implicitly or explicitly identify as the Age of Reason.

Anti-Skepticism and the Defense of Reason

Reason itself, of course, is not a stable universal concept but a historically determined notion whose definitions evolved over time. In the late seventeenth and early eighteenth centuries, *reason*, or *raison*, had several meanings. Derived from the Latin root *ratio*, it was related to the definition of man as a rational being, one possessing a "rational soul" (*anima rationalis*) as opposed to the merely "sensitive soul" (*anima sensitiva*) of animals. In its most literal sense, *reason* signified a faculty that was universal to human beings and distinguished them from other sentient beings. The first entry for *raison* in the *Dictionnaire de l'Académie françoise* (1694) defined it as "a power of the soul, by which man can speak and is distinguished from beasts."[39] César de Rochefort's (1630–c. 1690) *Dictionnaire général et curieux* (1685) described reason as a God-given faculty that helped human beings to preserve themselves, made them "masters of the world," and compensated for all of their "imperfections." Reason placed people above all other creatures, Rochefort argued, by allowing them to participate in God's "most noble perfection" through the contemplation of the most distant parts of the created universe.[40]

According to the majority of definitions, the distinction between humans and other living creatures consisted in the ability of the former to generalize and to form categories of universals on the basis of particular observations. Rochefort's *Dictionnaire général et curieux* and César-Pierre Richelet's (1626–98) *Dictionnaire françois* (1680) both defined *reason* as the "power of the soul that distinguishes the false from the true."[41] A reasonable person was someone who possessed "sense and judgement" or was "wise" and "judicious."[42] A person deprived of reason, by contrast, had "entirely lost good sense and . . . fallen into dementia" and had become similar to a beast, according to the *Dictionnaire de l'Académie françoise*. *Reason* also referred to the ability to argue coherently and provide a proof or demonstration.[43] The 1762 edition of the *Dictionnaire de l'Académie françoise* added another clause to the entry "Raison," suggesting that reason was also "the faculty of drawing conclusions."[44] By observing individual occurrences, the mind could construct patterns and generate universal determinations about those occurrences. Reason was thus seen as the capacity to reflect on individual sense perceptions, to draw causal inferences, to make generalizations, and to think abstractly.

While most thinkers agreed that reason was a faculty unique to human beings and described its various operations in similar ways, they debated its powers, limitations, and appropriate applications. Antoine Furetière's (1619–88) *Dictionnaire universel* (1690) defined *reason* as "the first power of the soul that discerns the good from the bad, the false from the true." However, the entry immediately noted that "reason is often a misleading guide." Furetière's definition distinguished between "mysteries of the faith that cannot be proved by reason," because they were "above reason, and not against it"; geometrical proofs that were "demonstrative" and "convincing"; and "other sciences," in which demonstrations were "merely probable and plausible [*vraisemblables*]."[45] The *Dictionnaire de l'Académie françoise* defined the term *reason* as "the good sense" and "the proper use of reason," implying that the word referred both to the faculty and to the appropriate use of that faculty.[46] The rules for the "proper use of reason," such as the law of identity, the principle of noncontradiction, and the ordering of mental operations, appeared in a variety of early modern textbooks on logic. As Antoine Arnauld (1612–94) and Pierre Nicole (1625–95) announced in the opening of their highly influential *Port-Royal Logic* (1662), reason was a faculty that enabled people to distinguish the false from the true, the light from the dark, and to navigate the path toward an exact and certain knowledge. By meticulously and methodically applying the rules of logic to their reflections, people could avoid both error and skepticism, thereby perfecting the faculty of reason and guiding it toward the truth.[47]

The ability of reason to act as a means to and a guarantor of true and certain knowledge was by no means undisputed. The philosophical skeptics often challenged the validity of indubitable logical principles by pointing to instances in which the inner workings of logic appeared to unravel and fail. They insisted that the mind relied on imperfect senses and drew conclusions on the basis of questionable and uncertain evidence. The skeptics thus maintained that human reason was a frequently fallible and generally inadequate tool for obtaining a reliable knowledge about human nature, the world, and humanity's place in it.

This conclusion had implications both for philosophy and for religion. Fideistic skeptics attempted to demonstrate the weakness of natural reason in order to champion supernatural faith in the Christian revelation as the only true source of certainty. Their opponents, however, insisted that by questioning the rational basis of religion, the fideists intentionally or unintentionally subverted Christianity. Indeed—and this is perhaps the most unexpected element in this story—the majority of thinkers who championed the powers of human reason during the first half of the eighteenth century did so in order to defend the rational foundations of revealed religion against such skeptical attacks. While many of these opponents of skepticism believed that they lived in an enlightened age, they perceived the dangerous consequences that Pyrrhonism could have both for the intellectual and moral improvement of humankind and for the foundations of their faith. They rallied against the so-called enemies of reason both by attacking their allegedly unenlightened opponents and by reformulating the criteria of certainty and probability. If we are thus to continue associating the

Enlightenment with the self-reflexive confidence in the powers of human reason, we certainly have to acknowledge the important role played by the religious opponents of skepticism.

Historical scholarship about the skeptical revival and its influence on eighteenth-century figures such as David Hume (1711–76) and Immanuel Kant is quantitatively impressive and qualitatively outstanding. Richard Popkin offered the most extensive and authoritative interpretations of the origins and influence of early modern skepticism. The final edition of his *History of Scepticism* traces the evolution of this philosophical school from the Renaissance to the early eighteenth century.[48] Popkin's interpretations remain widely influential, and his general observations continue to inspire studies on particular skeptical philosophers.[49] However, Popkin's declared affinity for his protagonists' philosophical views and his suggestion that the "confidence" of the thinkers of the French Enlightenment was "too strong to see any message in the pyrrhonian tradition" are problematic for a historical understanding of the role of skeptical thought in this period.[50] Indeed, later in his career Popkin himself revised his view to suggest that various forms of philosophical skepticism were "more pervasive" in Enlightenment philosophy than he had initially claimed.[51]

Recent reconsiderations of Popkin's initial interpretation of the declining role of skepticism in eighteenth-century thought have offered new avenues for exploration. These studies have shown that while Enlightenment philosophers rarely agreed with the full conclusions of Pyrrhonian skepticism, many embraced aspects of skepticism and recognized the limits of human understanding.[52] Jonathan Israel's impressive account of the Enlightenment and of its origins stresses the important role of heterodox ideas in undermining the foundations of established theological systems. Israel identifies the rationalist ideas of Baruch Spinoza (1632–77)—rather than philosophical skepticism—as the main source of intellectual change, but he also depicts Pierre Bayle (1647–1706) and other skeptics as close allies of the so-called Radical Enlightenment.[53] In addition, scholars have presented Bayle as a progenitor of the Enlightenment and traced the influence of his views regarding religious toleration, civil society, and philosophical certainty on Voltaire (1694–1778) and other philosophes.[54]

While these accounts have offered important contributions to intellectual history, many suffer from one common deficiency. By overemphasizing the importance and influence of philosophical skepticism, scholars have tended to offer unintentionally triumphalist narratives of skepticism and its impact. The nature and influence of the assertions of the skeptics have received significant attention, while anti-skeptical arguments have been dismissed as having no agency and have been generally relegated to the background. As a result, skeptical ideas have frequently appeared in a sort of intellectual vacuum, as though they evolved through discussions among the skeptics alone rather than out of debates within the diverse intellectual community of the time. An analysis of anti-skeptical claims will enrich our understanding of eighteenth-century thought by explaining how the debates about the powers of human reason actually developed in the context of the learned culture's multifaceted discourse.

In studying the refutations of philosophical skepticism, this book presents the vital but lesser-known side in the debates surrounding Pyrrhonism, and it highlights the important role that the opponents of skepticism played in framing essential deliberations of the Age of Enlightenment. By focusing on ideas and on figures for their importance at the time rather than for their resemblance to modern notions or their current philosophical appeal, this book reveals the variety and vibrancy of intellectual discourse in this period. Such a historical analysis does not seek to undermine the important role of skepticism or of other radical philosophical ideas, but it places them in a wider context of the debates and concerns that preoccupied the learned world of the eighteenth century. Ultimately, the nature and origins of the alleged confidence in the powers of human reason will be better understood when viewed not as an inevitable outcome but as a product of animated disputes among thinkers who knew little about the fate that awaited their intellectual culture.

Locating Anti-Skepticism

The revival of skeptical philosophy set down the deepest roots in the French-speaking world, making France the protagonist in any discussion of skepticism and anti-skepticism. Following the revocation of the Edict of Nantes in 1685, a number of prominent Huguenot intellectuals left France for Switzerland, England, the Dutch Republic, and various German principalities. The French émigrés remained in close contact with their Catholic counterparts in Paris through private correspondence. A number of French works were published in England and in the Netherlands because of the relatively lenient censorship in those countries. As the learned cultures of Europe became more integrated in the late 1600s, thinkers engaged in debates surrounding skepticism began to draw on the arguments of their foreign counterparts.

While France and the French-speaking world are at the center of this story, England remains an important point of reference for debates about the powers and limits of human reason. As we will see, English natural philosophers appropriated the arguments of philosophical skepticism in the early seventeenth century and deployed these arguments to critique Aristotelian Scholasticism. At the same time, they advanced a program of experimental philosophy that emphasized observation and induction over the a priori methods of Continental rationalism. By conceding their ignorance about the underlying nature of reality, the English natural philosophers were able to incorporate some of the skeptical arguments while forgoing the ultimate conclusions of Pyrrhonism. The tradition of experimental philosophy and empiricism thus defused some of the debates about skepticism—at least until Hume's intervention—while the rational systems of Descartes and his followers attracted the brunt of the skeptical critiques.

Delimiting the years of intellectual disputes is a difficult task. Philosophical concepts have complex and longstanding origins, and they rarely appear or disappear suddenly. Any chronological delimitation is thus partly arbitrary yet necessary for coherent enquiry. This book focuses on the period between 1697, the year of the first appearance of Pierre Bayle's famous *Dictionnaire historique et critique*, and 1772, when the publication of the *Encyclopédie* was fully completed. Historians consider the controversy surrounding the *Dictionnaire* to be the apex of the *crise pyrrhonienne*, while the *Encyclopédie* is frequently depicted as the ultimate expression of the Enlightenment's confidence in the power of human reason. These two works thus serve as logical limits for the investigation of such an apparently dramatic transformation. A broad chronological scope helps to account for the gradual nature of intellectual change. The debates about the powers and limits of human reason did not cause an abrupt mental shift, as Hazard has suggested, but instead led to a protracted modification in views of the purposes and scope of rational enquiry.

This book begins by exploring several distinct though frequently overlapping intellectual circles in order to establish the various motivations and strategies of thinkers who were concerned with the threat of Pyrrhonism. The early chapters thus examine the full spectrum of the discourses surrounding philosophical skepticism. Chapter 1 offers a brief history of the revival of ancient skepticism and explains why many eighteenth-century thinkers saw it as such a dangerous and controversial philosophical stance. It also outlines the broad intellectual spectrum of thinkers who identified themselves as the opponents of skepticism and considers the rhetorical strategies these thinkers employed in order to undermine skeptical claims. Chapter 2 discusses the complexity of interpreting Pierre Bayle's influential formulation of skepticism and places him in the context of his debates with his *rationaux* opponents in the Dutch Republic. In chapter 3 the focus returns to France, where attempts by Catholic thinkers and anti-skeptics to refute Bayle continued well into the mid-1700s. Chapter 4 explores the reactions to the posthumous publication of Huet's skeptical treatise and explains why Huet's seemingly pious arguments appeared so controversial to the intellectual world of the 1720s. Chapter 5 describes how, following the appearance of the first French translation of Sextus Empiricus's *Hipotiposes pirroniennes* (1725), thinkers attempted to provide accommodations to skeptical critiques by proposing verisimilitude and probability as sufficient goals of rational inquiry. Chapter 6 examines the common strategies deployed by critics of skepticism in Switzerland, the Netherlands, and Prussia and shows how intellectuals concerned with refuting Pyrrhonism reassessed the nature and limits of humanity's rational faculties.

The last four chapters investigate how the debates between the skeptics and their various opponents functioned in the context of various disciplines and fields of knowledge. Chapter 7 focuses on debates in epistemology and describes a fundamental shift from a search for metaphysical certainty to an increased emphasis on moral certainty and probability. It investigates the philosophical criteria that anti-skeptical thinkers offered to undermine the radical claims of their opponents, considers the principles they held to be indubitable and self-evident, and probes the fundamental assumptions about the nature of reality and of human knowledge that made such principles reliable. Chapter 8 examines the debates concerning the nature and composition of matter, and chapter 9 looks at the contest between Cartesian and Newtonian accounts of planetary motion. The disputes highlighted in these two chapters present a particularly curious case of the interaction between skepticism and anti-skepticism, because it was natural philosophy—above all other disciplines— that offered the most resilient model for accommodating and simultaneously mitigating the claims of Pyrrhonian skepticism. Finally, chapter 10 reveals the strategies thinkers of the early Enlightenment adopted to defend the historical tradition in which they all developed. It explains how an intellectual culture reconstituted the foundations of historiography in response to skeptical assaults and reveals how this culture rethought its approaches to textual and material evidence about the past.

The dialogical interaction between skeptical claims and anti-skeptical rebuttals led to a gradual reexamination of the most basic epistemological principles. First, the debates about the limits of rational understanding transformed philosophical and historical enquiries by leading intellectuals to abandon the quest for absolute certainty and to accept probability as an adequate compromise. Second, these disputes fundamentally changed the nature of skepticism by making its claims more mitigated and reserved. Instead of embracing a complete suspension of judgment in all questions, Enlightenment thinkers avoided the ultimate conclusions of philosophical skepticism but deployed its claims as tactical weapons of criticism. The chapters that follow shed light on these fundamental intellectual transformations.

PART ONE

THE SPECTRUM OF ANTI-SKEPTICISM

CHAPTER ONE

The Walking Ignorant

The Skeptical "Epidemic" in the Eighteenth Century

The Rediscovery of Pyrrhonism and the Fideist Tradition

Although the arguments of ancient skepticism dealt exclusively with philosophical matters, they had significant implications for religious questions in early modern Europe, where theology and philosophy were deeply interrelated. Consequently, the revival of skepticism during the Renaissance and its proliferation during the seventeenth century must be understood in the context of Reformation debates about the proper sources and criteria of religious knowledge.[1] The transposition of philosophical claims about the weakness of human reason onto theological questions could serve simultaneously as a defense of the Catholic Church's indispensable role as the only rightful interpreter of God's word and as a challenge to the rational foundations of Christianity. This tension would define the controversial attitudes toward philosophical skepticism in subsequent debates about the nature of human understanding.

Until the sixteenth century, Cicero's (106–43 BCE) *Academica*, Lactantius's (240–320) *Divinae institutiones*, and Saint Augustine's (354–430) *Contra academicos* were the main sources of philosophical skepticism.[2] The translation of the ancient works of Sextus Empiricus offered an alternative known as Pyrrhonian skepticism (named after its alleged founder, Pyrrho of Elis). The distinction between the two forms of skepticism dates back to ancient Greece, where thinkers had formulated one of two general claims: the first set of assertions, associated with Academic skepticism, proposed that no certain knowledge was attainable; the second set, defined as Pyrrhonian skepticism, maintained that there was insufficient evidence to determine whether any true and indubitable knowledge was attainable.[3]

Academic skepticism aimed to demonstrate that no dogmatic proposition— one that claimed certainty about the real nature of things—could be verified with absolute conviction. The Academics claimed that the evidence of any proposition had to be based on either sense perception or rational reflection, and they argued that both faculties were unreliable. Consequently, they maintained that complete certainty was unattainable and that all knowledge was probable at best. The Academic school derives its name from the evolution of the Platonic Academy, and its founding tenet was articulated in the third century BCE in the famous Socratic observation "All I know is that I know nothing."[4] This formulation, generally attributed to Arcesilaus (c. 315–c. 240 BCE) and Carneades (214–c. 128 BCE), was passed down in the works of Cicero and Saint Augustine.[5] While the Academic school had a long intellectual tradition, its tenets were generally not applied to theological matters.

Pyrrhonian skepticism traces its origins to Pyrrho of Elis and his student Timon of Phlius (c. 320–c. 230 BCE). Considering both the dogmatists and the Academics to be extreme, the Pyrrhonians proposed to suspend judgment on all questions that seemed to rely on conflicting evidence. For them, skepticism was a state of mind, not a philosophical commitment to a particular set of views. Indeed, the Pyrrhonians maintained, the proposition that nothing could be known with certainty, if drawn out to its full conclusion, would have to include itself: nothing could be known with certainty, including the assertion that nothing could be known with certainty. By suspending judgment with respect to all philosophical questions, a Pyrrhonian skeptic would then achieve a state of *ataraxia*, peace of mind or quietude.[6] The basic surviving text of this ancient school, generally called the *Pyrrhonianae hypotyposes* (*Outlines of Pyrrhonism*), was written by Sextus Empiricus at the beginning of the third century in Alexandria.[7] Sextus also composed the *Adversus mathematicos*, in which he subjected logic, mathematics, astrology, and grammar to skeptical refutations. Unlike Academic skepticism, which influenced the Middle Ages through the filter of Saint Augustine's attempted refutations, Pyrrhonian skepticism remained virtually unknown until the rediscovery of Sextus's manuscripts in the fifteenth century and the Latin publication of the *Outlines of Pyrrhonism* in 1562.[8] Within a century and a half, Pyrrhonism would displace the Academic tradition as the primary articulation of ancient skeptical thought, and the term *Pyrrhonism* would become virtually synonymous with *skepticism* in philosophical discussions.[9]

Almost immediately after its reappearance, Sextus's *Outlines* became a tool used by both Catholic and Protestant theologians in the debates surrounding the role of natural reason in interpreting scripture. Some Catholic apologists saw Pyrrhonian arguments about the weakness of human reason as powerful counterclaims against the Protestant insistence on the principle of *sola scriptura* (by scripture alone), the notion that all religious truths necessary for salvation were contained in the Bible and that Christians could obtain this knowledge through individual readings of the Holy Writ. By emphasizing the weakness of human understanding, some Catholic theologians attempted to preserve the indispensable role of the Church in interpreting the Word of God. The Protestants, in turn, argued that the Catholic Church's interpretations of scripture were still performed by fallible human authorities who could not claim to offer absolute certainty in theological matters.

Within both Protestant and Catholic theology, there existed a significant division between those who believed that major theological doctrines were rationally demonstrable and accessible to human reason and those who thought that given the fall from grace, humankind was incapable of understanding God's will without supernatural revelation. The theological disagreement derived from the tension between the self-proclaimed followers of Saint Augustine and those of Saint Thomas Aquinas (1225–74). Many early modern Augustinians stressed the fatal consequences of the fall, arguing that it inherently corrupted human understanding and that people could never obtain true and certain knowledge without divine guidance. The Thomists generally disputed such a negative view of the human condition. They remained confident that true and certain understanding, including proofs of the existence of God, could be arrived at a posteriori, from the experience of the external world.[10]

Among French Catholics, this distinction manifested itself in the clash between the Jansenists, who tended to be more pessimistic about the capacity of the unguided human mind, and the Jesuits, who largely held a more optimistic view of reason's abilities.[11] Within the Huguenot community, there was an analogous split between the fideists and the *rationaux*. The former sought to demonstrate that humans were incapable of understanding God's designs and intentions. They pointed to the apparent incomprehensibility of many scriptural passages, and they sought to liberate theology from philosophical debates. Often, they questioned the very foundations of metaphysics, logic, and natural philosophy. The latter argued for a less antagonistic opposition between reason and faith, claiming that the fideists undermined Christianity by doubting the rational bases of religious truths.[12]

Michel de Montaigne's "Apologie de Raimond Sebond," in his *Essais* (1580), is considered to be the first major early modern presentation of Pyrrhonian thought. Montaigne was one of the earliest thinkers to use skeptical arguments to support Catholicism against Protestant reform. The work claimed to defend the fifteenth-century Spanish theologian Raimond Sebond (c. 1385–1436), who had maintained that all the articles of the Christian religion could be demonstrated by natural reason. Montaigne's "defense" of Sebond was in fact a refutation. He first presented a theory of Christianity that relied exclusively on faith and then attempted to demonstrate that all reasoning was unsound, showing that Sebond should not be blamed for his theoretical errors.[13] Montaigne did not oppose the use of reason to support belief, but he concluded that faith did not depend on any rational arguments. Given the feebleness of human reason, Montaigne maintained, any philosophical claim made in defense of faith had to assume the truth of divine revelation. He argued against Protestant appeals to the principle of *sola scriptura*, criticized some of his fellow Catholics for selectively subjecting certain doctrines to doubt, and urged his readers to "either submit completely to the authority of our ecclesiastical government or do without it entirely."[14]

Montaigne's was a crucial statement in the context of Reformation and Counter-Reformation currents because it provided a skeptical basis for the defense of the authority of the Catholic Church against the critiques of the Reformers. The concept of *scriptura sola* stipulated that interpretive authority beyond scripture was superfluous, since each believer could arrive at an individual understanding of truth by reading the Bible. This argument directly challenged the Catholic reliance on the doctrinal interpretation of the Church, and it led Catholic apologists such as Francisco Suarez (1548–1617) to emphasize that the meaning of scripture was not as obvious and transparent as some of the Protestants had contended. Suarez insisted that the Bible could be understood only with the aid of the inspired authority of the Church.[15] In order to combat the rationalist critiques of the Calvinists, Gentian Hervet (1499–1584), the humanist secretary to the cardinal of Lorraine, assisted in the translation and publication of and wrote the preface to the 1569 Latin edition of Sextus Empiricus's *Adversus mathematicos*.[16] In the preface, Hervet argued that by exhibiting the sheer difficulty of understanding the natural world, Sextus's system would demonstrate to the Calvinists the futility of applying human reason to supernatural matters.[17]

By posing a series of skeptical difficulties with respect to scriptural interpretation, these and other Catholic thinkers sought to challenge reason as the criterion that distinguished true faith from false belief and to propose the authority of the Church as the only guarantor of religious truth.[18] Although they generally relied on Pyrrhonian arguments less frequently than their Catholic counterparts, Protestant thinkers similarly deployed skeptical claims to dispute the infallibility of the Church.[19] By challenging all rational foundations of religious belief, some Catholic apologists appeared to undermine the foundations of Christianity.

This potential consequence would create significant intra-Catholic tensions in post-Reformation thought.

Despite its unintended pitfalls, Montaigne's formulation of Christian Pyr-rhonism was expanded in the seventeenth century by the priest and philoso-pher Pierre Charron (1541–1603), who combined skeptical arguments with the major anti-rationalist currents in Christian theology. In *Les trois veritez* (1593), Charron argued that because of humanity's "weakness and the greatness of God," reason could not furnish a "sufficient demonstration" of God's existence and God's nature.[20] For Charron, God was unknowable for two reasons: because he was infinite and because humankind was incapable of knowing anything with certainty. Human beings thus had to rely on faith in the Christian revela-tion and on the Church's interpretation of scripture. Like Montaigne, Charron attempted to show that Christianity was the only true religion and that the Catholic Church represented its only veritable interpretation.[21]

Along with Charron, the prominent fideistic skeptic François de La Mothe Le Vayer (1588–1672) continued to champion the tradition well into the 1600s.[22] In *Opuscule, ou Petit traité sceptique* (1646), La Mothe Le Vayer questioned the human ability to know with certainty any natural truths about the real world. He cited the fallibility of the senses, the human inability to recognize the truth, and the absence of any criteria of truth as the major sources of the weakness of human reason.[23] He maintained that people could not obtain an objective knowledge of the real world but could only know their surroundings subjec-tively and imperfectly. In the *Soliloques sceptiques* (1670), La Mothe Le Vayer denied that man was a rational animal, claiming instead that he was an "animal desiring knowledge" but never able to attain it.[24]

By revealing the full extent of human ignorance, La Mothe Le Vayer argued, Pyrrhonism would persuade humankind of the futility of rational inquiry and of debates in natural philosophy.[25] It would also demonstrate the absence of any absolute truths within the general system of human knowledge, which was "nothing but a collection of opinions contested by those who have time to exam-ine them in depth."[26] Moving against the intellectual currents that gave increased attention to natural philosophy, La Mothe Le Vayer equally opposed Baconian empiricism and Cartesian rationalism. He saw them as fashionable systems that had become popular primarily because of their novelty, and not because they offered any actual enhancement of the ability to understand the physical world.

Much like other fideists, La Mothe Le Vayer asserted that given their fee-ble reason and untrustworthy senses, human beings had to accept faith in the Christian revelation as the only source of true and certain knowledge.

He believed that in addition to saving man from an interminable search for truth, skepticism proved useful for religion:

> Those who possess humility and ignorance at all times are much better accommodated [to receive the lights of faith] than those who are in spiritual darkness. The dogmatists, on the contrary, who have never had a stronger concern than to make others appear ignorant, became uncontrollably lost [in spiritual matters]; and their presumption of having enough light of understanding to overcome every manner of obscurity blinds them with every step that they advance into the shadows that humanity cannot penetrate. I find that skepticism is of no little use to a Christian soul, because it makes the soul surrender all those magisterial opinions that Saint Paul so strongly detests.[27]

Comparing the "soul of a Christian skeptic" to "a field cleared and purged of bad plants," La Mothe Le Vayer contended that total skepticism allowed human beings to attain a perfect belief in the essential tenets of Christianity.[28] A skeptic's mind would not hold any opinions contrary to the true faith, because it would have accepted the fallibility of natural human reason. The soul would have no choice but to turn toward faith in revelation for certainty and peace.

In the late seventeenth century, fideist arguments were also taken up and popularized in the Protestant context by the controversial philosopher and prolific journalist Pierre Bayle. Although a Protestant, Bayle claimed that he followed the fideist tradition of Montaigne and Charron, and he consistently voiced concerns about overly rationalist approaches to Christian theology.[29] The *philosophe de Rotterdam*, as he came to be known, made an explicit plea for the usefulness of Pyrrhonism in promoting religious belief. Although he began his article on Pyrrho by claiming that Pyrrhonism was dangerous to theology and religion, he concluded on a very different note:

> When one is able to grasp fully the ways of suspending judgment described by Sextus Empiricus, one sees that this logic is the greatest effort of subtlety that the human mind could accomplish; but at the same time, one sees that this subtlety is unsatisfactory: it confounds itself; for if it were solid, it would prove that it is certain that one must doubt [all things]. There would then be some certainty, one would have some sure rule of truth. . . . The reasons for doubting are themselves doubtful: one must doubt whether it is necessary to doubt. What great chaos and what a torment for the mind! It thus seems that this unfortunate state is most appropriate for persuading us that our reason is a path that leads us astray, since when it displays itself with the greatest subtlety, it plunges us into such an abyss.

The natural conclusion of this ought to be to renounce this guide and to implore the cause of all things to give us a better one. This is a great step toward the Christian religion, for it requires that we look to God for knowledge of what we ought to believe and what we ought to do and that we enslave our understanding to the obedience of faith. If a man is convinced that nothing good is to be expected from his philosophical inquiries, he will be more disposed to pray to God to persuade him of the truths that ought to be believed than if he flatters himself that he might succeed by reasoning and disputing.[30]

Like La Mothe Le Vayer, Bayle contended that Pyrrhonism humbled the human mind and prepared it to accept the mysteries of the Christian faith more readily.

After the publication of the first edition of the *Dictionnaire*, critics attacked Bayle for offering expositions of various heretical doctrines. Bayle defended himself in the "Clarifications" that he added to the second edition, claiming that he aimed to demonstrate that the mysteries of Christianity were incomprehensible to human reason. Any attempt to resolve these mysteries philosophically would merely result in paradoxes:

It is evident that reason will never be able to reach that which is above it, for if it were able to provide answers to objections against the dogma of the Trinity and the hypostatic union, it would be able to understand these two mysteries. . . . It would therefore accomplish that which surpasses its powers, which is contradictory. It must therefore be admitted that it cannot furnish responses to its own objections and that they remain victorious so long as one does not appeal to the authority of God and to the necessity of submitting one's understanding to the obedience of faith.[31]

Bayle expressed the most fundamental fideistic argument and, at the same time, exposed his intentions. Like Montaigne, Charron, and La Mothe Le Vayer, Bayle argued that the most basic tenets of Christianity had to be approached through faith and not through philosophical enquiries. Pyrrhonism was useful for demonstrating the weakness of natural reason and consequently for leading people to find refuge in supernatural belief.

Bayle's explicit fideism was attacked by his contemporaries as an insincere argument, and many critics accused him of being a secret atheist. While his position ran contrary to the main currents of Calvinist theology, Bayle's faith-based defense of religion would be in some ways less controversial than the one undertaken by his Catholic counterpart Pierre-Daniel Huet. Known as one of the leading biblical exegetes of his time, the young Huet tried to reconcile pagan sources with the Bible and to provide a mathematical proof of the veracity of Christianity in the *Demonstratio evangelica* (1679).[32] He combined moral axioms taken from scripture with the structure of a geometrical proof: "I imagined a new path might be struck out, different from the trodden ones, but certain, plain, and direct, leading to a demonstration of that truth, not less clear and indubitable than the argumentative processes of geometricians, who boast that they do not persuade, but compel conviction."[33]

Despite this ambitious attempt, Huet had already begun to question the ability of human reason to provide true and certain knowledge about the surrounding world or to furnish demonstrations of the existence of God. In commenting on Blaise Pascal's (1623–62) citation of Saint Augustine's claim that "reason would never submit unless she perceived appropriate occasions to do so,"[34] Huet went even further: "He supposes that this submission should depend on reason, but it seems to me that, on the contrary, to submit reason to faith is more of a feat of faith than of reason. Reason and faith are equally imperious, and neither would ever agree to submit to the other unless it were done involuntarily, by violence and opposition. Therefore, one of the two must defeat the other, and it is up to faith to make reason submit, not otherwise."[35] In Huet's view, the struggle between reason and faith was much more contentious than Pascal had imagined. For him, reason had to be coaxed into submission, because it would never voluntarily accept its inferiority.

Huet embraced philosophical skepticism early in his scholarly career, but he was reluctant to reveal his commitment openly for fear of criticism. Indeed, when his treatise was published posthumously in 1723, it created an uproar among his closest friends. While Huet's pious intentions were shared by those who criticized his skeptical treatise, his tactics appeared excessively unconventional to them. Huet sought to persuade his contemporaries to abandon rational arguments concerning the existence of God and the immortality of the soul and to accept these fundamental articles of Christianity on faith alone. Reliance on supernatural belief was the only thing that could, in his view, prevent the complete overthrow of established intellectual and religious authorities.

The Varieties of Early Modern Skepticism

Religious apologists were, of course, far from the only intellectuals to appropriate the arguments of Sextus Empiricus for their own purposes. The claims of Pyrrhonian skepticism proved to be an appealing tool in a variety of debates in several fields, such as epistemology, natural philosophy, and biblical criticism.

One did not need to embrace the full conclusions of Pyrrhonism in order to deploy its particular arguments tactically in attempting to refute the positions of one's opponents.

One notable set of uses of Sextus's *Pyrrhonianae hypotyposes* can be seen in the various challenges to the Aristotelian natural philosophy that continued to dominate universities in early modern Europe. Marin Mersenne (1588–1648) and Pierre Gassendi (1592–1655) were two of the most prominent natural philosophers who employed some aspects of Pyrrhonism to present a challenge to the Scholastic paradigm. While rejecting the Aristotelian and Cartesian notions that the nature of reality could be known with complete certainty, Mersenne and Gassendi acknowledged the possibility of attaining probable knowledge that was based on the appearances of things. Mersenne actually composed an attack on Pyrrhonism entitled *La vérité des sciences contre les sceptiques ou pyrrhoniens* (1625). He argued that although the skeptics were correct regarding the impossibility of knowing the real essences of things, they erroneously rejected the idea that probable knowledge could serve as a practical guide for human activity.[36] Gassendi, who taught mathematics at the Collège royal in Paris, argued that although the senses could be unreliable, their errors could be corrected and their reliability increased.[37] In his *De vita et moribus Epicuri* (1647) and his *Animadversiones in decimum librum Diogenis Laertii* (1649), Gassendi tried to revive, popularize, and Christianize Epicurean atomism, proposing it as a new alternative to natural philosophy.[38] Although Mersenne and Gassendi did not accept the ultimate conclusions of the Pyrrhonians, these "moderate" or "mitigated skeptics" rejected the dogmatic principles of the Aristotelians and the Cartesians.[39] Despite their use of skeptical arguments for critical purposes, they sought to construct new physical and metaphysical systems. However, unlike the Christian Pyrrhonists, who were committed to skepticism for religious reasons, these thinkers embraced skeptical claims for purely philosophical and critical purposes.

These "mitigated skeptics" would find peers across the channel amidst thinkers, such as Francis Bacon (1561–1626), Joseph Glanvill (1636–80), John Wilkins (1614–72), and Robert Boyle (1627–91), all of whom endorsed new methods in natural philosophy.[40] Glanvill, Wilkins, and Boyle were all members of the Royal Society, whose motto, *nullius in verba* (take nobody's word for it), proudly rejected philosophical arguments that were made on the basis of intellectual authority, according to the spirit of Bacon's *Novum organum scientiarum* (1620). Like their French counterparts, Wilkins, Boyle, Glanvill, and their allies declared their epistemological stances to be the middle ground between total skepticism and dogmatism. They endorsed the experimental method in all explorations of nature.[41] Their deployment of skeptical arguments was thus tactical and rhetorical, used primarily to undermine established authorities.

Academic skepticism provided an alternative model for probabilistic philosophical enquiry, one that appeared to be between the extremes of dogmatism and Pyrrhonism. Simon Foucher (1644–96), a prominent critic of Cartesianism, claimed to occupy a middle ground between the two extremes.[42] Foucher contrasted the Academic philosophy with Pyrrhonism by claiming that the former recognized a number of principles as true and certain, while the latter continued to doubt all propositions. He maintained that the main goal of the Academic philosophy was to undermine existing prejudices and to bring philosophers back to "first principles" by making them "undertake the necessary reflections to acquire [true and] certain knowledge." Foucher advocated a suspension of judgment in philosophical enquiries until the "evidence of the truth" (*évidence de la vérité*) led one to a particular conclusion. He held that a continued search for true and certain knowledge was the only option open to philosophers, because one had to attempt to seek it even if one wanted to prove that such a task was futile.[43]

Thinkers frequently applied skeptical claims exclusively to philosophical questions and either contended that philosophical skepticism supported religious faith by humbling the mind or maintained that philosophical uncertainty had no implications for moral or religious matters. At the same time, skeptical arguments were not always appropriated for the most pious reasons. During the seventeenth century, several prominent freethinkers of high social standing were accused of using the rhetorical and logical tools of Pyrrhonian skepticism to question the established moral order. Dubbed the *libertins érudits*, this group included Léonard de Marandé, secretary to Cardinal Richelieu (1585–1642) and critic of the empiricist and experimental paradigms; Gabriel Naudé (1600–1653), librarian to Cardinals Richelieu and Mazarin (1602–61); Guy Patin (1601–72), the rector of the school of medicine at the University of Paris; Isaac de La Peyrère (1596–1676), secretary to the prince of Condé and author of the controversial pre-Adamite theory; and Samuel de Sorbière (1615–70), translator and editor of the works of Thomas Hobbes (1588–1679) and Pierre Gassendi. These humanist scholars had little interest in confessional quarrels. Many of them argued against witchcraft persecutions and criticized the general ignorance and superstition of their age.[44] Their detractors frequently accused them of engaging

in scandalous behavior, including gluttony, excessive drunkenness, sexual pro-
miscuity, and other acts offensive both to religion and to established morality.
The reputation for debauchery of the *libertins érudits* may have been greatly exaggerated by their critics, who argued that skeptical views in philosophy necessarily translated into moral relativism in practical life. While no *libertin* actually
expressed such positions, the vilification of their alleged dissipation created an
association between theoretical skepticism and practical immorality that complicated future debates about Pyrrhonism.[45]

Some skeptics did indeed apply Pyrrhonian doubt to religious matters and
questioned the veracity of the Christian revelation. Attempts to establish a definitive version of biblical texts from a variety of manuscript sources, along with
humanist methods of textual criticism, contributed to increasingly natural and
historical assessments of scripture and in some cases challenged its divine authorship. The earliest and most notable example came in Isaac de La Peyrère's
controversial works *Du rappel des juifs* (1643) and *Prae-Adamitae* (1655). Combining historical data from the Egyptian, Greek, and Babylonian cultures with new
accounts of voyages in Asia and in the Americas, La Peyrère argued that the
Bible accounted for the history of the Jews alone, and not that of all mankind.
He hypothesized that the world had existed for an indefinite period of time (and
certainly for significantly longer than the temporal framework proposed by the
Old Testament) and questioned the Mosaic authorship of the Pentateuch.[46]
Father Richard Simon (1638–1712), a biblical scholar of the Oratorian order who
frequently corresponded with La Peyrère, was deeply influenced by these theories. His *Histoire critique du Vieux Testament* (1678) maintained that the Pentateuch had been written over several generations. While he asserted his belief
in the divine inspiration of the Bible, Simon questioned the accuracy and the
stability of the existing versions of the text.[47]

Although these skeptical analyses of scripture were undertaken with pious
and even apologetic intentions, they informed the arguments of Spinoza's *Tractatus theologico-politicus* (1670). This notorious treatise explicitly denied any
divine inspiration in the authorship of the Bible, regarding it as little more than
a historical document. Spinoza contended that prophecy, the fundamental basis
of the Bible's claim to the understanding of God, was based on the imaginative
faculty and temperament of the prophets and was inferior to natural knowledge.[48] Faith in the veracity of scripture, then, was not the same as faith in God;
it was merely confidence in the reliability of the prophets, who were human and
fallible. Furthermore, he argued that the tradition of scriptural interpretation

had allowed theologians to impose their own meanings on various passages of the Bible. Spinoza maintained that the commandments of the Old Testament were written specifically for the Jews at a particular time and consequently had no universal applicability. Indeed, he remarked that the various ceremonial observances and laws prescribed in the Bible were incompatible with modern society, and he called for a rational basis for the formation of laws that would best maintain a stable political order.[49]

Popkin has argued that Spinoza's position was in fact diametrically opposite to those of the fideists and Christian Pyrrhonists, because it subjected religious knowledge to a skeptical critique, while it maintained a rationalist and anti-skeptical attitude with respect to metaphysical philosophy.[50] La Peyrère, Simon, and other Catholic apologists applied critical and skeptical arguments to scripture to undermine the Protestant doctrine of *sola scriptura* by demonstrating the inability of human reason to comprehend the Bible without the assistance of a divinely inspired authority. Spinoza, by contrast, pointed to the inconsistencies and difficulties in scripture in order to establish its inherent historicity and to question its divine authorship. It was this explicit turn that made Spinoza seem so pernicious to contemporaries and exposed the full implications of both skeptical and rationalist critiques of scripture.

Early modern skepticism thus encompassed a rather diverse set of epistemological, ontological, and religious opinions. There were self-avowed fideistic skeptics, such as La Mothe Le Vayer and Huet, who claimed to have abandoned a rational quest for philosophical demonstrations and theological proofs in favor of a reliance on supernatural faith. There were self-proclaimed Academic skeptics, such as Foucher, who, rather than following Sextus Empiricus and the allegedly extreme Pyrrhonian branch of skepticism, sought probable knowledge of the surrounding world. There were also those who, like Montaigne and Charron, combined elements of both the Academic and Pyrrhonian traditions. Despite the variety and abundance of these factions, it is important to remember that while philosophical distinctions between the different kinds of skeptical schools (or other schools of philosophy) may appear to be self-evident to contemporary scholars, early modern readers may have perceived these divisions in rather different ways. Since its revival in the early modern period, Pyrrhonism gradually became the dominant strain of philosophical skepticism in learned Europe. Pyrrhonism and skepticism became virtually synonymous in the minds of critics, who frequently used the terms interchangeably. Detractors derided all forms of this ancient philosophy and associated the critique of human reason with irreligion and immorality.

The Spectrum of Anti-Skepticism and the
Causes of the Pyrrhonian "Disease"

Just as *Pyrrhonism* served as an umbrella term, despite the equivocations at the time, for a number of divergent positions, anti-skepticism also represented a wide range of philosophical views. Opposition to skepticism emerged from an intellectually diverse group of thinkers, crossing confessional, philosophical, and geographical divides. The perceptions of the dangers skepticism posed to religion were common to Catholic and Protestant theologians alike, as both foresaw the pernicious implications for the rational foundations of religious belief. Even skeptics with seemingly pious intentions, such as Huet on the Catholic side and Bayle on the Protestant side, were sharply condemned by their confessional allies. Similarly, thinkers from divergent, even polar-opposite epistemological camps sought ways to disprove the ultimate conclusions of a skeptical philosophy that posed equally strong challenges to both empiricism and rationalism. By trying to answer the arguments of real—or imagined—skeptics and to formulate new criteria of certainty, philosophers from rival schools tried to demonstrate the superiority of their respective systems and the inadequacies of their opponents' principles.

Circles of thinkers attempting to refute skepticism appeared in France, Switzerland, the Netherlands, England, and Prussia. This was a European debate and dilemma. The motivations of thinkers who attempted to disprove Pyrrhonian claims varied dramatically according to the particular intellectual and geographical contexts. Anti-skepticism was not a unified school of thought. At the same time, the opposition to Pyrrhonism did bring together a wide spectrum of thinkers. The perception of a common enemy served as a powerful stimulus for a variety of intellectuals, and it drove them to attempt refutations of philosophical and religious skepticism. Consequently, anti-skeptical literature represented a varied and sometimes mutually incompatible set of principles.

Those who were concerned about the religious and philosophical implications of Pyrrhonian skepticism had always found its fundamental claim difficult to resolve in philosophical terms. By making their own conclusions inconclusive, the Pyrrhonians left their opponents in a difficult position. They transferred the burden of disproof to the dogmatic philosophers, while limiting their own responsibility to merely demonstrating the inconsistencies of the various dogmatic axioms and premises. The skeptics also enumerated the failings of the sensory apparatus and the flaws in the operations of the mind, and they offered abundant examples of how these faults led to erroneous and uncertain ideas.

Indeed, the feebleness of the understanding was a permanent defect of the mind.[51]

Despite the difficulty of answering such claims, eighteenth-century thinkers concerned about the apparent growth in the popularity of skepticism attempted to counter the Pyrrhonian challenge. In trying to explain the seeming intransigence and the paradoxical positions of their opponents, the anti-skeptics deployed a variety of rhetorical devices. They claimed that their adversaries were providing insincere claims that aimed only at marshaling negative arguments about particular positions without articulating positive and coherent philosophical views. While Pyrrhonians declared that the mind was in a state of permanent weakness, their critics maintained that the skeptics were the ones suffering from a mental disease.[52] They attributed the skeptics' insincerity to a moral and intellectual malady that was corrupting the hearts and minds of numerous intellectuals and that had dangerous effects not only on philosophy but also on society. In portraying Pyrrhonism as a mental derangement, many anti-skeptical thinkers likened the alleged disease to an epidemic that spread rapidly from one person to another, created a culture of incredulity, and led to a general moral disorder.

Alarmist warnings and apocalyptic predictions about the dangers of the Pyrrhonian plague that was engulfing the enlightened world of the eighteenth century filled pages of treatises and learned journals. Apologetic authors portrayed a steady growth in the ranks of skeptics, unbelievers, and libertines, who showed little respect for philosophical, religious, and moral truths. Many thought that this heterodox triumvirate of irreverence supported doctrines that mutually reinforced one another. Pyrrhonism served as the first step toward irreligion and immoral behavior, because it undermined the respect for intellectual authority and taught people to doubt the most obvious philosophical and theological truths. Intentionally or not, the skeptics opened a Pandora's box of unbelief.

Contemporaneous reactions offer a crucial insight into the learned culture of the early Enlightenment. Whether the critics of skepticism were accurate in their portrayal of a surge in heretical views or whether their remarks offer an exaggerated account is less important than the fact that a large group of Catholic and Protestant thinkers shared this outlook. Their perceptions shed light on the concerns and priorities of a significant segment of the intellectual community of this period. An examination of the metaphor of infection, used by so many opponents of skepticism, reveals some of the fundamental motivations of those who undertook refutations of Pyrrhonism. It explains why these thinkers saw skepticism not just as an intellectual problem but also as a potential threat to the existing familial, social, and political orders.

The metaphor of disease was nearly ubiquitous in apologetic texts of Catholic and Protestant theologians. The portrayal of skepticism as a pestilence that corrupted the minds and hearts of its victims served a dual purpose. First, it allowed the various opponents of skepticism to account for what they saw as a surprising rise in the popularity of such unsystematic and inconsistent philosophical views. Epidemiological vocabulary enabled these thinkers to portray Pyrrhonism not as a coherent position but as an unbalanced stance that because of its very nature did not permit itself to be refuted. This absolved the anti-skeptics, at least in part, from having to provide methodological responses to Pyrrhonism. Second, the metaphor offered rhetorical devices that allowed the opponents of skepticism to discuss the tangible effects that followed from theoretical Pyrrhonism. Their warnings emphasized the potential intellectual and social consequences of the spread of this philosophy, and they raised the stakes of the debates about the powers and limits of human understanding.

A typical example that reveals the essential elements of the disease metaphor appeared in an anonymous letter that was published in the Amsterdam-based Huguenot periodical *Bibliothèque germanique* in 1730. The author described Pyrrhonism as "a contagion that spreads itself and leads to a universal ravage" and enumerated its pernicious and widespread effects.[53] The letter claimed that skepticism, much like a plague, rapidly jumped from one "infected" person to another. It identified Bayle's *Dictionnaire* as the most obvious source of the epidemic. According to the article, this popular text was filled with arguments that were specifically intended to extend debates on controversial subjects and to leave readers in a state of doubt and uncertainty about even the most evident truths. The skeptical contents of Bayle's text affected readers in different ways, depending on their age, experience, and *humeur*, just as an infection produced varying reactions in different bodies.[54] Those in the greatest danger of catching the Pyrrhonian malady, the anonymous author argued, were readers who were the least educated in the philosophical and scholarly debates that Bayle's text addressed. After encountering a variety of superficial musings and anecdotes on all kinds of subjects, a semi-educated reader would feel confident in commenting on almost any questions. The faux intellectual would parrot Bayle's attacks against the most revered scholarly authorities without actually understanding the complexity of the debates that Bayle described superficially and with a great deal of bias:

He prides himself on being in a position to take on the whole world; he recites from memory the great passages of his author; he does not understand even one-half of them; he frequently mangles them, but his confidence is not at all shaken. His authority and aplomb impose themselves on another ignorant one, who in turn affirms the one who misled him in the errors and in the fantasy that he is a clever man. The contagion spreads in this way; one does not see one's own errors, because one sees many people equally mistaken, and after being misled by another, one in turn misleads a third person.[55]

The author singled out the *Dictionnaire* because he saw it as a text that not only easily deceived inexperienced readers down the road to Pyrrhonism but also transformed them into highly contagious carriers of the disease. This allowed Bayle's controversial text to spread the sickness by geometrical leaps, making it the source of a veritable Pyrrhonian plague. One did not even need to read the *Dictionnaire* to become infected by its subversive ideas.

The concern for the semi-educated reader reflects an important facet of eighteenth-century learned culture. According to available statistics, between 1686–90 and 1786–90 literacy rates in France increased from 29 percent to 47 percent among men and from 14 percent to 27 percent among women.[56] Similarly, book ownership grew throughout the century as texts became available in cheaper formats.[57] The rapid increase in the number of readers during this period coincided with the greater accessibility of philosophical debates through book reviews and digests offered in a variety of learned journals.[58] Controversial ideas that during the seventeenth century had been debated—frequently in Latin—primarily by a small group of theologians and philosophers could suddenly reach a wide audience. A growing number of salons and cafés provided venues for discussion and dissemination of the most recent scholarly developments, allowing those who could not access the actual texts firsthand to learn about them by word of mouth.[59]

The increasing variety of learned journals played a particularly important role in exposing readers to a vibrant intellectual culture. By allowing complex philosophical and theological discussions to spill beyond the limits of individual works, these relatively inexpensive periodical publications disseminated such arguments to wider, more diverse audiences. Frequently, intellectuals would take their private correspondence public, engaging in protracted exchanges on the pages of these journals. Periodicals also offered concise and timely reviews of voluminous works, and they often supplied French digests of books published in Latin and in other languages. This allowed readers to keep up with the latest developments in the Republic of Letters without having to devote excessive time or resources to the task. Finally, in a French-speaking community that was physically divided by the expulsion of the Huguenots in 1685, journals provided a way to maintain intellectual relationships across confessional boundaries. The increased direct and indirect exposure of the public to subversive texts such as Bayle's worried apologetic thinkers because audiences unaware of the rhetorical traps set by such thinkers were more likely to fall prey to various heterodox ideas in general and to Pyrrhonian skepticism in particular.

The Jesuit Jacques Le Febvre (1694–1755), who published a popular short dialogue entitled *Bayle en petit* (1737) against the Huguenot skeptic, argued that Bayle's dictionary was particularly dangerous to those who had no formal education in philosophy or theology. Since such readers saw Bayle's text as an objective and erudite source of information about a variety of subjects, they did not perceive the manipulative arguments and the ulterior motives of its author:

> But in a dictionary such as Bayle's one finds a summary of an infinite number of articles that pertain to religion, and one even finds reasons for and against [certain opinions]: many important questions are resolved there either well or poorly, and above all, the most specious objections are handled with great skill. One attaches oneself to this work, and having soon become semi-learned at a small cost, one believes oneself capable of reasoning about everything and even of embarrassing the most able professors, who are not always ready to refute everything before them.[60]

In Le Febvre's view, Bayle's *Dictionnaire* served as an intellectual shortcut that appealed to those who sought a superficial understanding of complex problems. The text was dangerous precisely because it passed over important difficulties in religious questions and gave oversimplified answers rather than leading readers to ponder such matters.

Le Febvre drew an analogy between Bayle's dictionary and a poison that threatened not only novice readers but even experienced theologians, who attempted to refute the text and expose its dangers to the public:

> Certain works that are capable of exciting impure passions cannot be placed with indifference into the hands of the whole world. Therefore, a professor who has no other goal but to discover the poison therein and to warn chaste readers cannot avoid reading such texts. Heretical books are too pernicious for simple believers, and thus they are equally dangerous for theologians who undertake the obligation

of refuting them. Is it not more or less as I said? If such nourishment is harmful to a weak stomach, then a healthy and robust man cannot consume it without damaging his health.[61]

Even trained theologians who read the *Dictionnaire* for the purposes of refuting its controversial arguments were not immune from being "corrupted" by the contents of the work.

In the preface to his *Remarques critiques sur le Dictionnaire de Bayle* (1748), which mimicked the notorious *Dictionnaire* in its layout, the Catholic Philippe-Louis Joly (c. 1712–1782) described the obstinate and deliberate ignorance of those who followed Bayle's teachings:

> Those willfully blind ones, whose number today is very great and whose lot is even more regrettable, have a boundless admiration for this pernicious author, [and they] run the risk of forever remaining in the darkness where they walk. If they wished to make use of their reason, they would see the colors with which their imagination represents to them their guide and oracle fade. But it is to be feared that they will never take a single step toward emerging from the error into which the sweet illusion of their senses cajoles them and promotes the corruption of their hearts. I would be happy if with my work I can at least prevent the poison from reaching those who until now have been safe.[62]

Joly saw Bayle's skeptical text as possessing an evil charm that clouded the minds of its readers and prevented them from either reasoning clearly or perceiving the internal contradictions of skepticism. As other opponents of Pyrrhonism before him had done, he equated the skeptical philosophy to a toxin that could spread like a plague with the help of the *Dictionnaire*.

The editors of the *Mémoires de Trévoux*, an influential Jesuit learned journal, also used the metaphor of disease in their review of the French translation of Sextus Empiricus's *Outlines of Pyrrhonism* (*Les hipotiposes pirroniennes*, 1725). However, the reviewer argued that skepticism was not as contagious as some other philosophies:

> Many intelligent people have remarked that of all the philosophical sects, Pyrrhonism is the least contagious one. There is no danger that people of good sense will ever become Pyrrhonians in practice, since one sees how, by the most glaring contradiction, Pyrrhonians themselves behave as if they do not doubt anything. Only religion can become the victim of this affliction of doubting everything. It does not sufficiently interest the majority of people, for whom the smallest

speculative doubt in this matter cannot, by the perversion of the heart, become really contagious and fatal in practice.[63]

It was skepticism's disconnect from the practical realities of life that made its tenets less contagious than those of other dangerous philosophies. At the same time, the author reasoned, by promoting an attitude of doubt in speculative matters, Pyrrhonism undermined religious belief.

Later in the same review, the Jesuit critic attempted to paint a portrait of a typical Pyrrhonian skeptic, who contradicted everyone and everything and denied the most self-evident propositions. He depicted the skeptic as a madman of sorts:

> But a Pyrrhonian is a kind of troubled and jabbering mind, who does not respect anything, who agrees with no one, including himself, with whom, whatever side one takes [in a debate], one should expect to be contradicted, harangued, and refuted at length. He doubts, and he absolutely wants you to doubt everything: that which is demonstrated and that which is not, that which you see and understand, that which good sense dictates, that which reason approves, that which religion inspires. He wants us to doubt whether it is daytime at high noon, whether two and two make four, whether there is Providence, whether there is a God, whether there are [other] men.[64]

The reviewer presented the self-avowed supporters of skepticism as unreasonable to the point of absurdity. The Pyrrhonians shifted their positions and took the contrary side in any debate, not to prove anything but purely for the sake of contradiction.

Protestant intellectuals shared the concerns about the dangers of skepticism with their Catholic counterparts. Jean-Pierre de Crousaz, one of Bayle's most outspoken critics in the eighteenth century, used the metaphor of mental disease extensively in his eight-hundred-page *Examen du pyrrhonisme ancien et moderne* (1733). He described Pyrrhonism not as a coherent philosophical system but as a "derangement of the mind and of the heart." Crousaz diagnosed skepticism as a "disease that troubles the mind, that blinds it, and that casts it into obstinacy." His book depicted the Pyrrhonians as incensed and deluded people with insatiable appetites for contradicting any and all philosophical opinions. Crousaz was willing to admit, however, that their obsession rendered them skillful at poking holes in almost any widely accepted opinion.[65]

Crousaz located the historical origin of the skeptics' "derangement" in "the spirit of dispute that reigned among the Greeks [and that] contributed significantly to the establishment of Pyrrhonism."[66] He particularly blamed the Sophist philosophers, whose rhetorical acrobatics had been made notorious by Plato, for seeking to win philosophical arguments at any conceivable cost. Indifferent to the actual contents and implications of the questions they disputed, the Sophists, according to Crousaz, perpetuated endless disputations on any and every topic. He traced the sophistic arguments of the ancient Greeks to their eighteenth-century manifestations in the form of Scholastic disputations, a fundamental element of university education. He accused the pedagogical system of teaching students how to argue before explaining the important implications of philosophical and theological disputes: "One turned philosophy, and then theology, into an art of speaking much and thinking little, of never understanding the views of others, of taking their thoughts as backward, and of not understanding oneself."[67] In emphasizing the study of rhetoric and the formal aspect of arguments, teachers neglected to explain the actual content and background of the questions in dispute. Like other critics of skepticism, Crousaz believed that young and inexperienced minds were most susceptible to the Pyrrhonian disease.

Jean Henri Samuel Formey (1711–97), secretary of the Académie royale des sciences et belles-lettres de Prusse, wrote an abridgment of Crousaz's work entitled *Le triomphe de l'évidence* (1756). He also deployed medical language in describing the Pyrrhonians: "One might say that what they have is not a disposition; it is a malady. They have the same distaste for certainty and evidence as [when] certain afflictions of the body cause [allergies] to healthful foods; they love feeding themselves with doubt in the same way that one sometimes sees people whose constitution is disturbed devour chalk or coal."[68] Formey contrasted them with true skeptics, who "arduously seek the truth but do not wish to admit as veritable anything but that which truly is so."[69] These "diseased" Pyrrhonians—or "false" skeptics—reasoned insincerely, not wishing to admit what was plainly obvious.

Baron Albrecht von Haller (1708–77), a renowned naturalist and a corresponding member of the Académie de Prusse (as well as Crousaz's Swiss compatriot), composed the introductory remarks to Formey's *abrégé*. He equated philosophical skepticism with religious incredulity and attributed both conditions to the moral corruption and increasing superficiality and sensuality of his age: "These faults and these vices are so favorable to unbelief; unbelief, in turn, is favorable to them, and the contagion of this evil is so palpable that the insensitivity to it resembles the symptoms of a mortal gangrene."[70] In Haller's view, the sickness and corruption of individuals had spread across the entire contemporary society. Unbelief and skepticism went hand in hand with the immoral pursuit of sensual pleasures, one reinforcing the other.

The enemies of Pyrrhonism were surprised to see the spirit of skepticism and irreligion in what they otherwise perceived to be an age of unprecedented enlightenment and learning. The situation certainly appeared ironic: the number of skeptics seemed to be growing at a time when the greatest advances in natural philosophy were taking place.[71] Crousaz attributed the apparent popularity of Pyrrhonism to an inadequate educational system and to the superficial nature of philosophical contests, in which opponents sought to win not for the sake of truth but in order to gain recognition. Jacques Le Febvre and his Jesuit colleagues explained the appeal of skepticism by invoking the inexperienced nature of contemporary readers. The naturalist Haller, in turn, blamed what he saw on a general moral corruption of eighteenth-century society. He believed that there was a mutual reinforcement between atheism and Pyrrhonism, on the one hand, and hedonistic egoism and sensualist materialism, on the other.

The Anti-Social Symptoms of Skepticism and Potential Remedies

Apologetic opponents of Pyrrhonism often indicted it as an intellectual progenitor of atheism and hedonistic libertinism. They sought to demonstrate the wider implications of a phenomenon that to an untrained eye appeared innocuous. According to various opponents of Pyrrhonism, this so-called malady was pernicious not just for purely philosophical investigations but for society in general. They saw skepticism and its atheistic implications as destructive to public morality and consequently to the established social and political orders. In large part, their arguments were aimed specifically at Pierre Bayle's notorious claim that a society of atheists could be just as virtuous as a society of believers, and possibly more so.[72] To refute this claim, anti-skeptical thinkers highlighted the potential social consequences of the spread of Pyrrhonism by presenting dystopian visions of societies without religion.

Haller's critique focused more on describing the practical effects of atheism than on refuting Pyrrhonism philosophically. His "Discours préliminaire" offered dramatically pessimistic predictions for a culture that embraced "unbelief" or "incredulity" as the dominant faith. He depicted a society in which all the members lived solely for the satisfaction of their own individual needs and fulfilled no duties or obligations toward the larger community. In such a state of individual egotism, all social bonds would be ruptured. Families would dissolve because of infidelity, while children would be cruelly abandoned to their fates. Commercial exchanges would collapse owing to mutual mistrust among all parties; material self-interest would put an end to charity and neighborly assistance; kings and princes would engage in warfare to satisfy their vanity and greed.[73] Haller explicitly compared his dystopia to Hobbes's state of nature: "I believe that it is sufficiently demonstrated that this new wisdom is the ruin of [all] social life. It gives each man no other object than his own well-being, a purely sensual well-being. It puts the forces of all men in perpetual opposition, which must result in a state of war and universal enmity, a consequence sincerely recognized by Hobbes, and which cannot cease until religion comes to bring peace."[74] By equating Pyrrhonian skepticism with atheism and extreme egotism, Haller painted a vision of a sick and decadent future, warning readers about the potential practical dangers of irreligion.

Anticipating some of Haller's concerns, the anonymous contributor to the *Bibliothèque germanique* argued that a clear intellectual and moral connection united materialist hedonism, Pyrrhonism, and atheism. The author presented human nature as being divided between innate desires to satisfy bodily needs and seek physical pleasures, on the one hand, and a faculty of reason that God had implanted in humankind to moderate desires and act as a guide toward virtuous behavior, on the other. The insistence on the weakness of human reason was thus a surreptitious attempt to promote hedonism and libertinism. "Abandoned to the passions," an individual unchecked by reason would seek only sensory gratification and use other people as if they were means to the satisfaction of his or her fancies. By denouncing the utility of rational analyses in philosophical matters, Bayle and other Pyrrhonians knowingly led readers to embrace religious unbelief, irreverence toward authority, and libertinism.[75]

Crousaz described the increasingly popular Pyrrhonism not just as a plague but as a devastating fire that threatened the intellectual integrity and the moral compass of his contemporaries. Unlike those who defended Bayle as a fideist who had sought to defend religion, Crousaz argued that intentionally or not, the *Dictionnaire* produced pernicious effects: "Whether he [Bayle] foresaw these effects or whether they are due to the abuse that one made of what he had composed with completely different intentions is not the most important and the most pressing question. . . . When a fire engulfs several houses and is in danger of spreading across the whole city, one must rush to put it out instead of amusing oneself by disputing whether it was caused by the imprudence or by the malice of its authors."[76] Crousaz emphasized the real and impending nature of the Pyrrhonian threat to the religious, intellectual, and moral foundations of society.

The Pyrrhonian challenge to revealed religion was Crousaz's most pressing concern. He criticized fideist Christians, who called for a complete submission of reason to faith in theological questions. Crousaz maintained that by undermining the rational foundations of belief, they unintentionally destroyed the possibility of attaining a rational understanding of God and his nature. Such a rational and general conception of God, he argued, necessarily had to precede any supernatural belief. Bayle's arguments against reason were intentionally malicious, wrote Crousaz: they "fill the mind with doubts . . . place reason and faith in opposition . . . and perfect unbelief."[77] The only conclusion one could reach from reading Bayle's work was that it was written in such a way as to gradually accustom the mind to philosophical skepticism and religious incredulity. Bayle's examples did not present the Christian revelation as being incomprehensible to human reason because of its clear superiority. Instead, they pitted reason *against* revelation and enfeebled the authority of both. Why else, Crousaz asked rhetorically, would Bayle have attempted to demonstrate the inability of rational arguments to disprove the most monstrous heresies?[78]

Crousaz maintained that Pyrrhonism presented a substantial threat not just to religion but to the progress of human knowledge in general. By questioning the most self-evident truths and pretending that a logical equivalence existed between the most certain and the most dubious propositions, Pyrrhonians deliberately undermined any and all rational investigations.[79] For Crousaz, the Pyrrhonians sought to replace intellectual curiosity and a continued exploration of the world with ignorance and empty rhetoric. Repeatedly invoking the contrast between light and darkness, a contrast typically invoked by the philosophes themselves, he likened the Pyrrhonians to religious fanatics: both attempted to lead humanity into obscurity and ignorance. Like many of his contemporaries, Crousaz believed that God had endowed human beings with natural reason so that they could both improve their own condition by learning about the created universe and come to admire its creator more fully. By challenging the possibility of attaining such knowledge, Pyrrhonians intentionally diverted people from the path God had intended them to take and led them toward intellectual and spiritual darkness.[80]

Like his fellow opponents of skepticism, Crousaz portrayed Pyrrhonism as a potential menace to public morality and consequently to the established social and political orders. He saw reason not just as a foundation of religious truths but as the fundamental compass for human behavior, which generally steered people toward virtue. Crousaz condemned the *Dictionnaire* for examples of violence, debauchery, deceit, and vice that littered its pages and attracted readers by appealing to the baser instincts of human nature. He accused the skeptic of walking "the imagination of his readers through dangerous ideas" and offering new examples of deviant behavior for contemporary libertines. "In his own time," claimed Crousaz, "Mr. Bayle had eluded the accusations of Pyrrhonism and of atheism, which now make up a great part of his merit in the eyes of his supporters."[81]

The theologian Hubert Hayer (1708–80) and the lawyer Jean Soret (b. 1710), coauthors of the serial *La religion vengée* (1757–63), drew similar conclusions about the implications of Pyrrhonian skepticism—particularly of Bayle's arguments—on morality. By suggesting that ethical decisions concerned nothing more than the question of taste, Bayle and his disciples advocated moral relativism, making disputes about murder no different from debates about flavors.[82] "If the rules of morality were arbitrary," they contended, each person could design his or her moral framework. There would be nothing "essentially just," and there would be no difference between what is "morally good and bad."[83] Accusing Bayle of fomenting "sedition, revolt, and patricide," Hayer and Soret predicted that social and political anarchy would necessarily follow from skeptical philosophy.[84]

Opponents of Pyrrhonism also speculated about potential "cures" to the malady. The general consensus was that a remedy was difficult to find. Logical demonstrations appeared impotent to those who tried to reason with the skeptics. Since skepticism was a "mental derangement," those who suffered from it were either unwilling or unable to assent to the most basic and self-evident propositions. Nevertheless, perceiving the dangerous consequences, antiskeptical thinkers attempted to identify potential remedies that would either shake the Pyrrhonians out of their apparent delirium or prevent the epidemic from spreading.

The anonymous letter to the *Bibliothèque germanique* suggested that true Pyrrhonians had fallen so far into their delirium that lifting them out of it was highly unlikely. The author wondered whether their "derangement was voluntary, whether they took some pleasure in it, whether they stubbornly clung to their opinions, and whether they fed their vanity." The letter conjectured that it would be impossible to "bring [the skeptics] back from their confusion," because they intentionally attempted to ignore the most self-evident propositions presented to them.[85] The only potential remedy lay in getting the Pyrrhonians gradually reaccustomed to the basic rules of logic. However, the anonymous correspondent did not expect this to occur. The skeptics appeared to enjoy proposing contradictions, and they intentionally blinded themselves to the most self-evident truths. The author could not help but be moderately amused by their obstinacy: "I limit myself to listening to them and to instructing myself, by listening to them, in the different deviations to which the human mind is subject and in the confusions to which the passions carry it."[86] A skeptic's mental derangement, in the correspondent's view, was akin to an incurable sickness. Since the claims of the Pyrrhonians were inherently irrational and unanswerable, the author was absolved from answering them philosophically.

Other anti-skeptics shared this pessimism about overcoming Pyrrhonism through logic. The Swiss philosopher Jean-Bernard Mérian (1723–1807), who translated Hume's *Enquiry Concerning Human Understanding* (1748) into French in 1758, regarded the disease as completely "incurable": "I see absolute skepticism as an incurable evil, and the skeptic as a man who speaks in a language unknown to me and with whom I consequently will not enter into debate, since in order to understand one another in ordinary language it is necessary to agree on the meaning of terms, so in disputes it is necessary to agree on some principle. . . . Therefore in all cases the arguments against skepticism are insufficient and useless."[87] Mérian saw all attempts to reason with the Pyrrhonians as futile. Since they denied the most commonly accepted axioms, it was impossible to have a productive philosophical engagement with them.

Crousaz also voiced pessimism about divesting the skeptics of their love for contradicting any and every claim. He likened them to drunkards and religious fanatics, saying their minds were so clouded that they were simply impossible to engage in conversation. Their devotion to argument blinded them and led them to contradict even themselves.[88] However, Crousaz seemed to believe in a gradation of the disease that made treatment possible in certain cases:

> There are Pyrrhonians who are absolutely incurable. But there are also men who have some penchant for it and who are not impossible to bring back from it. Their sickness consists in not wishing to turn their mind toward self-evidence with sufficient effort and in preferring to ponder [various] difficulties. It seems to me that one does not pay attention, as one should, to the nature of their malady, and one does not take all the necessary precautions to cure them, [which could be accomplished by] calling them to [undertake] great efforts of attention [and focus] on ideas to which one does not come easily and that are contested by a great number of dogmatists.[89]

Thus, while some skeptics were hopelessly diseased and denied everything, others could be cured gradually. Crousaz advocated engaging skeptics in debates that would unsettle their deranged minds instead of punishing them for their embrace of universal doubt.[90] He outlined a potential remedy to the condition in the introduction to the *Examen*: "It is not completely impossible to bring the skeptic back from his deviation and to cure him of his malady. A Pyrrhonian . . . is not a Pyrrhonian all the time. One can therefore benefit from his good moments to accustom him to rely on evidence in order to give him some anxiety about his state and to open his eyes with regard to his own interests."[91]

Crousaz's prescription represented Pyrrhonism as a state of mind that took over the skeptics at some points, while being absent at others. He thus seemed to suggest that even if one could not cure the disease completely with a single treatment, there was still a possibility of improving the state of the skeptic's mind through repeated interventions. The primary aim of attempting to refute the Pyrrhonians, however, was to appeal to the wider reading public. Crousaz sought to inoculate potential victims of the skeptical sickness: "All that one should expect is to take advantage of whatever respect there is for reason among those who are weakened by the sophisms of the Pyrrhonists and to make them taste the clarity (*évidence*) that leads to certainty."[92] By demonstrating the internal inconsistency of skepticism, he hoped to protect inexperienced readers, who were at the greatest risk of succumbing to the sophistic musings of Pyrrhonism.

Refuting the Irrefutable

Making a rhetorical rather than a logical case against Pyrrhonism was quite a common strategy for apologetic thinkers. By portraying skepticism as a mental derangement, they gained several advantages. In the first place, *ad hominem* attacks that depicted the skeptics as irrational, insincere, and deranged freed the opponents of Pyrrhonism from having to disprove the actual arguments concerning the weakness of the human mind. By discrediting the skeptics, they absolved themselves of the responsibility to answer them philosophically. In the second place, by focusing on the supposed social and moral consequences that followed from the spread of skeptical ideas, especially those concerning religion, they raised the stakes of the debates. The arguments were no longer just about abstract philosophical questions; they were about the survival of the existing social and political order. This tactic appealed to readers and to authorities, enlisting the latter's assistance. In the third place, the association of Pyrrhonism with irreligion, atheism, libertinism, hedonism, and materialism allowed anti-skeptical thinkers to present the philosophy of their enemies as the fundamental source of these other intellectual maladies. The anti-skeptics were preaching to the choir, because they reinforced the negative descriptions of Pyrrhonism that were largely shared by those who opposed it.[93] In order to appeal to a wider reading public and to prevent the spread of the Pyrrhonian plague, apologetic authors would need to adjust to the tastes of their audience and offer their refutations in new forms.

The continuous discussions of the religious, political, and intellectual dangers of Pyrrhonism demonstrate the extent to which highly educated thinkers perceived it as an acute problem for their learned culture. Because of the persistent popularity of Pyrrhonism, and particularly of Bayle's *Dictionnaire*, opposition to skepticism continued to be one of the major currents in the apologetic literature of the eighteenth century. Many thinkers saw skepticism as an underlying cause of both the increasing sway of subversive philosophies and the decline in religious belief. As we will see, the opposition to skepticism, though frequently unified by a concern about rising irreligion, emerged among a philosophically and religiously diverse group of thinkers all over Europe. The attempts by the broad coalition of religious apologists, Cartesian dualists, and even materialists to refute Pyrrhonism would shape the issues and concerns of eighteenth-century intellectual culture. The interaction between skepticism and anti-skepticism would ultimately moderate and qualify the very meanings of the terms *reason* and *rationality*, redefining the powers and the limits of human understanding. In the chapters that follow, we will explore the evolution of these debates.

CHAPTER TWO

Pierre Bayle

Bête Noire and the Elusive Skeptic

The "Bayle Dilemma"

As is apparent from the many attempted refutations of Pyrrhonism, eighteenth-century thinkers most identified this philosophy with Pierre Bayle and his *Dictionnaire historique et critique*. It was the appearance of Bayle's controversial text, above all else, that prompted the concerns about the dangers of skepticism that we encountered in chapter 1. While Pyrrhonism had a well-established tradition in early modern France, it was not until the publication of the *Dictionnaire* that thinkers identified skepticism as a disease and became so deeply preoccupied with refuting it. Their concerns were certainly justified. Bayle's massive *Dictionnaire*, in its several editions, was the most widely owned book in French private libraries in the second half of the eighteenth century, and it was also translated into English and German.[1] Critics and supporters alike reproduced numerous passages from this text, allowing it to penetrate various areas of eighteenth-century learned culture.

Bayle's skeptical ideas first encountered fierce criticism and opposition from his fellow Huguenot émigrés in the Dutch Republic. An exploration of the debates surrounding Bayle's skepticism in this setting will help to explain the philosophical and religious context in which his skeptical claims acquired such a potent force. The main arguments presented against Bayle by his closest peers in the Dutch Huguenot circles foreshadow the attempted refutations of skepticism in general and of Bayle's Pyrrhonism in particular later in the eighteenth century. These earliest disputes also outline the major themes and stakes in the debates about the powers and limits of human understanding and about the proper relationship between faith and reason.

As the founder and editor of the prominent learned journal *Nouvelles de la République des Lettres*, Bayle, in exile, became one of the most significant links among French-speaking intellectuals across Europe. To friends, he was an admirable example of the rare combination of erudition, eloquence, and intellectual rigor. They viewed him as a shining beacon of religious toleration in a Europe that was suffering from a renewal of confessional animosities, as a champion of peace in a time of major wars, and as a defender of free expression in the face of severe censorship. To critics, as we have seen, Bayle was the voice of skepticism, irreligion, and libertinism. He was a sinister rhetorician who twisted logical arguments to confuse the most devout and pious believers. He was a dangerous Pyrrhonian skeptic and a covert atheist. This "double image" of Bayle, as Jonathan Israel has termed it, has persisted from the early eighteenth century to modern scholarship.[2]

The complexity and frequency of apparent tensions and contradictions within Bayle's texts are in themselves sufficient to render a "true" reading of his philosophical views nearly impossible. This ambiguity is complicated further by the fact that he has been read in so many diverse ways both by audiences at the time and by modern scholars that any attempt to link him definitively to a particular set of doctrinal beliefs becomes futile and unproductive. The various interpreters of Bayle have identified him as a skeptic, an atheist, a deist, a fideist, a libertine, and a progenitor of the Enlightenment.[3] Rather than trying to reconstruct the "real" Bayle, it would be useful, for historical purposes, to look at the variety of ways in which eighteenth-century intellectuals received and appropriated his ideas.

The problem at the crux of this debate is, ironically enough, an epistemological one. Whether one is dealing with Bayle, Voltaire, Hume, or other controversial figures, one will never be able to know with certainty what they actually thought. In Bayle's case, the issue is complicated further by the fact that he appeared to endorse a set of incompatible philosophical and theological views. It is thus nearly impossible to decide which opinion he entertained sincerely and which he advanced for the sake of argument. Perhaps we should leave the last word on the sincerity of his own religious beliefs to Bayle. While discussing the Dutch theologian Johannes Bredenburg's (1643–91) unsuccessful attempts to refute Spinoza's pantheism in remark M of his article "Spinoza," Bayle commented on the complex interplay between faith and reason:

> They maintained that the author of the demonstration was a Spinozist and consequently an atheist. As far as I could understand from hearsay, he defended himself by presenting the ordinary distinction between faith and reason. He alleged that just as Catholics and Protestants believe the mystery of the Trinity, although it is opposed by the natural light, he believed in free will, although reason

furnished him with strong proofs that everything happens by inevitable necessity and that consequently there is no religion. . . . One may exclaim that he is not sincere and that our mind is not such that it can take as true something that a geometrical demonstration shows to be false, but is that not appointing oneself as judge in a case where one's incompetence might be questioned? Do we have the right to decide what happens in the heart of another? . . . The abbé de Dangeau speaks of certain people who have religion in their minds but not in their hearts; they are persuaded of its truth, without their conscience being touched by the love of God. I believe we can say that there are also people who have religion in their hearts but not in their minds. They lose sight of it once they begin to search by employing human reason: it escapes into the subtleties and sophisms of their dialectic; they do not know where they are while they weigh arguments for and against it. But as soon as they cease disputing and do nothing but listen to the proofs of their feelings, the instincts of their conscience, the weight of education, etc., they are convinced of a religion, and they conform their lives to it as much as human weakness allows it.[4]

Popkin suggested that Bayle might have been describing his own complex relationship with religious belief in this passage.[5] Unfortunately for his interpreters, Bayle's true feelings will forever remain unknown. For this reason, it might be wise to shy away from passing judgments regarding his sincerity and take him at his word.

It is by no means the goal of this book to attempt to settle the interminable dispute about Bayle's intentions. His ideas were complex and "multivalent"[6] both for his contemporaries and for modern scholars. The crucial task, however, is to understand the reactions to his perceived skepticism in the eighteenth century. We cannot know with certainty what a complex thinker such as Bayle had in mind when he composed his grandiose *Dictionnaire*, yet we can determine with relative confidence how his contemporaries and near contemporaries reacted to his work. Such an analysis will shed light on how Enlightenment thinkers attempted to understand and deal with what they saw as skeptical and atheistic ideas contained in Bayle's texts.

Jurieu, Bayle, and the *Dictionnaire*

The first version of Bayle's dictionary appeared in 1692 as the *Projet et fragmens d'un dictionnaire critique*.[7] Bayle had begun the work as a set of corrections to what he perceived as the great number of factual errors in Louis Moréri's (1643–80) *Le grand dictionnaire historique* (1674). He sought to offer a "critical dictionary" that would "enlist under each name of a man or a city all the errors that had been disseminated about" them.[8] Bayle's self-declared aim was to provide a "touchstone for all other books." He hoped that his compendium of errors would serve as the "insurance board [*la chambre des assurances*] of the Republic of Letters."[9] After receiving mixed reviews, many of which criticized the tiresome and tedious nature of the text, Bayle modified his project. He adapted to the tastes of a reading public that was not necessarily interested in following the details of philological precision but instead sought concise and easily accessible information on a variety of subjects.[10] Following the model of his article about Zeuxis in the *Projet et fragments*, Bayle added a narrative section at the head of the critical remarks, transforming his intended critical dictionary into the *Historical and Critical Dictionary*.[11]

The resulting text, printed in October 1696 with a *privilège* from 1697, would have an original format. It combined historical sections that offered a "succinct narration of the facts" with long comment sections printed in smaller font in two columns below.[12] Bayle supported his claims with extensive citations and references to the sources that he relied upon. The commentaries served to elucidate the narrative and to correct errors, as in the previous project. However, these sections also presented provocative digressions and controversial philosophical reflections that exposed readers to the tangents of Bayle's thoughts.

Bayle's stated goal was not to produce a comprehensive reference work or to repeat information contained in other dictionaries but to offer a supplement to such texts. He justified his choice of subjects by claiming that he wanted to avoid both rehashing known facts about "Popes, Cardinals, emperors, and heretics" and duplicating the efforts of contemporaries who were working on national biographies in England and in the Netherlands.[13] Bayle distinguished his project from historical dictionaries that offered only general outlines of their subjects' lives, suggesting that he had tried to compile the most remarkable, personal, and sometimes scandalous elements of people's lives. He emphasized the disagreements and uncertainties concerning the details of various events: the closer one looked, the more facts seemed to unravel. Bayle also reinforced the sense of uncertainty by challenging accepted opinions, presenting several perspectives on the same question, and demonstrating the irresolvable nature of debates that were "capable of throwing most readers into continual mistrust."[14]

The controversy surrounding Bayle's skeptical magnum opus began just months after its initial publication. Bayle found himself engaged in a bitter dispute with Pierre Jurieu (1637–1713), a former friend and colleague and a fellow Huguenot refugee. Jurieu and Bayle had both taught at the Académie de Sedan

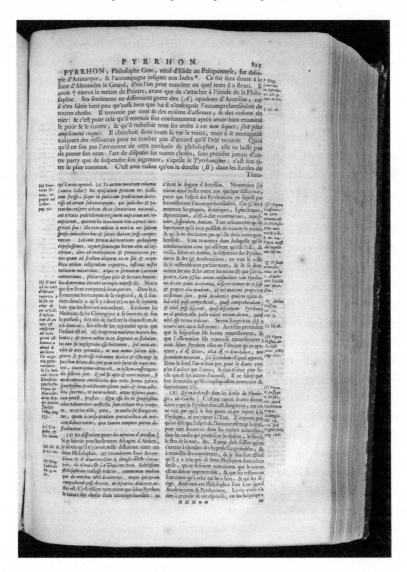

Fig. 2.1 "Pyrrhon," from the 1697 edition of the *Dictionnaire historique et critique.* Courtesy of The Newberry Library.

before moving to the École illustre in Rotterdam. Jurieu soon became a pastor at the Walloon church of Rotterdam and one of the most outspoken Huguenot refugees in the Netherlands. Jurieu and Bayle gradually fell out over both political and theological questions, such as the source and nature of religious certainty, the significance of biblical prophecies, and the legitimacy of Louis XIV's

(1638–1715) rule. After a series of bitter intra-confessional debates, Bayle and Jurieu came to occupy opposing ends of the political spectrum of the Huguenot refugee community. The irenic Bayle, who pleaded for religious toleration and a peaceful coexistence with Catholic France, loudly criticized the *dévot* Jurieu, who fervently upheld his interpretation of the Bible not only against Catholics but also against dissenting fellow Protestants. Jurieu also zealously called for an international Protestant front to depose King Louis XIV of France.[15]

Their intellectual rivalry lasted for more than two decades, but the publication of the *Dictionnaire* turned it into a full-scale scholarly war. Just months after the appearance of the first edition of Bayle's controversial text, Jurieu issued an acerbic pamphlet filled with anonymous letters condemning the work. While the *Jugement du public et particulièrement de M. l'abbé Renaudot sur le Dictionnaire critique de Sr. Bayle* (1697) remained unsigned, any informed reader in the late seventeenth century could easily identify Jurieu as the editor.[16] The text comprised anonymous letters about the recently published *Dictionnaire* that allegedly had been sent to the editor of the volume from Paris, London, Geneva, and other European cities. All of them condemned different facets of Bayle's grandiose work in the harshest possible terms. The letters were accompanied by several commentaries that summarized their major themes and points of criticism. In the preface, Jurieu vowed that he had received the letters—unsolicited by him—both from neutral observers and from those whom Bayle's text had explicitly attacked. He refused to reveal the names of his correspondents, claiming that he "did not wish to expose honest people to the ill temper of such a violent and angry author."[17] Jurieu's declared goal in circulating the various reactions to the *Dictionnaire* was to demonstrate that his own evaluation of Bayle's overall intellectual stance was consistent with the reading public's reception of his latest project.[18] This set of concurring opinions from so many diverse readers, Jurieu insinuated, offered a truly objective evaluation of Bayle's controversial text. Such a great variety of negative reactions to the *Dictionnaire* had the potential to sway the undecided members of the Huguenot reading public to side with the apparent consensus view.

In a surprising move, Jurieu placed at the beginning of the volume a report written by the Catholic royal censor, the abbé Eusèbe Renaudot (1646–1720), to the chancelier Louis Boucherat (1616–99). Renaudot had severely condemned the *Dictionnaire*, and his report was the main reason why Bayle's text would be banned in France until the death of the Sun King and the subsequent relaxation of censorship under the regency.[19] In this instance, Jurieu's tactical calculations and disdain for his Huguenot enemy seemed to outweigh any of the disagreements he may have had with the Catholic Renaudot. Although the report had been written for Louis XIV, whom Jurieu despised, he saw no problem with reprinting it for Huguenot readers.[20]

Renaudot's official account was followed by the extracts from anonymous letters and by Jurieu's summaries of the major themes of these criticisms; together they constituted a multipronged assault against Bayle. First, many of the readers claimed that Bayle's text was filled with irrelevant digressions on random topics.[21] Second, many letters accused Bayle of feigning erudition, citing ancient authors only in translation, and plagiarizing from relatively obscure writers.[22] This criticism was significant in the learned world of the early modern Republic of Letters. By claiming that Bayle had no direct knowledge of antiquity and by casting doubt on his use of sources, Jurieu, Renaudot, and the anonymous authors undermined his scholarly credibility—the basis of one's reputation in the Republic of Letters. The third set of censures concerned Bayle's malicious intentions and improper attacks against both historical and contemporaneous figures. This irreverent attitude toward the French monarchs, a letter from Paris argued, was "what particularly forced the chancelier to burn and to ban" the work.[23]

The fourth and most extensive type of criticism of Bayle's *Dictionnaire* concerned its mistreatment of religion in general and of Christianity in particular. One letter, addressed to the members of the Berg-op-zoom synod, claimed that Bayle's work was a more powerful tool for the propagation of atheism than Spinoza's controversial ideas could ever be.[24] Indeed, while some of Bayle's opponents had praised his refutation of Spinoza, Jurieu noted that the repudiation contained no trace of arguments based on Christianity. Instead, Jurieu maintained, Bayle spoke in purely deistic terms that could have been used by a Platonist or an Aristotelian.[25] By comparing the *philosophe de Rotterdam* to Spinoza, Jurieu cast Bayle as an intemperate unbeliever. Seeking to discredit him in the Dutch Huguenot community, he insisted that Bayle's ideas were dangerous to Catholics and Protestants alike. Jurieu declared that Bayle opposed all organized religion and revealed himself to be a libertine, a Pyrrhonist, and an atheist:

> The abbé [Renaudot] should regard this as being among the outrages the author makes against religion in general and not take it as a particular offense against popery. He quickly forgot the character of this author, though he had described him a few lines before as a libertine, a Pyrrhonian, and a common enemy of all religions. The abbé seems to have misread or forgotten the other works of this author. . . . We must remind him that [Bayle] does not begrudge other religions

any less than that which calls itself Catholic. This is a complete Pyrrhonian or a deist, whose main goal is to destroy all faith and all religion.[26]

Jurieu was referring to the *Avis aux refugiez* (1690), in which Bayle was allegedly more irreverent against the Calvinists than against Catholic theologians. Although it had been published anonymously, the *Avis* was one of the main reasons for which Bayle was dismissed from his teaching position at the École illustre in 1693. The sacking occurred largely because of Jurieu's condemnations. In the *Avis*, Bayle had directly attacked Jurieu's prophetic claims about the deposition of Louis XIV and pushed for moderation among Huguenot exiles. Bayle had insisted that calls for war against Catholic France were just as un-Christian as the Catholic persecutions of Protestants.[27]

Jurieu was incensed by the fact that Bayle's *Dictionnaire* had undermined both sources of religious certainty: authority and reason. Not only did the text cast doubt on the infallibility of the Catholic Church but it posed an even more aggressive challenge to the possibility of a rational analysis of the Bible. In Jurieu's view, Bayle implicitly demonstrated that various heresies could be just as true as the most solidly established religious doctrines, since all was equally uncertain and unknowable to the human mind: "There he wants to prove . . . that error or heresy are just as good as the real truth, because all is uncertain, all is obscure and impenetrable. . . . On the one hand, the foundation of the Roman Catholic religion, which is blind submission, is reversed; on the other hand, the foundation of the faith of the Reformed, which is [rational] examination, is ruined. Where, then, does that leave religion?"[28] Jurieu maintained that his skeptical opponent had a consistent record of employing Pyrrhonian claims to defend heresy and to present arguments that inevitably led to atheism. While Jurieu echoed Bayle's insistence on the supremacy of faith over reason, he contended that his opponent did all he could to subvert the authority of scripture. Bayle's claim that "one must believe the revelation and submit reason to faith" appeared hypocritical after he had "said all that can be imagined to weaken the authority of revelation and of the sacred authors."[29] For Jurieu, Bayle's skepticism and atheism were veiled in such a way that while pretending to be a devout Christian, he purposely misled his readers down a path of disbelief.

Jurieu took particular issue with Bayle's article on King David, claiming that it presented the author of the Psalms as a villain. Jurieu was also scandalized by the article "Pauliciens," in which Bayle had allegedly ridiculed the notion of original sin, comparing God's treatment of Eve to that of a "mother who had turned herself into a madam of her daughter by putting her in the circumstance in which the daughter could not do otherwise but yield [to advances] and be debauched."[30] One of the letters claimed that Bayle's dictionary was so conducive to promoting sexual libertinism that its title should have been "Of Ancient and Modern Brothels."[31]

The combination of the anonymous letters and Jurieu's reflections was nothing less than an act of academic aggression in the early modern Republic of Letters. The volume was a direct attack on Bayle's scholarly reputation, his religious beliefs, and his moral proclivities. Bayle gave a number of substantive replies to the accusations leveled by Renaudot, Jurieu, and the anonymous authors. He defended himself against the charge that his *Dictionnaire* was full of moral impurities and filthy stories by arguing that as a historian he had the right to recount true events even if they contained improprieties. He compared himself to Michel de Montaigne, stating that his *Dictionnaire* drew "on the poetic license of Montaigne's essays, both with respect to Pyrrhonism and with respect to the filth!"[32] Bayle similarly refused to leave out the immoral actions of various kings; by giving these examples and citing passages from licentious books, he explained, he had hoped to demonstrate humanity's extreme and universal depravity. He defended himself vigorously against the charges of atheism and libertinism, suggesting that he saw faith and not philosophy as the source of certainty in religious questions. Referencing the Paduan philosopher Pietro Pomponazzi (1462–1525), he stated that the immortality of the soul could be known only through divine revelation, not through philosophical inquiry.[33] He argued that the source of happiness and the best use of reason were found in the submission to faith.

This acerbic exchange marked just one episode in the intellectual war between Bayle and Jurieu, which lasted the better part of three decades. Jurieu would ultimately have the last word by publishing an anonymous pamphlet entitled *Le philosophe de Roterdam accusé, atteint et convaincu* (1706) months before Bayle's death. He repeated his general criticisms against his skeptical opponent, emphasizing what he saw as veiled attacks on Christianity. He contended that although all Calvinists maintained that reason should be submitted to faith, "none of them say that reason is in perpetual contradiction with faith . . . but that one light cannot be contrary to another."[34] Jurieu ended with the harshest possible judgment on the Huguenot skeptic: "I conclude that all the texts that have been written in favor of impiety are not nearly as dangerous as the writings of this man. The author of the book of the Three Impostors, if this work ever existed, the writings of Vanini the atheist, who was burned in Toulouse, those of Hobbes, and, finally, those of Spinoza and of all the Spinozists do not come near the poison of the writings of our philosopher for numerous reasons."[35]

Although Jurieu bitterly attacked Bayle throughout the latter part of their lives, the two men found themselves on the same side of the Calvinist theological debate.[36] Both appeared to agree that the best way to defend the truth of Christianity was not through rational demonstrations but through reliance on supernatural faith.[37] Despite his critiques of Bayle's skepticism, Jurieu claimed that human beings could not understand scripture without divine intervention.[38] If faith in the revelation were to depend on a rationalist analysis of the Bible, Jurieu maintained, one would end in total skepticism, since there would never be sufficient evidence to compel belief. He insisted instead that religious truth was something that was felt rather than discovered by reason.[39] Jurieu was also one of the most vocal millenarians of his time. He believed that the scriptures could be interpreted in such a way as to predict the downfall of Louis XIV and the deposition of the pope, who for him represented the Antichrist.[40] Although Bayle and Jurieu were both fideists, the former endorsed religious toleration and an irenic attitude toward Louis XIV, while the latter bitterly opposed such liberal stances, calling for an establishment of religious conformity and for a holy war against the Catholic monarch.[41] Jurieu's debate with Bayle concerned religious toleration and the Huguenots' relations with Catholic France more than it did theological or epistemological issues.

Bayle and the *Rationaux*

Although Jurieu was Bayle's most vocal Huguenot opponent during his lifetime, the *philosophe de Rotterdam* engaged in a number of equally significant debates with other Protestant intellectuals over the proper relationship between faith and reason. Theologically speaking, the divide between Bayle and the *rationaux* on this question was significantly wider than his differences with Jurieu.[42] This group of Protestant thinkers insisted that rational examinations of scripture provided the only reliable criteria of certainty in religious questions. Consequently, they saw Bayle's fideism as a direct threat to the very foundations of Christianity.

Jacques Bernard (1658–1718), a minister in Gouda, was one of the first authors to confront Bayle on the question of atheism. Bernard edited periodicals such as *Lettres historiques, contenant ce qui se passé de plus important en Europe* (1692–1728) and *Actes et mémoires des négociations de la paix de Ryswick*. He also served as editor of Bayle's *Nouvelles de la République des Lettres* from 1699 until 1710, and he offered his major critiques of Bayle in that learned journal. Bernard penned a series of replies not only to the *Dictionnaire* but also to Bayle's *Réponse aux questions d'un provincial* (1704–7), a multivolume work that contained discussions of the proofs of the existence of God and of the relative merits of atheism. Bernard insinuated that Bayle could have very well endorsed atheism, since he defended it so skillfully.[43] In another article, Bernard suggested that Bayle's real goal in discussing the superstitions and crimes of the ancients was to attack Christianity by comparing it to pagan religions.[44]

Bernard justified his suspicions of Bayle by citing the philosopher's repeated attempts to marshal arguments in favor of atheism and to demonstrate that "reason is opposed to the ideas that we have of the goodness and justice of God."[45] Bernard also objected to the fact that Bayle's *Réponse* had offered a false choice between only two possibilities (paganism and atheism) without stating that he was merely engaging in a *reductio ad absurdum*. He accused Bayle of excessive zeal in arguing that the existence of God was not demonstrable by rational means.[46] The ancients, Bernard contended, had arrived at the knowledge of the existence of God without the Christian revelation through rational proofs.[47] He cited Saint Paul's passage from Romans 1:21, claiming that the pagans had recognized the actuality of a perfect being prior to the revelation, but "they glorified him not as God."[48] By refuting the rational proofs of the existence of the creator and by showing that human reason was incapable of grasping his properties, Bayle had undermined (whether intentionally or not) the very possibility of religious belief: "He piles up the greatest difficulties he can against the immateriality of the soul; he defines the rules that one must observe in order to be able to assure oneself of the truth; and the result of all this is to cast us into perfect Pyrrhonism regarding the first principles of religion, which are the existence of God and the distinction between the soul and the body."[49]

Like Jurieu, Bernard took issue not only with Bayle's explicit argument that a society of atheists could be just as virtuous as a society of Christians but also with the implicit meaning of Bayle's statements and insinuations, both in the *Dictionnaire* and in other texts. In the minds of these two Huguenot critics, Bayle had presented atheism in such a way as to make it a viable option. Both argued that he sought to lead his readers toward unbelief by gradually and speciously undermining all sources of religious certainty. Bayle's Pyrrhonism was thus not an end in itself, the odd couple Bernard and Jurieu argued, but rather a means of promoting atheism by eroding the rational foundations of religion.

Such a view was shared by other notable Huguenot rationalists, such as Isaac Jaquelot (1647–1708) and Jean Le Clerc (1657–1736), both of whom challenged the theological aspects of Bayle's thought. Jaquelot, a Huguenot minister from the Champagne region who had taken refuge in Berlin, composed his reply to Bayle in the *Conformité de la foi avec la raison* (1705). The text offered a more tempered attack against Bayle than the works of Jurieu and Bernard. Jaquelot refrained from accusing Bayle of being a secret atheist and libertine.[50] Instead, he tried to prove that reason served as the basis of religion, to demonstrate the possibility of a rational examination of scripture, and to resolve the difficulties and contradictions posed by Bayle's *Dictionnaire*. In one of his chapters, Jaquelot specifically attempted to refute the implications of Bayle's article "Pyrrhon" by proving that rational understanding was not, in fact, contrary to faith. Since reason was a God-given faculty, it could not stand in opposition to divine revelation, although there could be instances in which divine truths were not accessible to it. By depicting a perpetual contradiction between reason and faith, Bayle inadvertently undermined religion. Such juxtaposition was dangerous because it "pushes men to atheism, to libertinism, and to the full renouncement of religion and of piety." Jaquelot insisted that one needed to "use reason in order to know the proofs of the divinity of the revelation." He rejected the notion that supernatural grace and a total suspension of rational judgment were necessary in order for people to accept both the divine origin and the contents of scripture. Indeed, one needed to consult reason in order to comprehend the most obscure elements of the Bible. Reason and faith were supposed to operate in conjunction with each other, rendering supernatural truths accessible to the human mind. Jaquelot addressed other difficulties posed by his skeptical opponent, such as the doctrine of the Trinity or of the incarnation, and he argued that Bayle's only conceivable goal in presenting these examples was to establish Pyrrhonism and weaken religion.[51]

A year later, Jaquelot published the *Examen de la théologie de Mr. Bayle* (1706) in response to the second volume of Bayle's *Réponse aux questions d'un provincial*. He continued to challenge Bayle on the questions of predestination and free will, as well as on the proper relationship between reason and faith. The work even contained a chapter entitled "That Mr. Bayle must be considered as a person who attacks Religion, because one finds in his work all that is necessary to destroy it." Despite the bold chapter title, Jaquelot claimed that he did not wish to discuss Bayle's intentions, but only the "consequences that come to mind and that result from multiple places in his books."[52] By focusing on what he perceived as the logical outcomes of Bayle's skeptical arguments about religion, Jaquelot could both sidestep the irresolvable question of the author's sincerity and show the apparent conclusions to which his assault on the rational bases of religion led. Jaquelot emphasized the perilous consequences of placing reason in perpetual opposition to faith and suggested that such an approach drove people to doubt the existence of God.[53]

On his deathbed, Pierre Bayle composed one final reply to his rationalist critics, the *Entretiens de Maxime et de Thémiste* (1707).[54] Bayle recapitulated the essential elements of his debates with the *rationaux* and reiterated his fideist stance, claiming that reason was incapable of accounting for seemingly inexplicable theological contradictions, particularly the problem of evil.[55] Since the persistence of evil in the world appeared to contradict the existence of an omnipotent and benevolent creator, Bayle maintained that all attempts to resolve this paradox rationally were futile. Giving the final word to Thémiste, Bayle defended his position and insisted that one "must resort to faith" to resolve apparent contradictions.[56] Human reason could not reconcile the conception of God as an infinitely good and infinitely powerful being with the existence of moral and physical evil, just as it could not reconcile the doctrine of predestination with the notion of free will. The only option was to abandon all attempts to explain these fundamental truths rationally. Bayle's Thémiste further maintained that since God was categorically superior to human beings, his designs and intentions could simply not be judged by the standards of human morality. Bayle insisted that Jaquelot had mischaracterized his fideistic views by suggesting that he had claimed that the Christian mysteries *were* contrary to reason. Bayle argued that he had merely demonstrated that the mysteries *appeared* contrary to reason, which was why he urged his readers to rely on faith in such matters and not to abandon reason entirely.[57] To the dismay of the reading public, the debate would end there. Jaquelot, much like Jurieu, would manage to have the final word, publishing a response a year after Bayle's death.[58]

Bayle's last work was an answer not only to Jaquelot but also to Jean Le Clerc, a prominent professor of philosophy in Amsterdam. Le Clerc, a tireless journalist who, like Bayle, edited several learned journals throughout his career, challenged his fellow Huguenot on the question of the proper relationship between reason and faith.[59] His last and most heated exchange with Bayle took place over the latter's *Réponse aux questions d'un provincial*, a text that appeared to make a powerful justification of atheism. Le Clerc drew a biting parallel between Bayle's laborious attempts to furnish arguments against the existence of a benevolent God and a subject who described his sovereign in the worst possible colors:

> He puts Christians in a situation in which they can neither prove that there is a beneficent God nor demonstrate the truth of the revelation to the atheists and the Manicheans. . . . He wants to make us believe that he is convinced that God is good (by inserting this claim here and there to throw some powder in the eyes of a simpleton) and that it is but a libel to claim that we have reason to doubt him. . . .

He creates a very villainous character, because he gathers all the objections against the goodness of God [and] presents them in the most specious manner possible. . . . It is as if someone had gathered all the most odious things that could be said about the behavior of his sovereign, defied all the other subjects to reply to them, and claimed that he was nevertheless persuaded that the behavior of the sovereign was irreproachable and that he remained his humble servant. . . . The prince would believe, with reason, that this man planned to rouse his subjects against him, and the subjects would have no better opinion of his fidelity even if he decried all accusations as libel.[60]

Bayle's pious fideism was nothing other than cleverly crafted dissimulation. The author's real goal was to undermine the very foundations of religious belief and to convert his readers to atheism.[61] By seeking to destroy every system of theology, Bayle left his readers no other option.

Much like Jurieu and Jaquelot, Le Clerc carried his dispute with Bayle beyond his opponent's grave, publishing a response to the *Entretiens* in 1707.[62] Claiming to defend not only his own reputation but Providence itself against the late *philosophe de Rotterdam*, Le Clerc accused Bayle of impiety, insincerity, and imposture.[63] He remarked that throughout his life Bayle had never intended to seek the truth; instead, he had invented every possible argument against religion.[64] He was most critical of Bayle's public indignation at the accusations leveled by his opponents and of the audacious aplomb with which the *philosophe de Rotterdam* advanced his assertions, calling it a "Pyrrhonian strategy of the Republic of Atheists."[65] Le Clerc was not the only one perturbed by the ideas that his opponent left to posterity.

Of course, Bayle was not the anticipated audience of these attacks. Even the replies that Jurieu, Bernard, Jaquelot, and Le Clerc published during the philosopher's lifetime were not intended primarily for him. Both Bayle and his critics sought to appeal to the broader learned community and to offer the most convincing theological and philosophical positions. Indeed, the debates became so bitter within the Huguenot *refuge* community precisely because each of these thinkers, including Bayle, wanted to offer *the* authoritative interpretation of the most crucial questions of the day. At the same time, the philosophical and theological issues at stake in these disputes were just as important as the public reputations of the respective authors. For reasons of substance and status, one could not let a challenge go unanswered.

Defending Bayle's Memory

Amidst the intense attacks that followed Bayle to the grave, his friends attempted to rehabilitate his reputation with respect to both his scholarly expertise and his controversial theological beliefs. The brothers Jacques Basnage (1653–1723) and Henri Basnage de Beauval (1657–1710) were the first to undertake a defense of the late Bayle's memory against his detractors in an anonymous eulogy published in their *Histoire des ouvrages des savans* in December 1706.[66] In discussing Bayle's historical Pyrrhonism, the unnamed author, now believed to be Jacques Basnage, argued that while many had accused the Huguenot skeptic of pushing "doubt and uncertainty too far," he "often had a reason for it."[67] The eulogist admitted that the *Dictionnaire* presented controversial and heretical opinions but suggested that Bayle's intention was not to advocate these views but to humble overly confident theologians: "His goal was to make those who make pronouncements on all religious matters with such pride and such certainty perceive that a ridiculous sect can make objections from which it is very difficult to escape and of which it is difficult to rid oneself. He wanted to mortify human reason or at least accustom it to never hastening in its judgments and to assenting to nothing without examination and understanding."[68] In the article preceding the eulogy of Bayle, Basnage de Beauval published a letter that enumerated the Catholic and Protestant theologians who shared Bayle's views and decried the bitterness of the attacks against him.[69] Nevertheless, the eulogist expressed the wish that Bayle had been more careful in discussing religion, because he had "let himself go too far in his spirit of doubt and of Pyrrhonism and pushed wisdom too far in looking for difficulties."[70]

Bayle's other friends also rushed to his defense, publishing the anonymous *Histoire de Mr. Bayle et de ses ouvrages* in 1715. They later reprinted this work under the name of the Jesuit Bernard de La Monnoye (1641–1728), along with seven other pamphlets that defended Bayle against his various accusers.[71] The piece attributed to La Monnoye upheld Bayle's scholarly reputation in the Republic of Letters. The author claimed that Bayle had lived a morally upright life and that he had never violated the principles of Christianity.[72] Another pamphlet, the anonymous "Exacte revue de l'histoire de Mr. Bayle," described Bayle as one of the foremost thinkers of the century. It accused both his *rationaux* and his Jesuit critics of libel and of trying to condemn the "heart and religion of this philosopher."[73]

The most robust defense of Bayle, however, came from Pierre Desmaizeaux (1666–1745), a Huguenot exile in England and a close friend of Bayle's. He would be the first to offer the philosopher's biography, in 1708 (in English).[74] Although a French translation would not be published until 1730 with a new edition of the *Dictionnaire*, the Francophone community appeared to be familiar with the text and made numerous references to it before that date. Desmaizeaux portrayed Bayle's skepticism as reasonable and mitigated:

> He perceiv'd things which others cou'd not spy; and finding no solutions for the Objections he discover'd, he left Matters undetermin'd. This Reserve brought him under a charge of Pyrrhonism. But if hereby be meant, that he wou'd not allow Evidence to be the Character of Truth, 'tis the most ill-grounded Accusation in nature. If it only means that he doubted of things which appear'd doubtful, and, in a word, always form'd his Judgments on the report of his Ideas; this is the greatest Honor can be done him. This kind of Pyrrhonism is the perfection of the Human Understanding.[75]

By presenting his protagonist's Pyrrhonism as a reasonable approach to philosophy, one that would be endorsed by most devout and sensible Christians, Desmaizeaux hoped to undermine the public perception that had been created by the *rationaux*.

Desmaizeaux also noted that contrary to the charges of atheism leveled by the late philosopher's detractors, Bayle had confessed to "his intimate Friends that he believ'd [in] a God, a Being infinitely Perfect; and always spoke of the other Mysterys of Religion just as the Reform'd do." The biographer reiterated that "almost all the Catholick, and the greatest part of Protestant Divines, openly maintain the same Doctrines concerning Predestination, Free-will, &c." Accusing the critics of "*Odium Theologicum*," Desmaizeaux blamed them for drawing conclusions that Bayle himself had disowned and for using those deductions to ascribe "pernicious Designs" to Bayle. Since the detractors were the actual authors of those claims, he asserted, the responsibility was theirs, not Bayle's. He lamented the fact that Bayle's enemies could not stop "railing abusive Language" at the *philosophe de Rotterdam* even after his death.[76]

Finally, in attempting to clear Bayle of charges of libertinism, Desmaizeaux stressed the philosopher's moral uprightness. Claiming that even Bayle's "bitterest Enemys cou'd never reproach him" for any faults, Desmaizeaux praised his virtuous behavior, "his Integrity, his Innocence, his Humility, his Temperance, his Equity, his Contempt of the World, [and] his Disinterestedness."[77] Desmaizeaux's conclusion could be read as an implicit allusion to Bayle's discussion of the relationship between virtue and atheism. The *philosophe de Rotterdam* had argued that religious belief had little to do with everyday behavior, since people did not always act out of the fear or love of God: "It should not be considered a paradox but as something quite possible that there are irreligious people who may be more strongly impelled toward a virtuous life by the springs of temperament accompanied by the love of praise and sustained by the fear of dishonor than others are impelled by the instincts of conscience."[78] In other words, Desmaizeaux may have been insinuating that even if Bayle's detractors were unwilling to acknowledge the sincerity of his religious belief, they would have to accept him as the primary example of a virtuous atheist.

Bayle's Enduring Legacy

As Elisabeth Labrousse has demonstrated convincingly, the intellectual battles discussed in this chapter are best understood when read in the context of intra-confessional Huguenot debates.[79] Indeed, she shows the deep divide within the Huguenot community between rationalist thinkers such as Bernard, Jaquelot, and Jean Le Clerc, on the one hand, and the allegedly fideist Bayle, on the other. The *rationaux'* reading of Bayle, as well as Jurieu's attacks on him, would foreshadow future critiques of Bayle by both Protestants and Catholics. However, even in the Protestant context, there remained some favorable readings of Bayle far into the eighteenth century. Although the *philosophe de Rotterdam* would remain a controversial figure, many trusted the sincerity of his theological views. Indeed, as late as 1716 the *Dictionnaire* was awarded as the prize to the best student in theology at the Reformed Académie de Neuchâtel. Similarly, the German count Nicolaus Zinzendorf (1700–1760) and other Pietists appeared to believe in the sincerity of Bayle's fideism.[80] This difference in interpretation among scholars is largely owing to the inter- and intra-confessional divergences inherent in Protestant theology.

These divisions became apparent not only in the debates about the proper relationship between reason and faith but also in discussions concerning the toleration of religious dissent, the Huguenot émigrés' relations with Catholic France, and even the divine right of kings.[81] Thus, depending on the theological, philosophical, and political side from which one approached Bayle's text, the *philosophe de Rotterdam* could be simultaneously read as a pious fideist, a liberal Calvinist, a witty libertine, and a crypto-atheist. These and many other labels would follow Bayle's complex legacy in the succeeding generations. His elusive *philosophical* skepticism was never in and of itself the aspect of his thought that most agitated Bayle's first critics. They opposed his alleged Pyrrhonism not because it seemed to undermine the foundations of established philosophical systems but because they believed that it struck a mortal blow to any possibility of establishing and supporting a rational foundation for religion. His skepticism, then, would be seen as a means to advance atheism and irreligion, not as an epistemological goal in itself.

Despite the many criticisms it faced, and in part because of them, the *Dictionnaire* continued to grow in popularity significantly after its author's death, going through nine different French editions between 1697 and 1741.[82] It was translated into English in 1710 and 1734 and into German in 1741. As we will see in the following chapters, theological and philosophical controversy surrounding Bayle's legacy would only intensify during the first half of the eighteenth century, as the allegedly growing waves of skepticism, deism, and atheism would continue to occupy the "orthodox" thinkers. For those attempting to stem this coming tide, Bayle would become a true *bête noire*.

CHAPTER THREE

The Specter of Bayle Returns to Haunt France

Bayle's *Dictionnaire* in Catholic Paris

In many significant ways, Bayle's intra-confessional debates with the Huguenot *rationaux* influenced the manner in which his skeptical works, particularly the *Dictionnaire*, were received in French-speaking Europe. However, the sharp differences between the religious, political, and intellectual situations of France and the Dutch Republic transformed the perceptions of his alleged Pyrrhonism, both for his admirers and for his adversaries. As the theological concerns of the intra-Protestant contests became transposed onto inter-confessional disputes, the stakes of the debates surrounding the implications of philosophical and religious skepticism changed. While the *rationaux* and Bayle competed both over their intellectual standing within the Huguenot community and over theological issues that were particular to Reformed theology, Bayle's French readers were often more interested in his treatment of Catholicism and of Christianity in general. As a result, the French Catholic critics of skepticism who sought to undermine Bayle's explicit and implicit claims deployed arguments that differed significantly from those of their Protestant counterparts.

Contrary to Labrousse's claim that the intellectual atmosphere in Paris was "alien to faith and fideism" in the 1720s,[1] it is quite obvious that the French reading public of that time had encountered a number of fideist Catholics since the revival of Pyrrhonism in the sixteenth century. Montaigne, Charron, La Mothe Le Vayer, and Huet had all endorsed systems of religious belief that relied on the submission of natural reason to supernatural faith. They had also advocated a total suspension of judgment in philosophical questions because of the mind's inability to know the surrounding world or its own operations with any degree of certainty. Consequently, the French learned audience was already predisposed to the counterintuitive combination of philosophical skepticism and religious belief that had so shocked some of Bayle's Huguenot critics.

The French Catholic readers were often unfamiliar with the confessional context that had surrounded Bayle's bestselling text, as Labrousse has suggested, and they perceived his attacks on Catholicism or on the rival claims of his Huguenot adversaries as assaults on all revealed religion.[2] However, Labrousse does not mention that this was precisely the same interpretation that Bayle's Huguenot opponents had advanced when they accused him of subverting Christianity. This indicates that the French Catholic perception may have developed not from the Parisian audience's unfamiliarity with fideism but from a combination of the peculiar and dramatic nature with which Bayle presented religious paradoxes and of the ongoing criticisms he faced from his rivals, who repeatedly accused him of attacking all of Christianity. Furthermore, the appropriation of Bayle's paradoxes by the *libertins érudits* and by the deists undoubtedly helped to reinforce the association between his Pyrrhonism and its irreligious implications.[3]

A final, perhaps most crucial element in the story of Bayle's reception in France is the change in the nation's political climate after the death of Louis XIV in 1715. Philippe II, duc d'Orléans (1674–1723), who served as regent to Louis XV until 1723, sharply mitigated his uncle's stringent censorship, allowing the reprinting of many books that had been banned in the preceding years.[4] He also lifted the restriction on the import of books printed abroad. In gratitude for the promotion of such a "spirit of freedom," the editor of the third official edition of the *Dictionnaire* (1720), the renowned Huguenot journalist Prosper Marchand (1678–1756), joined its publisher, Michel Bohm (d. 1722), in dedicating the text to the "enlightened" regent.[5] Due to the relaxation of censorship, the French reading public also became familiar with the first Greek-Latin parallel edition of Sextus Empiricus's collected works (1718),[6] a French translation of Sextus's *Hypotyposes pirroniennes* (1725),[7] and Huet's *Traité philosophique de la foiblesse de l'esprit humain*. While these texts were printed outside of France, they easily made their way across the border and into the hands of Parisians eager to read them. In addition to these controversial skeptical treatises, the French audience encountered a proliferation of the so-called clandestine manuscripts. These works expounded subversive ideas often associated with deism, materialism, and atheism, and they circulated in France from the end of the seventeenth century through the first half of the eighteenth. Because of the heterodox ideas they offered, they were seldom published, remaining anonymous and mostly in manuscript form to avoid detection and suppression. Nevertheless, their contents were disseminated widely and rapidly through extensive duplication.[8] Thus, after 1715, Parisian readers could turn to a variety of sources if they wanted to familiarize themselves with Pyrrhonism, deism, and other heterodox notions. Such a development in turn drove apologetic writers to offer more extensive refutations of what they perceived as an increasingly pernicious flood of subversive literature.[9]

This chapter explores the diverse ways in which Bayle's skeptical claims were received in the French context, especially from 1715 to the 1750s, and it reveals some crucial similarities to and differences from the Huguenot critiques. Catholic authors, particularly the Jesuits, adopted novel and peculiar strategies in their attempted refutations of Bayle's arguments. Frequently, they chose to point out the various deficiencies and inaccuracies of his scholarship rather than challenge his skeptical claims directly. They did so in part because many of their contemporaries read the *Dictionnaire* as an entertaining source of encyclopedic information and erudite knowledge. By trying to discredit both Bayle's scholarly credentials and the *Dictionnaire*'s reliability, his opponents hoped to reduce the destructive impact of his controversial views. These critical efforts would culminate in several anti-*Dictionnaires* that reveal some intellectual affinity and continuity between the goals and methods of erudite textual criticism and those of the *Encyclopédie* project. Both the Catholic critics of Bayle and the *encyclopédistes* were deeply concerned with expanding the reservoir of human knowledge.

Furthermore, the *philosophe de Rotterdam*'s claims about the weakness of human reason in general and its total inability to resolve supernatural questions in particular were not always antithetical to Catholicism. In some ways, Bayle's paradoxical examples made a strong case against the Protestant insistence on *sola scriptura* by showing how independent reason, unguided by the infallible Catholic Church, could trap itself in irresoluble difficulties. As we will see, the initially lukewarm attitudes toward Bayle's project would turn increasingly hostile over the course of the eighteenth century. The progressively polemical nature of debates between the philosophes and their opponents led to a growing polarization of the French learned culture, particularly on religious questions.[10] Furthermore, the intensification of the intra-Catholic contest between the Jesuit order, whose members generally embraced a rationalist stance on many issues of the creed, and the theologians of the Jansenist movement, whose views on these matters often approximated Bayle's, created greater controversy about fideist defenses of Christianity.

Mixed Reviews: Renaudot's Denunciation
and the Jesuit Flirtation with Bayle

Despite Bayle's best efforts to arrange for an edition of the *Dictionnaire* to be printed (and receive approbation) in France, his text was banned during his lifetime owing to the critical report by the royal censor, the abbé Eusèbe Renaudot. As we have seen, Renaudot's letter had been republished by Jurieu, who agreed with the essential critiques proposed by its author: Bayle's *œuvre* was a dangerous source of subversive ideas, and it undermined Christianity at every possible instance. The censor's main contention was that Bayle's treatment of religious questions could only scandalize readers and promote libertinism. Among the offenses of the *Dictionnaire*, he stressed the irreverent way in which the Huguenot skeptic had treated the sacred authors of the Old Testament, the improper remarks in the article "Adam," and the licentious comments about temptations faced by various saints and other revered biblical figures. Renaudot noted that Bayle often cited out-of-context passages written by the early church fathers (Saint Augustine in particular) in order to ridicule them.

While Renaudot acknowledged that Bayle's apparent Pyrrhonism was dangerous to both major confessions, he claimed that Bayle specifically focused on attacking the Catholic Church.[11] Renaudot's censure seems to undermine Labrousse's assertion that Catholic readers saw Bayle's critiques of Catholicism merely as attacks directed against all religion.[12] Indeed, the royal censor appeared to be very attuned to Bayle's assaults on the Church, arguing that the Huguenot émigré used selective evidence and presented rumors in such a way that Calvinists were "everywhere justified, and the Catholics blamed."[13]

Like Jurieu and the *rationaux*, he accused Bayle of promoting various doctrinal errors and heresies, such as those of the pre-Adamites, the Manicheans, and the Pelagians. By discussing them in sympathetic ways, Bayle lent them credibility. Although Renaudot was particularly angered by the treatment of Catholicism in the *Dictionnaire*, the royal censor concluded that Bayle's religious Pyrrhonism was injurious to all revealed religion: "And since the nature of his mind is a kind of Pyrrhonism in religion, it pervades all of this work in a way that must harm not only the Catholics but also the Protestants of good faith."[14] He made a nearly identical claim in his letter to the Huguenot journalist François Janiçon (1674–1730): "As to the rest, I do not believe that anyone could have made a report different from mine or concealed from M. Boucherat, the chancelier, that this book was full of things against religion, not only Catholic but also

Christian."[15] Like the *rationaux*, he found Bayle's skeptical ideas to be a significant threat to all religious belief and therefore unfit for publication and distribution in France.

Renaudot's report set the tone for how the self-proclaimed opponents of skepticism, atheism, and libertinism would speak about the *Dictionnaire*. For many, Bayle was the major source fueling these heterodox ideas. This attitude toward the Huguenot skeptic would gain momentum throughout the century, as "orthodox" defenders of the faith, Catholic and Protestant alike, explained how Bayle's ideas could be appropriated to advocate irreligion.

Not all French Catholics ascribed impious intentions to Bayle. In discussing the controversial *Réponse aux questions d'un provincial*, the editors of the Jesuit *Mémoires de Trévoux* praised Bayle's erudition.[16] They also admired his skill at playing the devil's advocate: "Mr. Bayle . . . wanted his own hopeless cause to make his eloquence shine. He proposed in his *Dictionnaire* the arguments of the Manicheans, [and] he lent them new reasons: the origin of evil, if one believes in it, is a pitfall that reason cannot escape without the help of revelation; and anyone who consults nothing but [one's own] natural lights will never reconcile the multitude of physical and moral evils that distress the universe with the idea of an infinitely good and omnipotent God."[17] Father René-Joseph de Tournemine (1661–1739), the editor in chief of the *Mémoires de Trévoux* and the likely author of the article,[18] did not seem to perceive Bayle's arguments or their consequences as particularly serious or treacherous. Tournemine offered an equally apologetic presentation of Bayle as a skilled rhetorician who "undertook a defense of skepticism to show off his mind and his ability to argue for and against anything" in his *Réflexions sur l'athéisme* (1713).[19] The Jesuit editor did not seem perturbed by the implications of Bayle's claims and did not appear to think that Bayle actually subscribed to the views that he had presented.

Tournemine continued his warm appraisal of Bayle in a note that followed the republished version Jacques Basnage's eulogy of the *philosophe de Rotterdam*: "Although we were forced to refute M. Bayle on more than one occasion, we were able to perceive that while we hated the errors, we sincerely loved the author. A true esteem was the only bond of friendship that we had for him."[20] Despite such kind words for his fellow journalist, Tournemine took the opportunity to make a theological claim about the superiority of the Catholic faith. He suggested that Bayle's controversial religious views should not be blamed on the ulterior motives of the late philosopher but on the method by which the Protestants approached religious questions: "His mind, too accustomed to dispute everything, became almost inaccessible to faith. This is the common effect of the Protestant method: it brings the most enlightened of its partisans to an almost complete incredulity, which they hide under the guise of universal toler- ance, and their excesses are the most conclusive proof of the need for an infalli- ble and present oracle to teach the truths of the faith."[21] For Tournemine, Bayle's Pyrrhonism and incredulity were a direct result of Protestant reasoning. Bayle did not stand out as a source of irreverence and skepticism; he was merely the victim of the errors of his particular confession.

As Pierre Rétat has suggested, the Jesuits may have had ulterior motives for praising Bayle's intellect. They seemed to like his disruptive and controversial arguments against other Protestant theologians, because the difficulties he pro- posed helped expose both the problematic nature of some of the Protestant te- nets, such as predestination and free grace, and the idea that the human mind could comprehend theological truths without the intervention of a divinely in- spired Catholic Church. On multiple occasions, the *Mémoires de Trévoux* brought up Bayle's arguments against the *rationaux*, such as Jean Le Clerc and Isaac Jaquelot, to demonstrate the weakness of their reasoning.[22] Indeed, a bitter theological quarrel among Protestants helped Catholics to justify their own approach to religion, and Bayle inadvertently agitated on their behalf.[23] The enemy of their enemies became their temporary ally.

Another possible explanation is that Tournemine and his fellow editors thought they could wet the powder in the barrel of Bayle's contentious ideas precisely by presenting his claims as uncontroversial. In dismissing Bayle's use of Manichean arguments as a simple exercise in rhetoric, Tournemine may have been seeking to undermine their significance and their danger. Similarly, by painting Bayle's apparent religious Pyrrhonism as a typical outcome of Prot- estant reasoning, Tournemine could make it seem like a quotidian view and detract from its potentially perilous implications.

Although the *Mémoires de Trévoux* was one of the major voices of Jesuit intel- lectuals in France, not all Jesuits agreed with the respect and reverence with which the journal treated Bayle at the time. Ignace de Laubrussel (1663–1730), a professor of theology and philosophy in Strasbourg, offered a harsh critique of Bayle, placing him among the leaders of the libertines. He described the *Diction- naire* as a "collection of major errors" and a "mosaic that, in its bizarre assort- ment of citations and in its serious and comical reflections, provides that from which one can create the most monstrous assortment of obscenities, monstrosi- ties, and atheism."[24] He argued that Bayle had "cleared the land and cultivated the roots of incredulity in us more than any other person; and that after weeding out faith in the mysteries, as being filled with thorns and contradictions, he planted the seeds of atheism."[25] Laubrussel enumerated the weapons that Bayle's texts provided to libertines and atheists. These included his arguments against universal consent to the existence of God, his claim that Christianity was not the best faith for maintaining a society, his presentation of Christians as violent zealots, and his assertion that reason furnished nothing but contradictions when it considered the mysteries of religion.[26]

As Bayle's works gained greater popularity in French learned circles, even the Jesuits of the *Mémoires de Trévoux* began to change their initial evaluations of Bayle's skepticism. In discussing the appearance of the third edition of the *Dictionnaire*, the editors seemed wary of the dangerous messages contained in the work and criticized the regent for allowing it in France: "Would posterity, which will find there such crude obscenities, such badly disguised impieties, which will see there the Holy scriptures, God, and religion bluntly attacked, believe that the booksellers who printed it were Christian and that Christian magistrates allowed its printing? Is it sound policy to inspire unbelief and authorize debauchery, to rattle the surest foundations of states, to break the ties of society, which are religion and morality?"[27] Bayle's role as devil's advocate no longer seemed harmless to the editors, who questioned the wisdom of sanctioning new editions of the *Dictionnaire*. As the loosening of censorship allowed the proliferation of subversive literature that appeared to pose threats to the religious and moral orders, the Jesuits of the *Mémoires de Trévoux* decided that they could no longer afford to play with fire.

Some critics thought that the relaxation of censorship measures was actually a deliberate attempt by the regent to promote unbelief and immorality. When recalling the regency period in his *Mémoires*, Cardinal François Joachim de Pierre de Bernis (1715–94) specifically mentioned the pernicious influence of the *Dictionnaire* on faith and morality:

> All those who thought boldly about religion have the right to like the regent. He allowed a new edition of Bayle's *Dictionnaire* to be dedicated to him, [and] this dangerous book passed into the hands of the whole world; by reading it one became a savant cheaply. One learned from the scandalous anecdotes; one saw the objections [against religion] presented in the full light of day. . . . The spirit of incredulity and of libertinism circulated together in the world. The irreligion of the regent and his debauchery easily found imitators in a nation whose own character is to slavishly imitate the virtues and vices of its masters; [moral] corruption became almost universal; one displayed materialism, deism, Pyrrhonism . . . ; it was no longer in good taste to believe in the Gospels.[28]

This, of course, was not the only accusation made against a regime that, compared with its predecessor, seemed to embody the most hazardous freethinking tendencies. The association of the *Dictionnaire* with the three-headed monster of skepticism, atheism, and libertinism was repeated so many times that it became almost a commonplace. As Bernis and Crousaz remarked, the admirers of this work were most often found among the members of high society who were not themselves savants or *érudits* but wanted to feign expertise in diverse subjects.[29]

Bayle's *Dictionnaire* in the Correspondence of Catholic Savants

While many French critics would continue to expose and disparage the harmful effects of Bayle's skeptical *œuvre*, some went beyond simple condemnations and actually analyzed the contents and the factual accuracy of the grandiose work. This was an alternative strategy for addressing the implications of Bayle's Pyrrhonian arguments. Rather than engaging his ideas in a polemical fashion, some French Catholic scholars attempted to discredit Bayle's erudition by showing that his scholarship was disorderly, inaccurate, and consequently untrustworthy. These critics perceived that many of their contemporaries saw the *Dictionnaire* as a major source of information about the past. By attacking Bayle's credibility and his scholarly aptitude, they sought to weaken the pervasive influence of his work and deprive it of its encyclopedic status.

One of the earliest efforts to provide a comprehensive analysis of the *Dictionnaire* was undertaken by Laurent-Josse Le Clerc (1677–1736), a Lyonnais scholar from the order of Saint Sulpice.[30] While serving as the director of the Séminaire de Saint-Irénée in Lyon, Le Clerc dedicated his life to humanist studies and critical scholarship. Before commencing a thorough examination of Bayle's work, he had already completed an extensive review of Louis Moréri's *Le grand dictionnaire historique* and composed a biographical supplement to César-Pierre Richelet's *Dictionnaire françois*.[31] Knowing Le Clerc's penchant for textual criticism, Mathieu Marais (1664–1737), a jurist in the Parlement of Paris and one of Bayle's most avid supporters in France, challenged him to undertake a critical examination of Bayle's *Dictionnaire*.[32] Although Le Clerc would publish his *Lettre critique sur le Dictionnaire de Bayle* in 1732 and attach his comments on the *Dictionnaire*'s various articles to the 1734 edition of the controversial text, his first reactions appeared in his letters to Marais.

While Europe had rapidly embraced print culture, it is vital not to underestimate the importance and diversity of correspondence networks in the eighteenth century. Letters provided a means to extend scholarly debates beyond published treatises, allowing intellectuals across Europe to probe the philosophical principles of their allies and adversaries. Thinkers would often write to close friends asking them to pass along their questions and objections to those authors with whom they were not directly acquainted, thereby expanding the epistolary networks even further. Frequently these exchanges were published in journals or in edited volumes, allowing the reading public to witness the protracted versions of philosophical debates. In many significant ways, an analysis of such correspondence sheds light on the intersecting intellectual circles of thinkers who shared similar concerns and reveals the most pressing topics of the day.[33] The triangular correspondence of Marais, Le Clerc, and Jean Bouhier (1673–1746) serves as an excellent example.

Both Marais, in Paris, and Le Clerc, who lived in Lyon, exchanged letters with Jean Bouhier, the president of the Parlement of Bourgogne in Dijon. A prominent literary and judicial scholar, Bouhier had built up a vast correspondence network across Europe.[34] In their missives, the two men appealed to Bouhier as to an independent authority, making their respective cases about Bayle's worth and legacy and soliciting his judgment on the matter. Marais and Bouhier had been discussing Le Clerc's forthcoming critique of Bayle since the end of 1724.[35] Before Marais received Le Clerc's extensive examination of the *Dictionnaire's* accuracy, the two thinkers had already exchanged some impressions regarding the importance of the text and Bayle's character. Marais had complained to Bouhier about Le Clerc's depiction of the *philosophe de Rotterdam,* "You will find an ugly portrait that he paints of Bayle, and he is so little disposed to forgive that he wants to present him as a depraved man."[36] Bouhier expressed curiosity about Le Clerc's long letter to Marais and asked Marais for a copy. In wording this request, Bouhier appeared to maintain a neutral stance in the debate about Bayle. He said he wished to read the critique because "in these kinds of battles, there is nothing to do but learn, and he [Le Clerc] assures me there will not be any bitterness toward the deceased."[37] Marais, in turn, suggested that while he looked forward to reading the critical letter about his late friend, he did not intend to respond, since Le Clerc would find errors in Bayle's work even if there were none.[38] Le Clerc's long-awaited critique would finally be in Marais's hands just one day later.[39]

Le Clerc began his meticulous examination with a long introduction. He remarked that he had been preparing corrections of the *Dictionnaire* for a long time but wanted to send Marais some initial remarks since he would not be finished soon.[40] Le Clerc's major line of censure concerned the quality of Bayle's uncritical use of sources and his excessive copying from various authors. In discussing the article "Alegambe," Le Clerc faulted Bayle for taking large sections of the text from the Protestant savant Adrien Baillet (1649–1706) without analyzing the content of what he had reported: "This is precisely what I find reprehensible in Bayle. In thousands of places he seeks nothing but to empty his notebooks . . . without discussing the strengths and weaknesses, the true and the false."[41] Le Clerc pointed out numerous instances in which Bayle had relied on incorrect information or made an uninformed use of his sources. He also attacked Bayle's claim that his only responsibility as a scholar was to provide correct citations: "Is this not, Monsieur, a maxim directly opposed to the first principles of what we call precise criticism? . . . Where would we end up, Monsieur, if every historian abandoned criticism and declared that without being himself the guarantor of facts, he aspired only to certify the accuracy of his citations and claimed that it was up to those whom he cited to verify them?"[42] By absolving himself of the responsibility to check the validity of his sources, Bayle had renounced the right to call himself a legitimate scholar. Rules of learned criticism obligated him to check the accuracy of the information he recorded. It was not sufficient to reproduce what readers could find for themselves. Le Clerc took a similar stance on Bayle's uncritical use of sources in the *Remarques* on Moréri's dictionary.[43] He suggested that Bayle's actions could in fact merit his being known as a plagiarist.[44]

In effect, by describing the *philosophe de Rotterdam* as a bad historian, Le Clerc sought to undermine what he perceived as a dangerous thinker in a novel way. Rather than denouncing him as a mischievous and clever proponent of skepticism and atheism, Le Clerc tried to expose Bayle as a fraud. He sought to show Marais that his idol was not an able scholar but a poor critic. This invalidated the very contents of the *Dictionnaire*: far from being an erudite encyclopedia, it was merely a sloppy work filled with basic errors and factual inaccuracies.

Unlike most detractors of the *Dictionnaire*, Le Clerc did not emphasize the atheistic implications of the work, mentioning them only once in the printed version: "I have said . . . 'his Critical Dictionary is full of features that tend to favor atheism, of dirty stories, of partiality toward the Huguenots and for Huguenot religion, etc.' . . . I made a choice. I limited myself to the errors of fact, without touching upon those of right, not wishing to make anything but a critical work, and not one about theology or [religious] controversy."[45] By shying away from the topic, Le Clerc managed to avoid repeating Bayle's controversial ideas and exposing the reading public to subversive arguments and irreverent passages. Instead, he could focus on challenging the quality of the *philosophe de Rotterdam*'s historical scholarship.

Although he mostly ignored the religious implications of Bayle's *Dictionnaire* in the published version of his critique, Le Clerc did, nevertheless, raise the subject of Pyrrhonism and atheism in his long letter to Marais. His examination of Bayle's intentions revealed a new line of critique, one that would later be taken up by fervent anti-skeptics such as Crousaz:

> Atheism is the most enormous of all the crimes, and one should never suspect anyone of it unless one finds it determined by proofs of the greatest force. But it is one thing to accuse man of being an atheist, and another thing to say that a lot of remarks favoring atheism came out of his mouth and from his pen. It happens all the time that people, [owing to the] mistake of [their inner] lights or of [their] reflections, [or] often because of a certain libertinism of the mind or of the heart, offer discourses that are completely contrary to religion without actually being atheists. This even happens with people who are not unintelligent. Bayle himself made this distinction in different parts of his *Dictionnaire*.[46]

Le Clerc was referring to Bayle's distinction between atheism in speculative matters (*l'athéisme spéculatif*) and atheism in the practical sphere (*l'athéisme pratique*).[47] Le Clerc claimed that whether or not Bayle was actually an atheist, his arguments about the possibility of virtuous atheism and his objections to the possibility of rational demonstrations of the existence of God were equally damaging to religion. The author's intention was irrelevant if the effects of his claims were subversive.

Unlike critics who contended that Bayle was a secret atheist and libertine who sought to weaken religion, Le Clerc moved past the irresolvable debate about Bayle's conspiratorial motives and analyzed the arguments and their consequences on their own merits. He reached conclusions that resembled those of the *rationaux*, but he largely avoided *ad hominem* invectives. Nevertheless, Le Clerc leaned toward the view that Bayle was a crypto-atheist, giving three reasons for his opinion. First, Bayle's texts contained a "certain element of Pyrrhonism in the matter of religion" that pointed to "a man whose goal was to infect and destroy the most essential truths, rather than to support and defend them." Second, "thousands and thousands of people of every kind" questioned Bayle's faith. Finally, various "libertines . . . drew arguments from Bayle" and thought that "he believed only when it was convenient."[48] Like many other critics, Le Clerc accused Bayle of attempting to extend the arguments of philosophical skepticism to religion in order to undermine the faith. More importantly, however, his reflections provided a rebuttal to Bayle's Pyrrhonism by offering a significant claim about the nature of certainty and the possibility of establishing the high probability of particular facts. In the case surrounding Bayle's religious views, Le Clerc maintained that a consensus among multiple witnesses and the contents of the *Dictionnaire* amounted to a preponderance of evidence against the controversial philosopher. This line of reasoning would become quite popular in refutations of Pyrrhonian claims about the uncertainty of philosophical and historical knowledge.

As Marais had already indicated to Bouhier, he would not reply to Le Clerc's six-hundred-page critique. Marais seemed to be annoyed by the number of minutiae contained in the letter of the "hypercritique."[49] He also disapproved of the insinuations about Bayle's atheism. Suggesting that Le Clerc went "too deep into [Bayle's] conscience, where he should not search at all," Marais questioned whether Le Clerc had "made the effort to read Bayle's four justifications."[50] In addition, he seemed unimpressed with the thoroughness of Le Clerc's scholarship, suggesting that by focusing on minor errors, Le Clerc had overlooked the beauty and grandeur of Bayle's *œuvre*. Bouhier replied that "it would be folly to answer the abbé Le Clerc point by point."[51]

This reaction reveals the great divergence between Marais's and Le Clerc's perceptions of the *Dictionnaire*. For the former, it was a literary masterpiece that could be read for entertainment as much as for information. For the latter, it was a poorly researched encyclopedic project that failed to fulfill the basic demands of the genre. Le Clerc assumed that his contemporaries used Bayle's text as a reliable source of factual information. He thus saw it as his scholarly duty to fix the errors in the *Dictionnaire* and to expose it as a work of superficial scholarship. His corrections would be used by later critics of Bayle and would be representative of the encyclopedic projects that became increasingly common in the eighteenth century.

In answering Le Clerc, Marais took a more civil tone than he did in his letters to Bouhier. He maintained that considering the impressive number of authorities whom Bayle cited in his work, there were bound to be some errors. Granting Le Clerc the analysis of Bayle's Protestantism as a given, he cast the remainder of the erudite critique as a friendly correction of mistakes in the text: "If you purge him of his factual errors, Monsieur, how much more admirable you make him and what a service you render to his friends, who would like to see him perfect. I would like to have this critique already, place it in the margins of my [copy of the] *Dictionnaire*, and identify everywhere the critic of the critic. I am far from being dissatisfied by your censure, Monsieur; it does nothing but augment my love for my friend."[52] Marais believed that by correcting the errors of the *Dictionnaire*, Le Clerc had helped to improve the text and make Bayle's research "unimpeachable."[53] In his reply to Bouhier, Marais expressed annoyance at Le Clerc and stressed that the various errors the Lyonnais scholar had discovered had in no way weakened his respect for Bayle's undertaking or his critical abilities.[54]

Exasperated by the lack of response from Marais, who had dismissively overlooked the months of efforts he had put into examining the text, Le Clerc ultimately decided to publish his corrections.[55] If he could not convince Marais of the defects of Bayle's work, Le Clerc would attempt to do so in the eyes of the larger learned audience. Although his main goal was to correct the factual accuracy of the *Dictionnaire*, the preface contained observations about the work's pernicious nature. Le Clerc expanded his original critique in the printed version of his letter, arguing that he did not wish to look inside Bayle's soul. It was evident, however, that the *Dictionnaire* was a pernicious work, because it "created many impious people."[56] As in his letters, Le Clerc emphasized the effects of Bayle's apparent skepticism rather than the philosopher's actual intentions.

Two years after the publication of his *Lettre critique*, Laurent-Josse Le Clerc would republish his work in a new format, alongside the sixth edition of Bayle's *Dictionnaire* (1734). As the publisher's foreword noted, it was almost unprecedented for such a voluminous work to be reissued so frequently in such a short time span.[57] Unlike previous editions, however, this one would contain Le Clerc's critical remarks at the end of each volume. Ironically, the sixth edition of the *Dictionnaire* was exactly as Marais had envisioned: the addition of the *Lettre critique* to Bayle's text rendered the work more exact and consequently more perfect.

The ultimately unsuccessful exchange between Marais and Le Clerc demonstrates the wide gulf that separated the two thinkers. To Marais, Bayle had been a close friend and a literary inspiration.[58] From his letters to Bouhier, it is apparent that the Parisian jurist admired Bayle's character, his erudition, his provocative wit, and his ideas. He thus saw it as a duty to defend his late friend's memory against the mounting accusations of irreligion and to uphold his reputation in the Republic of Letters. In fact, Marais had urged the Basnage brothers to compose an apology for Bayle as early as 1709.[59] To Le Clerc, Bayle was an impostor and a threat to the integrity of his profession. The *Dictionnaire* and other texts constituted not just an outrage for Catholics and a subversive promotion of skepticism, atheism, and libertinism. They were also an affront to critical scholarship. By neglecting to examine his sources and to verify the reported facts, Le Clerc argued, Bayle had failed in his essential duty as a journalist and a scholar, and he had helped to spread erroneous information to contemporaries and to posterity. Such disregard served to multiply errors and uncertainties about the past, thereby promoting skepticism.

Le Clerc had undertaken the critique because he wanted to lower Bayle's standing in the eyes of his most prominent supporters in France. Marais's dismissal showed that his approach was not successful in changing the minds of committed admirers of the *philosophe de Rotterdam*. However, it did open the way for a new strategy in addressing the fundamental problems posed by the *Dictionnaire* and its Pyrrhonism. Le Clerc's critique could also be read as an attempt to offer a more exact portrayal of historical facts, one that challenged the landscape of uncertainties presented by Bayle and damaged his skeptical claims in matters of historical scholarship. By demonstrating that one could arrive at a more certain knowledge of the past through a rigorous critical analysis of sources and a meticulous verification of facts, Le Clerc tried to chip away at Bayle's scholarly reputation and, more importantly, to undermine Pyrrhonism. His attempts to correct Bayle's factual errors would prove to be a popular and enduring strategy among Catholic apologists.[60]

The Anti-*Dictionnaire* Projects

Following Le Clerc's critical approach to Bayle's bestselling text, other French Catholics attempted to defuse the skeptical and irreligious implications that followed from the work by composing their own rival alternatives to the *Dictionnaire*. In the same year that Le Clerc published his *Lettre critique*, another critic of Bayle, the Jesuit Charles Merlin (1678–1747), issued his *Réfutation des critiques de Monsieur Bayle sur Saint Augustin* (1732). The *Réfutation* contained three distinct treatises and was meant to be a sample of a larger work in which the professor of letters, philosophy, and theology at the Collège Louis-le-Grand in Paris promised to give the public a full refutation of Bayle on matters concerning religion. The text was supposed to serve as an antidote to what he saw as the most irreverent and irreligious parts of Bayle's magnum opus. It would also resemble the structure of the infamous *Dictionnaire*: "These days one loves order and arrangement. This is why I also . . . believed that it was necessary to give my refutation in the form of a dictionary, where, following an alphabetical order, I compose a text with notes in the style of Bayle."[61] The promised anti-*Dictionnaire*, however, would never appear, because Merlin became involved in a protracted dispute with the Jansenists, whom he had accused of conspiring with Bayle.[62]

Merlin's goal was not unlike Le Clerc's, although his critique was confined to the defense of the church fathers, who he believed had been mistreated and slandered in Bayle's work.[63] He focused specifically on rectifying the misrepresentations of Saint Augustine and other sacred authors in the *Dictionnaire*. He offered both factual and interpretive corrections of Bayle's descriptions of the theological and philosophical positions of these revered authorities. Unlike Le Clerc, who had maintained a civil tone, Merlin did not conceal his disdain for the controversial philosopher. He frequently emphasized the apparent complicity between Bayle and his libertine followers and called him "the professor of the godless of our times."[64]

Merlin's most extensive treatise against the Huguenot skeptic was his *Apologie de David* (1737), in which he commented on the infamous article on King David in the *Dictionnaire*. Merlin's opening to the *Apologie de David* set the tone for the rest of the work. He maintained that Bayle had dealt a blow to religion "in the manner of the most dishonest and hypocritical libertine in the world."[65] Merlin corrected various chronological and factual mistakes in Bayle's account, suggesting that the Huguenot had maliciously altered scriptural passages in order to undermine the author of the Psalms.[66] He tried to exculpate David from the majority of the accusations by refuting them outright or putting the king's actions in their historical and cultural context.[67] By justifying David's behavior as a fulfillment of God's will, Merlin sought to weaken Bayle's premises about the incomprehensibility of divine grace. He believed that Bayle's arguments either led to fideist conclusions or, even worse, damaged the standing of one of the most revered biblical figures. In his conclusion, Merlin claimed that of all the irreverent articles in the *Dictionnaire*, the one on David harmed religion most severely: "Among an infinite number of things by which honest believers were scandalized when skimming through the *Historical and Critical Dictionary*, it is with good reason that the article on David particularly shocked them. One easily understood that it was written to weaken the foundations of revelation, while in the rest of the work the author does not leave anything else but revelation to refute the majority of impious systems.[68] Just as Jurieu had done many years before him, Merlin remarked that Bayle had dissimulated his Pyrrhonism in order to systematically undermine the rational foundations of religion and then to destroy faith-based arguments by showing the contradictions of scripture.

As the reading public became more diverse in terms of its educational background and began increasingly to turn away from formal philosophical treatises and toward fictional literature and didactic dialogues, defenders of religious orthodoxy adapted to capture the attention of this new audience. While Merlin was attempting to fight against the consequences of what he saw as Bayle's misrepresentation of sacred authors in short treatises and was aspiring to compose an anti-*Dictionnaire* to attract a wider audience, his Jesuit colleague Jacques Le Febvre (whom we briefly encountered in chapter 1) published a short and concise refutation of Bayle's essential tenets in the form of a dialogue. The professor of philosophy in Douai, and later head of the seminary in Cambrai, penned a rather short piece entitled *Bayle en petit* (1737). Comprising a conversation between a professor, a bookseller, and an abbé, the work attempted to give a digest of the most essential errors of the Huguenot skeptic.

In the foreword, the publisher himself admitted to having inadvertently acted as an "unfortunate instrument of certain poisoners of the public who through our hands passed the most pernicious and subtle poison into the Christian world." He urged his colleagues to stop distributing "a book so capable of corrupting the minds and hearts of people who are not very firmly convinced in religious matters."[69] Le Febvre set up a discussion between a professor, who represented the author's own point of view, and a bookseller, who naively asked about the dangers of Bayle's text. The two were later joined by an abbé, who first appeared to admire Bayle but came to see the pernicious nature of his ideas by the end of the conversation. The closing statements of the work mirrored the words of the publisher, as the professor despairingly declared his wish:

> I desire with all my heart that the curious [readers] and the booksellers took enough care of their health, the former by never buying any book capable of misleading them, the latter by not becoming poisoners of the public. However, curiosity and the spirit of vanity, of doubt, of libertinism blind the former; the greed for profit and sordid self-interest dazzle the latter, so that . . . despite all our critiques, the obscene and impious works of Bayle will always find booksellers who will sell them and readers who will read them.[70]

The abbé, newly convinced of the dangers Bayle posed, replied with cautious optimism, "And I believe that we will have the consolation of reducing the number of both."[71] The conclusion of Le Febvre's dialogue revealed a new outlook on the part of those who continued to oppose Bayle and his alleged religious skepticism. They no longer thought that mere refutations of his claims were sufficient for undermining the effects of Pyrrhonism in philosophy and consequently in theology. As we have seen, critics of skepticism attempted to paint Pyrrhonism not as a consistent philosophical system but as an affliction of the mind that preyed on those who lacked the intellect to stand up to the intricate arguments of subversive thinkers.

Given the growing number of readers who found the libertine and skeptical implications of Bayle's texts appealing, the goal for opponents of skepticism, as the anti-skeptic Crousaz had argued, was to stop or slow the increase in the ranks of the irreverent.[72] Thus, Le Febvre's professor, just like the publisher, was most concerned about the effect of the *Dictionnaire* on those who did not have a strong background in philosophy and theology. Calling Bayle's controversial text a "monster mothered by irreligion itself,"[73] the professor launched right into his tirade: "Did I not add that this was the most dangerous author for readers [who are] either extravagant philosophers or mediocre theologians? Did I not say that he favors Pyrrhonism in matters of religion, that he leads [readers] there little by little and with such pernicious skill that it is so well hidden that in the end, to be a deist or an atheist and a diligent disciple of Bayle is more or less the same thing?"[74] Le Febvre, like many other apologists, presented Pyrrhonism as a disease of the heart and of the mind, and he perceived the *Dictionnaire* to be a poisonous text that infected inexperienced readers.[75] While professional theologians could examine the skeptical texts without finding their ideas seductive, Le Febvre insinuated, those less familiar with the theological and philosophical canons were much more likely to be enticed by Bayle's arguments. It was thus incumbent upon experienced thinkers to prevent the reading public from succumbing to the harmful ideas articulated in Bayle's magnum opus. Le Febvre's appeal to publishers and booksellers was just another tactical maneuver in the war on skepticism and libertinism.

Like many of his fellow apologists, Le Febvre reprinted the most controversial passages from the *Dictionnaire* in order to prove the work's heretical nature. Ironically, although he called on publishers to prevent the dissemination of Bayle's bestselling text, the Jesuit professor provided readers with a digest of the most scandalous parts of his adversary's book. This was certainly not the intention of Bayle's critics, who merely sought to demonstrate the legitimacy of their own critiques by showing the contentious nature of the *Dictionnaire*. However, they inadvertently presented the very portions of the text they judged to be most irreverent and dangerous to segments of the reading public that might not have had direct contact with the book.

Le Febvre's professor drew largely on the arguments of Laubrussel, one of the first Jesuits to provide a systematic critique of Bayle. The professor consistently attacked Bayle for merely pretending to be a Calvinist, while secretly trying to undermine all Christianity.[76] Like Merlin, he saw the emphasis on the freedom of conscience and on the toleration of dissent in religious questions as the most dangerous elements of Bayle's philosophy. He argued that these principles led to heresy by allowing a great number of erroneous theological interpretations. By maintaining that "one cannot define heresy and that no judge may ever know with certainty whether the accused is a heretic or not," Bayle insinuated "that God demands nothing from man but the belief in what appears true" and consequently introduced "the most dangerous uncertainty into [matters of] religion."[77] In Le Febvre's view, Bayle's texts did not openly advocate Pyrrhonism, but the crafty author gradually ushered readers into a logical trap: "I do not claim that Bayle openly professed Pyrrhonism. He took care not to give such an advantageous position to his adversaries, who sought to convict him of irreligion and atheism. However, I maintain that he established Pyrrhonism throughout his work by the principles from which it follows naturally and that a student well trained in his school can be nothing other than a Pyrrhonian in the matter of religion."[78] Le Febvre equated Bayle's supposed Pyrrhonism with deism and atheism, suggesting that the three differed very little. He attacked the Huguenot skeptic for his explicit critiques of the infallibility of the Catholic Church and for his implicit challenges to Protestant tenets.[79]

Despite its lack of significantly new arguments against Bayle and his skeptical ideas, Le Febvre's *Bayle en petit* was reprinted just a year after its first publication.[80] The text would then be reissued in a third edition along with his *Entretiens sur la raison*, which served as a continuation of the dialogues.[81] The rapid appearance of new editions of the Jesuit's dialogues signaled the persistent demand for his text and the relative success of his apologetic strategies.

While Merlin and Le Febvre were never able to produce a full-fledged anti-*Dictionnaire*, their fellow anti-skeptic Philippe-Louis Joly finally brought the project to its completion in 1748, when he published the first volume of his *Remarques critiques sur le Dictionnaire de Bayle*. The work resembled the *Dictionnaire* both in its layout and in its grandiose size. The two in-folio volumes were meant to serve as antidotes to the text that continued to haunt orthodox thinkers, including the chancelier Henri François d'Aguesseau (1668–1751), who avidly followed philosophical debates and expressed his enthusiasm about Joly's work prior to its publication.[82] D'Aguesseau hoped that the text would be of service to reason as well as to religion:

> I strongly praise the zeal that has inspired in you the courage to attack a book so dangerous as Bayle's *Dictionnaire*, and I hope that you will succeed in making him lose credit that has no other foundation but the [careless] freedom of sentiments that reigns in this work, the desire to nourish doubts favorable to the human passions, and a spirit of irreligion that has become quite widespread recently in this country. You could not render a greater service to religion or to reason itself than to

convincingly censure an author who appears to have wished to build his reputation on the ruins of both.[83]

Having read excerpts sent to him by Joly, the chancelier perceived the significance and the potential of the forthcoming text. D'Aguesseau's invocation of "reason" is also noteworthy. Unlike most critics, who focused either on the religious consequences of Bayle's arguments or on the factual inaccuracies of the *Dictionnaire*, the chancelier saw a refutation of Pyrrhonism as having both religious and philosophical advantages. He presented the skeptics as ignorant, blind, superstitious, and unenlightened, contrasting them with those whom he believed to be pious and judicious scholars, such as Joly. Reason and religion, in his mind, mutually reinforced each other, and both needed to be defended from the Pyrrhonian assault of Bayle and his disciples.

Joly's *Remarques* mirrored the order and the layout of the *Dictionnaire historique et critique*, and the main part of the text offered alternate versions of Bayle's most controversial articles. According to a nineteenth-century editor of the *Dictionnaire*, the majority of the articles in the *Remarques* were copied from the texts of Laurent-Josse Le Clerc, Jacob Le Duchat, Charles Merlin, and other prominent critics who had already undertaken scholarly revisions of the divisive *Dictionnaire*.[84] In the preface, Joly himself acknowledged his debt to Le Clerc and Merlin, and he cited all of the authors who had undertaken critiques of Bayle's works.[85]

Like his Jesuit colleagues, Joly expressed concern that given the ubiquity of the pernicious text, a great number of unsuspecting readers would be exposed to the errors and dangerous ideas that it contained. He presented his project as an attempt to render a service to the reading public, one that countered the "ravages that his [Bayle's] writings had carried out for a long time in the minds of readers."[86] He described his task as a rather daunting one, claiming that it was difficult to overcome common prejudice. Attacking Bayle was always a risky undertaking, Joly remarked, because he had so many defenders: "Out of all accredited authors, I doubt that there is a single one more dangerous to attack than the one whom I combat. I perfectly understand the risk I run. I have foreseen all the murmurs and all the complaints that my enterprise will excite. . . . I know the blind prejudice that allows a great many people in this century to decide in his favor."[87] The tone of this passage suggests a peculiar role reversal. By presenting himself as the champion of reason against an army of prejudiced and deceived partisans of Bayle, Joly appropriated the metaphorical juxtaposition between light and darkness that was so characteristic of the language deployed by the philosophes. It was the Catholic apologist Joly who was combating the prejudice and irrationality of Bayle and his followers. It was they who blindly submitted to their idol's authority and took everything he wrote as the absolute truth.[88] Indeed, according to Joly's depiction, Bayle had virtually assumed the unassailable role of a new Aristotle (384–322 BCE). "I shall content myself with not regarding him as infallible," wrote Joly.[89] He attempted to show that the Huguenot archcritic was himself in need of being critiqued. By presenting Bayle as a false prophet and his followers as deluded fanatics, Joly sought to discredit both in the eyes of contemporary readers, even those who might be tempted to side with Bayle's critical approach. His preface thus appealed not just to the orthodox Catholic community, who, like d'Aguesseau, welcomed his efforts to defend the faith, but to a wider learned readership in Paris and beyond.

By this time, the *Dictionnaire* had gained renown outside of the French-speaking world. The first abridged English translation, from 1710, had not been very successful.[90] Pierre Desmaizeaux, Bayle's friend and fellow Huguenot émigré, worked on an improved translation and tried to provoke interest in Bayle's method of critical biography with texts on the latitudinarians John Hales (1584–1656) and William Chillingworth (1602–44). He explained that he wished to imitate Bayle's "Exactness and Impartiality," while avoiding his apparent offenses to religion and morality.[91] In 1734 two different English editions appeared. The first was Desmaizeaux's five-volume translation, titled *Mr. Bayle's Historical and Critical Dictionary* (1734–38). It featured his apologetic biography of Bayle and contained changes made in the French third and fourth editions.[92]

The rival edition was a ten-volume work titled *A General Dictionary, Historical and Critical: In Which a New and Accurate Translation of that of the Celebrated Mr. Bayle, with the Corrections and Observations Printed in the Late Edition at Paris is Included; and Interspersed with Several Thousand Lives Never Before Published* (1734–41). It was edited by Thomas Birch (1705–66) and differed significantly from Desmaizeaux's translation. Since Bayle "did not propose to compile a General Dictionary, and made choice of such Articles only as best suited his views, or for which he had materials already prepared," the preface stated, "he omitted a great many persons illustrious for their rank and dignity."[93] Following Bayle's layout, Birch and his coeditors added more than nine hundred biographical articles, most of which featured the lives of notable Englishmen. They even included an entry on Bayle, in which they discussed Bayle's life and career and went into detail about the controversies in which the Huguenot philosophe had been involved. They also added a number of critical remarks to some of his more controversial articles, such as "Manichéens," and "Pyrrhon."[94]

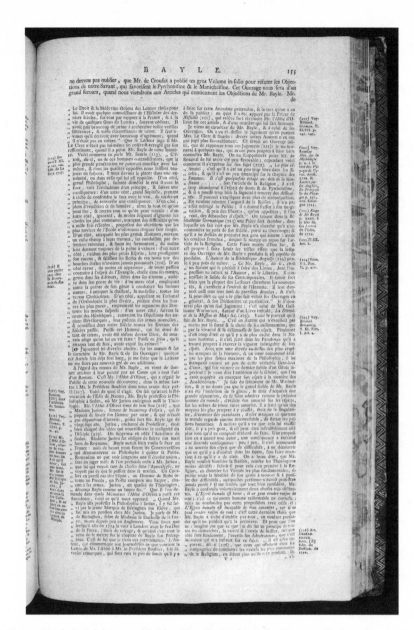

Fig. 3.1 "Bayle," with a note added by Chauffepié, from the *Nouveau dictionnaire historique et critique*. Courtesy of The Newberry Library.

A General Dictionary would serve as a model for the *Biographia Britannica* (1747–66) and the *Dictionary of National Biography* (1885), but it also had an interesting influence on the afterlife of Bayle's own project. In 1739 a group of Dutch booksellers commissioned the Calvinist minister Jacques-Georges Chauffepié to translate *A General Dictionary* into French, and after a hiatus, he completed the *Nouveau dictionnaire historique et critique* (1750–56). Chauffepié added, amended, or completely altered articles in order to criticize Bayle's views "in favor of Pyrrhonism or deism."[95] Suggesting that Bayle had failed "in his function as a critical historian," Chauffepié entirely rewrote the article on the Manicheans. Chauffepié suggested that Bayle, who had given a sympathetic presentation of the logically convincing nature of those who argued for the existence of two co-eternal principles, had misrepresented the Manichean position. The critic offered his own exposition of the sect's views and attempted to refute Bayle's claim that Manicheanism seemed to furnish a more rational explanation for the existence of evil than did the Judeo-Christian conception of God.[96]

Some of the more fascinating entries in the *Nouveau dictionnaire* concerned Bayle's own life. Chauffepié included a lengthy entry on Bayle's nemesis Pierre Jurieu, who had been the victim of slander, according to the critic.[97] Chauffepié added commentary notes to Birch's entry on Bayle, portraying him as more controversial and religiously heterodox than his English biographers had made him out to be. Chauffepié ended the entry with a heavy-handed judgment about the author whose dictionary he was supplementing. In his ambitious climb to the top of the Republic of Letters, Chauffepié argued, Bayle had presented numerous paradoxes, challenged established opinions, and erected his reputation on the "ruins of all other authorities." Despite his commendable "genius, erudition," and style, the entry concluded, Bayle's character remained in question because of his heterodox religious opinions and his dubious motives.[98] In an ironic twist, Chauffepié thus turned the genre against its inventor. He attacked Bayle in the critical notes of the very text that was meant to serve as a supplement to the ever popular *Dictionnaire historique et critique*.

The Persistent Need to Disprove Bayle

Some fifty years after his death, Bayle was still the subject of attacks by Protestants and Catholics alike. In spite of the increasing number of attempts to refute Bayle's skeptical arguments or demonstrate the inaccuracies of the *Dictionnaire*, or perhaps precisely because of them, the text continued to grow in popularity, going through nine different editions from 1697 to 1741. Ironically, one of these editions was published with the unintended collaboration of the very Jesuit scholars who sought to present Bayle's ideas as dangerous and worthy of censure. Furthermore, many of Bayle's critics reprinted the most controversial parts of his texts to prove to readers that their evaluations of the *Dictionnaire*'s pernicious nature were justified. Thus, they inadvertently familiarized an even greater part of the reading public with the work they were trying so hard to refute.

Some of Bayle's detractors hoped to reduce the influence of his divisive work by demonstrating its inaccuracies and errors to readers who saw it as a source of encyclopedic knowledge. However, these attempts do not seem to have proved successful in diminishing the popularity of the *Dictionnaire*. In fact, given Mornet's calculations of the holdings in French private libraries from 1750 to 1780, in which the rather expensive *Dictionnaire* occupies the undisputed first place, the critics' strategy may have had the opposite effect.[99] After all, as Bayle's ally Mathieu Marais had claimed, Laurent-Josse Le Clerc's critique had actually led him to reread significant parts of the work or to find new sections he had never seen before: "I know full well what will come of this great letter of 600 pages; there might be 600 corrected mistakes or more, and that will be 600 places that we will reread with great pleasure, because these factual errors will be surrounded by eloquent, lively, and enjoyable passages that will always make us admire the author who is being critiqued. It might even lead me to read passages that I had not read before."[100] Bayle's critics thus inadvertently increased his popularity among readers, undermining the very goal of their critical undertakings. By exposing an even wider public to the allegedly skeptical and heretical arguments of their archenemy, they unintentionally accomplished precisely what Le Febvre's publisher had hoped to prevent.

Partly because of the growing outcries in the Republic of Letters about the dangerous content of the *Dictionnaire* and partly because of the increasing number of subversive works that borrowed Bayle's arguments, the offensive against the controversial bestseller continued. By the 1750s the tone of Bayle's Catholic detractors had changed significantly. Long gone was the playful approach of Tournemine and his colleagues on the editorial board of the *Mémoires de Trévoux*, who had been amused by the theological difficulties Bayle posed to his fellow Protestants. Louis Bertrand Castel (1688–1757), one of the several chief editors of the Jesuit periodical in the 1720s and 1730s, published a much more acerbic portrait of the Huguenot skeptic in 1737.[101] The journal denounced him as a "deceiver" whose errors were the result of an "impure heart" and claimed that his works were full of "venomous skepticism."[102] Critiques continued from both sides of the theological divide. In the same year, the editors of the *Mémoires de Trévoux* published Béat de Muralt's (1665–1749) brief "Caractère de

Monsieur Bayle." The Swiss Pietist described Bayle as a "charlatan" who assumed different masks and feigned erudition to gain respect and popularity.[103]

Unlike Bayle's Huguenot critics, who had been concerned primarily with his treatment of theological questions that were particularly relevant in the Protestant context, Bayle's French Catholic detractors were more preoccupied with the implications of his arguments for their confession. Consequently, they sought to amend his representations of the church fathers and discuss the accuracy of his historical scholarship. Not infrequently, they used him as the example of the general danger of Protestantism: if the authority of the Church to rule in divine matters were overturned, one would end up with thinkers such as Bayle being given full reign to undermine the sacred foundations of all Christianity. Tournemine and some of his Jesuit collaborators initially saw Bayle's skeptical assertions regarding the inability of natural reason to comprehend supernatural religious truths as convenient attacks against the Protestant reliance on *sola scriptura*. However, as the Jansenist movement increasingly challenged the Jesuit order throughout the eighteenth century, Bayle's fideism appeared to pose a greater threat. By showing how his claims about the absolute primacy of faith could lead to atheism, Bayle's Jesuit critics could simultaneously attack their Jansenist opponents.[104]

As we will see in the next chapter, Bayle was not the only target of those who saw skepticism as a fundamental danger to religion. While he was the most noticeable advocate of Pyrrhonism, apologetic thinkers would attempt to refute all forms of skepticism, whether modern or ancient. As the foundations of philosophical and religious doctrines seemed to be crumbling under the attack of various irreverent authors, some religious intellectuals began to see danger all around them, sometimes even in their midst. Pyrrhonism appeared to be the primary source of irreligion to those concerned about the growing number of heterodox ideas, because it simultaneously challenged established authorities and questioned the accepted methods of attaining theological and philosophical certainty. If they hoped to stem the tide of unbelief, the opponents of skepticism would have to challenge Pyrrhonism directly by offering new criteria of certainty.

CHAPTER FOUR

Secret Skepticism

Huet's Fideistic Fumbles

Fideism and the Limits of Natural Reason

Skepticism did not only threaten orthodox learned culture from without. Pierre-Daniel Huet, who in his youth had attempted to provide a geometrical demonstration of the truth of Christianity, was revealed to have been a fideistic skeptic for the better part of his intellectual career with the posthumous publication of his skeptical *Traité philosophique de la foiblesse de l'esprit humain* two years after his death in 1721. This text startled and unsettled most of those who had considered Huet a friend. The work's explicit embrace of philosophical skepticism and its implications for philosophy and theology seemed incompatible with Huet's erudition and intellectual itinerary. The views articulated in the *Traité* seemed so distant from those expressed in Huet's earlier works that some of his contemporaries mistakenly argued that he could not have written the treatise. Huet's Jesuit friends were particularly appalled by his embrace of fideism.[1]

Although Huet's friends were stunned and disturbed by the posthumous revelation of his commitment to philosophical skepticism, he was far from being the only religiously devout thinker to have embraced such a seemingly counterintuitive set of beliefs. As we have seen, fideism had deep roots in French Catholic thought. The deist critiques of Christianity, together with a growing number of clandestine texts that undermined all forms of organized religion, rendered fideism an attractive refuge. By describing religious belief as a purely voluntary and strictly personal psychological phenomenon, Huet and other fideists attempted to remove the foundations of faith from the realm of philosophical speculations. Huet, like other fideists, believed that such a separation would shield religion from the increasingly rationalist currents of the late seventeenth and early eighteenth centuries. The immediate reactions to Huet's skeptical treatise revealed a deep anxiety about the potentially destructive influence of skeptical arguments on philosophy, on theology, and consequently on society. The bitterness of the disputes also reflected the growing polarization in the way Christian thinkers attempted to defend religion from new kinds of critiques.

The fideist position was, in many ways, a reaction to the theological and philosophical consequences of the decisions made at the Fifth Lateran Council in 1513. Prior to this council, the major axioms of Christianity, such as the existence of God and the immortality of the soul, were considered preambles to, rather than articles of, the faith.[2] During the late fifteenth century, a group of Italian philosophers commonly known as the Paduan Averroists claimed that neither the existence of God nor the immortality of the soul could be demonstrated by natural human reason; for them, faith was the sole source of such knowledge.[3] The arguments concerned neither the actual existence of God nor the immortality of the soul but rather the human ability to know these tenets with certainty through the use of natural reason. In response to such potentially dangerous claims, the Lateran Council declared the existence of God and the immortality of the soul to be naturally demonstrable, which made it an article of the faith that such natural proofs were compelling. By prohibiting philosophers from deviating in any way "from the true faith" in any principles or conclusions they presented to the public, the eighth session of the council in effect made fideism on such issues a heretical stance. All philosophers were obligated to "devote their every effort to clarify for their listeners the truth of the Christian religion."[4] Finally, the council sought to prevent any future challenges to the authority of the Catholic Church by limiting the study of philosophy to five years and allowing scholars to pursue further philosophical studies only if they studied theology simultaneously.

While Church authorities intended to reduce the controversy and debates surrounding the articles of Christianity, their decrees inadvertently generated increasingly heated disputes. For if the existence of God were demonstrable by natural human reason, then there could be, as René Descartes noted, "no greater task in philosophy than assiduously to seek out, once and for all, the best of all these arguments and to lay them out so precisely and plainly that henceforth the whole world will take them to be true and precise demonstrations."[5] Descartes's letter to the Faculty of Theology in Paris, written as a dedication to his *Méditations*, referred specifically to the obligations the Lateran Council had imposed on philosophers. Thinkers had to not only disprove those who claimed that the existence of God and the soul's immortality were not rationally demonstrable but also offer the best philosophical proofs of these articles of the faith.

As an unintended consequence of the decision made by Catholic authorities, the intellectual world of seventeenth-century France would be plunged into intense debates about and demonstrations of the existence of God. The Aristotelian Scholastics, who generally relied on Thomas Aquinas's five proofs, stood on one side of the debate. They generally formulated a posteriori justifications that were based on observations of the external world. Descartes and his disciples, by contrast, attempted to offer a priori demonstrations of the existence of God, without reference to evidence beyond the mind itself. Thinkers on both sides of this dramatic contest tried to present their proofs as the most certain and to explain why those of their opponents were faulty. The issues at stake concerned not just the significant philosophical and theological matters but also intellectual and institutional supremacy in the learned world. A philosophical system that could irrefutably demonstrate God's existence would ensure its own superiority.

Ironically, the inability of scholars to present fully conclusive proofs, coupled with their unwillingness to surrender perpetuated debates regarding the existence of God well into the eighteenth century, compounded refutation upon refutation and objection upon objection. Such disputes would prove mutually destructive to the arguments of all participants. The fideist position thus became increasingly appealing to those who wanted to withdraw from the intense theological quarrel among the Cartesians, the Aristotelians, and other schools of philosophy.[6] Instead of accepting the claim that the existence of God and the immortality of the soul were demonstrable by natural reason, they argued that both of these concepts could not be proved philosophically but could be established solely through submission to faith in the supernatural revelation. The late antique ecclesiastical author Tertullian (c. 160–c. 230) is generally considered to be the first protofideist, because he described Christ's death and resurrection in the following way: "The Son of God died; it is *immediately* credible because it is foolish. / He was buried, and rose again; it is certain because it is impossible."[7] This emphasis on the irrationality (and even the absurdity) of belief served to construct an inseparable barrier between faith and reason, thereby rendering any rational analysis of the Christian revelation impossible.

Huet seemed to think that the competing attempts to prove the existence of God and the veracity of religion were inadvertently undermining the foundations of Christianity. He vehemently opposed Descartes's proofs of God, which he saw as insufficient demonstrations that actually weakened religion rather than strengthened it. His *Censura philosophiae cartesianae* (1689) attacked Descartes's first proof of God by claiming that "our idea of an infinite and supremely perfect being, is itself finite and imperfect," although "Descartes would have us believe that this idea is so excellent and elevated that it not only far surpasses the perfection of our soul but could only be derived from God."[8] Because humans' conception of God was finite, it was necessarily and categorically different from him and could not reflect accurately the nature of a supremely perfect being. Huet similarly tried to refute the second proof, which was based on the clear and distinct idea of God's necessary existence, by claiming that there was no relation between ideas and objective reality.[9] The presence of a supremely perfect being in the mind could not, in itself, establish its actual and real existence; it could only testify to the necessary existence of such an idea in the mind: "From this it is obvious that this objective reality, which according to Descartes exists in the idea of an infinite and supremely perfect thing, is entirely inside our mind and in no way depends on the thing it represents."[10] Having relegated Descartes's proofs to an idealist level of certainty, Huet showed that the Cartesian God did not necessarily exist in the realm of objective reality. Descartes's infinite and supremely perfect being could be guaranteed only mental existence.[11]

Huet not only rejected the Cartesian proofs of God but also implicitly challenged the theological value of such demonstrations. His skeptical *Traité* even cited Thomas Aquinas's claim that natural human reason was a weak and inappropriate source of knowledge: "Things that may be proved demonstratively, such as the existence of God, the unity of God, and other similar points, are placed among articles we are to believe, as those preceding other things that are of the faith, and these must be at least presupposed by those who have no demonstration of them."[12] For Huet, rational verifications of God's existence inadvertently undermined faith in him. Since the Cartesian demonstrations appeared to be so easy to overturn, they inadequately defended the very basis of Christianity. The longer such philosophical and theological debates continued, the more speculative and feeble the defenses of the existence of God would become.[13]

Indeed, Huet also argued that the ultimate goal in the suspension of judgment in all philosophical questions was to prepare "the mind for the reception of faith."[14] He thought that adopting skepticism as a philosophical attitude would prevent bitter, divisive debates in natural philosophy and, more importantly, in theology: "Faith is a gift from Heaven that God is pleased to grant to those who do not trust too much in the forces of nature, nor presume too much about the power of their reason, nor espouse their own sentiments with excessive obstinacy, but diligently prepare their minds to receive it. And this is the effect produced by the art of doubting that we establish here."[15] Huet's little-known *Alnetanae quaestiones de concordia rationis et fidei* (1690) revealed his deep concern about this issue and definitively reconciled his skepticism and his Catholic faith.[16] He described his project in the following way: "I undertook the discussion of the very difficult topic concerning the agreement of Reason and Faith; or, what ought to be the province of reason in adopting faith; and how far the empire of faith over reason ought to extend."[17] Reason was merely a faculty that assisted human beings in obtaining a basic knowledge of their natural surroundings through perception and reflection. Faith, on the other hand, was a gift granted by God, and it alone could guarantee absolute truth.[18] Huet described a conflict between the two sources of knowledge, declaring that reason, "when she is turbulent and commanding, refuses to cede to other arbiters." The human mind became divided and turned to "sedition and tumultuousness," never resting in peace; tranquility could only be established under the guidance of faith, because "she [reason] must know herself, become aware of her weakness, and not aspire to give us happiness and eternal health, when we cannot even know truth through her."[19] Huet believed that natural human reason inhibited the reception of divine truth. This rational faculty was overly ambitious: it discounted its own limitations and attempted to exert its rule over human beings in both natural and supernatural questions.

Huet proposed that faith and reason should operate within different domains. The former should be concerned with all religious questions, while the latter should function autonomously without infringing on matters of faith.[20] Conversely, supernatural faith should not interfere in questions of natural philosophy.[21] As a consequence of such a division of mental labor, no conflict would exist between the two faculties, because each would be concerned with a particular realm of knowledge. Huet's system established a structural relationship in which reason would be in a position of obedience and subordination to things known by faith. He could thus defend the veracity of supernatural truths without reference to abstract proofs: "I believe that God is three in one not because of reason but because of the first revealed truth."[22] The supernatural world could coexist with the natural one. Philosophical disputes about religious matters would cease, as philosophers would no longer attempt to prove concepts that could be certain only through belief in the Christian revelation.

The *Quaestiones* appeared, logically and temporally, between the *Censura* and the *Traité*. While the *Censura* explicitly challenged Cartesianism, it also implicitly attacked the presumption of reason. The *Quaestiones* relegated this faculty to a separate and unequal position with respect to faith. The *Traité* struck the final blow to the powers of natural understanding, demonstrating its utter feebleness.[23] This continuity of themes reveals Huet's plan for a "greater work," an intellectual project that comprised these treatises and culminated in the *Traité*.[24] Huet admitted that his love and esteem for ancient philosophy had led him to explore ancient sects in depth. His studies had ended, however, in exasperation and disillusionment with the discipline:

> And as this science [of philosophy] is boundless, wandering into immensity beyond the limits of time and creation, whilst the human mind, cooped within narrow bounds, depressed to earth, and involved in thick darkness, attempts by the aid of its reason to break forth into the light, and to seize upon the arduous summits of truth, I proposed to enquire how high it could raise itself by its own powers, and what aids were to be sought for it from faith. These exalted studies long, much, and not unpleasantly, exercised my mind; and the accumulated product of my labors was swelling to a great bulk, when I thought it would be more useful, and better accommodated to common understandings, if it were divided into parts, and brought under certain head.[25]

By "parts" Huet meant the *Censura*, the *Quaestiones*, and the *Traité* (which he purposely excluded from the memoirs). All of these texts combined skeptical arguments with a fideistic outlook, in opposition to the increasingly rational and naturalistic current of philosophical theology in the late seventeenth and early eighteenth centuries.

Huet's *Traité* and the Jesuits of the *Mémoires de Trévoux*

Despite his pious intentions, Huet's project was not widely appreciated, as reactions to the *Traité* in Huet's correspondence reveal. While his friends perceived the sincerity of his arguments, they disparaged his fideism and his apologetic methods. Huet sent a manuscript of the *Traité* to his friend Charles de La Rue (1643–1725), a Jesuit preacher and orator, and he soon received a less than favorable reply. La Rue urged Huet to suppress the more shocking and controversial parts of the treatise, warning of the potential "public fury" it would ignite against Huet.[26] La Rue also predicted the reaction of Huet's comrades: "You will see the greater part of your friends either declaring against you or at least not daring to defend you. . . . This truth is not so important that you, in its defense, must take on the whole world."[27] La Rue's warning illuminated Huet's reasons for not publishing the *Traité* and accurately predicted the future outrage it would inspire. Huet's status and his personal relationships required a certain amount of discretion with respect to religious controversies.

As La Rue had predicted, Edme Pirot (1631–1715), the Sorbonne censor, was appalled by the *Traité* manuscript and troubled by the consequences of Huet's skepticism. Pirot wrote that by claiming the impossibility of attaining true and certain knowledge through natural reason, Huet had undercut the fundamental tool of Christian apologists and undermined belief instead of buttressing it.[28] By denying that reason was a source of certainty, Pirot argued, Huet had also challenged the authority of faith:

> I doubt that after overthrowing all certainty provided by reason, there is any place for that given by faith. If reason cannot conduct itself [to certainty], how can it leave itself to win by the designs of belief? In the end, there must be some certainty that is not that of faith. . . . All the Holy Fathers refuted the imagination of the pagans concerning the history of their Gods and the superstition of their cults; they made evident the contradiction and the folly that existed in all that the idolaters supposed, and they used nothing else for it but human reason. When they had to maintain Christian truths against the objections of the unbelievers, they responded to reason with reason itself, and they always said that there was nothing in what religion professed but that which conformed to reason.[29]

While praising Huet's erudition and his intellectual rigor, Pirot staunchly opposed the publication of the *Traité*. Pirot tacitly urged that the text be kept out of the public light: "I know that this book that you have entitled as the fourth part of the *Alnetanae quaestiones* is nothing but a *jeu d'esprit*; that you never intended to publish it and that you only worked on it to try your hand at the matter, seeing full well that if it were published, its conclusions would be feared and one might abuse it."[30] The censor predicted that the work would unintentionally undermine its author's sincere intentions and serve as a source of incredulity for those who did not share Huet's piety.

Pirot's prognosis proved to be remarkably accurate. When the *Traité* was finally published in 1723, it received striking criticism from Huet's other friends and colleagues. Many refused to admit that Huet could have written the work until the abbé Pierre-Joseph Thoulier d'Olivet (1682–1768), the late scholar's friend, produced the original manuscript in Huet's hand.[31] Others were dismayed by the *Traité*'s content and distraught over Huet's conclusions.[32] It is difficult to know whether the expressed public reactions were sincere or feigned, given that Huet had already circulated a manuscript of the work among his friends.

The *Traité* received the greatest scrutiny in the Jesuit *Mémoires de Trévoux*. The review of Huet's work was most likely coauthored by the natural philosopher Louis-Bertrand Castel (1688–1757) and the poet Jean-Antoine du Cerceau (1670–1730).[33] The reviewers questioned the attribution of the text to Huet and scrutinized its motives. They claimed that the title and intent of this work clashed "with the name and character of the illustrious author" and suggested that the text had actually been penned by "some incensed Pyrrhonian who wished to give credence to an outdated doctrine by using the name so respectable to savants and to honest people." The reviewers proposed that the presence of the text "among the papers of the famous bishop of Avranches" did not mean that he was its author or that he accepted its arguments.[34] The review questioned the attribution, hinting that d'Olivet himself could have been the author. The critics asked why Huet had never raised these ideas with his best friends and never mentioned the skeptical treatise in his memoirs. They also inquired how it was possible for a man who had written so many dogmatic works and contributed so much erudite research to embrace Pyrrhonism. The reviewers then speculated about the potential identity of the true author of the work: "If the editor of this work had been a little familiar with personalities and with probabilities, he would have chosen, as the hero of this novel, some of those clever-witted men without consistency [*beaux esprits sans consistance*], who flutter ceaselessly from paradox to paradox, from hypothesis to hypothesis, from fiction to fiction; one of these anti-*érudits* who haughtily brag that they turned Parisian cafés into schools of ignorance and good taste."[35] This was a portrait or a caricature common to apologetic literature of the period. Whether such people actually existed in the learned world of the 1720s or served as imagined straw men is difficult to determine. However, their frequent invocation in apologetic literature indicates that like the ancient Greek Sophists (as described by Plato), they were perceived as an actual menace to intellectual life. The use of "anti-*érudits*" exhibits an important distinction between the learned Huet and the supposed skeptical impostor. The Jesuit critics saw their Pyrrhonian opponent as an enemy of learning, which is precisely why they could not conceive that Huet could have been the author of the controversial treatise.

After attempting to show that Huet had not in fact written the *Traité*, du Cerceau and Castel undertook a critique of the actual text. They described the author as a "sophist grammarian" whose book was nothing but a "regurgitation of Sextus Empiricus," and they highlighted the internal contradictions that "fought against the most obvious evidence and renounced all religion, all principles, all society, and all common sense." The review ridiculed the author for his logical inconsistencies, especially for writing a book that professed that there was nothing to learn and that ignorance was a virtue. The reviewers did not view the author's Pyrrhonism as self-referential. They did not think that the writer's extremely confident belief in the weakness of the human mind could be reconciled with his embrace of skepticism.[36] They seemed confused by the author's underlying goal, since the work appeared to vacillate and "to take the middle ground between the Pyrrhonists and the dogmatists." While in the first book the author "goes so far as to make us suspect all the means by which the truth can enter our mind," the second book "brings him back to the certainty of faith and of good sense, but in the third one he returns a greater Pyrrhonian than ever."[37] By presenting the *Traité* as an inconsistent work, du Cerceau and Castel hinted at the possibility of a soft interpretation of its tenets and highlighted its incoherent defense of philosophical skepticism.

The reviewers saw the answers to the objections as particularly bizarre and inconsistent, because the author embraced the role of both "an incensed Pyrrhonian and an overzealous dogmatist at the same time."[38] The critique focused on the first book because it allegedly revealed the "sterile basis of the Pyrrhonian subtlety."[39] It was particularly ironic that the writer pretending to be Huet "forgot that he wished to be a Pyrrhonian" and not only employed a number of dogmatic definitions of terms such as "understanding, idea, thought, reason, [and] truth" but also based his very first proof on scripture and on the church fathers:

> For although scripture and the sacred authors warn us of the limits and the weakness of our mind, of the vanity of our sciences, of the great difficulties in our investigations, they are very far from telling us that God deceives us, that our senses give us one continuous illusion, that we do not know if there are bodies, if it is day at high noon, if two and two make four, and that we must doubt everything; furthermore, it is known that the [church] fathers always fiercely fought the Academic [skeptics] and even more so the Pyrrhonians, far from favoring their impious and bizarre system.[40]

Refuting the author's use of scripture and of the sacred authors in the *Traité* was crucial for Castel and du Cerceau, since these sources were the most essential building blocks of Christianity. If the Pyrrhonians were allowed to appropriate the Bible and the patristic authors, their arguments would have a seemingly pious undertone, and they would be able to deploy sacred texts in overthrowing the foundations of religious belief.

Curiously, the Jesuit reviewers invoked the argument against the fallibility of the senses that had been used by Descartes in the *Méditations*. Descartes had argued in the Sixth Meditation that *if* the information provided by the senses did not correspond to external stimuli that were the causes of those sensations, then the sensations had to have been placed in the mind by some other entity. Since this would render God a deceiver, which was a metaphysical impossibility,

Descartes had asserted, the only available conclusion was that the sensations were actually caused by external objects.[41] As we will see, this argument would be used by many anti-skeptical thinkers in their attempts to refute Pyrrhonian doubts about the correspondence between ideas and their objects.

The critics' second major point of contention involved a refutation of Pyrrhonism on a practical level. They claimed that when it came to everyday actions, it would be "pure folly" to act upon skeptical tenets.[42] In discussing book 2 of the *Traité*, Castel and du Cerceau approved its departure from radical skepticism:

Not only does the author come close to religion and to faith in the second book; he also makes an attempt to come nearer to good sense, from which his first book was far removed. He says that although we cannot know the truth nor have any certainty, it is nevertheless necessary to follow probabilities in the ordinary conduct of life and to behave as if we had full confidence in [the truth of] appearances. He agrees that we need to take a detour to avoid an encounter with a column, with an untamed bull, or with a precipice, as do those who believe that all these things are real. In such a way, Pyrrhonism is reduced here to a pure speculation for which there was no need to make such noise and to confuse all of humankind.[43]

The reviewers pointed out that even the most radical skeptics, who denied the possibility of knowing whether the senses provided accurate information about the external world, still acted as if they did not doubt their own sense perceptions. They also suggested that full-fledged Pyrrhonians scarcely existed, because people were "naturally more likely to dogmatize than to doubt everything." Most self-proclaimed skeptics either denied knowledge in some particular sphere (such as theology or the sciences) or adopted this philosophy because "when one comes to feel that one is ignorant of something, one concludes, and looks for reasons to prove, that others [also] understand nothing."[44] The critics denigrated Pyrrhonism by presenting it not as a legitimate and coherent school of thought but as one that merely undermined specific areas of human knowledge without actually accepting the final conclusions that resulted from its own principles.

The abbé d'Olivet, whose eulogy of the bishop of Avranches preceded the actual text of the *Traité*, defended the attribution of the text as well as his friend's reputation. A year after the scathing review in the *Mémoires de Trévoux*, d'Olivet published an apologetic work that attempted to refute the Jesuit critic's censures point by point. He scoffed at the review's tone and insults, asking whether "he would not regret expressing himself so harshly" if it turned out that the author was indeed Huet.[45] D'Olivet claimed that Huet not only had translated the work from Latin into French but had left behind several manuscripts of it. In addition, he confirmed that the late bishop had shown this work to a number of friends, including the Jesuit La Rue, whose letter to Huet had warned against a potential backlash if the text were published. D'Olivet even cited a letter from Huet to another friend that explained his reasons for withholding the work from publication.[46]

The attribution of the *Traité* was a crucial matter both for Huet's allies and for critics concerned with the spread of Pyrrhonism. Huet had been one of the foremost scholars in the Republic of Letters, known for his vast erudition and for his moral probity. By allowing him to be designated as the author of the skeptical *Traité*, the opponents of Pyrrhonism would have to concede one of two propositions: either that Huet had dissimulated his belief for a better part of his life or that it was possible for a person both to embrace philosophical skepticism and to remain religiously devout. If the former were found to be true, then the reputation of one of the most prolific scholars of the past century would be tarnished. If philosophical skepticism and belief turned out to be compatible, then the moral case against Pyrrhonism—according to which skepticism was tied with irreligion and immorality—would suffer a major setback.

Because of the stakes of the dispute about the authorship of the *Traité*, the abbé d'Olivet also defended his friend's sincerity and his Christian faith.[47] He regretted that Catholic intellectuals had "treated such a man as Huet in a way that one might treat a Bodin or a Spinoza" for having properly identified faith as the God-given and consequently infallible source of knowledge.[48] He saw no reason to think that Huet's commitment to *philosophical* skepticism and his religious belief were in any way incompatible. According to d'Olivet, many people "filled with a sincere zeal for religion" believed that Huet's motives had been pure and that "he rose up against the supposed power of the human mind during the reign of detestable metaphysics, whose conceit forms so many unbelievers."[49]

Among other intellectuals, d'Olivet was referring to the Jesuit Jean-François Baltus (1667–1743), who had sent him a positive review of Huet's *Traité* that would be published in the *Bibliothèque françoise* in 1727. Baltus, who had taught humanities in Dijon and theology in Strasbourg before becoming the rector of several French universities and a censor of books in Rome, defended the late bishop's motives. He suggested that Huet's main goal in undermining reason had actually been to strengthen the authority of the Church. If one "were convinced that one's reason was too weak to reach, on its own, the great truths that are the object of our religion, one would be obligated to resort to authority for instruction."[50] While Baltus defended Huet's intentions, he also argued that "one cannot suspect a great and learned priest . . . to have wanted, in any way, to favor the outlandish doubts and uncertainties of the Pyrrhonians and the Academics."[51] He saw Huet's motives as purely religious and corroborated the author's claims about the sacred sources of skepticism by citing passages from scripture and from Eusebius (c. 260–c. 340), Saint Augustine, and other patristic sources who pointed to the weakness of the human mind. Not only were "divine truths" inaccessible to human understanding, Baltus insisted, but "it is folly and a punishable temerity to attempt to understand them, and even more, to not believe them, since one does not understand them."[52]

Despite such apologetic efforts on behalf of the late Huet, the Jesuits continued to rebuke both the *Traité* and its defenders. In 1727 Castel and du Cerceau published a response to d'Olivet in which they argued further against his attribution of the work.[53] They maintained that Huet could have copied and translated the text without being its author. The Jesuit critics also claimed that Huet had not published the work that was found among his papers precisely because "he recognized it as dangerous for a great number [of people] and not intended for the public."[54] Emphasizing that they had nothing but the deepest respect for the late bishop, Castel and du Cerceau explained that their harsh words were intended for the anonymous impostor who had published the text.[55] They also lashed out at the translator of Sextus Empiricus's *Hipotiposes pirroniennes* for comparing Huet to Montaigne, Charron, and Bayle in the preface:

> In truth, this illustrious prelate finds himself well misplaced there, since the anonymous translator places him immediately after Charron and Montaigne and directly next to Mr. Bayle. These are the features that are, if the apologist is not aware, the ones that make all good people moan [out of frustration]. But it shall not be said that the famous, the erudite, the pious bishop of Avranches followed in the steps of the Bayles, the Charrons, or the Montaignes and approved of the pernicious sect of the empiricist miscreants.[56]

The critics, who—speaking in the singular—pronounced themselves the "sworn enemy of Pyrrhonism,"[57] fought so resolutely against the attribution of the *Traité* to Huet precisely because they did not want the late scholar to fall into this group of fideists. If Huet were to be classified among them, not only would the skeptical treatise gain credibility but fideism itself would have a defender who could not be suspected of secretly promoting atheism. The Jesuit critics did secure a way to safeguard their claims in case the text did turn out to be Huet's. If d'Olivet proved to be correct, he would "have the pleasure of having unnecessarily sullied a great man, allegedly his friend, and of having caused a great scandal for religion" by willingly revealing views that the late bishop himself had been responsible enough to hide from the world.[58]

Crousaz and the Protestant Critique of Fideism

Huet's efforts were opposed not only by the Jesuits but also by Protestants. In his refutation of ancient and modern Pyrrhonism the anti-skeptic Crousaz dedicated the last section of his enormous text to Huet. Unlike Castel and du Cerceau, who had considered Huet a valuable ally, Crousaz did not belabor the issue of the authorship of the skeptical *Traité*. Instead, he sought to disprove the seemingly pious propositions of all fideistic skeptics, who called for the submission of reason to faith. Such arguments, in his view, overlooked the rational foundations of religious belief and took for granted the ideas that natural reason had provided. "Those who labor for the establishment of Pyrrhonism," the Swiss critic contended, "needlessly try to cover up their malicious plan by saying that they have no other goal but to humble reason." Faith alone was an insufficient guarantor of the truth, he insisted, and a rational understanding of God had to precede any supernatural belief in his existence and his goodness. It was "necessary to already have an idea of God in order to be able to assure oneself that" the Bible really was the true source of divine teaching "by comparing what we learn from it with the idea" of God.[59]

This notion, known as the "preamble of the faith" (*praeambula fidei*), had been advanced by Thomas Aquinas in the *Summa contra gentiles* (1264). It stipulated, against the claims of fideists such as Huet, that the knowledge of God's existence could be arrived at by natural reason and had to logically precede any of the articles of the faith.[60] For Aquinas and Crousaz, people arrived at this knowledge not through the reading of scripture but through a metaphysical investigation of causes and effects, which led them to comprehend the necessity of the first cause of all being. Belief in the Christian revelation was then based on the complete compatibility between the rational idea of a perfect being and the contents of the Bible.

By disputing the certainty of the rational knowledge of God, the fideists appeared to advocate an entirely irrational and unfounded faith. Absolute fideism, Crousaz argued, was not a tenable theological stance: either supernatural belief assumed some basic rational propositions as true, in which case it was not entirely irrational, or the belief was wholly unfounded. In the former case, the fideist claims would merely prove themselves to be incoherent. In the latter, the foundations of Christianity would be undermined, because there would be no way of distinguishing between religious fanaticism and the one true faith.[61] If reason were relegated from the realm of religion, one would never be able to offer an objective proof of the truth and the sanctity of scripture.[62] With the intensity of belief and of devotion serving as the only criterion of religious veracity, Christianity would be placed on the same level as other faiths. The representatives of all revealed religions, including Judaism and Islam, "brag and boast about the grace of Divine Revelation, which makes them convinced of the truth of their religion." "By what right," Crousaz asked, "will a Pyrrhonian presume that the Jew and the Muslim are mistaken and that it is he who is correct in his beliefs, [while] the others are vainly mistaken?"[63] Only the use of reason could objectively demonstrate Christianity's truth and its superiority, he insisted.

Crousaz mocked Huet by concluding that the fideist's resistance to adhering to a particular philosophical sect should have extended to his religious commitments.[64] It followed logically from Huet's reasoning, Crousaz proposed, that the multitude of religions should have led the skeptic to conclude: "I should thus not embrace any religion for fear of erring in my choice, and I will regard them all as equally doubtful."[65] Crousaz questioned the intentions of skeptics such as Bayle and Huet, who explicitly sought to strengthen the foundations of the faith by attempting to show the weakness of human reason. Contrary to their avowed intentions, he contended, the fideists merely played into the hands of the unbelievers by providing arguments against the rational basis of Christianity.[66]

Crousaz questioned how someone of Huet's intelligence would not perceive that "Pyrrhonism, rather than driving toward faith, leads directly to libertinism." Any person could perceive the moral consequences that followed from the kind of doubt Huet advocated: "If all is uncertain, why bother, and why not abandon yourself to your fantasies, when you can do it with impunity? What do we have to fear after death? Would it not be a great injustice to condemn men for having neglected to regulate their conduct according to the proper moral principles after forcing them to be born without the possibility of assuring themselves of any rules or principles?"[67]

Having chastised Huet for his insincere and self-interested defense of skepticism, Crousaz then proceeded to give a point-by-point refutation of the late bishop's Pyrrhonism. He particularly challenged Huet on the grounds that his arguments were not self-referential. For instance, the *Traité* provided definitions of terms without expressing any doubts about their meanings.[68] At the same time, by refusing to admit the veracity of even the proposition that one must doubt all things, Huet and his fellow skeptics left the door open for the possibility that it was they who were mistaken.

The skeptic doubts and makes it a rule to always doubt. Can we obtain any certain knowledge? "I doubt it," he says; is it impossible to assure oneself on this point and know with certainty that one must doubt? "I doubt that as well," [he replies]. Therefore, when you accuse those who claim to know something of deluding themselves and of being mistaken, it is possible that that you accuse them falsely and that it is you who are mistaken and refuse to admit it. One sees that Pyrrhonism is a heap of contradictions.[69]

If the Pyrrhonians were correct about the necessity of doubting all things, they had to have advanced at least one certain proposition. Such inconsistency would lead to the unraveling of their entire project. This argument was central in attempted refutations of skepticism. Crousaz and other anti-Pyrrhonians believed that by showing the utter incoherence of skeptical arguments, they could prove that Pyrrhonism was nothing but a collection of contradictory negative claims. It was in vain that Huet had tried to prove the veracity of skepticism, Crousaz reasoned, since his deduction would negate itself. The late bishop could not have it both ways. He could not argue that nothing could be known with certainty without subjecting his own conclusion to the same verdict. Mocking Huet's insistence that the senses yielded imperfect knowledge of the world, Crousaz suggested that a publisher should have given Huet several badly printed pages of his book and claimed that they were in perfect condition.[70]

Two years after the publication of Crousaz's text, the German Johannes Egger (1695–1736) undertook his own refutation of Huet's *Traité* in his *De viribus mentis humanae disquisitio philosophica anti-huetiana* (1735). Egger claimed that he had been inspired by Crousaz's *Examen du pyrrhonisme* and that he wanted to compose a shorter, more accessible anti-skeptical work.[71] In its title and its text, Egger's work mirrored Huet's notorious treatise. Egger, who was a professor of philosophy at the Académie de Berne, went through each chapter of the *Traité* and tried to refute its arguments. He did not present new or original claims, and much of his refutation borrowed arguments from Crousaz's text. However, his rendering the anti-skeptical arguments into Latin made it available to a greater audience, particularly to students in German universities.

The Winter of Discontent with Philosophical Uncertainty

Huet's pious intentions were shared by those who chastised his skeptical treatise. His tactics, however, appeared excessively unconventional to them. Despite such a perception, Huet's fideistic skepticism presented one of the most orthodox reactions to the naturalization of theology in the seventeenth century. Huet sought to persuade his contemporaries to abandon rational arguments concerning the existence of God and the immortality of the soul and accept these beliefs on faith alone. This was the only way, in Huet's view, to prevent the complete overthrow of orthodox intellectual authorities. Although Huet denounced human reason, his humanist pursuits indicate that he thought some remnants of truth could be found in antiquity. He took the "losing" position in the *Querelle des Anciens et des Modernes*. By arguing that ancient sources possessed significantly more value than modern ones ever could, Huet stood against the intellectual currents of his time and doomed himself to relative oblivion. Huet is thus a tragic figure: he understood the dangers presented by rationalism to traditional authorities, but he was disparaged for his efforts to mitigate such hazards by those who claimed to represent those very authorities. He was forgotten by posterity for his relative orthodoxy and censured by his friends for his perceived heterodoxy.

The controversy and scandal that followed the posthumous publication of the *Traité* signaled the unease with which Huet's contemporaries faced the challenge of Pyrrhonism, which appeared to be permeating the learned culture of the early eighteenth century. Whether it was in print, in lecture halls, or in the streets and cafés around major universities, thinkers defending various philosophical schools perceived a unified attack of Pyrrhonian skepticism against their epistemological systems, their metaphysics, and even their philosophical theologies. Protestants and Catholics alike saw threats to their demonstrations of the existence of God, especially to those based on a posteriori reasoning that posited the existence of a first cause as the only possible explanation of the perfection of the universe. The growing unease among these philosophically and religiously diverse thinkers would prompt new efforts to grapple with philosophical skepticism, not only in France but also in England, Switzerland, Prussia, and the Netherlands. The crisis was European.

CHAPTER FIVE

A New Hope

The Critics of Pyrrhonism Strike Back

The Popularization of Sextus Empiricus

The proliferation of skeptical literature in the 1720s brought the *crise pyrrhonienne* to its climax, forcing thinkers concerned with the intellectual and religious consequences of Pyrrhonism to undertake refutations and formulate new criteria of certainty. At the same time, opponents of skepticism, both Catholic and Protestant, began to articulate arguments that could moderate the ultimate conclusions of the Pyrrhonians and offer new criteria of certainty. Some abandoned the notion that absolute metaphysical certainty was attainable, seeking instead to establish degrees of probability. Others attempted to show that one could employ Pyrrhonian arguments for critiques of unfounded dogmatism without accepting their full implications. Critics of Pyrrhonism thus attempted to disarm this seemingly dangerous philosophy by adopting some of its methods, while rejecting its ultimate conclusions. This chapter details attempted refutations of Pyrrhonism during the apex of the *crise pyrrhonienne* in the 1720s and 1730s, revealing new trajectories that anti-skeptical arguments took.

In 1725, two years after the posthumous publication of Huet's *Traité philosophique de la foiblesse de l'esprit humain*, a French translation of Sextus Empiricus's *Pyrrhonianae hypotyposes* appeared on the scene. This would be the first full vernacular edition of a text that was almost single-handedly responsible for introducing ancient Pyrrhonism in early modern Europe.[1] The anonymous translator, identified later as the Swiss mathematician Claude Huart,[2] incurred significant criticism for making the tenets of the ancient skeptic accessible to a wide audience. Before this translation, the Pyrrhonians' founding text existed only in Latin and Greek editions and was accessible only to a highly learned audience. A vernacular edition of *Hipotiposes* rendered it approachable to a much larger segment of the reading public, thereby increasing its pernicious influence, in the eyes of critics.

The Fabricius edition of 1718 had already received mixed reviews. The *Journal des savants* praised the editor for a meticulous compilation of the parallel Greek and Latin texts and commended the presentation of overlooked ancient schools of philosophy. At the same time, the critic admonished Sextus's overarching project: "In explaining the principles of the skeptical philosophy with great clarity, Sextus reveals how vain and unjust such a sect is if it claims to prevent a serious search for the truth." What could be "more frivolous," the reviewer asked, "than to engage in formulating weak objections against the most evident things that one never dares to doubt in the regular conduct of life" and to "remain in doubt and uncertainty with regard to facts that are . . . supported by the strongest and most probable reasons?"[3]

Jean Le Clerc, one of Bayle's primary *rationaux* opponents and the editor of the Amsterdam-based *Bibliothèque ancienne et moderne*, published a more positive evaluation of the text, suggesting that it taught people not to be overly credulous and not to rely excessively on established authority in philosophical questions. By forcing readers to question the foundations of their opinions, Sextus's skepticism was suitable for "curing those who hold blind admiration for antiquity and [established] authority." The author of the piece argued that if such a "spirit of credulity" persisted, then "truth and untruth would be put on an equal footing," and "the whole earth would be covered in darkness."[4] The reviewer saw Pyrrhonian skepticism as a critical tool that was useful for providing distinctions between fact and fiction and for furnishing a rational basis for various beliefs and opinions.

At the same time, he also argued that Sextus's presentation of Pyrrhonism led to the risky conclusion that "we are not in a state to distinguish the true from the false," because it denied any criterion of certainty that could help to make such a distinction. It left all decisions up to fancy and intuition and made mathematically certain propositions epistemologically equivalent to the purest fictions. Such an outcome, the reviewer asserted, "would destroy all religion and all civil society among men."[5] The critic also related the dangerous claims of self-avowed fideists:

> There have always been many people, not just among the Pagans but also among Christians, who have tried to introduce strange notions under the pretext of Religion, and they were applauded by others who claimed to be devout. Under the pretext of humbling Reason, they placed Faith in opposition to it, and they were not ashamed to claim that one must renounce all common notions to be a Christian, as if these common notions could be contrary to the Revelation or as if the

Author of the Revelation could contradict the Creator of the lights of reason, that is to say, [as if God could] be inconsistent in his instructions![6]

Although he did not mention Bayle by name, the reviewer deployed an argument commonly used against Bayle by Le Clerc and his other *rationaux* opponents. The consequence of opposing reason to faith, they had argued, was to propose an inconsistent God who violated the very principles that he himself had established.

The *Bibliothèque ancienne et moderne* review distinguished between a useful, mitigated skepticism that helped in a critical evaluation of received ideas and a dangerous, extreme skepticism (*pyrrhonisme outré*) that placed all truth claims about the world on the same level of uncertainty. The critic summarized the major arguments of the *Pyrrhonianae hypotyposes* and suggested that a skeptical attitude would be useful for most contemporaneous schools of philosophy: "It must be admitted that our modern dogmatists would be well served to take a few doses of the medicine of the ancient skeptics in order to learn to suspend their judgment more frequently than they do."[7] The reviewer also acknowledged the usefulness of suspending judgment in theoretical questions, such as the interaction between mind and body and the relationship between sense perceptions and objective reality.

At the same time, the critic pointed out the functional impossibility of remaining in a state of total indecision with respect to practical matters. He dismissed speculations that the physical world did not exist independently of human perception, suggesting that "such niggling does not merit a response, because even those who engage in it are themselves convinced that it is nothing but deception."[8] The reviewer thus emphasized the insincerity of the skeptical suspension of judgment with regard to questions of practical behavior, employing the commonly used argument that the skeptics never acted in accordance with their philosophy. Furthermore, he opposed the central claim of skepticism regarding the absence of a basic criterion of truth. Sextus had argued that since such a criterion would require a criterion of its own, any philosopher attempting to find it would be trapped in an infinite series of proofs. The critic proposed that the self-evidence (*évidence*) of propositions could serve as such a criterion, although he conceded that not all principles could be demonstrated in this manner.

Despite these and other reservations, the critic readily admitted that a prudent withholding of judgment remained a useful and necessary tool that allowed people to recognize the inconclusive nature of the human understanding of the world. One must never conclude that a view was true, he noted, simply because it was an entrenched and widely shared belief. Only a philosophical demonstration could provide sufficient certainly.[9] By declaring humanity's knowledge of the world to be provisional, one could escape the infinite number of errors into which ancient and modern schools of philosophy had fallen. These mistakes, he believed, would eventually be corrected:

> A time will come when physics will be nothing other than a collection of [true and] certain natural phenomena, and there will be agreement that their first causes are unknown [to us]. One will understand better than ever that there is a God who made all things with extreme wisdom and with infinite power, but one will [also] admit that the inner workings of his creation are no better known [to us] than they were two or three thousand years ago. In this regard, one will become a bit of a skeptic, and one will make fewer mistakes by admitting ignorance in cases in which it must be recognized.[10]

The *Biliothèque ancienne et moderne* review spanned more than one hundred pages. It summarized the arguments of the *Pyrrhonianae hypotyposes* and of the other treatises contained in the edition, while offering refutations of them. Although the review disagreed with Sextus's ultimate conclusions, it placed the ancient author in the context of his actual debates with his contemporaries and presented his system as a useful antidote to philosophical dogmatism. The effort by Jean Le Clerc's journal to offer a substantive, often sympathetic presentation of Sextus's ancient skepticism is curious, given the editor's vocal opposition to Bayle. Le Clerc's personal animus toward Bayle could certainly account for the difference in the journalist's treatment of the two skeptics. Another possible explanation is that Le Clerc and his fellow editors wished to control how Sextus's infamous skeptical treatise would reach readers who were unable or unwilling to read the Latin text. By moving away from a discussion of the extreme conclusions of Sextus's system and presenting it as a useful critical tool, perhaps the *rationaux* editors hoped to alleviate the book's potentially harmful effects.

Reactions to the 1725 French translation of Sextus were significantly more critical. The Jesuit *Mémoires de Trévoux* offered a very cold welcome to this vernacular edition, claiming that Sextus's disrespect for "the sacred and the profane" should lead people to "regard with indignation those who for some time have attempted to bring this author back onto the scene, sometimes in Greek, sometimes in Latin, and now in French."[11] The article focused on chastising the anonymous translator and his preface. The reviewer questioned the motives of the translator, comparing him to "authors who exposed in full force the objections of the enemies of religion" in order to refute them: "What does that make of an author who maintains that there is no response to these claims, that is, to the sophisms of the skeptics, and who, despite this, reports their arguments while doubting that they can be refuted?"[12] The review implied that the anonymous translator could have had sinister ulterior motives for popularizing Pyrrhonian arguments. The translator's own claim—that he sought merely to present the assertions of the skeptics without approving them—seemed far-fetched to the *Trévoux* critic.[13] The reviewer went on to attack Pyrrhonism and its adherents, describing the familiar figure of a hypothetical extreme skeptic as a "troubled and jabbering mind who does not respect anything, who agrees with no one, including himself," and who doubted the most obvious truth, such as "whether two and two make four."[14] The Jesuit reviewer was unconcerned with familiarizing the readers with the actual arguments of the text. In fact, he noted that he would "not give an account of Sextus's work, since the text is neither new nor unknown."[15] Instead, he offered a full-fledged attack on Pyrrhonism and its advocates. He maintained that the skeptics never reasoned in good faith, that they engaged in circular arguments and equivocations, and that they altered their positions whenever it suited them.

The sections concerning the possibility of proving the existence of God were the only parts of the *Hipotiposes* with which the review dealt specifically. The critic noted that the translator had explicitly critiqued this section of Sextus's text in vain, since all the other arguments advanced by the ancient skeptic led readers to doubt the existence of God. If one could not be sure that one's perceptions of the external world corresponded to anything real, then one could no longer infer God's existence from the apparent perfection of the universe.[16] The critic suggested that if the skeptics explicitly advocated doubt with respect to the evidence provided by their sense perceptions, then they implicitly, if unintentionally, promoted uncertainty about religious matters. He argued that no matter how much Sextus's translator may have wished to disguise the ancient philosopher's attempts to cast doubt upon the existence of a supreme being, it was evident from the text that Sextus, like other pagans, had no clear understanding of God's essential attributes and that he "attacked all [notions of] Providence by the ordinary sophisms of contemporary atheists."[17]

The most extensive and detailed refutation of Sextus, however, came not from Catholic critics but in Jean-Pierre de Crousaz's *Examen du pyrrhonisme*. The Swiss logician dedicated a significant portion of his colossal text to exposing and refuting Sextus.[18] He challenged the ancient philosopher on multiple issues: his epistemological skepticism, his arguments against the possibility of proving the existence of God, his claims about the existence of motion and extension, and his alleged endorsement of moral relativism. Yet Sextus's most significant failing, for Crousaz, was his insincerity. The Swiss critic believed that the ancient skeptic had not actually endorsed the Pyrrhonian principles that he advanced. The orderly nature of his exposition appeared, in Crousaz's view, to contradict directly his arguments about the uncertain nature of human knowledge. Similarly, Sextus began his work by giving his readers clear definitions that would allow them to follow his arguments systematically. He had argued so clearly in favor of skepticism, Crousaz asserted, because he sought to persuade his readers and attract new disciples, a goal he shared with his dogmatic opponents despite his claims that all philosophers engaged in vain attempts to learn the truth. Crousaz claimed to have caught the ancient Pyrrhonian in a self-contradiction. By attacking particular methods in natural philosophy, Sextus implicitly assumed both that there was a better way of understanding the physical world and that there existed an objective reality independent of human perception. If such assumptions did not underlie the skeptic's critique, then it was an entirely nonsensical argument.[19]

Crousaz contended that rather than embracing the full conclusions of his skeptical philosophy, Sextus had merely adopted contradictory positions in order to undermine his opponents. His goal had been to win the philosophical battle by challenging the various claims of his rivals without concern for the truth. To Crousaz's displeasure, Sextus had misused his rhetorical skills in order to improve his reputation at the cost of plunging the learned world around him into ignorance and "darkness."[20] Crousaz passed a harsh judgment on such self-serving motives. Sextus had enumerated the various divisions and contradictions among philosophical schools in order to demonstrate that all opinions were fallible. His ulterior motive, however, had been to attract adherents and disciples to his side.[21] Thus Sextus's intellectual project had been a purely destructive one, as he had subverted all attempts to acquire true and certain knowledge of the world and to establish ethical frameworks.

Redefining Pyrrhonism and Mitigating the Threat

Not all reactions to the reemergence of Sextus Empiricus and his version of Pyrrhonism were entirely negative. Friedrich Wilhelm Bierling (1676–1728), a professor of philosophy and theology at the University of Rinteln, offered both a novel approach to the study and writing of history and a unique interpretation of the varieties of philosophical skepticism in his *Commentatio de pyrrhonismo historico* (1724). He began his work by attempting to dispel the notion that Pyrrhonism amounted to a complete rejection of certainty. He argued that Pyrrho and his disciples had been significantly misinterpreted and that their actual objective had been merely to challenge the untenable positions of their dogmatic interlocutors and to force them back toward a middle ground. He saw the hyperbolic doubt of the Pyrrhonians as a *jeu d'esprit* and as a tool used to ridicule unfounded philosophical claims.

Effectively, Bierling was attempting to clear the name of Pyrrhonism in a learned culture in which calling someone a Pyrrhonian was equivalent to calling that person an atheist or a libertine. He noted that he was well aware of the derision associated with the ancient school and its support for universal doubt. In order to undermine this perception, Bierling attempted to redefine the term *Pyrrhonism* by using Sextus Empiricus's tripartite classification of all philosophical schools. The first set was made up of dogmatic philosophers, such as Aristotle, Epicurus (341–270 BCE), and the Stoics, who believed that they had arrived at the true understanding of things through their inquiries. The second group included the Academics, such as Clitomachus (187–110 BCE) and Carneades, who, after an unsuccessful search for the truth, declared that it could not be found and abandoned their efforts. According to Bierling, Sextus placed the skeptics in the third category, describing them as those who, despite not having found the truth, continued their search.[22]

By repeating this classification, Bierling sought to present Pyrrhonism as a pragmatic school of thought and to weaken its alleged association with radical and universal doubt. In his *Dissertations sur la recherche de la vérité* (1693), Simon Foucher, who had openly considered himself a follower of the Academic tradition, had made a similar case concerning the goals of skepticism. Far from abandoning all attempts to understand the world, he suggested, the Academic philosophy consisted in the continuous search for the truth: "We could even call it [Academic skepticism] the philosophy of all times; since it consists in searching [for the truth], it is not unreasonable to attribute to it all the good and solid things that the investigations of all the centuries could acquire. One can consider it as the main path toward the truth, others being nothing else but particular roads by which the dogmatists get lost in the confusion of their prejudices."[23] Foucher rejected Sextus's claim that the Academics had abandoned all inquiry. However, his description of the aim of Academic skepticism strongly resembled Bierling's interpretation of Pyrrhonism. In both cases, the authors emphasized that the chief aim was precisely not to abandon the search for truth but to continue it gradually and methodically.[24]

Bierling further claimed that the critics had either completely misunderstood Pyrrhonism or accepted the fictional accusations made against it by other philosophical sects at face value. He suggested that Pyrrho, despite being known as the head of the Pyrrhonians, had not actually gone further than seeking to advance a tamed version of skepticism: "You might ask: what does moderate Pyrrhonism consist in? I designate three rules to you: investigate carefully; judge prudently; and thus refrain from judgment while examining and refuse to delve into obscure things."[25] Bierling attempted to present Pyrrhonism not as a radical school whose adherents advocated universal doubt but as a judicious method of approaching philosophical questions.

It was the other philosophical sects, Bierling insisted, that provided inaccurate and exaggerated descriptions of their skeptical opponents, painting them as radical, unreasonable, extravagant, and morally corrupt. They had accused Pyrrho both of intellectual insincerity, for rejecting the most certain principles, and of moral corruption, for undermining fundamental ethical doctrines. Bierling contended that it was a common practice among ancient philosophers to circulate vicious rumors about the private lives of their adversaries to demonstrate the supposed practical and moral failings of their tenets. He compared the reports that Pyrrho's enemies had fabricated about him to the allegations the Stoics had disseminated about Epicurus and his hedonistic practices. The Protestant scholar attempted to rehabilitate Pyrrho's personal reputation by stressing that far from teaching his disciples to ignore all moral rules, he had urged them to follow the customs and ethical standards of their societies and to remain loyal to their countries. He further noted that although many people acknowledged the veracity of established moral tenets, they consistently violated them anyway. Thus, even if the skeptics really denied the truth of established moral or religious orders, such a rejection was not necessarily connected with behavior.[26]

Nor was Pyrrhonism a simple rejection of established principles, according to Bierling. He criticized Descartes for providing a caricature of skeptical doubt in his *Méditations*. Since Descartes had rejected as false those things that he believed to be uncertain, he was effectively offering a dogmatic proposition: "Holding as false those things we doubt offends the first principles of reason. One who holds things as false denies their truth; one who denies maintains or establishes something; one who denies [therefore] does not doubt."[27]

Bierling also questioned the actual existence of true Pyrrhonians, arguing that it was improbable that any philosopher in history had sincerely agreed with the full implications of Pyrrhonian skepticism and doubted the veracity of every single proposition. Instead, he contended, Pyrrhonism offered a rhetorical strategy and a method for invalidating the unfounded positions of dogmatic philosophers, who went too far in their assertions. Aiming to "instruct and harass the dogmatists," the skeptics "pretended to doubt even the most plainly evident principles" and transferred the "onus of proving things" onto their opponents.[28] In Bierling's view, Pyrrhonism had been misunderstood; its use of hyperbolic doubt had mistakenly been seen as a sincere position, not as a rhetorical device. The Pyrrhonians had formulated such extreme propositions about the uncertainty of all knowledge only in order to confound and frustrate their opponents. Those who "agree with Pyrrhonism are not really Pyrrhonians," Bierling argued. Rather than obscuring human knowledge of the world, skepticism offered an essential way of guaranteeing its relative accuracy: "The weapons and arms of wisdom are to doubt prudently; the muscles and arms of ignorance are either to blindly negate or affirm anything or to settle utterly nothing even though there are evident reasons for reaching conclusions."[29]

Bierling presented Pyrrhonians not as dangerous and irreverent thinkers but as clever rhetoricians who sought the probable nature of things through un-prejudiced examinations. Citing Bayle's famous dictum "I know too much to be a Pyrrhonian, I know too little to be a dogmatist," he argued that a reasonable doubt was a perfect middle ground between dogmatism and complete skepticism, which were equally unreasonable.[30] Having established the limits of human knowledge and the appropriate place for uncertainty, Bierling also criticized those who sincerely advocated complete skepticism. He suggested that such people were worthy neither of being despised nor of being refuted; instead, they were to be mocked and ridiculed.[31] Thus, by distancing what he saw as a reasonable and mild Pyrrhonism from radical skepticism, Bierling attempted to reappropriate the term and clear its name.

Bierling's *Commentatio*, which was an expanded version of his *Dissertatio de pyrrhonismo historico* (1707), received quite a lengthy and favorable review in the *Bibliothèque germanique*.[32] Making the essential arguments of the Latin text available in French, the reviewer praised Bierling's theoretical approach and his masterful use of examples.[33] Bierling's effort to recast the goals and the methods of skepticism, in particular Pyrrhonism, and to redefine the term *Pyrrhonism* itself would prove to be a new strategy for both the supporters and the opponents of skepticism.

Common Sense and Verisimilitude: Claude Buffier's Answer to Pyrrhonism

In the same year that Bierling tried to redeem Pyrrhonian skepticism and prove its methodological usefulness, the Jesuit Claude Buffier (1661–1737) undertook a different kind of approach in his *Traité des premières véritez* (1724).[34] Buffier's

"Avertissement" emphasized that the "knowledge of the first truths [had] never before merited more attention," since contemporary debates called for a reliable "method of verifying" human knowledge.[35] He sought to articulate the best ways of demonstrating the most essential truths against "common prejudice, the confusion of the schools, and the danger of certain fashionable savants or philosophers." He saw the ability to prove these "first truths" as the "key to all knowledge."[36] Buffier's treatise was published just one year after the appearance of Huet's skeptical tract, but he did not single out Huet, Bayle, or others, but instead spoke of "the skeptics" in general.[37] Nevertheless, he appeared quite concerned about the proliferation of Pyrrhonian claims and perceived the need to offer a substantive refutation of skepticism. Buffier was critical of the ineffectiveness of some of the arguments made by other critics of skepticism. For example, he stressed that the invocations of principles such as "two plus two equals four" and "the whole is greater than the part"—two examples of self-evident truths that were often enlisted to show that absolute Pyrrhonism was entirely untenable—did not actually communicate any concrete information about objects outside of the mind. These propositions merely established internal truths based on the principle that "such a thing is such a thing."[38] Such tautological truisms, in his view, did little to address the actual epistemological arguments presented by the Pyrrhonians.

Buffier began by elucidating what he believed to be the first and most indubitable principle, which he identified as the individual perception of one's own existence. Drawing on Descartes's *cogito* argument, he proposed that the skeptics had questioned this plainly obvious fact in vain: "It is a waste of time to try to make them understand their folly and to explain to them that if they doubt everything, they [must exist], since one cannot doubt without existing."[39] He found the skeptics equally unreasonable in their denial of the existence of physical bodies. As the second indubitable and necessary principle, Buffier proposed common sense (*sens commun*), which he defined as "the disposition placed in all men by nature that leads them to make common and uniform judgments about the different objects of their own intimate feelings and of their own perceptions."[40] This essential predisposition allowed human beings to form basic conclusions about the surrounding world with relative certainty. Thus, a rational person could not doubt plain and obvious facts, such as the existence of other human beings, the difference between truth and falsity, and the distinction between mind and body. He proposed that while people could disagree about matters of taste owing to different predilections, common sense nevertheless led them to agree about most fundamental questions.[41]

While Buffier maintained that the perception of one's own being was absolutely certain and indubitable, he conceded that the knowledge of objects outside the mind through sense perception was not perfect, attaining only "a very high degree of probability."[42] He accepted the skeptical claim that the senses could lead to faulty judgments in some instances but argued that in the majority of cases no one could reasonably contest that "the senses give us the certainty of actual sensations" caused by external objects, "which cannot be doubted."[43] However, sense perceptions could not, according to Buffier, serve as the criteria of truth, because they merely discerned the way things appeared, without being able to penetrate their inner natures or their essences.[44] Admitting that "the truth" was not always attainable with certainty, Buffier proclaimed that human beings should seek "that which most closely approaches it . . . which we call probability."[45] He proposed a series of rules for establishing degrees of probability and for determining factors that gave propositions greater or lesser verisimilitude. These criteria applied to the investigations of the natural world and to human testimonies. They helped to establish a chain of certainty by which probability could come close to approximating the truth: "These are, more or less, the different degrees of verisimilitude that according to their extension and considerable number render our opinion more similar to the truth. . . . [Thus] if all the circumstances aligned in such a way that our opinion perfectly resembled the truth, without recognizing anything dissimilar from it, such an opinion would be not only probable but true."[46] Buffier argued that probability should be sought in questions in which the truth was unattainable, particularly in matters of "pure speculation," in which it was useful to suspend judgment until the preponderance of evidence supported a particular interpretation.[47]

Buffier's analysis of the origins of human knowledge drew on John Locke's (1632–1704) *Essay Concerning Human Understanding* (1689). Locke had famously disputed Descartes's doctrine of innate ideas, and he argued that all knowledge came into the mind only through the senses. All ideas were the products of sensation—a process by which objects in the external world imprinted themselves onto the organs of sense—and of the mind's reflection upon those sensations. Locke had distinguished between real and nominal essences. Real essence was the "constitution of the insensible parts" of a body or the actual nature of objects as they existed independently of human perception. It was the unknown combination of matter that produced observable qualities. Nominal essences, by contrast, were the abstract ideas that the mind formed by identifying common characteristics and properties shared by several objects. Nominal essences were the apparent natures of things, but they were the only source of information about the world. The mind could not know the real essences of things; it "could only suppose their being without knowing precisely what they are," Locke insisted.[48] People generally presumed that the nominal essence of a thing represented its real essence, but according to Locke, the latter remained completely inaccessible to the mind and the correspondence between the two could not be established with certainty. All judgments about the world had to be based on the former. In many ways, this account resembled the epistemological critiques advanced by skeptics such as Foucher, Bayle, and Huet. Indeed, some eighteenth-century thinkers even accused Locke of promoting a theory of knowledge that led directly to skepticism.[49]

Nevertheless, Locke's arguments offered a way to integrate skeptical claims into an epistemology that avoided the ultimate conclusions of Pyrrhonism. Locke's work became known on the Continent rather quickly.[50] Parts of the *Essay* were made available to French-speaking readers in 1688—even before its official publication in England—through an abridgement provided by Jean Le Clerc's *Bibliothèque universelle et historique*.[51] A full French edition of the *Essay* appeared in 1700 with the help of Pierre Coste (1668–1747), a prolific translator and Huguenot *émigré* in England.[52] An abridged French version of Locke's text followed in 1720.[53]

Buffier became acquainted with Locke's *Essay* through the Coste translation, and his epistemology of common sense relied heavily on Locke's claims.[54] In a chapter titled "Remarques sur la métaphysique de M. Loke," Buffier praised the English philosopher for being "the first [thinker] of this time who attempted to untangle the operations of the human mind." He contrasted Locke's epistemology, which began with the study of simple ideas and was based on reality, to the rationalist systems of Descartes and Malebranche, which he likened to philosophical fictions (*romans*).[55] At the same time, Buffier criticized Locke for designating knowledge that seemed certain according to the testimony of the senses as merely probable.[56] He also found Locke to be equivocal on the use of the terms *reason* and *innate principle*. Buffier noted that while no ideas could come into the mind without experience, it was unreasonable not to admit the existence of the first truths (*premières vérités*).[57]

Buffier's *Traité des premières véritez* was an attempt to incorporate skeptical critiques into an epistemological framework that appeared to combine elements of Cartesian rationalism with Lockean empiricism.[58] His argument about the viability of an epistemology that contented itself with probability was so influential that it made it into the article "Vraissemblance" (1765) in the *Encyclopédie*.[59] Without attacking specific authors, he tried to formulate a new theory of knowledge and to mitigate the claims of skeptics such as Huet and Bayle. Buffier's and Bierling's emphases on limited skepticism called for a via media between dogmatism and radical Pyrrhonism.

Crousaz: The Self-Proclaimed Mortal Enemy of Pyrrhonism

While Bierling and Buffier appeared to cede some ground to Pyrrhonism, Jean-Pierre de Crousaz, whose polemics we have already encountered, decided to tackle what he saw as the most dangerous intellectual threat to contemporaneous society head on. It would not be unfair to claim that Crousaz was the eighteenth century's most outspoken opponent of both ancient and modern skepticism.[60] He was a devout Huguenot who remained in close contact with the Parisian intellectual world throughout his career and was even inducted into the prestigious Académie royale des sciences as a corresponding member.[61] In addition to his influential works on logic, on the relationship between mind and body, and on aesthetics, Crousaz composed the vast *Examen du pyrrhonisme ancien et moderne*. This text sought to refute the arguments of philosophical skepticism both as articulated in their ancient form by Sextus Empiricus and as presented in their modern formulation by the arch-Pyrrhonian Pierre Bayle in his *Dictionnaire*.

Crousaz was by no means a reactionary opponent of the radical ideas of Bayle. He vehemently opposed the persecution of the skeptics (and of others who held dangerous opinions) and claimed that their positions should be refuted, not suppressed.[62] Crousaz was hardly a supporter of Aristotelian theories and methods of education. His philosophical views combined Cartesian metaphysics, Lockean epistemology, and some elements of Newtonian physics.[63] Consequently, he is an excellent example of a relatively moderate Enlightenment thinker who sought to defend his intellectual culture from what he perceived as the pernicious effects of Pyrrhonism on religion, on morality, and on learning.

Nor was Crousaz an obscure member of the Republic of Letters. He was one of the most eminent logicians of his time. The prominent English historian Edward Gibbon (1737–94) called Crousaz's *New Treatise of the Art of Thinking* (1724) "a clear and methodical abridgement of the art of reasoning, from our simple ideas to the most complex operations of the human understanding." Gibbon noted that this text had prepared him to tackle the ideas of Locke and Bayle.[64] Indeed, the Swiss philosopher's treatise on logic was quite popular. It went through four French editions from 1712 to 1741 and was even translated into English in 1724.[65]

Crousaz's vibrant publishing career was complemented by a lifelong commitment to teaching. He served as a professor of philosophy and mathematics and was appointed rector four times at the Académie de Lausanne (1700–1724 and 1738–49). He taught the same subjects at the University of Gröningen (1724–26) before being selected as tutor to Prince Frederick II of Hesse-Cassel (1720–85), a position he held until 1732. Given his interest in logic and his dedication to pedagogy, it is not surprising that Crousaz was drawn to issues of philosophical skepticism and became one of the most outspoken opponents of this doctrine. He perceived Pyrrhonism as a grave danger not only to his personal and cherished views but also to the future of the intellectual world in which he participated. This awareness was further reinforced by the urging of Cardinal André-Hercule de Fleury (1668–1751), who implored Crousaz to offer a refutation of skepticism and to expose the threat it posed to morality and to religion.[66]

Crousaz composed the *Examen* between 1720 and 1724 but did not publish it until 1733.[67] The text was divided into three unequal parts: the first part examined the origins of skepticism and described its characteristics; the second analyzed the works of Sextus Empiricus; the third and largest part argued against the ideas of Bayle. This last part was also divided along topical lines, addressing the tenets of Pyrrhonism with respect to particular questions, such as the existence of God, the nature of the soul and its interaction with the body, the tension between free will and predestination, and historical certainty. It also included a chapter on Pierre-Daniel Huet's skeptical treatise. Three objectives underlie the essential traits of Crousaz's anti-skepticism. First, Crousaz sought to diagnose the causes and the symptoms of skepticism, explaining the philosophy's growing popularity in his own time. Second, he carefully outlined the dangers of Pyrrhonism to religion, to morality, and to the pursuit of knowledge in general. Third, he attempted both to refute the arguments of Sextus Empiricus and Pierre Bayle, demonstrating that skepticism was philosophically and practically untenable, and to provide foundations for the acquisition of true and certain knowledge about the surrounding world.

Before undertaking his critique of Pyrrhonism, Crousaz attempted to explain its popularity in an age that was experiencing unprecedented progress in almost every area of human knowledge.[68] He saw the effects of this destructive philosophy manifest themselves in academic and social life. He accused Pyrrhonism of infecting European intellectual culture, of promoting irreligion and immorality, and even of triggering the financial collapses in the cases of the

South Sea Bubble and the Mississippi Bubble.[69] As noted earlier, Crousaz saw several causes for this counterintuitive skeptical development. Above all else he blamed the educational system for producing skilled rhetoricians instead of training knowledgeable philosophers. He also censured those who took part in intense theological disputations for undermining the sources of religious certainty.[70]

Crousaz maintained that the ineffectual educational methods of the time had produced scholars who were prone to formulating erroneous metaphysical systems without adequately analyzing the premises on which such systems were based. Lacking sound philosophical foundations, these systems easily collapsed under scrutiny, leaving their advocates disillusioned: "A man who made mistakes on several occasions is discouraged, and in order to avoid having to foreswear his findings, he limits himself to finding probabilities. Then, the ridiculousness of those who were stubborn in their own errors affirms his place in the party of doubt. This is how Pyrrhonism established itself in those times and continues to establish itself today."[71] Pyrrhonism offered a convenient consolation for such thinkers, allowing them to excuse their own intellectual deficiencies by referring to the universal fallibility of human reason.[72]

Crousaz's depiction of the intellectual culture of his time offered a striking portrait of an early eighteenth-century paradox, and it echoed the attitude of Pierre Villemandy's observation that begins this book. On the one hand, Crousaz believed, as did Villemandy and many of his contemporaries, that the current age had reached an apex of learning, particularly in natural philosophy and the sciences.[73] On the other hand, he perceived a general decline in the standards of education and a concomitant rise in superficial learning, which led to the proliferation of skepticism. Bayle's *Dictionnaire*, for Crousaz, was both a source of dangerous ideas and a scholarly model of superficiality that was being emulated by many around him.

In undertaking his refutation of Pyrrhonism, Crousaz also pointed to the discrepancy between the Pyrrhonians' philosophical arguments and their practical behavior. While they claimed that nothing could be known with certainty and called for a suspension of all judgment, they did not act in accordance with such a position, because it was "so contrary to nature" that it was "impossible to maintain it continuously." The skeptics behaved as if there really was an objective reality independent of their senses: they satisfied their bodily needs, sought comfort, and accepted the practical implications of cause and effect. "Ordinarily," Crousaz wrote, "they think and live more or less like others, and they do not take part in doubting and in affirming their doubts unless such opportunities arise." Crousaz believed that even the most deranged skeptic could not remain in a state of perpetual doubt.[74]

Crousaz also tried to discredit the skeptics by demonstrating the obvious internal inconsistency of their arguments and by showing that they were "in perpetual contradiction with themselves."[75] For Crousaz, the most fundamental logical failure of Pyrrhonian skepticism was that it was not self-reflexive in its methods. In attempting to refute others, the skeptics constantly abandoned their universal doubts and assumed the veracity of various particular propositions. While arguing against their opponents, Pyrrhonians accepted common definitions, logical conventions, and metaphysical axioms. Crousaz thought that he had caught the skeptics in a vicious circle from which they could not escape. He proposed that their endorsement of universal doubt was itself dogmatic. They did not actually believe that the assertion that everything must be doubted was itself in doubt. Effectively, the skeptics had painted themselves into a corner: "This proposition 'All is uncertain' is [either] true or false; if it is false, then you are wrong in maintaining it, and the opposite is true; if it is true, then there is some truth."[76] If the skeptical claim were correct, and true and certain knowledge of the world were indeed absolutely unattainable, then the skeptics would have offered the only certain proposition and therefore invalidated their own assertion. By their efforts to demonstrate the validity of the skeptical conclusion, the Pyrrhonians contradicted themselves and showed that at least some definite knowledge, however limited, could be obtained. Crousaz also pointed to what he believed to be an illogical leap in the reasoning of the Pyrrhonians. They deduced the necessity for universal doubt from a limited number of examples. They reasoned that since "many people had been mistaken, no one can be assured of anything," and they erroneously concluded that because human beings "could not know *everything*," then they "could not know *anything*."[77] The Pyrrhonians were thus guilty of a clear paralogism.

Crousaz argued against Academic skeptics such as Simon Foucher, who proposed that all knowledge was merely probable but advocated continuing investigations. The Swiss logician remarked that without basic criteria of truth, the skeptics could no more make conclusions about the probability of a particular proposition than they could about its certainty. Defining "the most probable" proposition as "that which most resembles that which is true," Crousaz asked, "How is it possible for me to judge whether an opinion has more or less the semblance of being true if I don't know the nature of truth?"[78] By making judgments with respect to probabilities, the skeptics assented to the basic notion that the mind was able to acquire at least some understanding both of the world around it and of its own mental operations. Only the most insincere Pyrrhonian would deny the moral certainty of universally accepted propositions.

Throwing a jab at his Catholic counterparts, Crousaz asserted that one could not arrive at certainty by relying on intellectual authority: "Thus, the voice of authority is not a barrier to oppose Pyrrhonism; on the contrary, the voice of authority, far from uprooting it from its foundations, instead gives rise to uncertainty and doubt." He suggested that no human authority, however respected and revered, could ever obtain the Pyrrhonians' assent. Even the doctrines of Saint Augustine and of Saint Thomas Aquinas, both of whom were deeply (if diversely) revered in the seventeenth and eighteenth centuries, had produced debate and disagreement among their contemporaries.[79] Indeed, as noted earlier, Crousaz had maintained that even the divine nature of scripture had first to be proved by rational arguments.

Crousaz suggested that the self-evidence (*évidence*) of philosophical propositions was such a criterion of certainty. Although the Pyrrhonians contended that each party to any given debate could claim to have the more convincing proof, Crousaz suggested that the superior argument was almost always apparent if one examined the quality of the supporting evidence.[80] "We respect *évidence*," he proclaimed, because "it is a light that enlightens us by its own force; it does not need anything else to come to its aid in order to enlighten us and to make us see."[81]

Crousaz's language throughout the *Examen* invoked the contrast between light and darkness. As a philosopher and pedagogue, he saw enlightening students and readers as his fundamental duty. Pyrrhonism, on the other hand, cast people into the depths of darkness and ignorance. The opposition to skepticism was thus central to Crousaz's larger intellectual project. He believed that through an ordered examination of available evidence, humankind could improve its knowledge of the surrounding world, which in turn would provide greater support for the existence of God.

In concluding his voluminous refutation of Pyrrhonian skepticism, Crousaz proposed both religious and practical justifications for a continued pursuit of knowledge about the world. He rhetorically asked the fideists, who advocated a total submission of reason to faith, whether the contemplation of God's creation was not the most noble and suitable task in which human beings could engage. The study of the natural world, after all, not only enriched one's knowledge of the created universe but also fortified the foundations of both revealed and natural religion by uncovering the nature of God himself. Man's natural state was curiosity, he contended, not ignorance and doubt: "Are we not obligated to work for our own enlightenment? To neglect working for one's perfection, to neglect putting oneself in a position to be able to do the greatest possible good for oneself and for others—would this not be a moral evil?"[82] Crousaz's stance against Pyrrhonian skepticism was thus both religious and practical. He saw it as a danger to the foundations of religion and of morality, as well as an obstacle to the improvement of the human condition. However much he may have differed from the philosophes, he certainly shared this humanitarian concern with them.

Crousaz's project attracted significant attention across Europe. Richard Popkin has argued that "reviewers were not impressed" by Crousaz's effort and that his "great crusade against skepticism was ridiculed and answered" in 1739 by the anonymous author of the *Apologie de monsieur Bayle*.[83] Yet Popkin's analysis overlooks other significant reactions to the text. In fact, far from disparaging Crousaz's effort, the editors of all the major learned journals offered lengthy reviews praising the *Examen*'s goals and its arguments. For instance, the Amsterdam-based Huguenot *Bibliothèque raisonnée* declared that "the reading of this book can be useful for learning to distinguish what is certain from what is not, for confirming the most important truths . . . and for saving from doubt those who were left to venture there in good faith."[84] The journal devoted two extensive overviews to the *Examen*, analyzing the value of the work's counterarguments to skepticism. Similarly, although the editors of the Jesuit *Mémoires de Trévoux* did not like Crousaz's arguments against the role of intellectual authority, they praised the Protestant scholar's decision "to attack the common enemy."[85] These and other reviews reflect the significance of Crousaz's project as it was perceived by his contemporaries.[86]

Crousaz actively corresponded with the leading intellectuals in the Republic of Letters, such as the perpetual secretary of the Académie royale des sciences, Bernard le Bovier de Fontenelle (1657–1757), as well as the chancelier Henri François d'Aguesseau, Cardinal André-Hercule de Fleury, the abbé Noël-Antoine Pluche (1688–1761), the jurist Jean Barbeyrac (1674–1744), and the physiologist René-Antoine Ferchault de Réaumur (1683–1757), among numerous others.[87] Many of his correspondents praised his efforts to refute skepticism. Even before the publication of the *Examen du pyrrhonisme*, the abbé Jean-Paul Bignon (1662–1743), head of the Bibliothèque du roi, commended Crousaz's labors and appeared to share his view about the potential dangers of skepticism:

The book you plan to present to the public this autumn cannot be anything but very important. The spirit of Pyrrhonism has spread too far, and there are few ideas that have such pernicious consequences. You are correct in saying that Bayle's works have contributed greatly to rendering it more known. It is much easier to deny everything, or at least to place everything in doubt, than to deepen each question and to weigh the different reasons that might render specific knowledge either indubitable or uncertain; but I understand what an effort it must have been for you to compile all the different places where Bayle scattered his dangerous principles.[88]

In addition to serving as the royal librarian, Bignon was an ordained priest of the Oratorian order, the secretary of the Académie royale des inscriptions et belles-lettres, and one of the editors of the *Journal des savants*. He maintained a continuous correspondence with Crousaz and commended his attempts to refute Bayle, claiming that they would be "applauded by all those who have the interests of religion at heart."[89] Confessional differences mattered little to Bignon in this case, because he regarded Crousaz's project as beneficial to the rational foundations of all Christian denominations.

Cardinal André-Hercule de Fleury, who served as the first minister to King Louis XV (1710–74), shared Bignon's assessment of Crousaz's undertaking. He proclaimed that Bayle's works should be "burned by the hands of the executioner."[90] Writing to Crousaz several years after the publication of the *Examen*, Fleury shared his perceptions of the intellectual climate:

> The church fathers regarded the philosophy of Pythagoras, of Socrates, of Plato as a kind of preparation for the reception of the Gospels, whose many truths were taught by these great men. But I fear that we cannot say today that modern philosophy, or rather ancient philosophy renewed, is not the harbinger of the destruction of the universe. The absurd and impious doctrines of fatalism and Pyrrhonism establish themselves with great prejudice against religion, even natural religion, and against good sense. One banishes the Revelation as an effect of credulity or of superstition, which owe their sources to fear and to the baseness of the mind. Monsieur, you are, in truth, infinitely commendable for opposing yourself to the torrent that inundates the public.[91]

Fleury, along with other opponents of skepticism, saw a clear association between Pyrrhonism and materialist determinism (or fatalism, as Fleury called it). He also praised Crousaz for his refutation of Gottfried Wilhelm Leibniz's (1646–1716) controversial hypothesis of pre-established harmony[92] and for his labors in avenging contemporary philosophes' attacks on religion.[93] Fleury adopted the apocalyptic terminology of those who likened skepticism to a

plague or a contagion. Much like Bignon, he looked past confessional differences in his praise of Crousaz's defense of Christianity, seeing the Huguenot as
a valuable ally in the war against irreligion, which threatened both confessions
equally.

Crousaz also found supporters among various Protestant communities outside of France. The Swiss naturalist Albrecht von Haller, who taught medicine at
the University of Göttingen, shared his Catholic counterparts' concern for the
apparent conspiracy against religion and for the "corruption of mankind."[94] He
offered to translate parts of the *Examen du pyrrhonisme* into German in order to
make it more accessible to readers in the German principalities. He claimed that
"a work of this nature is necessary in Germany," where people were "not in the
state to defend themselves against his [Bayle's] artificial trappings." The Swiss naturalist declared that he would be pleased to "contribute, even as a secondhand
source, to the defense of the truth in an age when superstition and atheism are
making such great progress."[95] Haller's abridged translation would be published
in 1751 as *Prüfung der secte die an allem zweifelt* with the collaboration of Jean
Henri Samuel Formey, the perpetual secretary of the Académie royale des
sciences et belles-lettres de Prusse in Berlin.

Formey had also been in touch with Crousaz regarding his project, and he
proposed an abridgement of the *Examen*. Recognizing the importance of the anti-
skeptical text, Formey said that he had "decided to make a synopsis of the work"
in order to "to derive more fruit from this reading." He suggested that since "an
in-folio [edition] makes for very long reading for most people," a summary of
Crousaz's arguments might prove to be more accessible to a broad spectrum
of readers.[96] Because the cost of Crousaz's eight-hundred-page in-folio edition
made his audience fairly limited, printers were not all too eager to undertake
the publication of Formey's abridgment. It would finally be issued in 1756 under
the title *Le triomphe de l'évidence*.[97] By making the *Examen* easier to understand
and more affordable, the abridgment increased both the dissemination and the
impact of Crousaz's arguments. Haller wrote the "Discours préliminaire" to the
text, in which he underlined the dangers of skepticism and the importance of
religion to the maintenance of a stable society.[98]

Crousaz's attack on Pyrrhonism was expensive, extensive, unwieldy, and
complicated. It also reproduced a number of skeptical arguments that Crousaz
was attempting to refute. His *Examen* reprinted long sections of Bayle's *Dictionnaire* and Sextus's *Hipotiposes*. Despite its shortcomings, however, Crousaz's
massive anti-skeptical treatise was successful in presenting Pyrrhonism as a
legitimate threat to the intellectual and moral fabric of European culture. His

various correspondents across Europe recognized and shared the anxiety about the dangers that Pyrrhonian skepticism appeared to pose to the philosophical and theological foundations of their shared learned culture. Crousaz's *Examen* thus functioned as a call to arms to all those who shared his concerns. As we will see in the following chapter, numerous thinkers took up the challenge of refuting the ultimate conclusions of skepticism while, at the same time, seeking new sources of certainty.

CHAPTER SIX

The Berlin Compromise

Mitigated Skepticism and Probability

The Persistence of Pyrrhonism

The threat of Pyrrhonism did not seem to fade as years passed. Bayle, Huet, and other prominent skeptics had died, but their works continued to cause a stir in the Republic of Letters. Together with the growing popularization of philosophical materialism—which denied the existence of God and of the immaterial soul and postulated a purely material universe—skepticism appeared as a gateway philosophy that paved the way to more dangerous philosophical and theological views. This perception existed not only in Catholic France, where Pyrrhonism had set its deepest roots and acquired its most vocal exponents, but also in other parts of Europe, particularly those that attracted Huguenot refugees. While Paris remained the epicenter of the *crise pyrrhonienne*, debates about the powers of human reason also took place in other intellectual milieus, including the Netherlands, Switzerland, Prussia, and England. Huguenot thinkers, who remained in close contact with their French counterparts and who were deeply affected by the intense intra-Protestant debates between Bayle and the *rationaux* in the early part of the century, continued to undertake refutations of the *philosophe de Rotterdam*. Pyrrhonism's unrelenting threat to philosophy and to Christianity demanded new attempts to reformulate criteria of certainty in response to skeptical claims about the weakness of human reason.

Efforts to overcome Pyrrhonian challenges in the mid-eighteenth century illustrate how European thinkers reassessed the nature and the purposes of humanity's rational faculties. Increasingly, the moral case against skepticism would be combined with an appeal to pragmatism. The probabilistic approach to philosophical questions, deployed by Buffier and Bierling, continued to gain momentum and attract new supporters. Thinkers concerned with the far-reaching implications of Pyrrhonism grew progressively more willing to distinguish between different levels of certainty and to adopt more nuanced views about the powers and limits of natural human understanding. This chapter explores the motivations and intellectual itineraries of the major figures involved in these debates outside of France, paying particular attention to thinkers at the Académie royale des sciences et belles-lettres de Prusse in Berlin. It also shows how the concern with the religious and philosophical consequences of skepticism led to the formulation of new criteria of certainty.

David Renaud Boullier and Cartesianism

Catholic and Protestant thinkers appeared equally concerned with finding solutions to the skeptical crisis, which they believed could undermine the faith. In addition to Crousaz, one of the most prominent opponents of Pyrrhonism among the new generation of Huguenot *rationaux* was David Renaud Boullier (1699–1759), a Huguenot theologian and minister in Amsterdam and, later, in London.[1] In 1737 he published a second edition of the *Essai philosophique sur l'âme des bêtes* (1728), to which he attached his new *Traité des vrais principes qui servent de fondement à la certitude morale* (1737). In these two texts, both written as refutations of Pyrrhonian skepticism, Boullier attempted to formulate a set of principles that could lead to relative certainty in philosophical questions. He also applied these principles to metaphysics, natural philosophy, and history, demonstrating how they actually functioned on a practical level.

Unlike many of his contemporaries, Boullier did not necessarily think that the eighteenth century was witnessing a climax of Pyrrhonism. He suggested that one potential source of skepticism was the overabundance of competing theories and explanations in natural philosophy. He used the example of the struggle among the Ptolemaic, Tychonian, Newtonian, and Cartesian conceptions of the cosmos to demonstrate how a diversity of rival theories actually increased the uncertainty about the nature of the created universe.[2] He believed that the human mind was created by God in such a way that it constantly sought to explain visible effects by "imagined causes" (*causes imaginées*), or, in other words, by formulating hypotheses. Boullier defined a hypothesis as consisting "in the free arrangement of diverse supposed causes, from which one derives, in an orderly manner, the explanation of the diverse effects one sees."[3] The human mind organized multiple visible effects into a coherent pattern and then divined causes that best explained the existence of and the relationships among those various effects. The causes themselves remained invisible. Consequently, the mind could conceivably frame several viable possibilities, although only one explanation actually reflected the true nature of reality. For Boullier, skeptical doubt arose from an inability to decide among these multiple competing explanations. He thought that this problem could be solved by articulating clear criteria for selecting correct hypotheses. Such criteria would be applicable in any rational investigation.

Contrary to the views of a number of anti-Pyrrhonian philosophers, Boullier thought that there was no reason to assume that one could not argue with the skeptics. He did not see skepticism as a disease or a derangement of the mind, but, rather, as a conscious intellectual state. In his treatise on moral certainty and in his work on the nature of animal souls, Boullier attempted to articulate criteria so indubitable that even the skeptics could not contradict them. In the *Essai philosophique sur l'âme des bêtes*, Boullier took on both René Descartes and Pierre Bayle. He opposed the Cartesian hypothesis that animals were pure machines, devoid of a soul, reason, and sensation. At the same time, he argued against Pierre Bayle's *Dictionnaire* article "Rorarius," in which the skeptic appeared to eliminate any essential distinction between human beings and beasts. Boullier disagreed with the Cartesian model not because it was contrary to experience but because it failed to formulate an explanation that could overcome the hypothetical arguments of a skeptic.

The Cartesian claim that nothing stopped God from being able to create animals that acted based on purely mechanical principles had already been taken to task by the learned Jesuit Gabriel Daniel (1649–1728). In his *Voyage au monde de Descartes* (1691) Daniel had suggested that the logic of their argument necessarily led Cartesians to the dangerous conclusion that God could have created human beings that were soulless automatons. Daniel had reasoned that if animals were pure machines, there was no logical basis to assume that human beings were any different.[4] Once visible effects were no longer attributed to their most likely causes, the seemingly absurd hypothesis of human machines followed. After citing Daniel's assertion, Boullier wrote: "The silence to which one reduces the Cartesian becomes the triumph of the skeptic, who will be sure to admit the consequence to its full extent and to benefit from the difficulties that Father Daniel produces with respect to the existence of the human soul."[5] By offering a feeble explanation of a significant philosophical problem, Boullier claimed, the Cartesians actually gave an advantage to the Pyrrhonians. The latter could be silenced only with convincing arguments that were based on indubitable principles.

Unlike his allies, Boullier did not try to refute specific skeptical claims. Instead, he sought to solve Pyrrhonian challenges by articulating clear criteria of certainty. He distinguished between undeniable truths known with "metaphysical certainty" (*certitude métaphysique*) and those known with "moral certainty" (*certitude morale*). The former set of principles included the existence of God and the validity of various mathematical or geometrical principles (e.g., that two plus two equals four, that the whole is bigger than its various parts, and that a triangle has three angles). The latter set of principles were not absolutely definite or self-evident, but they could not be doubted sincerely by anyone who reasoned in good faith.[6] Thus, while the existence of God, for Boullier, was metaphysically certain, the existence of an external world that subsisted independent of human perceptions was not. Metaphysical truths were completely self-evident and undeniable in themselves, while moral truths depended on axioms and assumptions. Boullier offered two basic principles for attaining moral certainty and consequently overcoming Pyrrhonian doubt.

His first principle of moral certainty was based on Descartes's Sixth Meditation. Following Descartes, Boullier maintained that since God was not—and could not be—a deceiver, he would not have created a world in which observable effects led us to assume the reality of a cause that did not in fact exist. If it appeared as though animals acted on the basis of sense perceptions and reflections, Boullier reasoned, God would be a deceiver if it turned out, contrary to all evidence, that they were in fact unfeeling automata that had been wired to act in particular ways. Consequently, if one saw a clear and obvious connection between discernible effects and the most likely cause of those effects, then that cause necessarily existed. In the case that one was mistaken, God would have to be "the cause of our error" by assuming "the place of particular causes to which phenomena pointed . . . in order to deceive us." Because the notion of God as a deceiver contradicted the essential nature and properties of a perfect being, it was safe to conclude that "the agreement between the appearances that strike me and a simple cause that explains them, and that alone can explain them, proves the real existence of such a cause."[7] Thus, one could confirm the existence of the external world that corresponded to one's senses.

After establishing this first rule, Boullier proposed his second principle of moral certainty. He contended that in any attempt to explain natural phenomena, one always had to seek the simplest, most parsimonious explanations. A cause that was capable of explaining the greatest number of visible phenomena and of accounting for the connections among them in the most efficient manner necessarily had to be the real cause of those phenomena. "When one is moved to explain the phenomena of Nature," Boullier remarked, "the discovery of one simple principle . . . is sufficient to exclude the more complex hypotheses." He maintained that philosophical parsimony was a proof of the reality of the cause because it reflected the workings of divine wisdom, which always used the most efficient means available to govern the created universe. "This fertile simplicity, which brings all natural effects to one single source," he explained, "characterizes the wisdom of the Creator and through this becomes a principle of certainty in the search for causes." Boullier argued that the general conformity of opinions about the basic nature of the surrounding world (as well as a relative agreement about the truth of major historical events) was in itself evidence of the existence of an objective reality independent of human perception. How else, he asked rhetorically, could such agreement arise if not from independent judgments concerning the same objects?[8]

Ultimately, both of Boullier's rules of moral certainty depended on metaphysical assumptions about the nature of God. He based his criteria for explaining observable phenomena on two axioms: that God was not a deceiver and that he operated according to simple, general, and immutable laws of nature. Boullier argued that without these axioms about the nature of God, atheists and skeptics would not be able to secure a true and certain knowledge of any moral truths and would remain unsure whether their perceptions of the external world corresponded to the objective reality of such a world.[9]

Later in his career, Boullier continued to provide apologetic arguments for revealed religion in his *Lettres sur les vrais principes de la religion* (1741). He condemned the various attacks on belief from deists, atheists, and other "enemies of Christianity," and he attempted to persuade even "half-believers" (*demi-croyans*) to return to the flock of the faithful.[10] He also published a controversial work entitled *Le pyrrhonisme de l'église romaine* (1757). Composed as a series of epistolary exchanges between himself and the Catholic theologian Hubert Hayer, coauthor of the serial *La religion vengée*, the text featured mutual accusations of advancing total Pyrrhonism in religious matters. Hayer maintained that Protestantism led to competing scriptural interpretations, thereby promoting complete uncertainty. Boullier insisted that the Catholic belief in the possibility of obtaining an infallible understanding of God's word was faulty and inevitably resulted in a disillusioned skepticism about religious truths.[11] He proposed that personal certainty should be based on a rational evaluation of evidence and should replace the quest for absolute and metaphysical certainty.[12] Boullier admitted that this conviction was not, strictly speaking, a perfect assurance of the truth. Nevertheless, it was the highest attainable level of religious certainty for human beings, and it was more realistic than the Catholic quest for total certainty.[13]

Boullier's arguments foreshadowed systematic efforts to find a middle way between extreme skepticism and philosophical dogmatism. In his attempts to establish criteria of certainty and to stem the growing flood of critiques of revealed religion, Boullier went beyond making a moral case against Pyrrho-nian skepticism and repudiating it for its dangerous implications to morality and to religion: he attempted to reason with his skeptical opponents by offering philosophical arguments that he sincerely believed could persuade his interloc-utors to abandon their doubts.

Boullier's invocation of moral certainty resembled Bierling's argument for a reasonable Pyrrhonism and Buffier's emphasis on common sense and verisimil-itude. All three were early attempts to provide accommodations of and answers to skeptical arguments. While Bierling pointed out the many uncertainties that plagued philosophical and historical knowledge, he also redefined Pyrrhonism and mitigated its ultimate conclusions. Similarly, Buffier took quite seriously the Pyrrhonian arguments about the weakness of human reason and of the senses and sought to offer a new way of securing relatively certain knowledge about the surrounding world. Boullier, in turn, distinguished between degrees of certainty and moderated the ambitions of philosophical knowledge. They proposed reliance on probability and mitigated skepticism as practical solutions to the challenges posed by skeptical philosophy. As we will see, this approach would be embraced by a number of thinkers over the course of the eighteenth century. By adopting the methods of Pyrrhonism, while rejecting its ultimate conclusions, many of the participants in the debates about skepticism would endeavor to disarm this seemingly dangerous philosophy.

The Marquis d'Argens's Mitigated Skepticism and Lockean Empiricism

While Buffier and Boullier had attempted to moderate the conclusions of Pyr-rhonism primarily for religious reasons, this was far from the only motivation for eighteenth-century thinkers who advocated mitigated skepticism. Voltaire and Jean-Baptiste Boyer d'Argens (1703–71), neither of whom was known for religious piety, questioned the extent and limits of human understanding and came to embrace versions of moderate skepticism. Both relied heavily on Locke's *Essay Concerning Human Understanding* to advocate their own versions of skeptical empiricism. While Voltaire's use of Locke is well documented in historical scholarship, d'Argens's attempts to combine skepticism and empiri-cism are less well known. Nevertheless, they are crucial for understanding the gradual taming of Pyrrhonism in the mid-eighteenth century.[14]

D'Argens was born into a prominent aristocratic family in Aix-en-Provence, where his father served as attorney general (*procureur général*) at the Parlement of Provence. Despite his father's wishes, the young d'Argens dropped his pursuit of a legal education and decided to join the army. The young man's choice of profession and a series of scandalous adventures led his father to disinherit him. D'Argens heeded his father's wishes and went to study law in Paris, where he pursued his interest in painting and integrated himself into the vibrant intellectual life of the city. He rejoined the army during the War of the Polish Succession and was badly wounded near Philippsburg in 1734. Ignoring his father's orders to return to Provence and thus threatened with arrest, d'Argens fled to the Netherlands.[15] In The Hague (and later in Amsterdam) d'Argens traded the sword for the pen and began his literary career. He met Prosper Marchand, the prominent journalist who helped to publish the third edition of Bayle's *Dictionnaire*, who introduced him to the literary circle of French exiles and Huguenot émigrés as well as to his collaborator and publisher Pierre Paupie (d. c. 1755).

D'Argens's first philosophical work was the *Lettres juives* (1735–37), in which he imitated the style Montesquieu's (1689–1755) *Lettres persanes* (1721). The multivolume epistolary novel presented the correspondence between three fictional Jews who resided in different European capitals. Much like Montesquieu's Persian travelers, the *philosophes hébreux* discussed politics, religion, morals, and human nature, among many other topics, providing outsider perspectives on European customs and beliefs. D'Argens's correspondents were especially critical of what they perceived as the moral contradictions of Christianity and of religious persecution.[16] The *Lettres juives* proved extremely successful, appearing in at least ten French editions (many of them pirated) by 1739 and in Dutch, English, and German translations. It was this text that allegedly led Frederick II (1712–86) to make note of d'Argens and invite him to the Prussian court in 1742.[17]

While the *Lettres juives* raised questions about cultural and moral relativism, *La philosophie du bon-sens, ou Réfléxions philosophiques sur l'incertitude des connoissances humaines* (1737) addressed the nature of human knowledge. *La philosophie du bon-sens* followed the model of the increasingly fashionable histories of philosophy. The widely popular *Traité de l'opinion* (1733) of Gilbert-Charles Le Gendre, marquis de Saint-Aubin's (1688–1746), and André-François Boureau-Deslandes's (1689–1757) *Histoire critique de la philosophie* (1737) provided the best-known examples of this genre in the 1730s.[18] While Deslandes offered a history of philosophy that depicted a steady progress in human understanding, Saint-Aubin's *Traité* was more pessimistic about the possibility of such a gradual improvement.[19] Saint-Aubin, who had served as counselor at the Parlement of Paris and master of requests to the king (*maître des requites ordinaires de l'hôtel du roi*) before devoting his life to scholarly pursuits, claimed to write in the manner of a "moderate skeptic" and to demonstrate instances "when it was advantageous to suspend judgment." He positioned himself between Pyrrhonians, who "in trying to destroy the natural lights have pushed away reason" and refused to recognize evident principles, and the dogmatists, who had tried to appear "to have elevated themselves above uncertainty, which can only be overcome very rarely."[20] The multivolume *Traité* emulated Montaigne's and Bayle's styles by offering a historical overview of the varying opinions of ancient and modern thinkers on a wide range of topics, such as history, metaphysics, physics, and mathematics. The clash of diverse views in almost every sphere of human knowledge revealed the great number of errors to which people had subscribed, providing evidence of the inherent weakness of the mind.[21] Saint-Aubin articulated the pious and fideist intentions of his work, but the effect of the *Traité de l'opinion* resembled that of Bayle's *Dictionnaire*: it demonstrated the historicity, relativity, and uncertainty of philosophical and historical knowledge.

D'Argens shared Saint-Aubin's view regarding the historical relativity of human understanding. In his opening, he warned against the dangers of "gullibility" (*facilité de croire*) and the "vanity of wanting to know everything." He identified these as the "two sources of error and ignorance." D'Argens praised those who acknowledged the "great number of things that are above their understanding and to which the human mind will never be able to attain," and he emphasized the importance of distinguishing between truly doubtful things and those that can be learned.[22] D'Argens defended the middle ground between the "ridiculous opinion of the ancient Pyrrhonians" and the more judicious skepticism, praising the example that Montaigne had set in this regard. D'Argens also announced his agreement with Locke, noting that if he "were obliged to choose a party in philosophy," he would "not hesitate a moment to take a place under the standard of this great man."[23]

D'Argens contrasted the high levels of certainty that were attainable in geometry, algebra, astronomy, and mathematics, on the one hand, with the ambiguity of logic, metaphysics, and physics, "which dealt with general principles," on the other. Those who studied the former subjects could easily discover their errors and find a way to return to the truth. In the latter disciplines, however, "the mind could err with impunity, without fearing that it might be corrected." Although many of the questions were impenetrable, d'Argens lamented, "half-learned men [*demi-savants*] . . . wanted to pass their conjectures for true resolutions." The primary problem with logic, metaphysics, and speculative physics was that they did not rely on experience in order to confirm their propositions. Echoing the sentiments of Crousaz, d'Argens was especially critical of the Aristotelian Scholastics, who were in the habit of "spreading doubt on the clearest and most evident matters" and "accustomed to questioning the best-understood subjects." They were guilty of teaching the mind "to doubt the most certain things and to believe the most untrue things to be probable."[24] D'Argens insisted that the persistence of debates about the nature of God and of the human soul obscured the understanding of these questions and led people to doubt the existence of both. As we will see, the distinction between speculative and abstract knowledge, on the one hand, and empirically verifiable, observable facts, on the other, was central to new conceptions of rationality.

D'Argens's epistemology relied heavily on Locke. He followed many of the arguments of the *Essay Concerning Human Understanding* and described the mind as a tabula rasa with no innate ideas. All knowledge came by way of sensation and reflection. Sensations communicated notions of the sensible qualities of external objects to the mind. Reflections in turn furnished the mind with the "ideas of its own operations" and allowed it to form new notions by combining the various sense impressions. D'Argens appropriated the Cartesian *cogito* argument, framing it in Lockean terms. He claimed that it was more appropriate "to prove one's own existence by saying 'I feel, therefore I am' than by saying 'I think, therefore I am.'" The first idea of being had been produced by "the first sensation that made our understanding perceive our own existence."[25]

D'Argens's embrace of Locke's sensationalism led him to formulate his own version of epistemological skepticism. He attributed all the causes of errors and ignorance to a lack of ideas, improper connections between the notions that were acquired by the mind, and insufficient reflection upon them. The closer one looked, the more uncertain one's knowledge of the surrounding world appeared: "If we consider, in the first place, that the ideas we have by our senses have no proportion to the things themselves, [and] seeing that we do not have a clear and distinct idea of substance, even though it is the foundation of all the rest, we will easily recognize how few exact ideas we can have." D'Argens noted that numerous physical objects' composition and nature remained unknown on account of their distance from our view or their minute size. Humans' ideas about the surrounding world were based on conjectures formed from concepts that could very well be false. Indeed, the mind could not even fully comprehend the process by which it acquired and formed its ideas.[26]

Despite his skeptical outlook, d'Argens did not rule out the possibility of obtaining probable knowledge of the surrounding world. He insisted that the certainty of judgment depended on the accord between the evidence provided by the senses and the objects they represented. In some cases the evidence was so clear that there could be no uncertainties. In most instances, however, one had to assess the probability or verisimilitude (*vraisemblance*) of propositions according to the available evidence. All beliefs and judgments, according to d'Argens, were formed according to "what we see as having the appearance of the truth." In order to achieve some level of certainty, he argued, the mind needed to formulate several basic first principles or axioms from which it could proceed to more complex ideas.[27]

D'Argens concluded by delineating clear limits to the powers of understanding, but he maintained an optimistic tone. While the mind remained in "perfect ignorance" about the "principal secrets of the nature of things," it could still obtain probable knowledge that was sufficient for formulating rules of conduct in daily life. According to d'Argens, "Divinity had confined our understanding within such narrow bounds" in order to "give us occasion to distrust ourselves and others." The faculty of reason, which human beings had received from their creator, did not have "the privilege of discovering the sources and causes of things" but was only a "means for distinguishing" what was good from what was bad for them. For d'Argens, humans' "natural light" did not reveal many hidden mysteries, but it also prevented them from believing many false ideas.[28]

D'Argens's text received great praises from Voltaire, who had also admired the *Lettres juives* and continued to call d'Argens "Mon cher Isaac," a reference to one of the characters in the epistolary novel.[29] Voltaire predicted that *La philosophie du bon-sens* would be a huge success. He praised d'Argens "in the name of all those who think" for daring to voice "courageous truths." Voltaire also declared, "I agree with you on almost everything . . . you have the mind of Bayle and the style of Montaigne."[30] As Nicolas Correard has recently suggested, d'Argens and Voltaire shared a similar outlook about the powers and limits of human knowledge. Both thinkers dismissed the conclusions of radical Pyrrhonism (*pyrrhonisme outré*), especially those that cast doubt on the existence of the external world. Both expressed reservations about the utility of speculating on metaphysical subjects, and they deployed skepticism as a critical tool that undermined the reigning philosophical systems. They seem to have agreed on the advantages of adopting a Lockean empiricist epistemology and were extremely critical of contemporaneous rationalist systems, particularly of Descartes and Malebranche. Indeed, Correard suggests that Voltaire's intellectual relationship with d'Argens is crucial for explaining how the former reconciled Locke's empiricism with Montaigne's skepticism.[31]

Their early correspondence suggests that Voltaire saw in d'Argens a kindred spirit who criticized political and religious institutions and shared many of his philosophical views. Their epistolary friendship continued to flourish during Voltaire's extended stay at Cirey in the second half of the 1730s. Voltaire had also been in contact with the newly crowned Frederick II, and he urged d'Argens to come to Berlin and join the likes of Pierre-Louis Moreau de Maupertuis (1698–1759), Francesco Algarotti (1712–64), and Christiaan Wolff (1679–1754). Describing Frederick II as the "Marcus Aurelius of the north," Voltaire praised Prussia as the "fatherland of all those who think."[32] The Prussian monarch soon followed with his own offer, and d'Argens relocated to Berlin in 1743. Two years later he would become the director of the Class of Belles-Lettres at the newly inaugurated Académie royale des sciences et belles-lettres.[33]

The Battle with Pyrrhonism at the Académie de Prusse

Established by Frederick I (1657–1713) in 1700 as the Electoral Brandenburg Society of Sciences and reformed by his grandson in 1744 to include the Nouvelle société littéraire, the Académie royale des sciences et belles-lettres de Prusse gradually attracted prominent intellectuals from around Europe. French was the official language of this newly formed body, and there were a number of French-speaking scholars at the Académie thanks to Frederick II's policy of attracting notable, often controversial intellectuals. Among these were Swiss and French Huguenot thinkers who maintained close ties with their Parisian colleagues. Members included highly respected philosophers such as Maupertuis and Wolff and more outspoken figures such as the materialist Julien d'Offray de La Mettrie (1709–51), the marquis d'Argens, and of course Voltaire. Frederick II's reputation as an enlightened monarch who tolerated provocative opinions appealed to many members of the Republic of Letters, and it explains Voltaire's early enthusiasm for Prussia's new monarch. Some of these prominent figures were forced to leave France after their controversial writings struck the wrong chord with the political regime, and Frederick II readily welcomed them at his court in an attempt to boost the intellectual prestige of Prussia. Several members of the Académie de Prusse would play a crucial role in the debates surrounding skepticism during the eighteenth century.[34]

Jean Henri Samuel Formey, whose attempt to popularize Crousaz's massive refutation of Pyrrhonism we encountered in the last chapter, was on the front lines of the struggle against Pyrrhonism. Formey was born in Berlin in 1711 to a family of Huguenot émigrés from France. After studying at the Collège français in Berlin and serving as pastor at a French Huguenot church in Brandenburg, Formey returned to his alma mater as a professor of rhetoric and philosophy. He became a member of the Académie in 1744 and was named the *secrétaire perpétuel* four years later. During his career, he consistently opposed what he perceived as the radical materialism and skepticism of his age.

Formey undertook his first major attack on irreligion in the *Pensées raisonnables* (1749), a refutation of Denis Diderot's (1713–84) deistic *Pensées philosophiques* (1746). Reprinting the most provocative passages from the anonymous work, Formey identified the author as an atheist and a Pyrrhonian. He argued that by questioning the existence of God, atheists sought to bring mankind to the level of beasts, who operate without any knowledge of their origins or purpose.[35] Although the treatise aimed to counter Diderot's allegedly atheistic views, it also offered a scathing critique of skepticism. Formey addressed Diderot's distinction between "skeptical atheism" and "true atheism."[36] Defining the skeptic as "a person whose doubt covers everything without exception," Formey insisted that such a person had less "integrity than an atheist, who in rejecting the existence of God does not neglect to recognize the force of natural duty." The atheist was "only in error with respect to the existence of God," while the skeptic's " 'maybe' does not even value the demonstrated notions that the Atheist in question can obtain from universal morality."[37] Formey classified skepticism as more debased than atheism—a position he rejected but attempted to disprove logically—and presented it as a disease. For Formey, the skeptics not only denied the possibility of learning any truths but actually saw learning as an utterly useless task.[38]

Formey further attacked the skeptics for reducing all truth claims to a purely subjective status, for creating an equivalency among all views and opinions, and for rejecting the notion that any principles could be considered universally valid. The skeptics "removed all the intrinsic certainty of the things we know, leaving nothing but the knowledge we gather by our personal dispositions" and reducing reason "to a telescope, to simple glasses that vary from one individual to another." Indeed, one of the major epistemological claims of Pyrrhonian skepticism was that the differences in opinions among various people and the mutability of views held by an individual made any objective knowledge impossible. Formey disputed the extent of the divergences and variances in human perceptions, suggesting that one "would not dare to contradict the calculations and the demonstrations of a mathematician or a geometrician by saying that you have glasses [that are] different from theirs."[39]

Formey also distinguished between what he called "true skepticism" (*vrai scepticisme*) and Pyrrhonism. He described the former as "the middle between two extremes" of absolute doubt and complete gullibility.[40] He even praised "true skepticism" as a "laudable position," defining it as "nothing other than an impartial and enlightened search for the truth [that] does not concern itself with obfuscating evidence or with squabbling [pointlessly] by demanding proofs in cases where the thing proves itself."[41] The goal of this "true skepticism" was to conduct a thorough and unbiased search for immutable veracities; Pyrrhonians, on the other hand, falsely called themselves skeptics, while "divorcing themselves from all that calls itself the truth."[42]

Although he undertook the abridgment of Crousaz's text, Formey was not as categorically critical of skepticism as his Swiss colleague. In addition to defending what he called "true skepticism," Formey expressed reservations about how far philosophical knowledge could reach. When answering Crousaz about his youthful flirtation with Pyrrhonism, Formey argued that philosophy "has always been, and . . . always will be, a theater of opinions." Recognizing a small number of "fail-safe principles" or "axiomatic truths," Formey insisted that other claims to truth were "nothing but hypotheses, with respect to which one can choose what is the most probable or suspend one's judgment." He placed philosophical knowledge and religious belief in two categorically distinct realms. The latter was not subject to skeptical doubt, Formey claimed, because its veracity and certainty were not based on speculative metaphysical claims, but on an emotional and an intellectual recognition that was patently different from philosophical and theoretical knowledge.[43] At the same time, in his multivolume *Le philosophe chrétien* (1752–57) Formey argued that a rational understanding of the world was "enlightened" by the "knowledge of God," and it battled the "shadows of ignorance" that drive human beings toward vice. He emphasized the importance of a complete concordance between reason and religion, arguing that without the former, belief turned into fanaticism.[44] He thus saw reason and faith as separate yet cooperating faculties.

Formey undertook another critique of religious skepticism and atheism in a short treatise entitled *La logique des vraisemblances* (1748). Conceived as a defense against the "enemies of religion," the work immediately renounced the goal of proving religious truths with metaphysical certainty and proposed that the debate be limited to probability.[45] Formey urged his readers to consider whether it was more likely that the existing world was so perfectly arranged by pure chance or by the design of an "infinite intelligence."[46] He asked a series of similar rhetorical questions regarding human liberty, the existence of an afterlife, and various testimonies from the Bible. In each case, he suggested that probability pointed squarely in the direction of the existence of God and of an immortal soul.[47] Formey conceded that one could not prove either the existence of God or the truth of Christianity metaphysically. However, he proposed that both were far more likely than a purely material universe devoid of a supreme being. Formey's arguments were more polemical than philosophical, and his conclusion reformulated Blaise Pascal's wager by pointing to the eternal punishment that unbelievers risked.

Formey's concerns about the consequences of skeptical attitudes toward religion were shared by Albrecht von Haller, who was perturbed primarily by the apparent rise of religious incredulity, as we have seen. The expanded version of his preliminary discourse to Formey's *Le triomphe de l'évidence*, entitled *Discours sur l'irreligion* (1760), attacked Julien d'Offray de la Mettrie's translation of Seneca's *Traité de la vie heureuse* (1748). Gabriel Seigneux de Correvon (1695–1775), a Swiss journalist and former student of Crousaz's in Lausanne, translated Haller's work from German into French. Correvon perceived a clear tie between La Mettrie's materialist deism and Pyrrhonian skepticism. Both philosophies undermined revealed religion and a rational understanding of the natural world.[48] According to Correvon, by casting doubt on matters such as the immortality of the immaterial soul, Pyrrhonian philosophy led one to conceive of a purely material and Godless universe. This, in turn, led to the dystopian society that Haller described so vividly.[49]

David Hume and His Critics at the Prussian Academy

As the perpetual secretary of the Prussian Académie royale des sciences et belles-lettres, Formey formed a wide circle of former students and colleagues who shared his goal of opposing the growing tide of irreligion and philosophical skepticism. As we saw, however, Formey kept an open mind with respect to mitigated skepticism and remained interested in a wide variety of philosophical opinions. Among his many projects—and, ironically, as a part of his continual crusade against skepticism and unbelief—Formey organized the translation of David Hume's works into German and French. He felt that by exposing Hume's skeptical views to a wider audience, he would be able to refute him decisively. Formey thought that banning and decrying controversial works such as Hume's actually raised the public's interest in them. It was precisely such bans, he claimed, that made books popular by appealing to the morbid curiosities of readers who were excited to encounter allegedly dangerous texts. The difficulty of procuring prohibited books made readers more attentive to the ideas they contained.[50] Thus, Formey's goal in overseeing French and German translations of the text was to make the book more widely available and consequently less interesting to those who sought controversial texts.[51]

According to Hume, his *Treatise of Human Nature* (1738–40) did not receive as much attention as he had hoped, for after its initial publication, it fell "dead-born from the press without reaching such distinction as to excite a murmur among the zealots."[52] The Scottish philosopher decided to reissue the work in a series of shorter essays under the title *Philosophical Essays Concerning Human Understanding* (1748, better known by its alternative title, *An Enquiry Concerning Human Understanding*).[53] This second text was significantly more provocative than the *Treatise of Human Nature*. It not only made a robust case on behalf of epistemological skepticism and questioned the ability of the human mind to determine the hidden causes of observable phenomena but undermined the status of Christianity by challenging biblical accounts of miracles. The *Essays* questioned the possibility of knowing the nature of God and made a number of controversial and irreligious claims that Hume would make more explicit in the posthumous *Dialogues Concerning Natural Religion* (1779). Hume's assertions and their far-reaching philosophical and theological consequences installed him, in the eyes of his contemporaries and of modern scholars, as the most prominent successor to Pierre Bayle. In fact, Richard Popkin once wrote that Hume was "the only living skeptic" in the mid-eighteenth century.[54]

To Formey, Crousaz, Haller, and other opponents of skepticism, such a claim would have seemed obviously inaccurate, since they perceived a steady rise of Pyr-rhonism and irreligion all around them. Because Hume's *Essays* appeared to both advance Pyrrhonian skepticism and attack Christianity, Formey decided to issue an extended critique of the work. He did so in a five-part review of the German translation that was undertaken at his request by Johann Georg Sulzer (1720–79), a mathematician at the Prussian Academy.[55] Although he described Hume as "a lively and profound genius" and "the English philosopher of the century,"[56] Formey believed that one of Hume's main goals was to "lead his readers to skepticism or, even more so, to Pyrrhonism."[57] He warned that "the same spirit of doubt that is the key to a healthy philosophy becomes, when pushed beyond its just limits, the plague from which one gives in . . . to doubting for the sake of doubting." Remarking on the affinities between Hume and Bayle, Formey argued that the "fourth essay contains the foundations of all the objections that this philosopher, emulating Bayle, has wished to gather on the most important philosophical questions."[58]

For Formey, there were a number of similarities between the arguments and aims of the two skeptics. In his account of Hume's treatment of miracles,

Formey accused the Scottish philosopher of undermining the epistemological status of witness testimonies and indirectly attacking Christianity: "The Christian Religion, he claims, has a superior order of knowledge, being founded on Faith and on the miracles of Grace, which do not need to be proved by human testimony, since a true believer has an intimate sentiment of it. One knows this language is nothing but veiled irony. Mr. Bayle took the glory of inventing [this device] away from the English philosopher; it is the general maneuver by which the adversaries of Religion wish to separate entirely the interests of faith from those of reason."[59] Hume, just like Bayle, had dissimulated his claim for a non-rational epistemological status of Christianity with the ulterior motive of undermining its rational foundations. Formey thought that both skeptics insincerely argued for the special status of religious faith, while asserting that sense experience was the only source of knowledge about the world.

Formey probed Hume's *reductio ad infinitum* claim regarding the possibility of discerning causes on the basis of observed effects. The problem could be solved, he thought, both by attempting to discern patterns in the apparent causes and effects of phenomena and by a priori reasoning about effects that must necessarily result from particular causes. Formey also questioned the possibility of "curing skepticism with skepticism," because such a solution only helped Hume extend philosophical uncertainty. He described Hume's account of the Academic philosophy as the most "sane" and practically useful of his positions. While it exposed the prejudices and fantasies of philosophers as pure speculations, it "did not infringe on practice and did not disturb the springs of human life."[60]

Formey contested Hume's claim that the majority of people's actions were undertaken on the basis of instinct and not as a result of rational reflection. He said that the Scottish philosopher took this argument too far in stressing the importance of instinct and in comparing human beings to animals. "By showing that brutes cannot be raised to [have] reason," Formey wrote, "he has no other goal than to make men descend to [the level of instinct]" and to demonstrate that human beings do not act in accordance with rational decisions. Formey saw this as an error: "Man never determines himself but in virtue of following ideas, but the consequence that he derives is sometimes so rapid and even so obscure that he cannot perceive how he arrived at it."[61] While people might make choices without sufficiently evaluating available information, they nevertheless depended on reasoning and not on pure instinct. In his preface to the French translation of Hume's *Philosophical Essays Concerning Human Un-*

derstanding, Formey argued that habit and reason did not necessarily have to stand in opposition, since habit was "nothing other than a principle on which one may base many just [and probable] conclusions."[62]

At every point, Formey fervently disputed Hume's claim—a position central to epistemological skepticism—that there was no necessary connection between external objects and the sensations they produced in the mind: "The effect of sensations, the nature of the determination of the will, and the actions that result each time particular objects present us with particular ideas are as dependent on one another as the conclusion of an argument is dependent on the premises. If the logic of sensations and volitions is not as certain as that of syllogisms, it is only because the difference is relative to our understanding, but there is in one and in the other the same foundation of intrinsic certainty."[63] Formey suggested that while one could not establish with metaphysical certainty a causal relation between objects in the external world and ideas in the mind, the observable pattern between effects and their apparent causes provided sufficient evidence of their connection.

In his preface to Jean-Bernard Mérian's French translation of Hume's *Essays*, Formey offered a brief sketch of the history of philosophy.[64] He noted that while the past century had seen the appearance of brilliant minds such as Descartes, it also had witnessed an increase in the number of intellectuals who made a logical leap from "our ignorance in certain matters to a universal ignorance" and who professed that the mind "can find nothing but errors."[65] Following Crousaz's analysis of eighteenth-century learned culture, Formey suggested that a number of contemporary "distinguished writers" made a career of proposing various objections and of "planting seeds of doubt and uncertainty" all around them.[66] He included Hume among these thinkers, criticizing his *Essays* and claiming that Pyrrhonism pervaded the text and undermined the foundations of both "natural and revealed" religion.[67]

The majority of Formey's preface was dedicated to Hume's treatment of the miracles described in scripture. Hume had disputed the veracity of supernatural events by arguing, as many deists had, that a supernatural event contradicted the regular and uniform laws of nature that experience had demonstrated.[68] He also questioned the reliability of the witnesses who reported the miracles by asking whether it was more believable that the inviolable laws of nature had been broken than that the witnesses reporting them had lied. Hume consequently claimed that human testimony could not offer satisfactory and reliable proofs of miracles.[69] Formey noted a contradiction between Hume's epistemological skepticism and his view of miracles. The Scottish philosopher had already denied the possibility of knowing whether perceptions corresponded to an external world and consequently the ability to determine whether there were uniform laws of nature.[70] Since a miracle was commonly defined as "an occurrence that opposes the laws of nature," one needed to recognize that such laws existed and that "there are certain forces whose effects conform to known and invariable rules." Hume was thus "exposed to the forces of his own objections," because he took great efforts to persuade readers "that there are no forces in nature and that one is never allowed to say that something is an effect of another thing or that it is not."[71] Hume appeared to contradict his own Pyrrhonian claims about our ignorance of the laws of nature in his attempt to refute the possibility of miracles.[72]

Formey also maintained that Hume's critique of witness testimony made impossibly high demands on the quality and number of witnesses who could give convincing accounts of miracles.[73] In order to counter the rejection of the certainty of miracles, Formey proposed probability as a sufficient criterion of certainty and the only practically attainable one. It was a criterion that Hume himself seemed to endorse.[74] Formey advocated applying the principle of verisimilitude to natural philosophy and to historical events.[75] He suggested that while complete certainty was unattainable in such matters, probability was superior to the hyperbolic doubt that Hume advocated with respect to religion and to the understanding of the natural world.

Formey accused Hume of exaggerating uncertainty and providing insincere reasons to doubt even in cases in which doubt appeared unreasonable. In one of the critical notes he inserted in the translated text, Formey engaged Hume on the issue of causality. He suggested that humans' alleged "ignorance" with respect to "the essence of things, the hidden action, the secret mechanism that ties causes with their effects," did not "infringe on the certainty of the effects we expect from particular causes." Each time one placed a pot of water over a strong flame, one was certain that it would boil, just as one was certain that if the water were removed to a sufficient distance from the fire, it would not boil.[76] Such an example, Formey insisted, established "the necessary connection of all that takes place in nature"; one did not need to account for the essence of various forces and operations in order to perceive their existence.[77] Hume's skeptical critique of causality was thus irrelevant for the majority of questions. Formey accepted the probabilistic nature of philosophical and scientific explanations, but he maintained that Hume hyperbolically manipulated arguments to advocate a nearly universal suspension of judgment.

Beyond True and False: Mérian's Concessions to Pyrrhonism

Formey's attempted refutation of Hume reveals an increasing turn away from a moral case against skepticism and toward pragmatic arguments about the sufficiency of *vraisemblance* in philosophical and even religious questions. Jean-Bernard Mérian, who had translated Hume's skeptical work into French, continued this trend. Having completed his doctorate at the University of Basel in 1740, Mérian traveled to Amsterdam and eventually to Berlin. The mathematician Pierre-Louis Moreau de Maupertuis, president of the Prussian Academy, invited Mérian to be a member of the Class for Speculative Philosophy in 1750.[78] Unlike many of his colleagues at the Académie, Mérian did not discuss Pyrrhonism's dangerous consequences to religion and to society, but focused exclusively on questions of epistemology.[79]

In one of his first essays on the subject, Mérian returned to Descartes's *cogito* argument, made more than a century earlier in the late thinker's Second Meditation. Mérian wished to resolve what he saw as a fundamental problem that this claim created for debates about the possibility of obtaining true and certain knowledge. After discarding all acquired ideas and refusing to admit the testimony of his senses, Descartes found himself in a state of hyperbolic doubt that made him question his own existence. However, Descartes reasoned that even if he had been completely deceived about everything that he had believed to be true, he could not doubt the existence of his own thought. If the surrounding world and indeed his own body were not real, but merely notions implanted in his mind by a malicious and powerful deceiver, there still had to be a mind that was being misled. Therefore, Descartes concluded, thought and, consequently, a "thinking thing" (*res cogitans* or *chose pensante*) must exist. Descartes remained aware of his thinking process, and by virtue of that awareness he concluded that he existed. Thus, for Descartes, the unceasing reflection upon one's own existence served as the philosophical guarantor of that existence.[80]

Many of Descartes's contemporaries saw this plunge into and logical reemergence from hyperbolic doubt as an attempt to defeat Pyrrhonian skepticism on its own terms. However, Mérian found the argument both invalid and ineffectual for refuting skeptical claims. He began his essay by suggesting, as several other critics of Descartes's proof had done, that the *cogito* argument referred to a mental state that had already passed. Consequently, in relying upon it, "we would never be assured of our present existence, only of the past one."[81] He claimed that Descartes's conclusion happened to be correct by chance and that his meditation was merely a grammatical exercise, not an actual proof. Mérian described the *cogito ergo sum* argument as not only "vicious and full of soph-istry" but also an insufficient "mechanism to convert a skeptic." By pushing "skepticism to such a point as to place his own existence in doubt," Descartes had gone "beyond the reach of our reasoning." Unable to "agree with us on any principle," he was unlikely to "bring about anything positive." By attempting to demonstrate such an evident fact as one's own existence, a thinker offered the skeptic interlocutor a considerable advantage by "burden[ing] oneself with the tacit obligation of demonstrating every proposition as [being as] self-evident as this one." Rather than disproving Pyrrhonism, Descartes had played right into the skeptics' hands by stretching the limits of doubt to the furthest possible point, one from which he could not successfully reemerge. By questioning his own existence, Descartes had destroyed the possibility of securing any true and certain knowledge. Further, he had reasoned poorly and inconsistently in his attempt to extricate himself from this state of universal doubt by suddenly assuming the existence of various axioms.[82]

For Mérian, direct debates with the skeptics were not productive, since Pyr-rhonians would always find ways to contradict whatever stance one took. Such a basic matter as one's own existence could not be verified philosophically, because it was an "intuitive truth." After showing the difficulties of proving the existence of the self logically, he concluded that the "knowledge of our being comes from neither reasoning nor reflection nor by any mediated path that al-lows us to conclude that we perceive it immediately and intuitively." Instead, Mérian defined "the perception of the self" as "the first act, an essential act of an intelligent being, such that while all other knowledge presupposes it, it alone does not presuppose anything."[83] The awareness of one's own existence was a prerequisite for intelligence and for any rational discussion, and it could never itself be in doubt.[84] Mérian insisted that "an idea of an intelligence that did not perceive itself is absurd and contradictory." One could conceive of an intelligence that perceived nothing but itself, but one could not conceive of an intelligence that perceived something in the world without at the same time perceiving itself.[85] Continuing from this awareness of the self, by relying on sense experi-ence one could then determine the existence of other objects and reflect on the operations of one's organs of sense. Mérian further maintained that the mind perceived all objects as individual entities and later formed generalizations based on discernible characteristics. Rather than debating the skeptics on the most elementary questions, as Descartes had attempted to do, Mérian sug-gested accepting some basic principles as self-evident and proceeding from them. By taking the mind's intuitive self-awareness as an axiomatic and unquestionable truth, he hoped to move the argument away from abstract debates about the most basic principles and toward more productive discussions of the practical limits of human understanding.

Elsewhere, Mérian addressed the relationship between external objects and their representations in the mind. He claimed that it was pointless to speculate about hypothetical ideas and urged his readers to consider only those notions that entered the mind through the senses.[86] One could not philosophically prove that ideas in the mind corresponded to objects in the external world. Instead, one had to rely on intuition to know that this was true.[87] People behaved as if ideas corresponded to reality, but such a conclusion was a philosophical leap of faith: "Let us believe in [the existence of physical] bodies if this sentiment pleases us; let us endow them with reality and with substance; but if we are philosophers, let us agree ingeniously that all this is nothing but an act of faith. . . . It is only with respect to [ideas] that our understanding operates, and external things, if any exist, are something else entirely."[88] Mérian thus accepted the position of the Pyrrhonians, who claimed that one could not know with certainty that ideas had any relation to the objects they represented. While they were philosophically correct, however, their claims had no relevance in the practical conduct of life.

Louis Isaac de Beausobre (1730–83), Formey's former student and a member of the Prussian Academy, offered a similar compromise in his *Pyrrhonisme du sage* (1754) and his *Le pyrrhonisme raisonnable* (1755).[89] In both texts, he elaborated on Formey's appeal for a restrained skepticism in philosophical enquiries. Son of the French Huguenot ecclesiastical historian Isaac de Beausobre (1659–1738), Louis Isaac de Beausobre attended the Collège français in Berlin, where he studied under Formey. His *Pyrrhonisme du sage* was condemned to be burned by the French parliament for its offense to religion.[90] Nevertheless, Beausobre edited the text and issued a second edition with a dedication to Frederick II a year later. Beausobre began by decrying the pitfalls of sectarianism (*esprit de secte*) in philosophy. Arguing that extreme skepticism was preferable to such factionalism, he described as *sectateurs* those who "believe all that they are taught without examination."[91] He suggested that prejudice served as the foundation of the majority of things one believed to be certain, and he particularly emphasized the pernicious influence of philosophical claims made on the basis of authority. Various sections of Beausobre's work did in fact resemble a skeptical treatise. He stressed the fleeting nature of human knowledge and claimed that there was not a single act of human reasoning that operated without error and no opinion or view that did not have both supporters and detractors.

He also pointed to the ephemeral and superficial nature of philosophical systems, which melted away like wax.[92]

At the same time, Beausobre acknowledged that some ideas seemed to be highly probable, and he maintained that it was "necessary to think and to live by following what appears most probable to us without imagining that it is the absolute truth."[93] Beausobre's "reasonable Pyrrhonism" resembled Bierling's defense of an epistemology concerned with obtaining probable certainty. Both emphasized the relative inconclusiveness of both rational and empirical knowledge and denounced what they viewed as a fruitless quest for metaphysical certainty. Increasingly, both skeptics and their opponents saw this variant of skepticism as an acceptable compromise.[94] Unable to refute the Pyrrhonians philosophically, their opponents agreed that a "reasonable skepticism" was a tolerable alternative. Those who favored skeptical arguments and emphasized the weakness of the human mind recognized that probability, not certainty, was an attainable end. The critical arguments of Pyrrhonian skepticism could thus be deployed without stretching those assertions to their fullest conclusions.

Unlike Boullier, Crousaz, and Formey, all of whom pointed to the inconsistencies of skepticism and tried to refute it philosophically, Mérian and Beausobre proposed conceding Pyrrhonian claims and moving beyond them. Moreover, Formey's and Mérian's critiques of skepticism display a shift away from reliance on Cartesian principles toward more empirical and probabilistic approaches. While Boullier and Crousaz continued to draw upon the *cogito* argument and Descartes's claim that a noncorrespondence between ideas and their objects would render God a deceiver, the Berlin Huguenots moved in a different direction. No longer invoking God as the necessary guarantor of absolute certainty, they sought to explain the practical methods of obtaining knowledge that best approximated the truth.

Formey, Haller, Mérian, and other anti-skeptical members of the Académie royale des sciences et belles-lettres pose a challenge to the frequently invoked opposition between religion and reason in the Age of Enlightenment. As the perpetual secretary of the Prussian Academy, the editor and contributor to multiple scholarly journals, a tireless correspondent, and a prolific author, Formey embodied many ideals of eighteenth-century learned culture.[95] Despite his critiques of skepticism and irreligion, he remained on good terms with the philosophes. Having conceived the idea of a universal dictionary as early as the 1740s, Formey sent his papers to the editors of the *Encyclopédie*. He contributed to as many as eighty articles, including "Athéisme," "Atomisme," "Création," "Dualité," "Dieu," and "Trinité."[96] He also attempted to offer a less heterodox version of his work in the

Dictionnaire instructif (1767).[97] Formey remained a devout Protestant and an opponent of irreligion, and he clashed with Voltaire, Rousseau, and Diderot over the importance of organized religion.[98]

While Formey was one of the most active and prominent philosophers of the mid-eighteenth century, Haller was at the forefront of the latest research in physiology. His investigations of the irritability of fibers inadvertently aided the formulation of vitalist and materialist theories of thinkers such as La Mettrie. Although Haller was very far from sharing La Mettrie's conception of a material soul, his attempts to challenge mechanistic explanations of behavior provided crucial evidence for materialists.[99] Mérian's contributions to philosophical debates and his efforts in translating Hume, with whom he deeply disagreed on so many questions, also render him a significant part of the German *Aufklärung*. Nevertheless, despite their scholarly achievements, their participation in the various intellectual projects of the Enlightenment, and their diverse views on epistemology, natural philosophy, and politics, all three remained committed to a defense of religion in general and of Christianity in particular. All three believed that undermining and overcoming the challenges posed by Pyrrhonian skepticism was essential to such a defense.

Skepticism and Certainty in the Mid-Eighteenth Century

The Berlin anti-skeptics were not alone in challenging Pyrrhonism. Some of the French philosophes also attempted to mollify the effects of universal doubt. In the article "Pyrrhonienne" (1765), the *Encyclopédie* editor Denis Diderot, whose materialist and atheist views were widely known, took a pragmatic stance with respect to both certainty and doubt. Diderot, who had penned the controversial and religiously irreverent *Promenade du sceptique* (written in 1746 but published only in 1830),[100] suggested that since all knowledge was related and intertwined, there was absolutely nothing that human beings could know with perfect assurance. One could always point to something unknown or debatable and extend the logical consequences of that obscurity.[101] At the same time, Diderot argued, reason had to be applied "soberly," and one sometimes needed to end disputations and arguments in order to avoid "floating in uncertainty." It was important not to allow the skeptics to push the rhetorical expression of doubt too far and to stop arguing once a relatively definite principle was established. Diderot claimed that he would not entertain the arguments of someone "who might deny the existence of bodies, the rules of logic, the testimony of the senses." He declared that he would ignore anyone who tried to engage in "pedantic speeches on the nature of mater, of understanding, of substance, of thought and on all other subjects that are inexhaustible." Absolute Pyrrhonism was neither a sincere nor a sustainable philosophical position, since the skeptics' theoretical stance never held in any practical matters. Pyrrhonians who claimed to doubt the reality of appearances or who obstinately advanced the possibility that they were the only living beings in the universe were arguing for the sake of arguing. It was useless, Diderot asserted, "to waste time on" debating with an opponent "to destroy an opinion he does not [actually] hold."[102]

Gradually, a compromise on probability or verisimilitude became an acceptable option in cases in which absolute certainty could not be obtained. Citing Claude Buffier, the *Encyclopédie* article "Vraissemblance" (1765) distinguished between practical and speculative questions.[103] In "matters of pure speculation" it instructed readers "to suspend judgment . . . except when degrees of verisimilitude are considerable," since one ran no risk by remaining undecided and it was "the character of a sensible spirit and a true philosopher to judge objects only by referring to evidence." At the same time, in practical matters, one had to be "contented with" accepting something that appeared probable "as true" and to act upon that decision, because inaction "would be the most pernicious and most impertinent of all sides."[104] Even authors composing religious apologetics agreed that in some cases one had to resort to verisimilitude in issues of faith in order to persuade the unbelievers both of the extremely probable existence of God and of the truth of Christianity.[105] Moral assurance would suffice.

Such declarations reflected gradual concessions to the major claims of philosophical skepticism. Over time, anti-skeptical thinkers had come to accept mild or mitigated skepticism as a suitable alternative to dogmatism and to extreme Pyrrhonism. Even the most outspoken anti-skeptic, Crousaz, conceded that a reasonable amount of skepticism could be useful, suggesting that "a prudent suspension [of judgment], far from aiding Pyrrhonism, [was] a great means to prevent it." It was by accepting arguments too quickly, without prudently analyzing the available evidence, that people had committed errors and consequently found themselves in a state of uncertainty. Crousaz argued that although a suspension of judgment was "appropriate in some cases, it does not follow that it should be universal."[106]

The perceived necessity to disprove skepticism was not entirely irrational. As the century progressed, the variety of subversive texts continued to grow. Most were not skeptical works, properly speaking. However, many apologetic thinkers saw Pyrrhonism as the root cause of other heterodox opinions, since skeptical critiques had, in their view, undermined the most fundamental philosophical principles and, most significantly, posed a great challenge to the rational foundations of religion. The critiques of skepticism persisted in part because it was almost impossible to refute the doctrine on its own terms. One could denounce it and demonstrate the moral implications that followed from it, but one could not, as Mérian noted, disprove the philosophical validity of skeptical arguments. Channeling the response of Diogenes the Cynic to Zeno's paradox of motion (which posited the theoretical impossibility of motion by claiming that one would continually have to get to a halfway point between where one was and where one was going and so *ad infinitum*),[107] Mérian suggested, metaphorically, that standing up and walking across the room was the only plausible way to end the argument. However, such solutions did not mollify Mérian's anti-skeptical allies, who saw Pyrrhonism as the relentless and fundamental cause of the growing moral and intellectual malaise of their society. They continued to seek philosophical solutions to skepticism.

Another reason for the persistence of debates about skepticism was its pervasiveness across various domains of European learned culture. Pyrrhonian challenges could be and in fact were applied to almost any subject: skeptics questioned the ability of theologians to prove the existence of God by rational means, they dared philosophers to explain the nature of the immaterial soul and account for its reciprocal relation with a material body, they doubted whether appearances and sense impressions corresponded to any objective reality in the external world, they questioned the theories of natural philosophy that purported to explain the nature of matter and the composition of the physical universe, and they even denied the possibility of knowing the past with certainty. The assault of Pyrrhonian arguments in multiple disciplines thus magnified this philosophy's apparent danger and inspired counterarguments not only among philosophers and theologians but also among historians and literary authors. Ultimately, these debates transformed skepticism, making its claims more mitigated and reserved, and also these particular disciplines, leading those who studied them to abandon the quest for absolute certainty and accept probability as an adequate compromise. The next four chapters describe this dialectical process in the context of debates about the origin of human ideas, the composition of the physical universe, and the nature of historical knowledge.

PART TWO

DISCIPLINING DOUBT

CHAPTER SEVEN

Matter over Mind

Dualism, Materialism, and Skepticism
in Eighteenth-Century Epistemology

Descartes and the Problem of Dualism

The skeptics' most fundamental arguments in favor of a suspension of judgment involved critical examinations of the mental faculties and of the senses. They claimed that the human mind was unreliable and inconstant because it was affected by bodily dispositions. The skeptics offered numerous examples of reason's inability to overcome logical paradoxes. By questioning the possibility of obtaining certain and reliable knowledge of the world through the senses, which were fallible, the Pyrrhonians made their case for a complete withholding of conclusions about both natural and supernatural questions. In order to give a credible and definitive answer to Pyrrhonian critiques, philosophers had to construct theories of knowledge that would be able to withstand such scrutiny.

René Descartes tried to provide one such answer to Pyrrhonism in the mid-seventeenth century. In attempting to prove philosophically the immortality of the human soul, Descartes proposed an essential distinction between the immaterial mind and the material body. In his view, the universe was composed of one uncreated and two created substances: God, who was an uncreated infinite substance; mind, which was a created and immaterial substance whose essence was thought; and matter, which was a created material substance whose essence was physical extension. Matter was subject to changes and modifications, which made it destructible. The mind, on the other hand, was immaterial and therefore not susceptible to physical transformations or to destruction.[1]

While this distinction allowed Descartes and his disciples to offer a philosophical demonstration of the immortality of the soul, the dualist conception of human beings posed fundamental problems for the theory of knowledge. How was it that an immaterial mind could perceive material objects through the senses and be affected by them? How could the mind issue commands to the body? Cartesian dualism raised challenging questions about mind-body interaction that would continue to occupy philosophers for the next century and a half and beyond.[2] The fundamental tension between substance dualism and inter-substantial interaction elicited numerous attempts to resolve the apparent quandary, producing theories that often undermined existing philosophical assumptions and theological doctrines.

The disciples of Descartes and their various opponents attempted to explain how an immaterial soul could interact with an extended and material body. However, skeptical thinkers used the ongoing disputes to their advantage. Simon Foucher, Pierre Bayle, and Pierre-Daniel Huet all emphasized the inability of philosophy to explain adequately either how sense experiences resulted in the formation of ideas or how an immaterial substance could direct the body to perform various activities. For these scholars, the problem of mind-body interaction thus served as a prime example of the weakness of the human understanding, which could not even account for its own operations. This chapter explores the evolution of the debates about the mind-body interaction and about the origin of human ideas. The outcome of these disputes, as we will see, reveals a major epistemological shift from a search for metaphysical certainty to an increased emphasis on moral certainty, probability, and verisimilitude in the French-speaking world of the eighteenth century.

Descartes himself had struggled to explain the relationship between mind and body. He saw the mind as a completely immaterial substance whose essence was thought, and he argued that it had no specific location in the body.[3] However, he also claimed in the *Dioptrique* (1637) that the pineal gland was the "seat of the common sense," and he suggested in his correspondence that it was "the principal seat of the soul and the place in which all our thoughts are formed."[4] This inconsistency remained present in Descartes's last work, *Les passions de l'âme* (1649). In article 30 of part 1, Descartes claimed that the soul was "joined to all of the body," and "it could not be said to be in any one part to the exclusion of others," since it was indivisible and lacked the properties of matter.[5] Nevertheless, he argued in the very next article that there was "a certain part of the body in which [the soul] exercises its functions more particularly than in all the others." This area was a "little gland" in the "innermost part of the brain."[6] In a letter to Princess Elisabeth of Bohemia (1618–80) Descartes confessed that "the things that pertain to the union of soul and body can be known only obscurely by the understanding acting alone . . . but are known very clearly by the senses."[7] This ambiguity in Descartes's own views prompted heated debates among his disciples.

For skeptics, Cartesian dualism presented a prime example of the inability of philosophy to provide the most basic explanation of human perception. The

Academic skeptic Simon Foucher was one of the first critics to claim, in his *Critique de la Recherche de la vérité* (1675), that it was impossible for material objects to be represented in the immaterial soul. The work was primarily an attack on Nicolas Malebranche's *Recherche de la vérité* (1674), but it also advanced Foucher's critique of the entire Cartesian system and articulated the outlines of his skeptical philosophy.[8] In discussing Malebranche's epistemology, Foucher argued that ideas could not represent objects because they could not be *like* the objects. Since the soul was purely immaterial in Descartes's and Malebranche's systems, it could not have any similarity to anything that was material or extended. Consequently, neither the senses nor ideas could "give us knowledge of things that are outside us."[9]

In his article "Pyrrhon," Bayle referred to Foucher's *Critique de la Recherche de la vérité* when discussing the new set of problems that modern philosophy furnished for theories of knowledge. Bayle recounted a dialogue between two abbés on the compatibility of skepticism and Christianity. The first abbé seemed astonished by the fact that Pyrrhonism still existed after the Christian revelation. The second abbé, who was not surprised by the persistence of skepticism in the modern world despite apparent advances in philosophy and the spread of Christianity, suggested that Cartesianism was actually to blame.

> I renounce the advantages with which the new philosophy has supplied the Pyrrhonians. . . . Cartesianism put the final touches on the work, and no one among our philosophers any longer doubts that the skeptics were correct in maintaining that the qualities of bodies that strike our senses are nothing but appearances. Each one of us can say "I feel heat in the presence of fire," but not "I know that fire is, in itself, such as it appears to me." This was the style [of reasoning] of the ancient Pyrrhonians. Today the new philosophy adopts a more positive language: heat, smell, colors, and the like are not in the objects of our senses; they are modifications of my soul; I know that bodies are not at all as they appear to me. One would have wished to exempt extension and motion, but it was not possible, for if the objects of [our] senses appear [to be] colored, warm, cold, [or] scented without being so, why could they not appear extended, at rest, or in motion without actually being so? Moreover, the objects of the senses cannot be the cause of my sensations; I could therefore feel cold and heat, see colors, figures, extension, and motion, even if there were no bodies in the universe. Thus, I have no solid proof of the existence of bodies.[10]

Bayle's abbé accused the philosophy of his time of furnishing new difficulties and supplying skeptical philosophers with a fresh arsenal of arguments. Cartesian dualism built a trap from which one could not emerge philosophically. After all, how could one prove that anything existed outside the mind if all judgments were based on information that was contained inside it? Bayle made similar observations in his article "Zénon," in which he suggested that extension and the three-dimensional nature of objects "could exist only in our minds . . . only ideally."[11]

Huet, who was one of the most outspoken opponents of Descartes and his various Cartesian followers, also took advantage of this predicament in his skeptical *Traité philosophique de la foiblesse de l'esprit humain*. He defined "truth of judgment" as the "agreement or correspondence" between the object of consideration, which existed outside human perception, and the concept or image of that object in the human mind.[12] Such a correspondence required knowledge of both the object and the idea of that object. However, since the mind could only know things through the ideas that it formed, the verification of an agreement between the two proved impossible.[13] Since ideas were immaterial and existed only in the mind, it was impossible to know, he contended, whether they actually represented something that really existed outside the mind. Huet cited the example of dreams and hallucinations to suggest that one could experience the presence of concepts in the mind without there being any corresponding object in the external world.[14]

These skeptical challenges posed fundamental problems not only for Cartesians but for all philosophical schools that embraced some form of substance dualism. For theological reasons, abandoning this notion would prove quite problematic. However, attempts to reconcile philosophical explanations of the mind-body interaction with fundamental doctrines of Christian theology would exacerbate tensions between these two intertwined realms of human knowledge.

Attempted Solutions within Cartesianism: Malebranche and Régis

The underlying tension between substance dualism and inter-substantial interaction led the disciples of Descartes to undertake attempts to resolve the apparent difficulty. In attempting to defend dualism while expanding the discussion of the mind-body relationship, these thinkers articulated rival interpretations of Descartes's positions. Historians of philosophy generally see these as divided between the empiricist and the idealist strains of Cartesianism.[15]

Pierre-Sylvain Régis (1632–1707) was one of the most notable exponents of the empiricist branch of Cartesianism, and his *Système de philosophie* (1690) was one of the most prominent and extensive expositions of Cartesian philosophy in the seventeenth century. Régis attempted to reconcile the mind-body problem both in his *Système* and in his reply to Huet's *Censura philosophiae car-*

tesianae (1689).[16] He answered Huet's objection by distinguishing between the mind (*esprit*) and the soul (*âme*): "The mind is nothing but thought that exists by itself and knows itself by itself, while the soul is thought that exists by itself and is joined to body."[17] Consequently, although the mind could cogitate independently, the soul depended on the body for most of its ideas.

While Régis downplayed the consequences of Cartesian dualism by stressing the intimacy of the union, Malebranche took the mind-body distinction to one of its logical conclusions by insisting that there could be no formal interaction between the two distinct substances. For Malebranche, each substance remained essentially the same as it was before the union. Because there was no necessary causal connection between mind and body, God was required to ensure interaction between them.[18] He was also the actual and only source of all human ideas. Consequently, the body and the soul provided occasions for divine action: "It is through them [our bodies] as the occasional causes that we receive from God thousands and thousands of different sensations that are material."[19] Defining an idea as "the immediate object, or the closest object to the mind, when it perceives something," Malebranche offered an emanationist epistemology. He concluded that human beings saw all things in God, who was "very closely united to our soul by his presence, in a way that one can say that he is the place of the minds, just as spaces are the place of bodies."[20]

Régis and Malebranche intensely debated the issue in the 1690s. Régis disputed the possibility of a union between God and particular souls. Such a union required interdependence between two substances. To suggest that souls were united to God was to suggest that God was somehow dependent on human souls![21] Malebranche attacked Régis's empiricism, claiming—just as the skeptics had done—that material extension could not act directly on the mind, because only ideas could modify thinking substance. He remarked that humans' notions were representative of objects only because it pleased God to create something that corresponded to them, and he asserted that the mind could form ideas even if they did not represent anything actually existing in the world.[22] Their bitter exchange continued for several iterations and attracted allies on both sides of the wide spectrum of interpretations inherent in Descartes.[23] Unintentionally, empiricist and Malebranchist Cartesians were doing the work of the skeptics with respect to each other.

Locke and the "Thinking-Matter" Controversy

While debates among French Cartesians continued well into the eighteenth century, they also attracted attention across the Channel. John Locke famously began his *Essay Concerning Human Understanding* by disputing Descartes's doctrine of innate ideas, arguing for an empiricist epistemology. Although Locke seemed to endorse a dualist conception of human nature throughout most of the *Essay*, he did not theoretically rule out the possibility that matter could be capable of thought. It was impossible to know, Locke argued, whether God had "given to Matter fitly disposed, a power to perceive and think, or else joined and fixed to Matter so disposed, a thinking immaterial Substance." The two options were equally easy for an omnipotent being to accomplish.[24] Although Locke made the suggestion in the context of explaining the limits of human understanding, his argument implicitly pitted divine omnipotence against the traditional conception of matter as inert and incapable of mental operations.[25] Locke did not believe that thought could be a property of matter, but he could not preclude the possibility that an omnipotent being operated in ways that were unknown to man.[26] The ambiguity arose from the fact that most readers approached Locke's statement as an ontological claim that speculated about the actual nature of reality. However, the argument could also be read as an epistemological statement about the unknowable nature of the mind's composition and operations.

Locke's *Essay* contained not only materialist implications regarding the nature of the soul but also potential skeptical inferences about the understanding of the world. As we saw in chapter 5, the English philosopher had distinguished between real essences, by which he understood the actual nature of objects as they existed independently of human perception, and nominal essences, which he defined as ideas about the apparent nature of things.[27] All judgments were based on nominal essences because people could only understand objects through the ideas they formed about them through sense perceptions and reflections. In other words, Locke's theory conceded the skeptical claim that the mind could not know with absolute certainty whether one's ideas represented objects such as they really were.

Voltaire played perhaps the greatest role in popularizing Locke's philosophy in the French-speaking world. His "Treizième lettre sur Mr. Locke" in the *Lettres philosophiques* (1734) praised Locke for elucidating "human reason as an excellent anatomist explains the springs of the human body."[28] Most of the letter discussed Locke's notion of the soul. Voltaire repeated the famous passage regarding the materiality of the soul, described the uproar it elicited, and defended his protagonist against accusations of irreligion.[29]

René-Joseph de Tournemine, the editor of the *Mémoires de Trévoux* and Voltaire's former teacher at the Collège Louis-le-Grand, was one of the first to engage the philosophe on his presentation of Locke's thinking-matter hypothesis.[30] He observed that the query entailed a category mistake by asking whether God could perform an act that was "contradictory" and "outside the realm of possibility." Thought was entirely incompatible with properties of matter. Matter, by contrast, was "divisible and composed of parts," and it could not perceive or judge objects. Such an operation required that the subject of perception be whole and indivisible.[31] Tournemine disputed that it would be as easy for God to join an immaterial soul to a material body as it would be to render matter capable of thought: the first option was metaphysically possible, but the second implied a self-contradiction.[32]

David Renaud Boullier, whose attempts to refute skepticism we have already encountered, also composed a lengthy review of the *Lettres philosophiques*, dedicating most of the discussion to Locke's view of the soul. He attacked Voltaire for emphasizing the controversial statement about thinking matter, and he suggested that Voltaire had seized upon this point in order to advance his own irreligious agenda. He remarked that the passage was appealing to libertines and unworthy of Locke's otherwise dignified memory. Accusing Voltaire of appropriating Locke's theories for his own impious purposes, Boullier concluded that the philosophe's depiction of Locke was inaccurate. He seemed to have "the appearance of a Pyrrhonian, even though he himself was far from Pyrrhonism."[33] Later in his career, Boullier took a more critical stance toward Locke and others who "maintain that the nature of substances is unknown to us" for emphasizing the ignorance and defects of the human mind.[34] If one followed their arguments to their logical conclusions, one would be "reduced" to becoming a Pyrrhonian, because "if substances are unknown to us . . . a universal uncertainty must follow from this ignorance."[35]

Locke's empiricist epistemology and controversial suggestion, as well as its popularization on the Continent, helped to fuel the continuing controversy about mind-body interaction. Although Locke himself did not belabor the contentious claim, Voltaire appropriated the statement and made it central to his presentation of Locke's philosophy. Voltaire's opponents saw the need to refute both him and, by extension, Locke because of what they perceived as the materialist and skeptical consequences that followed from the possibility of thinking matter.

Berkeley's Anti-Pyrrhonian Skepticism

The Irish philosopher Bishop George Berkeley (1685–1753) attempted to formulate an almost diametrically opposite response to Locke's empiricist epistemology in

his *Treatise Concerning the Principles of Human Knowledge* (1710). According to
Locke and other so-called materialists—those who believed that a physical world
existed outside the mind—primary qualities actually existed in physical objects,
while secondary qualities were merely the products of the primary qualities and
had no true subsistence outside the mind.[36] Berkeley conceded that secondary
qualities were only in the mind, but he questioned the validity of the claim that
primary qualities had objective existence. An extended object without any color
was just as inconceivable as a colored object without any shape. Since it was impossible to conceive of "Extension, Figure, and Motion abstracted from all other
Qualities," then it followed that all "other sensible Qualities" were "in the Mind
and no where else."[37] The distinction between primary physical and secondary
mental qualities was a fallacious one, since both subsisted only in the mind.

Berkeley contended that it was impossible to know whether anything actually existed outside the mind, since, as skeptics had claimed, all that could be
known was in the mind itself. Thus, even if the "materialists" were correct, and
various substances did in fact exist outside the mind, one would never be able to
perceive them. Since they were "unable to comprehend in what manner Body
can act upon Spirit, or how it is possible it shou'd imprint any Idea in the Mind,"
they could not explain "how our Ideas are produced."[38] Berkeley employed the
problem of mind-body interaction as another argument against the possibility
of perceiving a material world with an immaterial mind.

Although Berkeley employed arguments similar to those of Foucher, Bayle,
and other skeptics, his self-avowed goal, as the full title and the preface of his
text made clear, was actually to refute the Pyrrhonians.[39] Indeed, he believed
that the skeptics actually benefitted from the unconfirmable assumption that
ideas in the mind corresponded to objects outside it. The "most groundless and
absurd Notion" that "Real Things subsisted without the Mind" was, for Berkeley, "the very Root of Scepticism."[40] Uncertainty followed "from our supposing a
difference between Things and Ideas, and that the former have a Subsistence
without the Mind." Berkeley noted that the skeptics had always pointed to the inability of establishing a causal connection between the two and said that the "doctrine of Matter" had been "the main Pillar in Support of Scepticism . . . Atheism
and Irreligion."[41] As long as philosophers attributed "a real Existence to Unthinking Things," an existence "distinct from their being perceiv'd," they would never
be able to verify their subsistence outside the mind. Inadvertently, they would end
up becoming skeptics.[42]

Berkeley argued that the only way to overcome skeptical claims that questioned the possibility of knowing the true nature of the external world was by

establishing the foundations of all knowledge on a purely idealist basis. Since one could not prove the existence of anything external to the mind, it was reasonable to assume that there was nothing in the world other than ideas. Berkeley maintained that objects did not and could not exist except as ideas, since "the very existence of an unthinking thing consists in being perceived." One could not reason, properly speaking, about relations between objects, but only about relations between ideas. Berkeley defined "external" ideas as those that were "not generated from within, by the Mind itself, but imprinted by a Spirit distinct from that which perceives them."[43] He argued that human beings received ideas not from the external world but from God, who alone was responsible for producing a constant and coherent stream of thoughts in their minds.[44] Berkeley went beyond Malebranche's occasionalist philosophy. While Malebranche supposed God to be the source of all ideas, he still believed in the existence of external objects that corresponded to those ideas.[45] Berkeley completely eliminated the physical world, thereby establishing a direct connection between God and individual human souls.[46] His immaterialist epistemology also functioned as a demonstration of the existence of God and a proof of the immortality of the soul.

Three years after the publication of the *Principles*, Berkeley completed his popular *Three Dialogues between Hylas and Philonous* (1713). This text reiterated Berkeley's main arguments against skepticism in a new genre. After the first two dialogues, the "materialist" Hylas finds himself "plunged into the deepest and most deplorable Skepticism" as a result of his "Belief of material Substance."[47] In the conclusion of the third dialogue, Hylas declares his surprise: "You set out upon the Same Principles, that Academics, Cartesians, and the like Sects, usually do; and . . . it looked as if you were advancing their Philosophical Scepticism; but, in the End, your Conclusions are directly opposite to theirs." His interlocutor, Philonous, replies with a metaphor of a fountain. He suggests that "the same Principles which, at first View, lead to Scepticism, pursued to a certain Point, bring Men back to common Sense."[48] With this final exchange, Berkeley insinuated that all philosophical systems that attempted to establish the existence of an objective reality—one made up of material objects and independent of the mind—ultimately led to Pyrrhonian skepticism.[49] It was only by abandoning the material world and focusing on what could be known (the realm of ideas) that one could overcome skepticism and obtain a true and certain knowledge of the world.

Berkeley's arguments immediately found their way into the Continental debates about skepticism, as reviews appeared almost instantly in major Catholic and Huguenot periodicals.[50] The review of Berkeley's *Dialogues* in the Hague-based *Journal littéraire* brought up the issue of divine omnipotence. The critic insisted that Berkeley "will not convince [us] that God is not powerful enough to have created inanimate beings and to have made them capable, by means unknown to us, to act on minds and to produce ideas in them."[51] The inability to explain the interaction between matter and mind did not imply that such a causal relation was impossible. The supposition that the material world did not really exist made it seem as though God had misled human beings into believing that they were surrounded by a material world, when in fact God was the actual source of their ideas. It was unlikely that "God, having two possible ways of making men have ideas of sensible things, wanted to make them believe that he had employed means that he in fact had not."[52]

Tournemine added a section on Berkeley to the 1718 version of his reflections on atheism.[53] He contrasted Spinozism and materialism with the immaterialism of the Irish philosopher, suggesting that the latter was an example of a "novel effort [to promote] incredulity."[54] The Jesuit ridiculed it as an implausible theory of "the impious members of this sect" by which "all that we believe we see and feel" were but "phantoms of the mind."[55] The most dangerous implications of Berkeley's system were moral. Tournemine warned of what he perceived to be the dangers of radical subjectivism that followed from an epistemology according to which one could only be certain of one's own existence. If the ideas in one's own mind were the sole criteria of truth, and if one could not be persuaded that any of those ideas corresponded to an objective reality, then all social interactions would cease. Each individual would become self-absorbed and egotistical. Moreover, if people could not verify their own existence, it would be "impossible to believe in the truth of the existence of God."[56]

While most reviewers expressed bewilderment at Berkeley's immaterialism, the Scottish philosopher Andrew Baxter viewed Berkeley's approach as an endorsement of Pyrrhonism.[57] Baxter did not see Berkeley's self-declared goal of disproving atheism and skepticism as a sincere one, since his arguments seemed to do just the opposite.[58] He accused Berkeley of embracing a "willful, determined kind of Scepticism" by forcing himself to deny the reality of the material world because the demonstration of its actual existence was uncertain.[59] He questioned Berkeley's logical consistency and compared his arguments to those of the ancient Pyrrhonians: why was Berkeley attempting to demonstrate that nothing could be demonstrated?[60]

Despite his stated intentions, which certainly appeared pious, Berkeley's attempt to refute skepticism produced a substantial backlash both in England and

on the Continent. While his immaterialist system proposed to resolve the problem of inter-substantial interaction and provide a new explanation for the origin
of ideas, it led many to accuse him of surreptitiously promoting skepticism. His
denial of the actuality of an external material world undermined those who
wished to prove the existence of God based on the perfection of his creation.
Furthermore, as some suggested, Berkeley's propositions rendered God a deceiver who had led human beings to mistakenly believe in the existence of a
world that corresponded to their ideas.[61]

Leibniz and Pre-established Harmony

Berkeley was not the only thinker to be derided for the theological difficulties
posed by an attempted solution to the mind-body problem. The German mathematician and philosopher Gottfried Wilhelm Leibniz proposed another influential yet controversial resolution to substance dualism. Although he was educated at the University of Leipzig and spent only a few years of his life in Paris,
Leibniz remained fully involved in French academic circles. It was in the French
learned journals, most notably the *Journal des savants*, that he articulated the
controversial theory of pre-established harmony.

Although Leibniz was not a dualist, he began his "Sisteme nouveau" with
the assumption that the universe really was composed of two substances, as
Descartes had proposed. Unlike Descartes, however, he did not think that it was
possible for the mind and the body to interact with or influence each another.
Since they were metaphysically distinct, it was philosophically inconceivable,
within Leibniz's conception of what a substance was, that a material substance
could ever affect an immaterial one, and vice versa.[62] Although the two seemed
to interact causally, this was the result of a divine arrangement that ensured a
consistent and perpetual correspondence between the finite substances (each of
which continued to act only according to its own laws).

Contrary to Descartes, who had contended that the mind had both innate
ideas, which were present at its creation, and acquired notions, which were gathered by the senses, Leibniz argued that ideas could not possibly come into the soul
from the physical world. Being purely immaterial, they could arise only as the
products of the mind (or be created by God). By omnipotent design, notions in the
mind happened to represent, accurately and faithfully, the external world. Such a
solution, in Leibniz's view, rendered an attempt to explain inter-substantial interaction unnecessary.[63]

Leibniz attempted to clarify the system in a letter to Henri Basnage de
Beauval. He asked that his interlocutor imagine two clocks that were in perfect

accordance with each other and showed precisely the same time. There were three possible explanations for their synchronicity: they mutually influenced each other; someone was constantly adjusting them; or they had been made in such a way that they would constantly be in synch. The clocks served as analogies of the mind-body interaction. Dismissing all empiricist accounts (whether Aristotelian, Cartesian, or Lockean) as inexplicable and metaphysically impossible, Leibniz described Malebranche's theory of occasional causes as overly miraculous, since it required God's constant intervention.[64] He presented his own hypothesis as the most parsimonious explanation of the apparent interaction between mind and body.[65] God had created the world so perfectly that although each substance acted solely according to its own laws, it was in perfect concordance with the other by virtue of "a pre-established harmony."[66]

Leibniz's theory elicited a number of critical responses concerning its dangerous implications. Jean-Pierre de Crousaz was among the system's most vocal critics. In his critique of Alexander Pope's *Essay on Man* (1734), a work that had popularized Leibniz's metaphysics, Crousaz attempted to refute the Leibnizian system. He argued that Pope and Leibniz had made it seem as if the whole world were nothing but "an immense machine . . . composed of infinite others." According to their principles, all events were merely "inevitable consequences of the first movement that set them in motion."[67] Crousaz claimed that in such a system, the movements of the body and the operations of the mind were predetermined and followed a set of "necessary and inevitable" sequences. This annihilated free will and eliminated moral responsibility: "If all our willful actions are really the effects of causes to which we are subjected, we cannot be guilty, we should not reproach ourselves, and we have nothing to fear." If all human decisions and acts had been predetermined, then God alone was the "inevitable cause" of all humans' actions.[68] Consequently, all deeds that appeared to be morally evil, including the original sin, were actually "inevitable outcomes of an eternal chain of events."[69] The Swiss logician made similar arguments in his private correspondence, noting that Leibniz and his disciples were guilty of advocating a system of fatalism.[70] Crousaz saw Leibnizian "fatalism" as being on par with skepticism in terms of the dangerous consequences that followed from it, and he sought to "attack the two monsters."[71]

Crousaz's argument against Leibniz's theory of pre-established harmony was moral and not epistemological in nature. He and critics such as Voltaire, whose *Candide* (1759) served as a critique of Leibniz's theodicy, did not attempt to undermine the actual content of Leibniz's views.[72] Crousaz argued, rather, that despite their internal consistency, these theories, if pushed to their logical conclusions, resulted in a purely deterministic universe that clashed with basic assumptions about human nature and free will. Just like Berkeley's immaterialism, Leibniz's pre-established harmony and his theodicy entailed moral implications that neither a religious apologist such as Crousaz nor a philosophe such as Voltaire was willing to entertain.[73]

Anti-Spiritualism and Materialism

Some thinkers did voice explicit dissatisfaction with the philosophical and theological consequences that followed from substance dualism. The Swiss apologist Gaspard Cuentz (or Kaspar Künz, 1676–1752) unambiguously accused the systems of Descartes, Malebranche, and Leibniz of helping to promote skepticism and irreligion by contradicting common experience and emphasizing the complete immateriality of the soul. Cuentz contended that the paradoxes and inconsistencies inherent in their theories actually undermined all arguments for the immortality of the soul and helped Pyrrhonians by advancing easily refutable claims.[74] The "weakness of reasons derived from philosophy, on which, in undertaking to prove the absolute non-extension of our soul, the authors of the three systems and their adherents claim to base the dogma of the immortality of the soul," encouraged the Pyrrhonian libertines to question this fundamental principle. Cuentz argued that the notion of an immaterial soul could also "create more followers for their pernicious sect," while putting others at risk for "falling into complete and blatant incredulity." He thought that the various hypotheses "threw into uncertainty" those who would otherwise be receptive to self-evident proofs of the soul's immortality, thereby increasing the ranks of the skeptics.[75]

Alleging that he had based his theories on the principles advanced by Locke, Cuentz argued that it was quite possible for the soul to be both extended and immortal at the same time. Citing Locke's famous passage about the possibility of thinking matter, he defended the English philosopher against what he believed to be unjust accusations.[76] Cuentz proposed that a "non-extended being" was incapable of thinking or of causing movements of the body and that the soul was extended but imperceptible and indivisible. While the soul was not material as such, he maintained, it was "a being endowed with extension and power that thinks."[77] The soul was thus neither purely immaterial nor material but rather a "spiritual body," or complex matter that was arranged in such a way that it could feel and think. The soul was just like a watch; it had several parts that were organized in a complex manner and, as a result, could tell time.[78]

Although Cuentz's views appeared quite eccentric and contrary to orthodox theology, they represented yet another sincere attempt to offer a philosophical explanation of the mind-body interaction that adequately defended the existence of God and the immortality of the soul.[79] Cuentz often cited scripture in his arguments and insisted that his system was not only closer to the truth but also able to disarm Pyrrhonians, atheists, and libertines. He aimed to offer an explanation that prevented the skeptics from casting doubt on fundamental principles of Christianity.

Not all attempts to resolve the mind-body problem endeavored to accommodate Christian theology, however. Julien d'Offray de La Mettrie put forth a decidedly anti-theological theory of the soul with his materialist hypothesis. In 1745 he anonymously published his *Histoire naturelle de l'âme*, in which he offered his reflections on the interdependence of mind and body. Outrage over the work, which was immediately condemned by the Parlement of Paris, forced La Mettrie to flee to Leiden in 1747. The publication of his equally controversial *L'homme machine* (1748) quickly wore out his welcome in the Netherlands, and he was invited by Frederick II to move to the Prussian court in Potsdam. There he was allowed to continue his practice and his writings until his untimely death in 1751.[80]

Although La Mettrie admired Descartes's work in physiology, he faulted the Cartesians, the Malebranchists, and other contemporary metaphysicians for admitting "two distinct substances in men, as if they had seen and had counted them."[81] He openly advanced the thinking-matter hypothesis for which Locke had been so criticized. Indeed, citing Locke's argument, he suggested that it would be impious to deny divine omnipotence the ability to create matter that was capable of thought, even if one were not able to understand fully the properties of matter.[82] For La Mettrie, the proper question was not whether matter was capable of thought but whether matter could be *organized* in such a way as to be able to think. The human eye was able to see not because some spiritual ability enabled it to do so but because a fine arrangement of particles allowed light to be reflected and transmitted to the brain. When particles of matter were joined together in particular ways, they could perform complex functions such as sensation and thought.[83]

La Mettrie presented examples of the intimate interdependence of the soul and the body: both went to sleep simultaneously; the velocity of blood circulation affected the soul's ability to perceive; excited emotions in turn accelerated the heartbeat and the blood flow; drugs, such as opium and coffee, affected the operations of the mind as well as the operations of the body; and disease and sickness damaged the sharpness of the mind.[84] It was impossible to speak about the soul without taking physiology into account, since "all the faculties of the soul depend on the proper organization of the brain" and since "thought develops with the organs."[85] Thoughts, emotions, and other operations of the mind were based entirely on the physical constitution of the body and on the nature of the brain, La Mettrie contended. Ideas came into the mind through sensory organs and left traces in the brain tissues, thereby creating memories.[86] La Mettrie concluded that if physical conditions and physiological deformities clearly affected emotions and thoughts—which they did—then the soul (or the mind) was not distinct from the body, acting as a causal agent on it. Rather, it was a behavior of the body. What philosophers referred to as the soul (or spirit) was not an external cause but the effect of the complex actions of diverse parts of the body. Thoughts, emotions, and decisions to act did not stem from an individual spiritual entity; they were the products of sophisticated physiological interactions and combinations of matter.[87]

All evidence pointed to the fact that the soul was not distinct from, but heavily dependent on, the body, La Mettrie protested. It was in vain that philosophers tried to imagine and describe the soul as a distinct substance independent of physical influences.[88] Explicitly positioning himself in opposition to Descartes, Malebranche, and Leibniz, he maintained that the soul was extended. If the soul were not extended, as Descartes had claimed, then it "would not be able to act on the body, and it would be impossible to explain the union and the reciprocal interaction of two substances."[89] La Mettrie's solution to the problem of dualism was as radical as Berkeley's, though it presented a materialist system diametrically opposed to the Irish philosopher's conception. Indeed, La Mettrie saw the soul as a "term about which we have no ideas" that was used only to "name the part in us that thinks."[90]

In addition to advancing his materialist view of the human soul, La Mettrie also suggested how one should investigate the question. He argued that "experience and observation" should serve as the sole guides. The only reliable authorities on the question were physicians, who understood the mechanisms of the human body, rather than theologians, who did not comprehend the subject on which they expounded and who were "driven to a thousand prejudices" by their "obscure studies."[91] La Mettrie maintained that empirical observations and experiments alone provided credible information, while metaphysical speculations proved very little.[92] The "searches that the greatest philosophers undertook a priori . . . have been in vain," since the soul could only be understood a posteriori. It was only by examining the soul through the organs of the body that one could "attain the greatest possible degree of probability with respect to this subject."[93] Abstract invocations of an immaterial substance to explain human behaviors were equivalent to declarations of ignorance. Metaphysicians such as Descartes, Malebranche, and Leibniz had begun their investigations with the prejudiced supposition that the soul was immaterial, and they had erroneously attempted to proceed from this basic assumption to explain the nature of the soul based on what they believed it to be.[94] La Mettrie denounced what he saw as the pointlessness of metaphysical speculations that claimed to provide certainty, while in actuality obscuring the matter further. He described himself as a "frank Pyrrhonian" and endorsed a probabilistic approach in exploring human nature.[95]

La Mettrie's view that metaphysical speculations lacked practical utility reflected a growing discontent with abstract philosophy that became apparent in the writings of his fellow philosophes by the mid-eighteenth century. Similarly, the expanding and increasingly diverse reading public, often untrained in formal philosophy or theology, became increasingly uninterested in the progressively complex metaphysical systems that were being proposed. This trend is evident from quantitative studies that analyzed the changes in the types of works published throughout the course of the eighteenth century. As the decades passed, there was a gradual yet steady decrease in approbations and *permissions tacites* granted to works on metaphysics and devotional theology, along with a falling number of journal pages (as a percentage of all publications) devoted to reviews of these subjects.[96] This slow decline was offset by a rise in the number of texts devoted to history, politics and political economy, and the physical sciences.[97] The growing popularity of the philosophical novel (*roman philosophique* or *conte philosophique*) also played an important part in the relegation of theology and of metaphysics from the forefront of intellectual debates.[98]

"Confess Yourselves to Be as Ignorant as I":
Consensus, Probability, and Mitigated Skepticism

The various attempts to account for the mind-body interaction created powerful crosscurrents in the philosophical world of the eighteenth century. Pyrrhonism and other expressions of skepticism were not so much the causes of this development as symptoms of it. As Huet had claimed in the preface to his *Traité philosophique de la foiblesse de l'esprit humain*, there was "no end" to the "perpetual disputes of philosophers on all kinds of subjects."[99] How the immaterial and immortal soul interacted with the material and perishable body and the theological implications of the answers to this fundamental question were at the heart of the protracted metaphysical debates that we have witnessed. Hazard's supposed "crisis of the European mind" was thus a lengthy, drawn-out process, as philosophers grappled with the basic question of how it was that they really knew the world with certainty. The result, particularly in the French-speaking intellectual world, was the growing frustration with metaphysics and the gradual acceptance of probable, rather than certain and indubitable, knowledge as the only attainable goal.

The growing discontent with metaphysical approaches to the mind-body problem led to the increasing popularity of explicitly non-metaphysical (even anti-metaphysical) epistemological systems. The irresolute nature of debates about epistemology led some philosophes, such as Voltaire, to denounce the entire enterprise of understanding the true nature of the soul and of speculating about its composition. In his "Lettre sur Locke," he summarized the English philosopher's call to his critics: "At least confess yourselves to be as ignorant as I."[100] Since the mind could not imagine how a body could have ideas or how matter and spirit could interact with each other, it was best not to make dogmatic claims about the issue. Voltaire presented Locke's admission of ignorance not as a failure but as a virtue. He contrasted the English philosopher's intellectual humility with the presumptuous attempts to define the essences of spirit and matter. Despite the protracted disputes about "the nature and the immortality of the soul," the issue still could not be resolved, because "human reason is so little able to demonstrate by itself" the soul's immortality.[101]

Voltaire had done a great deal to popularize Locke's ideas in France through the *Lettres philosophiques*, but Etienne Bonnot de Condillac (1714–80) offered a more systematic presentation of Locke's epistemology and expanded on it to present a full-fledged sensationalist theory of the origins of human knowledge. Condillac was less controversial than Voltaire, d'Argens, and La Mettrie in his attempts to advance an empiricist epistemology. He remained loyal to his Catholic faith and maintained good relations both with philosophes such as Jean-le-Rond d'Alembert (1717–83) and Denis Diderot, who used many of his ideas in the *Encyclopédie*, and with the Jesuits of the *Mémoires de Trévoux*.[102] His efforts to articulate an account of the nature and origin of human ideas had a lasting influence on French philosophy.[103]

In his *Essai sur l'origine des connoissances humaines* (1746) and his *Traité des sensations* (1754) Condillac attempted to sidestep metaphysical issues, while offering explanations of the operations of the mind. Condillac opened the *Essai* with a jab at metaphysicians. He pointed out the irony that while metaphysics was supposed to be the most enlightening to the sciences, it was actually "the most neglected" field in France. Metaphysicians appeared to be "the least wise of all the philosophers," because their works failed to be instructive, being filled instead with "phantoms" and "confusions." He distinguished between two kinds of approaches to metaphysics. The first was "ambitious, seeking to penetrate all the mysteries, the nature, and the essence of things and the most hidden causes." The second method was more "restrained" (*retenue*). It demarcated clear limits and directed its investigations in accordance with "the weakness of the human mind." While the first approach constructed a delightful mirage that easily dissipated, Condillac claimed, the second was "as simple as truth itself." He associated Descartes, Malebranche, and Leibniz with the former method, while praising Bacon and Locke for undertaking the latter. According to Condillac, Locke was the only philosopher who had "limited himself to the study of human understanding and succeeded in that pursuit."[104] He praised Locke's and Bacon's focus on the role of the senses in the acquisition of human knowledge, contrasting them with Descartes, Malebranche, and Leibniz, all of whom professed to know the nature of the soul. One needed to study the mind, not to determine its nature but to distinguish the processes by which it operated, Condillac insisted.[105]

Condillac's position on the interaction between mind and body was less theologically controversial than Locke's, Voltaire's, and La Mettrie's. Because of the original sin, Condillac noted, the soul had become so dependent on the body that philosophers confused the two substances and imagined that the soul was "nothing more than the most subtle part of the body." The problem with such a view was that the body was not a single substance but "an assemblage or a collection" of substances. Repeating Tournemine's argument against Locke, Condillac insisted that the body "cannot be the subject" of thought, precisely because it was made up of many parts, while thought was "a single and indivisible perception." The abbé claimed not to know "how Mr. Locke came to assert that it is impossible for us to discover whether omnipotency has not given to some systems of matter . . . a power to perceive and to think." Whereas the English philosopher had insisted that he did not know the nature of matter or of thought, Condillac remarked that one did not need "to know the essence and the nature of matter" in order to resolve the question. "It is sufficient to observe," he noted, "that the subject of thought must be singular [and indivisible]," which was not the case with matter. While the soul was clearly distinct from the body, it was dependent on the body in its current earthly state, Condillac concluded. There was no evidence on which to base speculations about its disembodied condition, so it was necessary "to consult experience and to reason only from facts that one could not question."[106] Condillac's analysis cleared the argument of any possible theological controversy, while limiting the discussion to observable operations of the mind rather than to imperceptible causes or essences.

Condillac began his exposition from the same point that Locke had started from in his *Essay Concerning Human Understanding*. The abbé argued that according to the way the human mind operated, it was evident that all ideas were necessarily acquired and not innate. From the first moment of a human being's existence, "the mind immediately experiences a variety of sensations, such as light, colors, pain, pleasure, motion, and rest." These sensations constituted the mind's "first thoughts." The second step of human cognition involved the mind's reflection on the effects that the sensations produced in it. Ideas could come from only two sources: either immediately from the external world or from the operations that the senses produced within the soul.[107] It was evident from an examination of the content of human perceptions, Condillac remarked, that the source of our ideas about extension, color, shape, and other aspects of physical objects came not from within us but from something external to the mind. "It could not be doubted," he claimed, "that there are qualities in bodies that cause the impressions they make on our senses." As both skeptical and rationalist philosophers reminded readers, however, "the difficulty some claim to raise is whether these qualities bear a resemblance [or likeness] to what we feel."[108]

Condillac observed that Descartes and Malebranche had unfairly attributed error to sensations and presented sense experiences as "obstacles to acquiring knowledge." He noted that they had failed to explain their terms clearly, and he proposed to divide sensations into three distinct units: "the perceptions that we feel"; the connections, or "relations," that we establish between these perceptions and something that is outside us; and "the judgment that what we attribute to those [external] things really belongs to them." According to Condillac, error came not from the operations of the senses but from the mistakes of judgment that ascribed to objects properties that they did not have. For example, the mind commonly confused magnitudes or shapes of objects that were far away. Extended experience was required to correct such shortcomings in judgment. Memory and attention consequently played a particularly important role in Condillac's epistemology, as he attempted to explain the formation, retention, and corruption of ideas.[109]

The *Essai* largely followed Locke in exploring the operations of the mind, but it added emphasis to the role of language. For Condillac, the English philosopher had not paid sufficient attention to exploring the role that signs played in the formation of abstract ideas.[110] Condillac insisted that the process by which the mind forms signs was "one of the most essential operations in the search for the truth." He used the example of mathematics to show how the exactness of constructing a system of signs could lead to real progress in human knowledge. Signs were so important for organizing perceptions and for communicating that it was impossible to imagine that ideas without their signs were "something clear and determinate."[111] Signs compensated for the weakness of the mind, which could not "revive a great number of ideas and render them all the subject of [one's] reflection simultaneously." By combining several similar simple ideas under one general notion, the mind formed abstractions that offered it a broader perspective and allowed it to communicate with others.[112] Condillac used the example of gold to show how a single word referred to a set of notions about the size, shape, extension, density, and other properties of this substance. Signs thus allowed for the formation of complex ideas. Similarly, the mind could also combine several complex ideas, such as "mind" and "body, to form the idea of an animal. Without signs, people could not come to any understanding of the world, Condillac insisted. "Just as the qualities of objects would not coexist independently of us were it not for the objects in which they inhere," he claimed, "so the ideas of them would not coexist in the mind were it not for the signs in which they are united."[113]

While abstractions helped the mind to expand its knowledge of the surrounding world, they also led to a number of errors. Condillac remarked that some philosophers had forgotten that abstract ideas were the "products of the imagination" and erroneously assumed that they were "something real." He specifically attacked Descartes, who had claimed that some ideas had more objective reality than others. The reification of abstract concepts, such as "substance," "essence," and "being," among a multitude of others led philosophers into endless debates and contradictions. Condillac observed that this was a particularly acute problem in descriptions of the operations of the mind. He referred to Locke's observation that abstractions made philosophers assume that various mental faculties corresponded to real and distinct agents within the soul. Such false assumptions produced unnecessary speculations about "whether judgment belongs to the understanding or the will" or "whether the will is capable of knowledge or is only a blind faculty."[114] Condillac attempted to address these unnecessary problems:

> If by *the understanding* and *the will* philosophers only wanted to signify the soul considered in regard to particular acts that it produces or is able to produce, it is

evident that judgment, activity, and liberty would either pertain or not pertain to the understanding, depending on whether we considered a greater or a smaller number of its actions in speaking of this faculty. It is the same with the will. It is sufficient in these sorts of cases to explain the terms determining the notions we have of things by exact analyses. But philosophers, having been obliged to represent the soul by abstraction, have multiplied its being, so that *the understanding* and *the will* have undergone the fate of all abstract ideas.[115]

The problem, for Condillac, was in the abuse of language and of abstractions. Just as mathematics used clearly defined units that allowed one to perform elaborate calculations, so languages needed plainly delineated terms in order to avoid errors. Philosophers had turned "the understanding and the will into the phantoms that exist only in their imagination."[116] As a consequence of a lack of reflection upon the origins and function of abstract ideas, metaphysics had been cast into a great obscurity.

Human understanding, in Condillac's analysis, was made up of "a collection or combination" of several distinct "operations of the soul." It was not a faculty with a unique essence but rather a term used to describe a number of actions that the mind performed: "To perceive or to be conscious, to give one's attention, to recognize, to imagine, to recall, to reflect, to distinguish ideas, to abstract them, to compare them, to compose and decompose them, to analyze them, to affirm, to negate to judge, to reason, to conceive: all this is the understanding."[117] While Condillac in no way denied the existence of the soul, he offered a description that strongly resembled La Mettrie's claims. Both described the mind in terms of the operations it performed, and not with reference to its nature or essence. By focusing on the observable effects rather than on the underlying causes, Condillac attempted to demystify the powers of reason. He deconstructed the understanding into its constituent parts and analyzed them separately. He explicitly articulated this procedure in explaining the order one needed to follow in "the search for the truth." By beginning all examinations with simple ideas or with "complex ideas whose creation was known," one would discover the relations among ideas and perceive what followed from them. Consequently, "having begun with the most simple, we will imperceptibly rise to the more complex ones, and we will form a series of ideas so strongly connected with each other that we could never reach the most distant ones but by means of those that preceded them."[118]

Condillac assured his readers that this approach had two concrete advantages. First, by knowing the origin of the ideas upon which the mind meditated, one would be able both to proceed in an orderly fashion and to retrace all steps at any moment. Second, this method made it possible to "see plainly the boundaries of our knowledge, for we will find them as soon as the senses cease to furnish us with ideas and when the mind . . . is no longer capable of forming notions."[119] Condillac acknowledged the limits of human understanding that arose both from the mind's dependence on the senses and on signs and from its imperfect operations. However, he insisted that one could compensate for these inadequacies by recognizing them and by devising strategies to minimize errors. It would be more productive and enlightening, Condillac maintained, to shift the focus from contemplations of causes, natures, and essences to discussions of the perceivable operations of the mind's different faculties. This process involved breaking the mental processes down into different constituent parts and examining the means by which the mind constructed notions and made judgments. A clear awareness of the origin of its ideas and of the weakness of the mind would enable philosophers to avoid making errors and engaging in endless metaphysical speculations about topics such as the nature of the mind-body relationship. One could not hypothesize about the exact nature of the mysterious union, but one could certainly describe its consequences.

Condillac's Lockean analysis of the powers of human reason and of the origin of ideas had a significant influence on the way in which the *Encyclopédie's* editors approached these contentious questions. Like Condillac, they refused to engage in metaphysical discussions about the nature of the soul or to speculate about how it interacted with the body. The article "Ame" enumerated the various ancient and modern opinions on the nature of the soul, even citing the rather controversial views of Hobbes and Spinoza. The coauthors, Denis Diderot and the abbé Claude Yvon (1714–91), discussed the location of the soul, suggesting that the article could never be finished if it had to summarize all the different views. They claimed that while common experience pointed to a clear interdependence between the soul and the body, it was impossible to establish clearly where and how the immaterial soul interacted with the body.[120] The article "Idée," written by the Swiss mathematician Charles-Benjamin de Lubières (1714–90), also gave an overview of the difficulties involved in understanding how ideas "can imprint themselves in our soul." Lubières suggested that to answer this question it was necessary to know fully "the nature of the soul and of the body" and to "penetrate the inexplicable mystery of their union." The author presented a number of contemporaneous accounts of the origin of human ideas, including those of Descartes, Malebranche, and Leibniz, and entertained different counterarguments. The conclusion of the subsection on the origin of ideas proved rather inconclusive: "With a veil remaining over the nature of the soul, we can know neither what an idea is nor how it is produced," Lubières argued, predicting that the matter "will always be open to conjectures."[121] The abundance of competing theories, each with its own set of problems, and the persistent inability of the various philosophical systems to grasp the true nature of the soul and of the body rendered the exercise futile.

Many of those opposed to philosophical skepticism accepted the methods of their adversaries as useful in particular cases. They also agreed that a suspension of judgment was an inevitable outcome in questions such as that of the essence of spirit and matter. Nevertheless, they rejected the ultimate conclusions of the skeptics, seeking instead ways to overcome Pyrrhonian claims and to provide some new basis of epistemological certainty. As we have seen, those who attempted to offer a rebuttal to the Pyrrhonians acknowledged the virtual unattainability of metaphysical certainty (*certitude métaphysique*), while maintaining that a moral certainty (*certitude morale*) could still be secured.

Consensus and Common Sense

Anti-skeptical thinkers frequently invoked self-evidence (*évidence*) and common sense to suggest that there were basic knowable truths that were not and could not be doubted. Formey elaborated on the notion of "common sense" (*sens commun*) to formulate a more systematic way of evaluating the reliability of perception. In replying to the Pyrrhonian claim about the untrustworthy nature of the senses, Formey suggested that by accumulating multiple sense experiences with regard to the same object, one could have a better chance of establishing that object's existence and of ascertaining its properties. The concordance among various senses, such as vision, smell, and touch, provided sufficient conditions for moral certainty. Describing a hypothetical examination of a human corpse by touch, smell, and sight, Formey argued that "the agreement among these three senses demonstrates the existence and the state of this body as invincibly as reason itself could prove anything."[122]

Formey emphasized not just the agreement among the senses but also the concurrence among individuals as a means of establishing true and certain knowledge of the surrounding world: "When several people have the ability to submit a fact to be tested by all the senses that are appropriate to judge it, and they agree to ascertain the existence of this fact, the judgment of truth pertains to these people, and their unanimous statement serves as evidence of this fact."[123] In such a case, the relative certainty of the agreement among the senses was augmented further by corresponding testimonies, all of which improved the probability that the fact or object in question really did exist. The concordance among various observers with regard to perceptions of the external world thus increased the probability that the objective reality corresponded to individual perceptions of that reality.[124]

Formey's colleague Mérian, who translated Hume and attempted to offer practical rebuttals to skepticism, also suggested consensus among individuals as a reliable basis for establishing the existence and properties of objects in the surrounding world. He offered a specific example in order to question both Pyrrhonian and Leibnizian theories of perception. Proposing a case of a dozen people who were simultaneously observing "a bright moon in a serene sky," Mérian argued that "each visible point that radiates from the globe forms a perception in the mind of each spectator; and the collation of these perceptions forms a painting of the whole object, [which is] a spiritual [representation of the] moon." He rhetorically asked whether anyone could seriously claim that the group saw "twelve absolutely different objects" and "maintain, without complete absurdity, that none of these perceptions that enter into the composition of the image that is in my mind is similar to another in the mind of any of the other eleven people who are watching the same spectacle."[125] Mérian ridiculed the notion that different observers would perceive completely dissimilar images of the same object. After all, how was it that human beings could concur about the names and descriptions of things that they observed independently if those perceptions did not agree on the fundamental identity of the objects in question? By pointing to the existence of a general consensus about basic natural objects, Mérian thus undermined skeptical claims about the unreliability of human perception.

Debates about the source and nature of human ideas and the problem of mind-body interaction were by no means resolved by the mid-eighteenth century. However, the diversity of conflicting theories of mind, the philosophical and theological implications that followed from those theories, and the bitter and seemingly unending disputes among the defenders of the theories all led to a gradual decline in attempts to provide a fully metaphysical account of human cognition.[126] As could be seen in the case of thinkers such as Voltaire, La Mettrie, and Diderot, the learned world seemed to experience a gradual weariness with endless metaphysical speculations about the possibility of explaining the nature of the mind and proving the soul's immortality by philosophical demonstrations. Indeed, Diderot's *Encyclopédie* article on metaphysics (1765) called it "a contemptible science" to investigate matters in which "the object of metaphysics is limited to empty, abstract, and arbitrary considerations about time, space, matter, and spirit."[127]

The "Discours préliminaire" (1751) of the *Encyclopédie* began by addressing the origin of ideas. After presenting the Cartesian doctrine of innate ideas and Malebranche's occasionalist theory, Jean-le-Rond d'Alembert approached the issue pragmatically:

> Let us therefore believe without wavering that our sensations do in fact have the cause outside ourselves that we suppose them to have, because the effect that can result from the real existence of that cause could not differ in any way from the effect that we experience. Let us not imitate those philosophers of whom Montaigne speaks, who, when asked about the principle of men's actions, were still attempting to discover whether there are men [that exist]. Far from wishing to cast shadows over a truth recognized even by the skeptics, when they are not engaged in debates, let us leave the trouble of working out its principle to the enlightened metaphysicians.[128]

D'Alembert dismissed the metaphysical speculations about the origin of ideas, leaving the dispute to those who considered the abstract question worthy of further discussion. The implication of his dismissive statement, of course, was that any philosophical resolution to the problem did not impact the ability to discuss the source and nature of ideas on a purely practical level. For d'Alembert and his fellow *encyclopédistes*, skeptical doubts about the correspondence between ideas and objects in the external world, as well as metaphysical speculations about the nature and the role of the soul in this process, were irrelevant and distracting.

In some ways, Descartes's own hesitant explanation of the mind-body union seems to have made a full circle. In the letter to Princess Elisabeth, Descartes had suggested that the union was known not through abstract reason but through sensation and daily experience:

> Those who never philosophize, and make use only of their senses, do not doubt that the soul moves the body and that the body acts on the soul.... And metaphysical thoughts that exercise the pure understanding serve to render familiar the notion of mind, and the study of mathematics ... accustoms us to form very distinct notions of body, [but] in the end, it is by relying exclusively on the activities and concerns of ordinary life, by abstaining from metaphysical meditation, and by studying things that exercise the imagination that one understands the union of soul and body.[129]

Even the rationalist "father of modern philosophy" had to do admit that there were practical limits to philosophizing and that sometimes one simply had to accept intuitive certainty.

Skeptical arguments stimulated debates about epistemology, as advocates of different philosophical systems saw the need to provide definitive answers to those who questioned the possibility of securing true and certain knowledge of the world. While the imputation of irreligion was often made for rhetorical reasons, the prospect of being censured for presenting claims that ultimately led to skepticism weighed heavily on eighteenth-century philosophers. As we have seen, it was an accusation that was leveled against almost every thinker who attempted to resolve the problem of inter-substantial interaction and to determine the origin of human ideas. Increasingly, however, Enlightenment intellectuals accepted limited skepticism with respect to metaphysical explanations of human cognition, and they acknowledged that probable knowledge was the only realistically attainable goal. This was the same form of knowledge that Carneades, Cicero, and other Academic skeptics had thought they could secure.

CHAPTER EIGHT

A Matter of Debate

Conceptions of Material Substance in the Scientific Revolution

Skepticism and Natural Philosophy in the Age of Enlightenment

The debates about the origin of ideas and the nature of the human soul led many eighteenth-century thinkers to incorporate elements of mitigated skepticism into their epistemological frameworks. The moderation of epistemic ambitions also transformed the ways in which philosophers studied the physical universe. The assumption that all knowledge was probable and based on sense experience implied that the underlying structures of the natural world were not always accessible to the mind. Skeptics pointed to the uncertainty about whether the senses offered an accurate representation of reality. After all, how could one speculate about the properties of matter if one could not know whether objects outside the mind really existed and were actually such as they appeared? It was by accepting the uncertainty of such knowledge, however, that eighteenth-century thinkers began to use the methods of natural philosophy to formulate a new "standard of cognitive values" and a "model of rationality."[1]

The centrality of uncertainty in the investigations of the natural world is not always apparent in the progressive narratives the philosophes constructed about the "century of lights." According to many eighteenth-century depictions of the dramatic improvement in the knowledge of the natural world, the practitioners of natural philosophy and of the physical sciences from the previous century deserved the most credit for this great leap. The set of intellectual transformations identified by historians as the Scientific Revolution provided the greatest evidence to Voltaire, d'Alembert, and their contemporaries that they lived in a time of unprecedented progress in the ability of human reason to understand the surrounding world. The philosophes saw the new methods of natural philosophy, championed by the thinkers of the so-called philosophical revolution, as the founding principles of a new world-view. Indeed, J. B. Shank has convincingly argued that the philosophes "defined Enlightenment by constructing a highly politicized history of modern science as an act of self-justification."[2]

The philosophes offered carefully constructed histories of philosophy in order to legitimize their own intellectual projects. They depicted themselves as the rightful heirs of the so-called heroes of the philosophical revolution, and they established a hierarchy of those to whom they owed their greatest allegiances. Voltaire's *Lettres philosophiques* attempted to promote Locke's epistemology and Newtonian physics, while d'Alembert's "Discours préliminaire" postulated a clear line of philosophical succession. D'Alembert began with Bacon, who "after bursting so many irons . . . was still held back by certain chains that he could not or dared not break." Descartes, "who dared to show intelligent minds how to throw off the yoke of scholasticism," came next. Isaac Newton (1643–1727)—"that great genius," who "gave philosophy a form that apparently it is to keep,"—achieved the triumph of discovering the true laws of nature. Finally, Locke, who "undertook successfully and carried through what Newton had not dared to do" by creating a new metaphysics, topped this list of philosophical heroes.[3]

Despite such triumphalist narratives, natural philosophy was not impervious to skeptical critiques during this period. As we saw chapter 1, the major thinkers of the "philosophical revolution" of the seventeenth century had incorporated certain skeptical claims into their methodologies. Tactical deployments of mitigated skepticism allowed Bacon, Gassendi, and others to attack Aristotelianism and to present their natural philosophical programs as a prudent middle ground between Pyrrhonism and dogmatism. This model of enquiry, generally identified as "experimental philosophy," became increasingly appealing in the eighteenth century, when thinkers found it fashionable to reject the "spirit of system" (*esprit de système*).[4]

The incorporation of a skeptical perspective into theories of natural philosophy notwithstanding, prominent philosophical skeptics articulated genuine critiques about the possibility of attaining knowledge of the surrounding world. Pierre Bayle, most notably in his article on the ancient Greek philosopher Zeno of Elea, suggested that one could not truly prove the reality of extension and motion. Bayle's arguments framed a number of eighteenth-century debates, and they also were reformulated by Saint-Aubin and d'Argens, among others. Furthermore, thinkers from competing philosophical camps deployed certain skeptical claims to demonstrate why opposing theories failed to explain physical phenomena accurately. Although hypotheses about the nature of matter and the structure of the universe appeared more empirically verifiable than abstract theories of mind-body interaction, the competition among various physical theories left much room for uncertainty. As the Aristotelian Scholastics continued to lose hold over a learned world that increasingly looked to new intellectual authorities, representatives of various philosophical schools competed for followers. Each group sought to demonstrate its system's ability to describe the surrounding world in the most coherent, parsimonious, and theologically compliant ways. Seeking to explain the composition of matter and the laws of terrestrial and celestial motion, rival systems of natural philosophy failed to provide accurate and convincing explanations of observable phenomena. While rival schools tried to reveal the inadequacies of their opponents' views, the skeptics used the debates as examples of the inability of the human mind to understand the surrounding world with certainty.

The debates among various schools of natural philosophy and those between the skeptics and their opponents help to explain why the philosophes chose to endorse Lockean empiricism and Newton's theory of gravitation over Cartesian accounts. Locke and Newton provided models that helped to reconcile the skeptical critiques of reason with a progressive view of human knowledge. Locke's epistemology had formulated a program for scientific inquiry that willingly accepted the skeptical proposition that one could know the appearances of things but not their essences. Newton, in turn, rejected the Cartesian premise that scientific knowledge could begin with any a priori truths. He insisted that only the observation of particular phenomena and the organization of those specific observations into coherent generalizations could furnish relatively certain ideas about the universe. Locke's and Newton's admissions of the limits of scientific knowledge provided an epistemic model that informed the philosophes' approach to the study of nature and directly challenged various rationalist systems.

This chapter examines the debates about the essence and nature of matter, and the following one explores the contests between the Cartesian and Newtonian descriptions of the physical universe. Together, these two chapters explain the complex process by which eighteenth-century thinkers came to embrace a form of natural philosophy that claimed to privilege sense experience, observation, and experiment over abstract a priori speculations. Enlightenment natural philosophers accepted a new set of assumptions and methodologies as a result of their attempts to navigate between the extremes of dogmatic rationalism and Pyrrhonian skepticism, on the one hand, and among a wide range of possibilities offered by competing theories about the structure of the physical universe, on the other. The changes in the way thinkers understood the goals and limits of natural philosophy reveal the significant influence of the insights of epistemological skepticism on scientific inquiry. The gradual appropriation of skeptical claims allowed thinkers to criticize certain systems while embracing those that appeared to be more limited in their scope and ambition. Protracted contests over the nature of matter and the theories of planetary motion explain, at least in part, why the French scientific community of the eighteenth century gradually came to accept what Keith Baker has termed "epistemological modesty" and simultaneously rejected the "spirit of system."[5]

Bayle on Extension and Motion

Most scholars who present Pierre Bayle as a rationalist tend to focus on the implications of his skeptical arguments about religion. Antony McKenna and Gianluca Mori have suggested that Bayle deployed Pyrrhonian skepticism as a tactical device to guide his audience toward rationalist, rather than fideist, conclusions.[6] They argue that by showing the dramatic divergence between what had been dictated by reason and what was stated in scripture, Bayle sought to demonstrate the superstitious and irrational nature of Christianity and to persuade his readers to side with reason against the mysteries of revealed religion. Jonathan Israel has gone so far as to assert that Bayle was, "strictly speaking, neither a sceptic nor a 'fideist.'"[7] Israel has emphasized Bayle's so-called *rationalisme militant*, and he has insisted that Bayle "totally rejects skepticism . . . claiming pure reason as the sole criterion of what is true."[8] However, the difficulties that some of Bayle's articles posed for natural philosophy render the interpretation of Bayle as rationalist problematic, to say the least.[9] Indeed, scholars who present Bayle as a rationalist and as a secret atheist tend to focus on his critiques of religious questions, while ignoring the profound challenges he posed to contemporaneous theories of motion, of epistemology, and of cosmology, among others.[10]

As we saw in chapter 7, Bayle's article on Pyrrho questioned the distinction between primary and secondary qualities that had been made popular by several thinkers in the seventeenth century, including Bacon, Galileo, and Locke. Bayle had argued that it was not possible to maintain that primary qualities, such as dimension, motion, and size, actually existed in the objects, while secondary qualities, such as color and taste, were present only in the mind. Both types of qualities were subjects of the mind's perception, and their objective reality could not be guaranteed.[11] The article "Zénon d'Elée" went further by questioning problems concerning the void, infinite divisibility, and motion. Bayle presented Zeno's paradoxes of motion and his objections against the existence of extension, maintaining that they were philosophically difficult, if not impossible, to refute. The problems raised in the article on Zeno touched on the most heated controversies of late-seventeenth- and eighteenth-century natural philosophy: the nature of matter and extension, the existence of a vacuum, and the possibility of motion.

Seventeenth-century philosophers disagreed profoundly about how to explain the composition of material substance. According to Aristotelian metaphysics, matter was inert, incapable of organizing itself. Absent an external organizing principle, it remained disordered. The Aristotelians postulated that all living and immaterial things had a substantial form—a principle that united various accidental properties with the subject's essence. It gave each object or being its individual and universal "whatness" (*quidditas*). Although Thomas Aquinas and other Aristotelians had discussed prime or formless matter as a theoretical concept, they agreed that matter could never have actual existence without a form or organizing principle. The substantial form actualized formless prime matter, giving it real existence.[12]

Cartesian natural philosophy offered an alternative view according to which material substance was defined purely as physical extension.[13] Shape, density, and all other properties of objects were derived not from particular qualitative states—as the Aristotelians had insisted—but only from the arrangement of the objects' constituent parts. Although extended bodies could differ in density and shape according to the motions of these parts, "the earth and the heavens are made of the same matter," because there was "but one kind of matter in the whole universe." Descartes and his disciples sought to construct a mechanical system in which all explanations of natural phenomena could be provided with reference to physical interactions among extended bodies. According to Descartes's analysis in the second part of *Les principes de la philosophie* (1644), space was the same thing as corporeal substance. "The same extension in length, breadth, and depth that constitutes space constitutes body," Descartes argued. A vacuum, or "a space in which there is no substance," could not exist, because it was a self-contradictory notion that was entirely repugnant to reason. What one commonly referred to as an empty space, such as an empty water pitcher, was actually filled with air or another substance that was not immediately apparent to the senses.[14]

The third set of available explanations has been referred to by scholars as "corpuscularianism." These accounts included a broad spectrum of views, relied on different intellectual traditions, and in many cases derived from the ancient atomist theories of Leucippus (fifth century BCE), Democritus (c. 460–c. 370 BCE), and Epicurus. Epicureanism was made especially popular by Lucretius's

(c. 99–c. 55 BCE) *De rerum natura*, which was rediscovered in 1417.[15] The corpuscularian theory posited that all matter was composed of minute, indivisible particles that had distinct shapes and sizes. These corpuscles (or atoms) came together in different combinations and formed various objects and substances. In the seventeenth century, thinkers such as Pierre Gassendi and Robert Boyle attempted to make ancient atomist explanations compatible with Christian theology. The theory remained problematic in both philosophical and theological terms, however. Aristotelian and Cartesian natural philosophers had argued against the atomist hypothesis because it required the existence of a vacuum in which the atoms could move. Both schools insisted that the atomist theory was difficult to sustain because the very notion of a vacuum was a physical and logical impossibility. Furthermore, ancient forms of atomism, as they were described in *De rerum natura*, had denied the existence of a divinely ordered universe. By positing an eternal and chaotic world in which all existing entities came together by pure chance, the atomist hypothesis undermined the most essential demonstrations of the existence of God.[16]

Bayle suggested that Zeno's paradoxes could present more formidable challenges for his contemporaries than they did for the ancient Greeks, because a modern Zenoist could make use of new conceptions of extended matter. He insisted that the possibility of motion presupposed the existence of extension. Consequently, a Zenoist philosopher could easily disprove the former by demonstrating the impossibility of the latter: "It seems to me that those who would like to renew the opinion of Zeno should argue thusly: I. There is no extension; therefore there is no motion." Speaking from the perspective of a Zenoist, Bayle offered a logical demonstration of the impossibility of physical extension by refuting each of the three possibilities for its composition. For him, either extension was composed of mathematical points, or it was composed of atoms, or it was infinitely divisible. The first possibility could be easily ruled out, Bayle maintained, because "several nonentities of extension [*néants d'étendue*] joined together will never make up an extension." Since each individual point occupied no space, no collection of such points, however large, could add up to become an extended object. Likewise, Bayle quickly dismissed the second possibility—that extended substance was made up of "Epicurean atoms, that is to say, extended and indivisible corpuscles"—because every extended entity was necessarily composed of parts and consequently divisible unto infinity.[17]

The third and final possibility for the composition of physical extension, according to Bayle, was that it was infinitely divisible. The hypothesis of infinite divisibility was just as problematic, he insisted, because it was impossible to explain how a finite extended object could be divided into an infinite number of extended parts. Added together, these parts would necessarily constitute an infinitely large object, leading to a self-contradiction. As the hypothesis embraced by Aristotle, Descartes, and "almost all philosophy professors in all the universities for several centuries," it received the greatest attention in this section of the *Dictionnaire*. The *philosophe de Rotterdam* attributed the popularity of this view to the fact that all other alternatives appeared evidently false. "If there are only three ways of explaining a fact," he suggested, "the truth of the third [explanation] necessarily follows from the falsity of the other two."[18] All that the proponents of each theory had to do in order to prove the validity of their hypothesis was demonstrate the impossibility of the other two competing theories. It was by default, and not through any logical or physical demonstration, that the majority of natural philosophers embraced the theory of the infinite divisibility of matter, the skeptic insisted.

Bayle's arguments posed a fundamental challenge to contemporaneous theories of matter and accounts of motion. However, some scholars have insisted that Bayle actually endorsed specific hypotheses in natural philosophy. For example, Todd Ryan has maintained that the *philosophe de Rotterdam* sided with the Cartesian definition of extension and with the hypothesis of infinite divisibility.[19] Ryan quotes Bayle's review of James Darlymple's (1619–95) *Phylosiologia nova experimentalis* (1685) in the *Nouvelles de la République des Lettres*, where Bayle did indeed appear to embrace the hypothesis of infinite divisibility. Bayle maintained that "the hypothesis of infinitely divisible parts, however shrouded it may be by ruinous difficulties, is the least troubling of all."[20] Assuming, of course, that Bayle continued to hold the same views more than a decade later, when he published the *Dictionnaire*, his treatment of the Cartesian hypothesis hardly sounds like a ringing endorsement. The logic in this article, as in "Zénon d'Elée," seems quite similar. Bayle expressed his preference for the theory of infinite divisibility because other available explanations were more problematic. His support thus appears to have been an act of skeptical resignation with regard to accepting the Cartesian explanation of *res extensa*.

Jean Delvolvé, on the other hand, has depicted Bayle as an atomist primarily on the basis of the *Dictionnaire* article "Leucippe."[21] In this article, Bayle adopted a seemingly opposite view from the one he advocated in "Zénon d'Elée." He argued that the atomist hypothesis was difficult to refute. While the Aristotelians and the Cartesians offered strong objections to the atomist hypothesis, Bayle noted, they could "only claim a possible divisibility of all kinds of extension; as for the actual division, however, all sects are obliged to fix a limit to it at some point."[22]

The incompatibility of such interpretations comes from unnecessary attempts to treat Bayle as having held a stable and definitive view on this question. While it is possible to find specific sections in which he seemed to argue in favor of a particular position, it is not difficult to find writings in which such opinions are refuted or contradicted. Bayle's playful expositions of different philosophical opinions allowed him to describe the variety of possible views and to expose the weaknesses of each one.[23] Bayle could thus appear to endorse several contradictory opinions simultaneously, while in fact not fully embracing any of them. Indeed, the only stable line of argument that runs through all of the *Dictionnaire* in general and his discussions of natural philosophy in particular is that of philosophical skepticism. By overlooking the lengths to which Bayle went in order to demonstrate the weakness of human understanding not just in questions of religion but also in natural philosophy, and by refusing to take Bayle's skeptical claims seriously, scholars continue to ask questions that cannot be answered and perpetuate an irresolvable debate about his "real" philosophical views.

In the article on Zeno, not only did Bayle express doubts about the possibility of explaining the nature of extended substance but he questioned the existence of a material universe outside human perception. Having rejected all three possible explanations for the nature of extended substance, Bayle appeared to side with Zeno, claiming that it was "evident that the existence of this extension is impossible and that this extension exists only in the mind."[24] Similarly, he elaborated on the difficulties in explaining the origin of the motion of bodies, concluding the remark by distinguishing between one's belief in motion and extension and one's ability to explain that belief rationally. Bayle confessed that he felt "completely incapable of resolving all the difficulties that have just been presented." Because "the philosophical answers that can be made from them are far from solid," he assented to the "common opinion."[25] Bayle referred to Antoine Arnauld and Pierre Nicole's *L'art de penser*, which had used the paradoxical case of infinite divisibility to demonstrate the limits of rational understanding and to make the mind admit "that there are things that exist even though it is not capable of understanding them."[26]

In remark H in "Zénon d'Elée," Bayle addressed the question of the existence of matter. As in "Pyrrhon," he questioned the reliability of the senses as a basis for proving the existence of bodies. Since the senses deceived the mind about qualities such as shape, magnitude, and color, there was no reason to assume that they could not also deceive the mind about the existence of extension. Bayle summoned Malebranche's claims to dispute Descartes's argument that God would be a deceiver if bodies that presented themselves to the senses did not have an objective reality. This argument required one not only to demonstrate that God existed and was not a deceiver but also to prove that God had actually provided humankind with the assurance that he had created physical objects. Absent such a guarantee, God "would in no way be a deceiver even though no bodies might exist in reality."[27] Indeed, Bayle maintained, there were numerous instances in which the mind made mistakes, and none of these required the creator to engage in active and continued deception. Humanity's fallen nature, not God, was responsible for these errors. As with the problem of infinite divisibility, it was "absolutely necessary to have recourse to faith to be convinced that there are bodies," Bayle concluded.[28]

Another challenge to the possibility of motion came from theories about the nature of space and the existence of a vacuum. Bayle cited the argument of the ancient Greek philosopher Melissus of Samos (fifth century BCE), who had suggested that bodies could only move if there was a vacuum. It was impossible to conceive how one body could change its position within a plenum, because it would have to displace another object first. Since two bodies could not occupy the same space at the same instant, some amount of empty space had to exist in order to accommodate their initial displacement. Consequently, Bayle argued, either one had to admit the existence of a vacuum, as Isaac Newton and Christiaan Huygens (1629–95) had done, or one had to agree that motion was impossible. Aristotelian and Cartesian philosophers had argued that "nature abhorred a vacuum" and insisted that all empty space necessarily had to be occupied by extended bodies. The Cartesians maintained that the simultaneous displacement of different bodies made motion in a plenum possible.[29] Newton and Huygens, on the other hand, had insisted that "to deny the vacuum would be to deny a completely evident fact," according to Bayle's account.[30] As we will see in chapter 9, this disagreement also resulted in dramatically different conceptions of the cosmos and explanations of planetary motion.

Bayle admitted that although Newton's mathematical calculations appeared to demonstrate the existence of a vacuum, it nevertheless remained a concept "contrary to the most evident notions we have in our understanding." To posit the possibility of a vacuum was to admit "the existence of something about which we have no concept and that is repugnant to our clearest and most distinct ideas." Although Newton had insisted that a vacuum was absolutely necessary to account for the motions of the celestial bodies, Bayle noted, neither he nor Locke could adequately explain its properties. Defining it as "space distinct from bodes" and as an "immobile, indivisible, and penetrable extension," Bayle asked whether it was "a substance or a mode" and whether it was "created or uncreated."[31] The article "Leucippe" similarly addressed this problem, claiming that the new supporters of the existence of a vacuum could neither "deny that the arguments of the Cartesians against space being nothing are very strong" nor maintain that "space is nothing and that it is pure privation."[32]

The Huguenot skeptic referred to several other contemporaries who had offered theories about the possibility of a vacuum. The major opposition to the possibility of a void arose primarily on metaphysical grounds. A space that was empty of all substances and that had no discernible properties appeared to be a problematic notion. The Aristotelian Scholastics, for example, had defined space as a "privation of body" and insisted that, "properly speaking, the vacuum is nothing." The Dutch mathematician and physicist Nicolaas Hartsoeker (1656–1725) suggested that a vacuum could not exist because it was "completely contradictory to conceive of a pure nonentity [*un rien tout pur*] having properties that can only belong to something real."[33] However, Bayle noted, if one reasoned in the manner of the Cartesians and denied the possibility of a vacuum, then one had to explain how bodies came to be distinct from each other in a plenum.[34]

According to Bayle's account, the atomist Pierre Gassendi, who had defended the existence of a vacuum, had conjectured that the "extension of space is among beings that are neither corporeal nor spiritual." Finally, John Locke, although he was unable to define a vacuum, had maintained that it was a "positive being," meaning that it had attributes such as length, breadth, and depth.[35] Bayle sought to portray Locke as a skeptical ally who did not "believe that we know either what extension is or what a substance is." He referred to Locke's rhetorical questions about the proper definitions of *space, extension,* and *substance* and noted that the English philosopher found "himself answering the questions of Cartesians only by questions that he believes to be more obscure and more confusing than theirs." According to Bayle's assessment, the apparent advances in mathematics had actually strengthened the theoretical basis of Zeno's arguments against motion by showing that it was impossible in a plenum:

> The demonstrations of our new mathematicians—that there is a vacuum—have made them recognize that motion in a plenum is not something that can be understood. Consequently, they have accepted the supposition of a vacuum. It is not that they did not find it surrounded by several inconceivable and incomprehensible difficulties, but having to choose between two incomprehensible systems, they picked the one that repelled them the least. They chose to be content with mechanics rather than with metaphysics, and they even neglected the physical difficulties that came their way.[36]

As with the definition of substance, one had to choose from among seemingly inadequate and problematic explanations.

New mathematical theories, Bayle contended, appeared to expand the arsenal of Pyrrhonian arguments. On the one hand, the mind seemed to hold clear and distinct ideas regarding the impenetrability and divisibility of bodies that formed "the basis of mathematics." On the other hand, the mathematical demonstrations of the existence of a vacuum, which defined it as an "indivisible and penetrable extension . . . that has three dimensions, that is immobile, and that allows other dimensions to pass and repass through it," rendered all intuitive ideas about extension misleading.[37] Reason thus found itself lost in the labyrinth of its own making, unable to find its way out of the problems it had constructed.

In discussing potential refutations of Zeno's paradoxes, Bayle referred to the example of Diogenes the Cynic, who had stood up and walked across the room to disprove Zeno's paradox of motion. While witty, Diogenes's response had failed to explain how motion was theoretically possible. Bayle insisted that while no one, including Sextus Empiricus and Zeno, would reject the fact that bodies appeared to move through space, it seemed impossible to provide a philosophically adequate account of this phenomenon. The testimony of the senses clashed with the dictates of reason to produce uncertainty.[38] At each point in the article, Bayle stressed the arbitrary nature of the hypotheses concerning the composition of extended substances, the possibility of motion, and the existence of a vacuum. The choice among rival explanations, each of which posed as many difficulties as it appeared to resolve, ultimately led to the recognition of the "incomprehensibility of all things."[39]

The articles "Zénon d'Elée" and "Pyrrhon" pose serious problems for interpretations of Bayle that present him as a rationalist who used skepticism to subvert theological claims and indeed skepticism itself. If, as Israel suggests, the *philosophe de Rotterdam* was an ultra-rationalist, then why would he have subjected the nature of extension, the possibility of motion, and the existence of the physical world to the same scrutiny that he had applied to the doctrine of predestination and to the problem of evil? Human reason, for Bayle, not only failed to grasp the doctrines Christianity; it also appeared powerless in understanding the natural world. Presented with seemingly irresolvable paradoxes and incomprehensible difficulties, all the mind could do was acknowledge its own limitations and accept the existence of the external world on faith alone. Bayle's *Dictionnaire* marshaled an arsenal of claims concerning different theories of natural philosophy. By summarizing the views of ancient and modern thinkers without clearly endorsing any particular proposition, it enabled eighteenth-century authors to pick and choose examples that favored their cause. It also raised fundamental doubts about the ability to speculate about the underlying nature of the physical world.

Enlightenment Conceptions of Material Substance

Bayle's skeptical arguments about the nature and the divisibility of matter would have great resonance throughout the first half of the eighteenth century, as thinkers continued to debate these issues and as the competition between the Cartesian and the various atomist explanations escalated. The issues at stake were not only the physical composition of material substance but also the way in which mathematics and metaphysics were to be deployed in resolving these fundamental questions. While there were numerous episodes involving eighteenth-century debates about the nature and the infinite divisibility of matter, we will focus on those that took place at the height of the Pyrrhonian crisis. These disputes shed light on how the understanding of material substance shaped views about the powers and limits of human reason and contributed to the emergence of mitigated skepticism in natural philosophy.

The debates about material substance took place not only in highly learned treatises and at the meetings of scientific academies but on the pages of the popular learned journals as well. In September 1733, the editors of the *Mercure de France* printed a letter that posed an open-ended question about motion and the nature of matter.[40] The author noted that God's infinite power, as well as the nature of motion, allowed for the theoretical possibility that bodies could move at an infinitely rapid velocity. He noted that according to Bernard le Bovier de Fontenelle's *Eléments de la géométrie de l'infini* (1727), "all magnitude that was capable of being increased to infinity could be supposed as [actually] increased to infinity."[41] Even if one agreed with Louis-Bertrand Castel's distinction between geometrical and physical infinity, the letter insisted, it followed that a person could be transported from Paris to Constantinople and back instantaneously, so that the person would be in both places at the same time. Since a body would thus find itself in multiple places at the exact same moment, without being in any kind of intermediate state between them, one could not claim that extension was the essence of matter, as Descartes and the Cartesians had insisted. This body "could be in a state of penetrability, in a state of indivisibility," and "its essence would no longer consist in having parts; it would be whole everywhere and whole in each part [*tout dans le tout, et tout dans chaque partie*]." Having shown that none of these properties could be the essence of matter, the author asked readers to provide their own definitions of material substance.[42]

The marquis de Saint-Aubin, whose *Traité de l'opinion* offered a historical overview of the views and errors of humankind, was the first to attempt a response, and he became involved in a series of debates about this question.[43] He insisted that the ambitions of the human mind to reach beyond its limits pushed it away from the path to the truth and led it to devise problems that it could not solve. These included the essence of matter, the problem of infinite divisibility, and the very notion of infinity. Saint-Aubin noted that the entire problem rested on the misapplication of divine omnipotence to the laws of nature. He maintained that if the supposition that a body could be in several places simultaneously were true, "we would be forced not only to abandon physics . . . but also to renounce the faculty of reasoning." The author of the problem failed to account for the infinite divisibility of time, according to Saint-Aubin. Consequently, even if one allowed for the infinitely rapid velocity with which a person moved between Paris and Constantinople, that person would be present in the two places successively, at different moments, and never in both simultaneously. In the same way, a piece of burning coal that was rapidly moving in a circular motion merely appeared to be in all of the circle at the same time, while actually being at a different point at each particular instance. Our vision deceived us concerning the actual situation of this object.[44]

Saint-Aubin also disputed Fontenelle's notion of infinity and suggested that it was contradictory. He argued that "a magnitude that is capable of increase to infinity cannot be supposed to be actually increased to infinity precisely because it is potentially capable of this augmentation." Something that could always become bigger could not be imagined as actually reaching any possible limit of magnitude. In other words, "something that is inexhaustible could not be supposed to be exhausted." If the potential were actualized, a contradiction would follow. Saint-Aubin thus insisted that the geometrical notion of infinity remained an incomprehensible "labyrinth of the human mind" and that geometry was "filled with conclusions that could not be reconciled with natural notions." Since geometry was merely "a product of the human mind," it could not surpass the laws of nature but had to be formed in accordance with them.[45] Because geometricians often failed to recognize this fact, Saint-Aubin maintained, they frequently articulated erroneous and contradictory notions, such as the concepts of different orders of infinity and the infinite divisibility of finite objects. He concluded by noting that "the infinitely big and the infinitely small, both in geometry and in physics, were the products of reason" and did not actually exist in nature.[46] Saint-Aubin's examination did not just place clear limitations on the ability of human understanding to resolve the apparent contradictions posed by notions of infinity. It also questioned the epistemic status of geometry, which had been considered by many of his contemporaries as the most certain of all the disciplines. By showing that geometrical principles did not always correspond to phenomena observed in the natural world, Saint-Aubin undermined the discipline's revered status.

The abbé François Cartaud de la Vilate's (1700–1737) *Pensées critiques sur les mathématiques* (1733) went further in its attack on mathematics. Cartaud de la Vilate, who has been identified as a Pyrrhonian and who is best known for his *Essai critique et philosophique sur le gout* (1736), deployed skeptical arguments to dispute the degree of certainty mathematical investigations could attain.[47] He specifically rallied against the "idolatry" with which his contemporaries seemed to revere the discipline, and he denounced the "tyrannical" power of geometricians, who turned people into "slaves of their authority" without allowing anyone to examine the principles of mathematics. Modern geometricians, much like the pagan idolaters of antiquity, refused to seek the foundations of their beliefs. Cartaud de la Vilate also drew parallels between the unfounded assumptions of mathematicians, on the one hand, and the baseless superstition of those who believed in astrology and thought that the movements of the celestial bodies could have any effect on human behaviors, on the other. Finally, he compared mathematicians to members of dogmatic philosophical sects and religious cults, because both renounced all uncertainty and refused to have their principles evaluated by the "tribunal" of reason. Instead, geometricians presented mathematical truths as axioms or articles of faith, refusing to acknowledge that there were any uncertainties in their discipline.[48] The accusation of blind submission to authority was a common trope in the discourses of seventeenth-century natural philosophy, and Cartaud de la Vilate turned this rhetoric against the most revered discipline of the "philosophical revolution."

In order to arrive at the knowledge of true and certain principles, it was vital to subject all questions to thorough examination and to engage the strongest counterarguments, Cartaud de la Vilate insisted. One could not approach mathematics in the same way that one considered religious truths. One continued to believe in Christianity despite the incomprehensibility of its mysteries because faith was "an all-devouring fire that consumes all worries of reason" in religious matters. However, in questions that were related to the natural world, it was important to "consult the voice of examination [*la voix de l'examen*]" and to erect difficulties in order to obtain rational certainty. He referred to Bayle in suggesting that mathematics would not stand up to skeptical critiques, and he praised Montaigne, Bacon, Descartes, and Malebranche for clearing "the way to the truth by avoiding the one that led to error." Cartaud noted that geometricians were unwilling to seek the foundations of their certainty, they undertook shallow investigations, and they were content to compose "thousands of volumes of elementary geometry" without engaging with their skeptical critics. Similarly, Scholastic theologians endlessly discussed the nature of the mysteries and the sacraments and ignored the claims of deists and Socinians, who posed real difficulties for the rational foundations of the faith. Cartaud de la Vilate argued that the main goal of mathematics was to "guide us to the truth by the surest and most infallible ways" and to "reassure our reason" against the claims of the skeptics. The geometricians and the skeptics would mutually benefit from productive discussions, he claimed. While the former would arrive at more certain truths by adopting a circumspect and critical attitude, the latter would do well to attempt to find the truth rather than doubting all things.[49]

Cartaud de la Vilate began his skeptical critique by observing that geometricians erroneously assumed that the relations and figures they described corresponded to real objects in the external world. In order to be useful and true, ideas about geometrical relations needed to "inform us about the relations between real figures, that is to say, those that exist independently of our mind." Indeed, Cartaud de la Vilate insisted, geometrical speculations were useless if they remained idealized and divorced from metaphysical accounts of material and thinking substances. He proclaimed that the practitioners of geometry purposely sidestepped these difficulties in order to avoid being embarrassed by errors and paradoxes, and he insisted that the study of metaphysics necessarily had to precede and serve as the basis for the study of mathematics. Without an understanding of the nature of the external world, geometrical demonstrations were solipsistic, and they failed to refute the Pyrrhonians. Mathematical calculations in astronomy could predict the position of the celestial bodies with great accuracy, but they could not convince a Pyrrhonian who doubted the existence of the material world and dismissed such predictions and calculations as elaborately constructed fictions. Internal consistency did not guarantee the objective reality of these relations. Indeed, Cartaud proclaimed, the "true nature of geometry is less in raising us to high certainty and more in providing justification to our imagination."[50]

Cartaud also questioned the undisputed internal coherence of geometry and tried to demonstrate the variety of apparent contradictions and uncertainties that plagued the discipline. The most obvious example, for Cartaud, involved the disputes about the nature of infinitely large objects and about the infinite divisibility of matter. He cited Saint-Aubin's discussion of the topic in the *Traité de l'opinion* as an example, claiming that "ideas of infinity are pure suppositions without reality" despite serving as the basis of numerous geometrical principles. Cartaud de la Vilate invoked the authority of Fontenelle, who, despite having authored a work on infinity, remarked on the incomprehensibility of this concept to the human mind. He also referred to Bayle's article "Zénon" in summarizing the problems of infinite divisibility. Cartaud went on to demonstrate the uncertainty of several mathematical propositions, including those that dealt with parallel and perpendicular lines, measurements of the circumference of circles, and trigonometric calculations. The ignorance of these central issues left people in the dark about the nature of extension and about the possibility of motion, he concluded.[51]

Cartaud de la Vilate undermined the existence of any undisputed mathematical certainty by citing Bayle's article "Zénon," in which Bayle had observed the great number of disagreements among mathematicians. Cartaud de la Vilate also invoked passages from Huet, Pascal, and La Mothe Le Vayer, among others, who had made similar observations. Furthermore, he described contemporaneous debates among the members of the Académie royale des sciences about the geometry of infinitesimals to demonstrate the disagreement among mathematicians about basic principles.[52] Saint-Aubin's and Cartaud de la Vilate's observations about the uncertainty of mathematics took place in the context of intense disputes between Fontenelle and Louis-Bertrand Castel, among others.[53] The lack of unanimity on fundamental issues could "shake the foundations of geometry" and provide sufficient reasons to doubt the absolute certainty of mathematical principles. By siding with the skeptics, Cartaud purported to urge humility and introspection on the part of mathematicians.[54]

The critiques of mathematical certainty in the texts of Saint-Aubin and Cartaud de la Vilate reveal the extent of Bayle's influence on debates in natural philosophy. The paradoxes presented in the *Dictionnaire* continued to generate an arsenal of skeptical arguments. As an outspoken supporter of Locke's epistemology, d'Argens addressed the uncertainties of human knowledge in logic, metaphysics, and history, and he included an extended section on physics in *La philosophie du bon-sens*. D'Argens admitted a certain amount of progress in experimental physics, particularly with respect to the understanding of observable effects, but he maintained that knowledge of first principles remained hidden from view. The underlying composition of material substance, for example, continued to be a contested issue. While the Cartesians and the Gassendist atomists offered rival hypotheses to explain the underlying causes of natural phenomena, the debate appeared irresolvable. Did it really matter, d'Argens asked rhetorically, whether a vacuum existed or subtle matter occupied all of space? Nature allowed human-kind to learn only those things that were useful and necessary. D'Argens cited book 4 of Locke's *Essay Concerning Human Understanding*, in which the English philosopher had highlighted the imperfect knowledge of bodies that the mind possessed owing to the limitations of the senses.[55]

D'Argens ended with chapters on the nature of space, the existence of a vac-uum, and the essence of matter. He continued to contrast the Cartesian view that extension was the essence of material substance with the Gassendist hy-pothesis that associated matter with solidity and impenetrability. D'Argens pro-claimed the atomist view to be the more probable explanation. First, the choice of extension as the essence of matter seemed somewhat arbitrary; it was merely one of many attributes of material substance, and the essences of things were generally unknowable. Second, the Cartesian rejection of a vacuum forced these philosophers into the "absurd necessity of admitting infinite matter." Third, as Locke had argued, any outright denial of the existence of a vacuum impinged on God's omnipotence by suggesting that he could not annihilate material sub-stance to create space devoid of matter if he so desired. Fourth, not only was a vacuum possible because of divine omnipotence, d'Argens argued in the manner of Bayle's Zeno, but it was necessary to allow for the free movement of bodies, which would not be possible in a plenum.[56]

D'Argens also sided with Gassendi against Descartes on the existence of atoms and the question of infinite divisibility. He repeated Bayle's reasoning that it seemed difficult and indeed "absurd . . . to suppose that a thing bounded and lim-ited on every side could have infinite parts." The constant motion of atoms that joined or came apart led to the formation and destruction of various bodies and helped to explain the "perpetual change observed in all things." At the same time, the senses failed to perceive the atoms, and their existence was not empirically verifiable.[57]

Although d'Argens used many of Bayle's skeptical arguments, he seemed more willing to take sides in debates concerning natural philosophy, or at least to admit that some explanations appeared to be more probable than others. He de-clared that he was "not significantly more persuaded by the opinion of the Gas-sendists than by that of the Cartesians," because "something probable is not the same thing as something evident."[58] He concluded with a statement about the possibility of attaining true and certain knowledge in natural philosophy:

Here are the opinions of philosophers on the first principles of natural philosophy. . . . You see the uncertainty of their reasoning, for what evident consequence can they draw from such uncertain principles? . . . True natural philosophy is nothing more than experimental knowledge that reveals to us a great many secrets, whose first operations it is nevertheless impossible to know [because we] do not have . . . any idea of the way the active parts or the first movers of matter operate. Thus, Descartes explains an experiment by means of subtle matter; Gassendi by that of atoms and a vacuum; Newton by that of attraction; and so on. But why is it important to know precisely how the first principles operate, when we know that the manner of the operating certainly produces the effects that we seek and from which we derive all the advantages that we need? God, in concealing the first operations of nature from us, . . . has left us with experimental knowledge that is sufficient for our needs and that is accessible to those who have the curiosity and patience to apply themselves to it with diligence.[59]

While d'Argens echoed Bayle's skepticism with regard to the ultimate unknowability of the underlying principles of nature, he insisted that such knowledge was irrelevant. Contrasting useful knowledge of observable effects with the highly speculative hypotheses about first principles, d'Argens seemed to endorse the attitude of mitigated skepticism.

Voltaire, in his *Lettres philosophiques*, had already given a similar assessment about the ultimate mysteries surrounding the composition of matter in the "Lettre sur Locke." Voltaire claimed to be "absolutely ignorant" about what matter was and insisted that he could only "guess imperfectly some properties of it."[60] In *La métaphysique de Neuton* (1740), he similarly decried ambitious speculations about the essences of matter and praised the "modest" opinion of Newton, who "limited himself to believing that the elements of matter are matter, that is to say, extended and impenetrable substance, whose intimate nature man's understanding cannot penetrate."[61]

A much more extensive exposition of Voltaire's views on the nature of matter appeared in his *Éléments de la philosophie de Neuton* (1738). The text sought to continue the process, started by the *Lettres philosophiques*, of introducing French readers to Newtonian natural philosophy and making Newton's ideas accessible to a wide learned public.[62] Much like d'Argens, Voltaire reasoned in favor of the atomist hypothesis and against the infinite divisibility of matter. He argued that "if matter could be physically divided *ad infinitum* . . . there would be nothing but pores and no matter." Consequently, it "was not in reality physically divisible to infinity," which demonstrated the necessary existence of "indivisible atoms."[63]

In chapter 17 of the *Éléments de la philosophie de Neuton*, Voltaire likewise speculated in favor of the possibility of a vacuum, siding with Locke and d'Argens. He defined it as "space" or "the place of bodies" that was "extended in length, breadth, and depth." It was impossible to form an image of "incorporeal space," Voltaire argued, but it was possible to conceive of it mentally and to demonstrate "the impossibility of a plentitude and the necessity of the void." Voltaire contested the Cartesian definition of matter as extension, insisting that "all matter is extended, but all extension is not matter." By claiming that "matter and extension [were] the same thing," the Cartesian proposition inevitably implied that matter was infinite, although Descartes himself had defined the boundaries of physical extension as "indefinite." Without a vacuum, Voltaire noted, one could not possibly "conceive any limits to extension." Such a consequence rendered the existence and the nature of God problematic: if matter were infinitely extended, then one would have to conclude that God was material. "Space exists of necessity, because God necessarily exists," Voltaire insisted, but matter was a contingent and created being that "cannot be infinite."[64] In *La métaphysique de Neuton*, Voltaire reiterated the problem with the Cartesian hypothesis of the plenum, claiming that it invariably led one to conclude that matter was infinitely extended, that it was eternal and "existed by itself by absolute necessity," and that it was therefore God himself. This was, of course, Spinoza's conclusion in the *Ethics* (1677).[65] Voltaire, like Bayle, pointed to the fact that such atheist (or pantheist) conclusions necessarily followed from the Cartesian view of material substance and its properties.[66]

The nature of physical bodies remained a central issue of debate for natural philosophers of the eighteenth century, although most of the philosophes sided with Locke's and Newton's conceptions of material substance. The *Encyclopédie*'s "Discours préliminaire" offered an extended discussion of the properties of material bodies. D'Alembert identified "impenetrability" as "the principal property by which we distinguish between bodies and the indefinite portions of space in which we conceive them as being placed." Although the mind perceived other properties of bodies, impenetrability was the most fundamental one, because bodies could "act only insofar as they are impenetrable." One's sensations led one to believe that space was "a place occupied by bodies" and that it was "penetrable and immobile." D'Alembert disputed the Cartesian definition of matter as extension, suggesting that there were "two sorts of extension, one being impenetrable and the other constituting the place occupied by bodies." Consequently, bodies could be defined in the most general sense as "shaped and extended parts of space." D'Alembert went on to claim that "extension in which we did not distinguish between shaped parts would be a distant and obscure image in which everything would elude us because we would not be able to discern anything clearly."[67]

The article "Corps" (1754), also penned by d'Alembert, enumerated the different ways in which philosophers had conceived of physical bodies. The Aristotelians defined body as a composite of matter and form. The Cartesians classified it as "a certain part of extension." The Newtonians saw it as "a composite of hard, solid, heavy, impenetrable, and mobile particles" that were arranged in a particular way. The author did not explicitly endorse one of these three theories, although he devoted a significant part of the discussion to the Newtonian view of atoms.[68] The article "Matière" (1765), also by d'Alembert, gave a longer exposition on the nature of matter. D'Alembert explained that the Cartesians had designated "extension as the essence of matter" because "it is conceived before all other [properties] and because it is [a property] without which one could not conceive any other." He contrasted the Cartesian theory with Newton's atomist hypothesis, according to which all bodies, including light and fluids, "appeared composed of hard parts, such that hardness could be regarded as a property of all matter," no less essential to it than impenetrability.[69] The article "Étendue" (1756), written by Philibert Guéneau de Montbeillard (1720–85), questioned the definition of extension as the essence of matter. Claiming that the word *essence* was itself equivocal, the author argued that extension was not more essential than its other properties, although the idea of matter would be "incomplete" without taking extension into account.[70]

The articles "Divisibilité" (1754), written by d'Alembert (with contributions from Formey), and "Étendue" disputed the Cartesian hypothesis of infinite divisibility. Appearing to side with the Epicureans and against the Aristotelians and Cartesians, d'Alembert summarized the atomist position as follows: "Their strongest argument is that from the divisibility of all bodies or of all the parts of a body, even after all the divisions had been made, it follows that the smallest corpuscles are divisible to infinity, which according to them is an absurdity, because a body can only be divided into the actual parts of which it is composed. To suppose . . . infinite parts in the smallest body is to suppose an infinite extension." In effect, the article repeated the objection against infinite divisibility that had been raised earlier in Bayle's *Dictionnaire*. D'Alembert turned to the distinction the atomists had made between the "divisibility of physical quantities" and the "divisibility of mathematical" ones. While mathematical dimensions could be increased or diminished to infinity, the same did not hold for physical quantities.[71] In describing extension, Guéneau claimed that if one conceived of extension in a purely abstract fashion, one could suggest that it was divisible to infinity because one could always find numerical values to represent increasingly smaller parts of matter. However, when it came to actual physical extension, "which we knew through sense perception," it was "evident" that it was "not divisible to infinity, because after a certain number of divisions the phenomenon of extension vanished," being no longer perceptible to the organs of sense.[72]

Despite implicit endorsements of atomism and explicit condemnations of the Cartesian view of physical extension, the editors of the *Encyclopédie* retained a somewhat skeptical attitude about the ability of the mind to understand the essential properties of matter.[73] D'Alembert concluded the article "Corps" by stating that experience and observations led to the conclusion that "we do not, in effect, know the nature of bodies." If natural philosophers had some familiarity with the essence of bodies, they would be able to predict "a great number of effects that bodies that act on one another must produce." Since they could not accurately predict these effects, it was necessary to rely on experiments and observations. In closing, d'Alembert made another jab at the Cartesians:

> Have those philosophers who believe that they know the nature of bodies ever been able to predict, by relying solely on the reflections that have been made concerning bodies, at least one of the effects that bodies produce when acting upon one another? Even if one agrees with them that the nature of bodies consists in extension, they will not have advanced much, because we cannot deduce anything from this and we cannot foresee anything that happens in bodies; thus we must conduct our research by relying on experiments, as if we knew nothing about the nature of bodies.[74]

Thus, even if the Cartesians were correct in their definition of material substance, their assumptions provided little useful information. A priori speculations about the true essences of physical objects still needed to be confirmed through further study and observation, d'Alembert insisted. The philosophes' tendency to forgo metaphysical investigations into the essences or underlying structures of material substance mirrored their dismissal of speculations about the nature of the soul. Such questions needed to be either bracketed off or resolved empirically through observation. As we will see in the next chapter, many Enlightenment thinkers developed a very similar attitude concerning the structure of the cosmos and the nature of planetary motion.

CHAPTER NINE

War of the Worlds

Cartesian Vortices and Newtonian Gravitation in Eighteenth-Century Astronomy

---

Rival Explanations of Planetary Motions

In addition to debating about the nature of material substance, eighteenth-century thinkers engaged in ever more sophisticated speculations about the composition of the universe. Nicolaus Copernicus's (1473–1543) *De revolutionibus orbium coelestium* (1543) had unsettled a number of assumptions about the structure of the created world by departing from the closed, geocentric conception of the universe. The heliocentric system made the earth one of the many planets traveling in spheres around the sun. Copernicus had defined the outermost eighth sphere of his system as infinite, which meant not only that the universe now appeared to have no perceptible physical limits but that there were a great number of ways to account for its structure beyond the limits of the solar system. The growing acceptance of heliocentrism in the seventeenth century resulted in the gradual reconceptualization of the cosmos. Natural philosophers such as Tycho Brahe (1546–1601), Johannes Kepler (1571–1630), Galileo Galilei (1564–1642), Descartes, Newton, and many others formulated new hypothetical depictions of the universe.[1]

The plurality of hypothetical world systems eventually gave way to a two-way competition between Cartesian and Newtonian accounts during the first half of the eighteenth century. Voltaire's *Lettres philosophiques* captured the intensity of this philosophical and national rivalry: "In Paris one sees a universe composed of vortices of subtle matter; in London one sees nothing like this. Among us it is the pressure of the moon that causes the flow of the seas; among the English it is the sea that gravitates toward the moon. . . . According to your Cartesians, all happens by impulsion, which one hardly comprehends; according to Mr. Newton, it is by attraction, whose cause we do not know any better."[2] As J. B. Shank has masterfully shown, Voltaire's account of the national differences in the views of natural philosophy contributed toward the philosophe's goal of fashioning himself as an outsider to the Parisian intellectual circles. Voltaire certainly exaggerated the notion that everyone in France was a Cartesian, although it was true that a number of prominent members of the Académie royale des sciences, including Bernard de Fontenelle and Jean-Jacques d'Ortous de Mairan (1678–1771), did endorse Cartesian cosmology.[3]

The disputes between the Cartesians and the Newtonians revealed dramatic ontological and epistemological rifts in late-seventeenth- and early-eighteenth-century natural philosophy. The two rival explanations of the universe disagreed about the physical makeup of the cosmos, the causes of the circular motion of the celestial bodies, and the existence of the vacuum, among a number of other issues. The divergence between Newtonians' and Cartesians' explanations derived from contrasting epistemological approaches to the study of the natural world and from conflicting assumptions about the purposes of scientific enquiry. Their accounts offered two alternative conceptions of certainty, and they relied on different types of evidence and explanations. The evolution of the debates between the supporters of these systems not only helps to explain why Newton's theory of attraction prevailed over Descartes's fluid vortices; it also sheds light on the process by which a methodological and mitigated skepticism emerged as the prevalent attitude in natural philosophy by the middle of the eighteenth century.

At the most basic level, the difference between Descartes's and Newton's accounts resulted from differing explanatory mechanisms. Descartes offered an extensive account of the physical universe in the third part of *Les principes de la philosophie*. Although he agreed with aspects of Copernicus's, Kepler's, and Galileo's theories that removed the earth from the center of the universe, his views differed from previous conceptions in several significant ways. He posited a cosmos with an indefinite number of solar systems. The sun of our solar system was just one of many fixed stars, and the earth was just one of numerous planets in an indefinitely large universe. One could no longer speak of a heliocentric universe, since there was no single center.

The Cartesian cosmos was composed entirely of matter in motion. Although Descartes conceived of all matter in the universe as being identical and homogenous, he divided it into three categories of varying sizes and forms in the posthumously published *Le monde* (1664).[4] The first of these, which he called "the element of fire," was "the most subtle and penetrating fluid," whose particles did not have "any determinate size or shape." These particles, which were in a state of constant and rapid motion, collided with one another and with other bodies to produce heat and light. They were so small that there was "never a passage so narrow . . . where parts of this element did not penetrate . . . and fill precisely." Descartes called his second type of matter "the element of air." It was "a very subtle fluid" without a fixed shape, and it was often intermixed with the first type of element. Finally, Descartes judged the element of earth to be "much larger and to move much less swiftly" than the other two elements.[5] The difference in the magnitudes of the elements was based on the velocity at which their constituent parts moved.[6]

Descartes hypothesized that in creating the universe, God had divided all matter into equal parts and, using an equal force, put these parts into motion in two different directions: each celestial body moved around its own axis, and several such bodies revolved together around a common fixed star or sun. The sun resembled "fire in its motion," leading us to believe that it was "composed of a very fluid matter, whose parts were so extremely agitated that they carried the surrounding parts of the heaven along with them." Like other fixed stars, the sun did not "move from one place in the heaven to another." Rather, its parts moved in relation to the others.[7] The rapid rotation of the sun at the center of our solar system created a centrifugal force that caused the fluid matter to rotate around it in a circular motion.

The second major difference between Descartes's theory and all other accounts was in the way he explained the mechanics of the planetary motions. Since the Cartesian system did not allow for a vacuum, Descartes insisted that the spaces between the different celestial bodies were filled by a liquid—that is, the second element in his classification. Set in motion by the movements of the fixed stars, these fluid heavens "necessarily have to carry with them all the bodies they contain."[8] The planets and other celestial bodies thus swam in a series of interlocking fluid vortices (*tourbillons*) that rotated around the fixed stars.[9] This hypothesis not only helped to solve the problem of a vacuum but allowed Descartes to offer a mechanical explanation of planetary and local terrestrial motion. By exerting pressure toward the center, the revolving fluid matter kept the planets in their orbits around the sun and also pushed the heavy bodies that were circulating around the earth toward its center. For Descartes, weight, or gravity (*pesanteur*), was not an intrinsic quality of bodies but an effect produced by fluid dynamics. If the space surrounding the earth were indeed a vacuum, then the natural tendency of objects would be to float away.[10] By postulating a fluid medium that filled space, Descartes was able to offer an account that involved direct contact between the fluid matter and the planets and that did not postulate action at a distance.[11]

Although Descartes claimed that general metaphysical principles had to be established by reason, he also noted that particular effects had to be observed. "The power of nature is so ample and so vast," he observed in the *Discours de la méthode* (1637), and "its principles are so simple and so general," that it could operate through many different possible effects. In order to determine the specific effects and their causes, one had to have recourse to experiments.[12] In *Les principes de la philosophie*, he similarly argued that although we can know that all of the universe is composed of the same divisible matter, we cannot deduce the particular movements of individual bodies. Because God, in his omnipotence, could have organized nature "in an infinity of different ways, it is by experience alone, and not by the force of reasoning, that one can know which of all these ways he chose."[13] General metaphysical principles were established a priori, but particular effects had to be observed and verified. While reason allowed human beings to formulate hypotheses about natural phenomena by establishing the basic axioms, particular relations between objects had to be confirmed by experiments. Such a framework applied especially to the study of natural philosophy, which, in Descartes's view, concerned itself with particular mechanical laws. Thus, in physics, astronomy, optics, and other disciplines, one needed experiments to confirm hypotheses and to obtain knowledge of particular relations.[14]

The foundation for Descartes's conception of natural philosophy in *Le monde* rested on the assumption that the world could be entirely different from the way we perceived it. It was a common misconception, Descartes reasoned, that "the ideas that are the objects of our thought are entirely like the objects from which they proceed."[15] Consequently, the senses were not necessarily the most reliable means for understanding the surrounding world. There were all kinds of imperceptible phenomena that, in reality, explained a variety of effects that the mind perceived. Descartes used the example of fire to show that light and heat were produced by the rapid motion of miniscule particles of matter, a process that differed quite significantly from what the senses appeared to reveal. Similarly, he argued that sense experience led us to believe that there was empty space around us even though we were actually surrounded by air.[16] In order to secure clear and distinct ideas about the nature of the surrounding world, one had to formulate hypotheses and then verify them.[17]

While it seems true, as Stephen Gaukroger has insisted, that Descartes was not intending to advance a skeptical argument, his claim did, nevertheless, have skeptical implications.[18] By suggesting that the world was not at all as it appeared, Descartes followed a classic Pyrrhonian line of reasoning concerning the unreliability of the senses. Unlike the skeptics, of course, he thought that their defectiveness could be compensated by the proper application of the powers of human reason. By declaring sense experience to be an unreliable tool for explaining natural phenomena, Descartes privileged an a priori theoretical framework over an empiricist one.

Isaac Newton's *Philosophiae naturalis principia mathematica* (1687) relied on a different epistemological approach and consequently offered an alternative explanation of celestial and terrestrial motion. While Descartes posited a universe of uniform matter in a constant state of motion, Newton began with a different set of assumptions. His approach was based on the combination of the empirical observations of planetary motions with calculations that sought to describe the observed phenomena in terms of mathematical relationships. Newton's model posited celestial bodies as mass points that had no dimensions and that moved in a vacuum under the influence of external forces.[19] According to Newton's first law of motion, stated in book 1, "every body preserves in its state of rest, or of uniform motion in a right line, unless it is compelled to change that state by forces impress'd thereon."[20] The apparent movement of the planets in elliptical orbits led Newton to conclude that there existed a centripetal force "by which bodies are drawn or impelled, or any way tend, towards a point as to a centre." This force caused the planets to revolve around the sun rather than continuing in straight lines. He also posited that the force of attraction was universal and that all bodies exerted this force on one another.[21]

Various conceptions of gravity and explanations of attraction had appeared in earlier heliocentric accounts, such as those of Johannes Kepler, Galileo Galilei, Giovanni Alphonso Borelli (1608–79), and Robert Hooke (1635–1703), among others. The specific explanations of the causes of gravitation differed, but these theories generally assumed that the planets had a natural tendency toward the sun, and they frequently took magnetic repulsion and attraction as an obvious analogy of this phenomenon.[22] Newton's achievement—one recognized even by critics of the theory of attraction—was to determine through precise calculations how the force of gravity operated based on the masses of the celestial bodies and the distances between them. Although Newton did not purport to know the nature or cause of the physical force gravity, his theory described the precise movements of celestial bodies with mathematical certainty. He echoed Galileo's approach and assumed that if mathematical calculations could describe and predict natural phenomena accurately, they were as good as demonstrations of the physical cause of motion. Indeed, in the first edition of the *Principia*, Newton insisted that he was merely describing the mathematical principles of natural philosophy, rather than making any claims about the actual physical causes of natural phenomena. He relied on "mathematical demonstrations and quantitative empirical proofs" to validate his theory of universal gravitation.[23] By approaching the relations among the different celestial bodies in purely mathematical terms in book 1 of the *Principia*, Newton appeared to offer an idealized view of nature.[24]

Early critics of the *Principia* noted that Newton failed to explain the nature of gravity.[25] The brief review of the work in the *Journal des savants* praised Newton's text for its "precise and exact demonstrations" but insisted that they were "only mechanical" because Newton had considered the principles not "as a physicist but as a simple geometrician." Newton's explanation of "the system of the world" was based on "hypotheses that were, for the most part, arbitrary and that consequently could only serve as the foundation for a treatise in pure mechanics." The reviewer noted that Newton's account of the tides was based on the principle that "all the planets gravitate [*pesent*] mutually toward one another." The reviewer maintained that the "supposition is arbitrary," since "it has not been proved" and any supposition based on it could not reveal truths about natural philosophy.[26] For detractors, Newton's calculations seemed perfectly correct, but his project could not be classified as true natural philosophy because it failed to offer an account of causality.[27]

The Dutch natural philosopher Christiaan Huygens, who corresponded with Newton extensively, was one of the first to offer a critique of his theory on the grounds that the force of attraction did not offer an appropriate mechanical explanation.[28] His *Discours de la cause de la pesanteur* (1690) addressed the causes of attraction. For Huygens, as for the Cartesians, "nature operated through secret and imperceptible ways in steering objects that we call heavy toward the earth, and no matter how much attention or industry one might employ, the senses will never be able to discover anything." Nevertheless, Huygens observed, philosophers had continuously tried to determine the cause of this effect, and many had decided to "attribute it to some internal and inherent quality" of bodies that made them move toward the earth. He praised Descartes for recognizing that the cause of attraction had to be external to the objects and for seeking explanations in "principles that do not exceed the capacity of our mind."[29]

Huygens demonstrated the theoretical viability of the Cartesian theory through the famous experiment in which he placed a piece of wax in a rotating bucket of water. When he brought the bucket to a sudden stop, the water continued to rotate and the piece of wax gradually moved toward the center of the fluid vortex. According to Huygens, this experiment seemed to demonstrate that fluid dynamics could account for the apparent heaviness (*pesanteur*) of planets and of terrestrial bodies.[30] Having described the theoretical viability of fluid vortices, Huygens went on to examine Newton's hypothesis. He admitted that there were admirable elements in Newton's system, and he acknowledged that the gravitation of the planets toward the sun and of the objects toward the earth was an empirical fact. However, Huygens concluded against Newton's theory of universal attraction because the cause of attraction "was not at all explicable by any principle of mechanics or by any rules of motion."[31] Huygens was less diplomatic in a letter he wrote to Leibniz claiming that Newton's principle of attraction appeared "absurd." He was baffled that the English natural philosopher "could have undertaken such difficult research and calculations, which have nothing but this principle as their basis."[32]

It was a veritable clash of methodologies in natural philosophy. For Newton, rational mechanics consisted in the observation of particular phenomena, from which one deduced general laws. For Huygens and the Cartesians, nature had to be explained through mechanical accounts that made reference to physical contact between objects.[33] The Newtonian theory of gravity posited the reciprocal action of celestial bodies across a vacuum, which made it an example of the crudest mysticism in the eyes of many critics. They argued that Newton was misguided in presuming the existence of a vacuum and that he was also guilty of reasoning, in the manner of an Aristotelian, that physical objects had intrinsic essences, such as gravity or attraction.

A significant epistemological difference between the Newtonian and the Cartesian approach to natural philosophy was at the heart of the substantive disagreement about the structure of the universe. Descartes and many of his disciples assumed that sense experience could not, on its own, provide an accurate account of the underlying structures of the physical world. In seeking explanations in terms of microstructures of matter, the Cartesians privileged the knowledge of causes over the observation of effects.[34] This is why the Cartesians so vehemently insisted that Newton had to account not just for the observable effects of gravity but for its underlying cause as well. Newton, on the other hand, sought to explain phenomena "in terms of their systematic relations with other phenomena" and not in terms of a fundamental structural reality.[35] Since he did not think that the mind could penetrate beyond the information that had been furnished by sense perception, Newton opposed the formulation of causal explanations that could not be verified empirically. Following in the tradition of experimental natural philosophy, Newton and his supporters insisted on the application of the inductive method to the study of nature. When combined with Locke's systematic analysis of the source of human knowledge, Newtonianism provided a new appealing model for understanding the natural world.[36]

In effect, Descartes's and Newton's natural philosophies rested on rival conceptions of methodological skepticism. Descartes assumed that the physical world was not as it appeared, and he considered the senses to be unreliable guides to the study of nature. At the same time, he thought the mind could improve its understanding of its surroundings by arriving at clear and distinct ideas about the underlying structures of reality. By contrast, Newton and Locke constructed their understanding of the world on the assumption that the underlying essences of things were not accessible to the mind directly. As Locke had insisted, one had to be satisfied with understanding the "nominal essences" of things.[37]

Newton responded to his detractors in the "General Scholium," added to book 3 of the 1713 edition of the *Principia*. He directly addressed the controversy surrounding the competing theories of gravity and vortices.[38] One of the biggest problems concerned the inability of the Cartesian *tourbillons* to explain how comets could be carried "with very eccentric motions through all parts of the heavens indifferently, with a freedom that is incompatible with the notion of a Vortex." Indeed, Newton had already demonstrated that Descartes's system was incompatible with Kepler's laws of planetary motion in book 2 of the first edition.[39]

Newton also used the "General Scholium" to expatiate on his theory of gravity and his general approach to natural philosophy. He noted that the force proceeded from the "quantity of the solid matter" that the different bodies possessed.[40] Newton also famously expressed his unwillingness to speculate about the underlying cause of gravity:

> But hitherto I have not been able to discover the cause of those properties of gravity from phaenomena, and I frame no hypotheses. For whatever is not deduc'd from the phaenomena, is to be called an hypothesis; and hypotheses whether metaphysical or physical, whether of occult qualities or mechanical, have no place in experimental philosophy. In this philosophy particular propositions are inferr'd from the phaenomena, and afterwards render'd general by induction. Thus it was that the impenetrability, the mobility, and the impulsive force of bodies, and the laws of motion and gravitation, were discovered.[41]

Newton's refusal to speculate about the underlying causes of the force of attraction was at the heart of his disagreement with Huygens, the Cartesians, and others who embraced a rationalist mechanics. He insisted that while one could not doubt the existence of this universal force, the human mind remained incapable of fully comprehending the workings of nature. Bounded by its limited experience of the surrounding world, the understanding could not learn all the ways in which God could have arranged the universe.[42] Newton's natural philosophy thus relied on some arguments of mitigated skepticism both to criticize alternative theories for overextending their explanatory ambitions and to justify the limits to the scope of his own explanations.[43]

Roger Côtes's preface to the 1713 edition of the *Principia* was more combative than Newton's text. The natural philosopher offered a direct critique of the Cartesian hypothesis and distinguished it from Newtonian principles.[44] Côtes divided all schools of natural philosophy into "three classes." The various followers of Aristotle, who made up the first group, "affirm that the several effects of bodies arise from the particular natures of those bodies" without explaining the origin of those natures. The Peripatetics, according to Côtes, had been "entirely employed in giving names to things and not in searching into things themselves." Côtes placed the Cartesians, who were not explicitly named, in the second class. He credited them with "laying aside that useless heap of words" and "going on from simple things to those which are more compounded." However, Côtes criticized them for taking "a liberty of imagining at pleasure unknown figures and magnitudes and uncertain situations and motions of the parts; and moreover of supposing occult fluids freely pervading the pores of bodies." With these "fallacious conjectures," the Cartesians "run into dreams and chimeras, and neglect the true constitution of things." Using unfounded hypotheses "as the foundations on which they build their speculations," they composed "an ingenious romance." Within Côtes's classification, only the third class of natural philosophers, who "profess experimental philosophy," who "assume nothing as a principle, that is not proven by phenomena," and who "frame no hypotheses," offered "the best way of philosophizing." Proceeding by a "synthetical and analytical" method, these thinkers observed various natural phenomena and "deduce by analysis the forces of nature, and the more simple laws of forces; and from thence by synthesis, they show the constitution of the rest."[45]

Côtes naturally included Newton among the third group, praising the natural philosopher who "has given us a most illustrious example, by the explication of the System of the World, most happily deduced from the Theory of Gravity." He called out the critics of Newton, who, according to Côtes, were "too much prepossessed with certain prejudices and . . . unwilling to assent to this new principle and . . . ready to prefer uncertain notions to certain [ones]." He went on to provide his own justifications for the alleged certainty of Newton's theory.

It was a "law of nature universally received by all philosophers" that bodies at rest remained at rest or moved in a straight line at a uniform velocity unless acted upon by an external force—as was stated in Newton's second law of motion. Consequently, in the case of bodies that moved in curved lines, there necessarily had to be "some force operating, by whose repeated actions they are perpetually made to deflect." The observation of the movements of celestial bodies, combined with the mathematical calculations that demonstrated that the celestial bodies revolved "with an equable motion in concentric circles," made it quite apparent that the planets were subject to a centripetal force. This force was "always directed towards the center of [the planets'] orbits," according to Côtes. The centripetal force that produced planetary orbits appeared to be the same as the force of gravity that attracted different bodies toward the earth, as was manifest from the revolution of the moon and from pendulum experiments. Since it was evident that the celestial bodies attracted one another mutually, and since it was axiomatic that "effects of the same kind . . . take their rise from the same causes," Côtes concluded that all particles of matter must possess "attractive forces" that were proportional to their masses.[46]

Côtes also countered the Cartesian charge that gravity constituted an occult cause, saying that "it is plain from the phaenomena that such a virtue realy does exist." It was more accurate to doubt the existence of Descartes's "imaginary vortices," which were supposedly composed "of a matter entirely fictitious and imperceptible to the senses." Côtes admitted that the cause of gravity remained unknown, but he did not regard this as a sufficient reason to conclude that it was either occult or miraculous. He warned that those who disputed gravity on such grounds "should be careful not to fall into an absurdity that may overturn the foundations of all philosophy." Every causal explanation could be reduced to a more simple principle, but one could not expect a detailed mechanical account of the simplest cause. Although the underlying cause of gravity remained unknown, Côtes argued, Newton's theory did a better job of explaining natural phenomena than did the vortex hypothesis. He noted that the Cartesians neither explained why the planets moved at different rates nor gave an accurate account of the comets. The supposed fluid dynamics of the vortices appeared to create more problems than they solved. Côtes qualified Descartes's hypothesis as "ridiculous and unworthy of a philosopher, since it is altogether without foundation, and does not in the least serve to explain the nature of things."[47]

From the 1720s to the 1740s, the contest between Cartesian and Newtonian descriptions of the universe became a matter not just of cosmology but of larger philosophical, historical, and, some might argue, national importance. Because of the dramatic difference between methodological approaches to the understanding of the surrounding world, Cartesian vortices continued to enjoy strong support in France and on the rest of the Continent, while Newton's theory of universal gravitation was still subjected to criticism and interrogation. In constructing the narratives of the century of light, which was founded on the "philosophical revolution" and the emergence of modern science, the philosophes made use of this rivalry in order to advance their own conceptions of the powers of human understanding and the ultimate purposes of natural knowledge.[48]

One of the most notable critiques of the Newtonian system appeared in Fontenelle's eulogy of Newton, delivered to the Académie royale des sciences in 1727.[49] After a brief summary of Newton's early life and education, Fontenelle quickly proceeded to the discussion of the *Principia*. He described it as a "book in which the most profound geometry serves as the basis for an entirely new physics." Fontenelle explained that Newton had interpreted Kepler's observations and calculations of the motions of the celestial bodies as the "physics of the whole world," noting that the moon was attracted to the earth by the same centripetal forces that attracted the earth to the sun. He praised the English natural philosopher for his geometrical calculations, which were "necessary for untangling the chaos of relations" among the celestial bodies. It was astonishing, Fontenelle remarked, that from "a theory so abstract, formed from many particular theories . . . conclusions that are always in conformity with the facts established by astronomy are born."[50]

Fontenelle then moved to address the contentious issue of attraction. He observed that the cause of heaviness (*pesanteur*) remained unknown, even to Newton, although the English natural philosopher seemed "to determine *pesanteur* to really be an attraction." This was at the heart of Fontenelle's criticism: "He constantly uses this word [*attraction*] to describe an active force in bodies, a force that is truly unknown and that he does not claim to define." After all, the idea that physical bodies could have such "active forces" had been "banned by the Cartesians" and condemned by "all the other philosophers." Indeed, Newton had brought back the force of "attraction and the void[, which had been] banished from the physics of Descartes, and banished forever according to appearances." Fontenelle argued that for Newton, "attraction is a principle that operates throughout all of nature and is the cause of all motions." According to Fontenelle, Newton had admitted his ignorance of the cause of attraction in order to save himself from the charge that the force was "an occult quality of the Scholastics."[51] In the *Théorie des tourbillons cartésiens* (published anonymously in 1752 but written much earlier), Fontenelle similarly condemned the notion of gravity.

Claiming that "mutual attraction is an essential property of bodies" was akin to admitting all that was "opprobrious in the old scholastic philosophy."[52] The Cartesian view of natural philosophy was central to Fontenelle's critique of Newtonian attraction. The notion of active forces and of action at a distance smacked of the crudest Aristotelian metaphysics.

Fontenelle's *éloge* of Newton juxtaposed the theory of attraction with Descartes's *tourbillons*. He insisted that "both were geniuses of the first order" who derived their physics from the novel conceptions of geometry, and he concluded the comparison on a conciliatory note:

> But the first [Descartes], taking a daring leap, wanted to place himself at the source of everything, to make himself the master of first principles through some clear and fundamental ideas, [and he] descended to the phenomena of nature and to the necessary consequences. The other [Newton], being more timid or more modest, began his journey by relying on phenomena in order to ascend to unknown principles, [and] he resolved to admit only those things that could reveal the chain of consequences. The first proceeds from what he understands clearly to find the cause of what he sees. The second proceeds from what he sees to find its cause, whether clear or obscure. The evident principles of the first do not always lead to phenomena as they are, [but] the phenomena did not always lead the second to sufficiently evident principles. The barriers [*bornes*] that could arrest two men of such stature on their opposite roads are not the limits of their own minds but the confines of the human mind itself.[53]

Fontenelle's attempt to mediate the posthumous rivalry between the two philosophical giants reflects the eclecticism of his own thought. He was hardly a devout Cartesian: although he sided with the Cartesian vortices, he departed from Descartes's metaphysics and method.[54] The skeptical conclusion to Fontenelle's comparison reveals his own methodological skepticism.[55] As his posthumously published *Fragments d'un Traité de la raison humaine* and *De la connoissance de l'esprit humain* (1766) revealed, Fontenelle remained deeply skeptical about the powers of the human mind. He noted that the ancient philosophers (meaning Aristotle) had not been altogether wrong in claiming that "everything in the mind came from the senses." He disputed the notion of innate ideas, claiming that even the most basic axioms were formed by repeated experience of the world.[56] Fontenelle also noted that the nature of reason was "as unknown to us as everything else." He posited a double source of errors: "not only does the true nature of things not fully show itself" to the understanding but the mind "operates in diverse ways" when dealing with its ideas.[57] As Marsak has argued,

Fontenelle seemed to subscribe to the common-sense empiricism that had been made popular by Claude Buffier in the 1720s.[58] Consequently, he navigated among the various available methodologies, while remaining critical of the contents of Newtonian physics.

Other members of the Académie royale des sciences, such as Joseph Privat de Molières (1677–1742), Pierre Bouger (1698–1758), and Johann Bernoulli (1667–1748), among others, attempted to reconcile elements of the Newtonian and Cartesian systems. On the one hand, Cartesianism seemed to provide more acceptable philosophical explanations of the underlying causes of *pesanteur* than did Newtonian gravity. On the other hand, Newton's calculations appeared to give a more accurate account of the observed phenomena. Furthermore, the Cartesian hypothesis of fluid dynamics had difficulty explaining the effects of resistance and accounting for the elliptical orbits of the planets.[59] Comparisons between the Cartesian and Newtonian theories of planetary motion became increasingly popular in the 1730s, but not all thinkers unequivocally favored Newton. The contest between the two rival theories continued to hang in the balance as observers saw advantages and problems for each theory.

The second edition of Le Gendre de Saint-Aubin's popular *Traité de l'opinion*, from 1735, included a lengthy section on the two hypotheses.[60] Saint-Aubin offered a relatively evenhanded comparison of the two thinkers. According to him, while Descartes guided the mind "from simple truths to more complex ones" and "descended from principles to phenomena and from causes to their effects," Newton appeared to address only the most able geometricians and algebraists and based his theory on the examination of phenomena. Descartes was interested in "discovering why things are the way they are." Consequently, he formulated a hypothesis that "explains phenomena as much as possible through general, constant, and uniform laws." Newton, on the other hand, "appeared more preoccupied with examining how things are." While Descartes "engaged by brilliant ideas and plausible conjectures," Saint-Aubin continued, Newton "claimed to subdue you with obscure demonstrations and frightening calculations." Descartes "sought only to enlighten the mind," but Newton was "perfectly aware" that human understanding "was always disposed to admire what it did not comprehend."[61]

Saint-Aubin enumerated both the well-known Newtonian objections to Cartesian vortices and the problematic assumptions that were central to Newton's theory. He concluded that the latter seemed to offer more accurate accounts of the movement of comets and of motion in general. At the same, the theory of attraction—"the axis" and the "general foundation of Newton's system"—was not without problems. Saint-Aubin repeated the most common criticisms of the English natural philosopher's system, noting that the concept of attraction appeared contrary to everyday experience and that the idea of physical influence in a vacuum seemed contradictory. He refused to endorse either theory but argued that while Newton's account of certain planetary motions seemed more in accord with experience, Descartes offered a "general philosophy" that explained all natural phenomena.[62]

Saint-Aubin's description indicated a relatively level playing field between the two accounts, but the tide began to turn in favor of Newtonian explanations during the first half of the 1730s. This happened in part because of the manner in which Newton's French popularizers advanced his cause. One of the most notable shifts in favor of Newton occurred with Pierre-Louis de Maupertuis's publication of his *Discours sur les differentes figures des astres* in 1732.[63] Maupertuis, who would become the director of the French Académie royale des sciences and the first president of the Prussian Académie royale des sciences et belles-lettres, included a chapter on the metaphysics of attraction in his text. According to his analysis, the Cartesians attempted to explain all natural phenomena, including *pesanteur*, by appealing to the principle that "a moving body that encounters another has the force to move it." While this principle had the "advantage of simplicity," it encountered "great difficulties" when it came to "the detailed level of phenomena." Newton, on the other hand, "marvelously explains all the phenomena" by establishing "a different principle of action" according to which "parts of matter gravitate [*pesent*] toward one another." Unlike the Cartesian explanation, which ran into difficulties at the level of particulars, Newton's account appeared confirmed and substantiated when one went into greater detail.[64]

Maupertuis conceded the accusation leveled by Fontenelle and others that the principle of attraction made many "fear to see the rebirth of the doctrine of occult qualities in philosophy." He defended the English philosopher, claiming that "Newton never saw attraction as an explanation for the *pesanteur* of some bodies toward others." For Maupertuis, Newton "had often asserted that he used this term only to designate a fact and not a cause, that he only used it to avoid systems and explanations." Refusing to speculate about causes, Newton merely insisted that whatever attraction might be, "it was always a primary fact from which one must proceed to explain all other facts that depend on it." One could certainly study the observable effects of gravity without knowing the causes and while "leaving the search for the cause of this tendency to the more sublime philosophers," Maupertuis insisted.[65]

Maupertuis proceeded to argue that although the human mind had little knowledge of the real properties of matter, it had the unfortunate tendency to jump to conclusions. "It would be ridiculous," he insisted, "to assign to matter properties other than those we discover by experience." However, it might be "even more ridiculous to wish, after seeing such a small number of properties hardly known to us, to dogmatically exclude all others." One could only definitively reject the existence of "those properties that are contradictory" to the notion of matter.[66] If one reasoned according to experience, and not according to some a priori notions, then one certainly could not exclude the possibility that bodies had a tendency to gravitate toward other bodies. The way properties inhered in matter "would always remain a mystery to us." Assuming the rhetorical position of a skeptic, Maupertuis further suggested that Newton's theory of attraction and Descartes's hypothesis of impulsion were equally obscure notions. It was quite possible to doubt the accuracy of both accounts and to insist that "God himself" sets bodies in motion.[67] He concluded the chapter on attraction by arguing that although such arguments did "not prove that there is attraction in nature," they did show that it was not "metaphysically impossible." Since it was "neither impossible nor contradictory," one was entitled to determine whether it was confirmed by natural phenomena.[68]

The subsequent chapters of Maupertuis's *Discours* explored the intricacies of the Cartesian and Newtonian explanations. The Cartesian account, although appearing "quite simple at first glance, proved to have many drawbacks upon closer examination." Maupertuis enumerated the difficulties that surrounded the *tourbillon* hypothesis. He observed that the velocities of the vortices were not able to adhere to both of Kepler's laws of planetary motion simultaneously. He concluded that in order to make the theory work, one had to assume that the fluid was of different densities in different places and that there was "an interruption of movements in the different layers of the solar vortex." Similarly problematic was the explanation of why objects fell straight to the earth and did not flow sideways—as one would expect from Descartes's claim that the fluid matter circulated around the earth "in the direction parallel to the equator." For Maupertuis, proponents of the *tourbillons* had to resort to Huygens's solution and assume that there were several streams of "ethereal mater" that flowed in different directions within the earth's vortex.[69] All this rendered the Cartesian explanation quite difficult to reconcile with the observable phenomena.

The advantage of the Newtonian system, Maupertuis argued, was that it neatly resolved these problems. Beginning by demonstrating geometrically that "if a body in motion is attracted toward a moveable or an immovable center, it must cover equal areas in equal times," Newton showed that this was exactly how the planets revolved around the sun. The system appeared to successfully adhere to both of Kepler's laws and to fit with all the observed phenomena: "To suppose this [centripetal] force and its law is not to construct a system but to discover the principle whose observed effects are its necessary consequences. One does not establish gravity [*pesanteur*] toward the sun in order to explain the course of the planets; the course of the planets shows us that there is gravity toward the sun." Newton's demonstration appeared as an inevitable outcome of observation. Maupertuis touted the appealing simplicity of a principle that seemed to explain a wide variety of phenomena, and he concluded with an implicit rhetorical nod to Galileo's *Discorso sopra i due massimi sistemi del mondo* (1632). He declared his own ignorance on the nature of gravity and impulsion and stated a lack a preference for either system, asking "the reader to judge whether attraction was sufficiently proven by the facts or was a gratuitous fiction."[70] As Shank has pointed out, Maupertuis successfully offered a strong critique of Cartesian vortices without explicitly declaring himself in favor of Newtonianism.[71]

While Maupertuis made a relatively subtle case for Newton's theory of universal gravitation, Voltaire engaged in a more aggressive campaign to promote the ideas of the English philosopher during the 1730s. Indeed, his *Lettres philosophiques*—a work the marquis de Condorcet claimed "began a period of revolution" (*époque de revolution*) in France—did more than just popularize the ideas of Locke and Newton.[72] The text was, as Shank has called it, the "manifesto of the Enlightenment," and it designated the duo of English thinkers as the philosophical founding fathers of the "century of lights."[73] Voltaire's "Lettre sur Descartes et Newton" began by enumerating the differences between the theories of the two philosophers. Unlike Fontenelle, who had given a fairly balanced presentation of the achievements of both Descartes and Newton, Voltaire showed a clear preference for the latter. Although Voltaire's portrait of Descartes was, on the whole, positive, the philosophe maintained that Descartes had fallen into error concerning the "nature of the soul," "the proofs of the existence of God," the structure of "matter," "the laws of motion," and "the nature of light." In a backhanded compliment to Descartes, Voltaire proclaimed that "nature almost made him a poet," as he "was born with a shining and strong imagination." According to Voltaire, Descartes "abandoned his guide and gave himself entirely to the spirit of system [*esprit de système*]." He developed the tendency to form arbitrary hypotheses, after which "philosophy became no more than an ingenious romance that only appeared to resemble the truth for the ignorant."[74] Associating hypotheses in metaphysics or in natural philosophy with fictional narratives or romances became a common way to undermine their validity.

In the "Lettre sur le système de l'attraction" Voltaire addressed the theory of attraction and the rival vortex hypothesis. After giving an unsympathetic presentation of the *tourbillons* and summarizing Newton's objections, he announced that the English philosopher had "destroyed the Cartesian vortices." Voltaire told the apocryphal story of how Newton, upon seeing "fruits fall from a tree," had discovered the "power that forces heavy bodies to descend." He summarized Newton's observations and calculations about the relationship between the quantity of matter and the distances between celestial and terrestrial bodies. Finally, he attempted to defend the English natural philosopher against critics who had equated the theory of attraction with occult qualities and had wondered "why he did not employ the word *impulsion*, which is so well understood, rather than the term *attraction*, which is incomprehensible." Voltaire echoed Maupertuis in noting that neither concept provided a perfect idea about how bodies interacted. For both allies of Newton, the English philosopher was simply describing "an indisputable effect of an unknown principle, a quality inherent in matter" whose cause had yet to be discovered. Voltaire compared Newton's discovery to that of an anatomist who explained that the human arm moved as a result of the contractions of the muscles. Would people be "less obliged" to the anatomist for his discovery, Voltaire asked rhetorically, "because he did not know the reason why the muscles contact?"[75]

Voltaire's *Éléments de la philosophie de Neuton* appeared four years after the *Lettres philosophiques* and went into significantly greater detail about Newton's natural philosophy. In addition to addressing planetary motion and the theory of gravity, the text also dealt with Newton's theory of light. Émilie du Châtelet (1706–49), one of the most gifted natural philosophers of the eighteenth century, made a very significant contribution to the text, assisting Voltaire with the more technical aspects of Newtonian physics.[76] The book proved to be a hit with the reading public. A pirated Amsterdam edition appeared before Voltaire was even able to get an authorized French version into print.[77] It was followed by a 1738 London edition that included Voltaire's corrections. Another English edition, which included *La métaphysique de Neuton* as the first part, appeared in 1741.

By this time Voltaire appeared much more confident in affirming Newton's theory of universal gravitation than he had been in the *Lettres philosophiques*. He proclaimed that "centripetal force, attraction, gravitation is an indubitable principle both of the course of the planets and of the fall of all bodies," and he praised Newton for advancing demonstrations and calculations that had "seemed to be outside the reach of the human mind."[78] Nevertheless, he retained the attitude of skeptical empiricism.[79] In discussing the first principles of matter, he concluded that "if one is allowed to say attraction is probably the cause for this adhesion and continuity of matter, this is what one would advance as the most likely [*vraisemblable*] explanation." Voltaire insisted that experience and observation should put an end to metaphysical disputes.[80]

Voltaire's and Châtelet's popular presentations of the principles of Newton's philosophy played a critical role in paving the way for the acceptance of Newton in France. Voltaire succeeded in persuading many contemporaries that the Newtonian theory of gravitation was the more probable explanation, even if the underlying cause of the attraction between bodies remained unknown.[81] By presenting Newtonian attraction as a more likely explanation—or at the very least a less problematic one—than the Cartesian vortices, Voltaire and Maupertuis both stressed the relative advantage of Newton's theory without making claims about its absolute veracity. The rhetorical emphasis on verisimilitude and the privileging of observation over metaphysical speculation about unobservable causes made Newtonianism appear as the more pragmatic approach to natural philosophy.

Other supporters of Newton would use analogous strategies when comparing the two systems. Willem Jacob van 's Gravesande's (1688–1742) popular textbook introduction to Newton's philosophy—titled *Physices elementa mathematica* (1721, translated into French in 1742 and 1746)—opened with an implicit allusion to Cartesian hypotheses. He warned readers not to admit "some fiction of our mind as truth" and cautioned against "the vanity of reasoning upon fictitious hypotheses." It was only through an "assiduous study" of nature, the Dutch mathematician argued, that we might achieve gradual progress in the understanding of the world and "determine the limits beyond which our understanding could not extend." According to 's Gravesande, most errors in natural philosophy were the result of "the immoderate desire to make progress in physics and the shame of confessing our ignorance." Noting that people had no a priori ideas of the properties or essences of bodies, he declared that "human intelligence is bounded within narrow confines."[82] The laws of nature could be discovered through phenomena, but the knowledge of causes was frequently inaccessible. Newton's approach recognized these limitations and provided a method suitable to them. By discovering the laws of nature through observable effects, using "induction" to confirm that these laws were general, and reasoning "mathematically" with respect to the rest, one could attain relative certainty in physics.[83]

Similarly, in his *Traité des systèmes* (1749) Etienne Bonnot de Condillac noted that the debate between the Cartesians and the Newtonians came down to a disagreement over which of the two laws of motion God had decided to resort to when he created the universe and set matter in motion. The Cartesians seemed to overreach when they insisted that God necessarily had resorted to impulsion and not attraction, although they were no more privy to God's ways than the Newtonians. Condillac claimed that although "neither of the hypotheses had an advantage over the other," Newton's explanations appeared to have fewer difficulties and were "more in accordance with observations." At the same time, he admitted that one "might never be assured that [Newton's hypothesis] was the true system of the universe."[84]

D'Alembert praised Newton's discoveries, but he added that "perhaps [Newton] has done more by teaching philosophy to be judicious and to restrict within reasonable limits the sort of audacity that Descartes had been forced by circumstances to bestow upon it."[85] In the article "Attraction" (1751), d'Alembert described "Newtonian attraction" as "an indefinite principle . . . by which one refers neither to a kind of particular action nor to a physical cause of such an action, but only a general tendency . . . whatever its physical or metaphysical cause might be." The knowledge of causes was not necessary, because the "effects are before the eyes of the whole world."[86] By contrast, d'Alembert noted, Descartes had depicted an imaginary world in the minutest detail, going so far as to speculate about the shapes of imperceptible particles. He questioned the confidence with which Descartes had described how God must have arranged all parts of matter and the aplomb with which he had declared that God could not have created certain things, such as the vacuum. D'Alembert quoted Fontenelle's warning about the "danger of hastily formed systems, to which the human mind gives in all too easily and which, once established, become opposed to new truths."[87]

The contrast between Newton and Descartes as articulated by Newton's advocates was clear. While the Newtonians speculated merely about appearances, the Cartesians purported to describe the works of the creator. The latter erected a robust and interconnected philosophical system, whereas the former emphasized the provisional nature of scientific knowledge. The Newtonians retained epistemological modesty, while the Cartesians sought to know too much. In light of the increasingly fashionable denunciations both of metaphysical speculations and of the *esprit de système*, Newton's philosophe supporters presented his theories and his method as models for a true and enlightened natural philosophy.

The Scientific Revolution Devours Its Children:
Descartes and the *Esprit de système*

Newton's philosophical triumph over Descartes in the *Encyclopédie* was a final act in a rivalry between radically different visions of the natural world. It was also an explicit recognition of a *fait accompli*. During the 1730s and 1740s the Cartesian hold on natural philosophy was beginning to yield to the Newtonian current that was strengthening in France and on the rest of the Continent. Descartes's first supporters had been extremely effective in promoting his metaphysics and natural philosophy despite opposition from traditional intellectual authorities. They had managed to penetrate both university curricula and new scientific societies in the second half of the seventeenth century. By 1720 Descartes's *Méditations metaphysiques* had made it onto the list of required texts at the Sorbonne, where the work was praised for illustrating the teachings of Plato in a "remarkable way" and bringing them "closer to the Christian doctrine."[88] It was partly because of this initial success that Cartesianism found itself on the outside looking in when Voltaire and d'Alembert composed the philosophical origins of the "century of lights." The French philosophes acknowledged Descartes's important place among the foremost contributors to the rise of modern philosophy and admitted that Cartesianism had offered the necessary step in the progressive emergence of the human mind "from barbarism."[89] However, they also pointed out the numerous errors of Cartesian metaphysics and natural philosophy, explicitly preferring the methods and theories of Locke and Newton to those of their compatriot.[90]

There were several reasons why the philosophes threw Descartes under the proverbial carriage and undertook a conscious effort to marginalize his contributions to the rise of modern philosophy. As Cartesianism was integrated into the intellectual establishment in France, it also became an obvious target for those who sought to challenge that establishment. As we have seen, Protestant and Catholic theologians came to rely on Cartesian arguments in order to prove the existence of God and the immortality of the human soul against materialist theories. The alliance between Christian theology and Cartesian metaphysics seemed to place the latter in a position analogical to that previously held by Aristotelian Scholasticism. Through the association with these apologetic thinkers, Descartes became a proxy target for many of the philosophes. Furthermore, Cartesianism bequeathed to the philosophes a number of difficult ontological problems that appeared nearly irresolvable. These included the problem of mind-body interaction, the hypothesis of animal machines, and the *tourbillon* theory. Finally, the Cartesian insistence on accounting for natural phenomena with reference to a priori principles might have appeared problematic for a learned culture that was deeply challenged by skeptical arguments.

Indeed, Locke's and Newton's epistemologies seemed to fit the philosophes' methodology better than Cartesian rationalism. Wary of both the difficulties posed by Pyrrhonian skepticism and the futility of protracted metaphysical debates, Voltaire, d'Alembert, and other philosophes emphasized not only the extent but also the limits of human reason. Just as Locke's account of the origin of ideas sidestepped metaphysical speculations about the true nature of the soul and the real essences of things, so Newton's theory of planetary motion appeared to deal solely with appearances, without delving into the underlying causes of gravity. Both thinkers made all conclusions probable, provisional, and always subject to correction on the basis of subsequent observations. By supporting such critiques of metaphysical speculations and embracing what they saw as a pragmatic empiricism, the philosophes established their intellectual genealogy and their raison d'être in the learned world of the eighteenth century. Voltaire, d'Alembert, and their partisans embraced a view of philosophy that emphasized practicable and useful knowledge over abstract reason. One had to delimit scientific enquiries and to leave aside all speculations that "increased the uncertainty of human knowledge."[91] As Giorgio Piaia has suggested recently, " 'Reason' of the great metaphysical systems [had] given way to the 'reasonableness' of the Enlightenment."[92]

Within this new scheme, Cartesianism appeared overly rigid, systematic, and ambitious and thus unreasonable. Locke's withdrawal of speculation about the essences of things and Newton's refusal to "feign hypotheses" appeared to be more fruitful (and more marketable) models. In describing Locke, Voltaire praised his "modest philosophy," which was "conscious of its own Weakness," contrasting him with Descartes, who was "hurried away by that spirit of system [*esprit systématique*] that blinds the greatest men."[93] D'Alembert made a nearly identical contrast when he praised the English philosopher's "reasonable metaphysics" and warned about the dangers "of the natural temptations that prevent us from holding ourselves within bounds when we engage in metaphysical speculations."[94] For both, Cartesianism was guilty of perpetuating the *esprit de système* that had made Aristotelian philosophy so detestable. Lockean and Newtonian theories, by contrast, avoided such petty philosophical partisanship and claimed to provide useful knowledge of the surrounding world.

Of course, there many in the scientific community were not swept away by the wave of Newtonianism. The Jesuit Louis-Bertrand Castel, who had been an editor of the *Mémoires de Trévoux*, presented himself as a neutral observer and arbiter of two imperfect systems.[95] Castel's text engaged in a comparative analysis of Newton's and Descartes's systems, pointing out the advantages and weaknesses of each. He explicitly lamented the partisan nature of the debates surrounding physics and planetary motion and insisted that each side misrepresented the arguments of the other. While the Newtonians blamed the Cartesians for giving into hypotheses, the Cartesians could object that the Newtonians philosophized by blindly submitting to the articles of faith and by accepting undemonstrated concepts such as the force of attraction and the vacuum. Castel appeared to have greater sympathy for the "most servile Cartesians," who, while reasoning according to Descartes's principles, nevertheless "measure the likelihood [*vraisemblance*] and unlikelihood [*non-vraisemblance*]" of various propositions independently. By contrast, the members of the "Newtonian sect" simply followed the calculations and arguments of their master: "Newton had thought for them, reasoned for them, and philosophized for them."[96] Castel's larger critique of Newtonianism had to do not just with science but, more generally, with the alleged servility of Newton's disciples. Using the type of rhetoric that had been commonly deployed against the Aristotelian Scholastics, Castel accused the Newtonians of embracing the *esprit de système*.

The concept of a philosophical system emerged from the increasingly popular histories of philosophy. This genre had emerged during the Renaissance and reflected the fascination with antiquity and its various schools of thought. The contents, goals, and scope of seventeenth- and eighteenth-century histories of philosophy varied greatly and included a diverse set of approaches. Many of these texts, such as Saint-Aubin's *Traité de l'opinion*, Boureau-Deslandes's *Histoire critique de la philosophie*, and Johann Jakob Brucker's (1696–1770) *Historia critica philosophiae* (1742–44), provided historical overviews of ancient and modern schools of philosophy. While some authors presented narratives of the progress of the human mind, others engaged in more evenhanded comparisons of the ancients and the moderns.[97] Still other texts, such as Condillac's *Traité des systèmes*, offered critical analyses of contemporaneous philosophical systems.

Condillac's work, in particular, provides crucial insight into the philosophes' attitude toward metaphysics and abstract reason in the mid-eighteenth century. His distinctions between the different systems were not just analytical or historical but also reflected the author's philosophical commitment to Lockean empiricism. He distinguished between "abstract systems" (*systèmes abstraites*), which were "based on nothing but abstract principles . . . [and] had nothing but suppositions as their foundation," on the one hand, and systems that were grounded in the observation of particulars, which were verifiable by observation and experience, on the other. The former included "systems," or schools, such as Cartesianism, Leibnizianism, Malebranchism, and Spinozism, all of which were constructed on logical deductions from first principles. These systems were based either on a priori axioms or on undemonstrated hypotheses. Condillac insisted that while "abstract notions were absolutely necessary for ordering our knowledge," they could not carry the mind to the knowledge of particulars.[98] According to Condillac, since all knowledge began with the senses, it was a mistake to assume that such principles were anything other than the product of generalizations drawn from specific observations.[99]

For Condillac, philosophers who began their studies by endorsing abstract assumptions about nature were going about things backwards. By allowing such abstract principles to dictate their understanding of the world, he maintained, these thinkers deployed a "sterile" method that was wrongheaded in at least two ways: First, they wrongly supposed that principles that were true in one instance were true in all instances. Second, they deployed analogical reasoning incorrectly, assuming that what held true for *one* set of natural relations held true for *all* sets of natural relations. Finding themselves "in the middle of a labyrinth," these thinkers proposed "general principles in order to discover the exit" instead of patiently exploring their surroundings. A philosopher's arbitrary preference for a particular principle led him to erect an entire edifice of unfounded propositions and to attempt to convert others to "his favorite system." Condillac cautioned against philosophical systems that purported to explain everything theoretically instead of following the actual phenomena of the natural world.[100]

Condillac echoed Locke in condemning the "ridiculous" use of abstract principles, suggesting that the majority of the arguments "among metaphysicians were merely disputes about words." He censured this approach as "an obstacle to the art of reasoning" that "blinds the imagination by the inflexibility [*hardiesse*] of the consequences to which it leads," "seduces the mind" by unreflectively appealing to the passions, and "gives birth to and feeds an obstinate support for the most monstrous errors [and] for the love of dispute." Much like Crousaz, who had blamed the spirit of dispute for creating a fertile ground for the spread of skepticism, Condillac warned that the intense critiques to which the supporters of the different systems subjected one another made people "perceive the uncertainties into which" these debates led. Persuaded that no better method existed, one adopted no system at all and consequently "fell into another extreme" of assuming that true and certain knowledge could not be attained. These uncertainties were compounded by the fact that "abstract principles" served as "an abundant source of paradoxes."[101]

Following his introductory condemnation of "abstract systems," Condillac attempted to describe and refute their particular manifestations in the learned world of his time. His *Traité* appeared when the enthusiasm for Locke was at its highest in France and the rationalist systems of Descartes, Malebranche, Leibniz, and Spinoza were under the attack by prominent philosophes.[102] Condillac attributed the general fault of all existing abstract systems to the "habit of reasoning concerning badly determined principles."[103] All the rationalist thinkers, according to Condillac, erroneously attempted to articulate ambitious metaphysical accounts of the hidden causes of things. The specific errors that Condillac found resulted from this faulty methodology. He attacked the Cartesian notion of innate ideas, claiming that this principle not only failed to offer an accurate epistemology but also led to grave mistakes in the understanding of the physical world. He likewise argued against Malebranchian occasionalism, suggesting that "instead of explaining things by natural causes," the supporters of this view "made God descend into the machine, such that each effect appears to be produced by a miracle." Condillac described Leibniz's theory of monads as a typical and symptomatic mistake of abstract systems that attempted to explain "vague notions and unknown things" by invoking invented obscure concepts. Finally, he claimed that Spinoza had deployed Scholastic verbiage and had offered a confusing, indeed nonsensical definition of substance. It was an error on the basis of which Spinoza had constructed the rest of his system. Spinoza's definitions were vague, his axioms were inexact, and his descriptions of the world were merely the products of his imagination, the critic asserted.[104]

Having concluded his critique of abstract systems, Condillac proceeded to articulate his positive views for the advancement of learning. He addressed the general usefulness of hypotheses in explaining the natural world. Hypotheses could be either good or bad, depending on how accurately they explained observable phenomena and provided new knowledge. For Condillac, hypotheses could be true under two conditions: if one had exhausted all other possible explanations concerning a particular question and if one had a criterion by which to confirm or reject the chosen supposition. They were most useful and appropriately applicable in mathematical investigations, because the mind had "exact ideas" concerning numbers and could easily discover errors in its reasoning. Hypotheses also proved to be fruitful in astronomy. Through extensive observations, meticulous calculations, and steady corrections, astronomers continuously increased their knowledge of celestial motions. As a result, they were able to account for a growing number of phenomena with reference to increasingly simple systems.[105]

By contrast, hypotheses proved to have a more problematic role in physics, given humanity's limited perspective on the surrounding world. Thinkers had employed hypotheses to demonstrate the "first elements of things," to explain "the origin of all phenomena," and to account for the "mechanism of the whole world." However, most of these attempts had proved inadequate or at least incomplete. Although new experiences continually increased humans' knowledge of nature, there were always new phenomena to uncover. Some things remained hidden from view, while others were too distant to be observed properly. The ignorance of these and other objects, Condillac remarked, rendered humankind unable to learn the "true causes of things" and led people to devise a system that explained everything in a parsimonious fashion.[106] Unable to accept the great number of unknowns, natural philosophers furnished unfounded and arbitrary conjectures concerning what could not be observed. They began from uncertain principles and attempted to "penetrate the nature of extension, of movement, and of all bodies." Indeed, although even the operations of the human body remained a mystery, some philosophers attempted to speculate about the workings of the entire universe. Condillac criticized such speculations, claiming that they were rarely based on sufficient observation. By conjuring up a single principle that accounted for all phenomena, some natural philosophers let their imaginations run wild and came to resemble poets who invented fictions to substitute for facts they did not know.[107]

The contrast between the methods of astronomers and those of natural philosophers was central to Condillac's analysis.[108] The former engaged in measurements and calculations, while the latter deduced the workings of the universe from general principles. Progress in physics could occur, Condillac prognosticated, only if the principles of natural philosophy were based on extensive observation of a wide range of phenomena. It was only after observing a sufficient number of effects that philosophers could come up with laws and generalizations that accurately described the complex workings of nature. Most importantly, Condillac insisted, nothing was to be admitted as true unless confirmed by properly conducted experiments.[109]

Condillac's *Traité des systèmes* appeared just two years before the first volumes of the *Encyclopédie*. D'Alembert's "Discours préliminaire" echoed many of Condillac's sentiments about abstract systems in metaphysics and natural philosophy and about the proper role of hypotheses. D'Alembert's introduction decisively condemned the *esprit de système*. The philosophe observed that the "taste for systems" had been almost entirely banished from philosophy and that the "spirit of hypothesis" had now brought more disadvantages than positive results. While the *esprit de système* could serve as a useful start toward the knowledge of nature, d'Alembert proclaimed, it was "almost never capable of leading us to the truth on its own." The editor of the *Encyclopédie* extended the desire for straightforward and pragmatic investigations to physics:

> [The spirit of system] can glimpse the causes of phenomena when enlightened by the observation of Nature, but it is for calculations to assure, so to speak, the existence of these causes by determining exactly the effects they can produce and by comparing these effects with those that are revealed to us by experience. Any hypothesis without such a support rarely acquires the degree of certitude that ought always to be sought in the natural sciences and that is so seldom found in those frivolous conjectures honored by the name "systems."[110]

D'Alembert went so far as to assert that the "use of systems" was "dangerous" in the sciences. He urged that physics should be confined to "observations and calculations," that medicine should be limited to "the history of the human body, of its maladies, and their remedies," and that chemistry should focus on "the composition and the experimental decomposition of bodies." He insisted that "all sciences [should] be confined, as much as possible, to facts and to consequences deduced from them [and should] leave nothing to opinion except when forced to."[111]

The denunciations of the *esprit de système* and the coinciding calls to delineate boundaries to scientific enquiry strongly resembled the pattern of the evolving debates about epistemology and the nature of the human soul. Just as protracted contests over the mind-body relationship and the origin of ideas resulted in a gradual decline in metaphysical speculations about the soul, so disputes over the properties of matter and the nature of the cosmos produced a healthy consensus about the necessity of limiting the scope of scientific investigations. The philosophes criticized Leibnizianism and Cartesianism, whose adherents claimed to offer ambitious rationalist explanations of physical phenomena and of human nature.[112] By emphasizing the need for extensive observations of natural phenomena and claiming ignorance about the hidden causes of perceptible effects, the combination of Newtonian physics with Lockean epistemology appeared to provide the optimal model for natural philosophy. Much like Pyrrhonian skepticism, which had emerged as a response to the dogmatic schools of ancient Greece, the mitigated skepticism of the Age of Enlightenment was the outcome of clashes between ambitious philosophical systems of the late seventeenth century. It offered a practical middle way between the futile quest for absolute certainty and complete resignation to extreme Pyrrhonian doubt.

The philosophes' embrace of Lockean Newtonianism continued the tradition of seventeenth-century experimental science, which had internalized several key assumptions of philosophical skepticism. The mitigated skeptics of London's Royal Society had sought an alternative to excessive dogmatism and absolute doubt. Eighteenth-century philosophes had similarly attempted to navigate among a wide variety of philosophical systems that sought to determine the nature of the surrounding world with absolute certainty while avoiding the pessimistic conclusions of Pyrrhonism. It was this difficult path that ultimately led many philosophes to emphasize the probable nature of all knowledge and to call for a suspension of judgment in questions in which the basis for making conclusions was insufficient.[113] By making all conclusions provisional and subject to future revisions based on new observations, Voltaire, Condillac, d'Alembert, and other philosophes outlined their visions for the steady yet restrained progress of human knowledge.

CHAPTER TEN

Historical Pyrrhonism and Its Discontents

The Origins of *Pyrrhonisme Historique*

The revival and proliferation of philosophical skepticism in the early modern period affected not only philosophy and the natural sciences but also humanist disciplines, particularly history. While scholars have discussed the impact of the skeptical revival on philosophy in great detail, Pyrrhonism's influence on historiography has received significantly less attention, particularly in Anglophone literature.[1] Despite the growing popularity of history as a genre during the eighteenth century, historians began to face significant challenges from several sides. Skeptics and other critics questioned the purposes and methods of historical practices, cast doubt on the reliability of the most respected authorities, and questioned the possibility of obtaining true and certain knowledge of the past. Debates about historical certainty had been a prominent topic since Renaissance humanists began to develop new critical methods of source analysis. The polemical disputes of the Reformation had injected new explosive issues, including questions about Church history and hagiography. The debates of the late seventeenth and early eighteenth centuries, however, combined these previous concerns with a systematic philosophical and theological critique of received traditions and established epistemological assumptions. Philosophical skepticism thus played an essential role in changing the terms and nature of the debates about historiography in a period when Europeans were becoming increasingly self-conscious about their own place in the process of historical development.

In the first set of critiques, Descartes, Malebranche, and their disciples began to question the epistemological status of historical knowledge and to compare its allegedly feeble standing with what they saw as the infinitely more reliable certainty of mathematics and natural philosophy. In the *Discours de la méthode*, Descartes openly questioned whether historical knowledge was reliable or even useful as a source of moral examples. He maintained that fables distorted the historical record through exaggerations and omissions, pushing the imagination to conceive impossible things. Furthermore, for Descartes, an interest in the past was itself pernicious. He insisted that "if one is overly curious about things that happened in past centuries, one usually remains very ignorant about things that are happening in this one."[2] The Cartesians also questioned the reliability of historical evidence and, in the view of antiquarian scholars such as Pierre-Daniel Huet, denigrated the very usefulness of humanist scholarship.[3] Indeed, Descartes's critique of received traditional knowledge in the *Méditations* challenged the certainty one could expect to obtain in the study of history. Cartesians insisted that knowledge based on human testimony was categorically inferior to knowledge derived from rational examinations of the natural world.

Another set of historical critiques was leveled against the veracity of the accounts related in the Bible. These attacks both questioned the divine authorship of scripture and scrutinized its accounts of miracles. As noted, Isaac de La Peyrère's controversial and condemned *Prae-Adamitae* challenged the universality of biblical accounts, suggesting that scripture was solely a relation of Hebrew history. Similarly, the Oratorian Richard Simon's *Histoire critique du Vieux Testament* raised a number of queries about the factual reliability of scripture. Baruch Spinoza not only attempted to disprove the very possibility of miracles but also maintained that the Bible was merely a historical document. The critiques of sacred history provided ample material for deists, who challenged the status of revealed religions in general and of Christianity in particular. By disputing the historical reliability of scripture, these attacks cast doubt upon the entire corpus of Western history and undermined belief in its providential nature.[4]

The humanist practices of source criticism that attempted to establish the authenticity of ancient and medieval writings complemented these critiques. They culminated in the notorious claim made by Jean Hardouin (1646–1729), the Jesuit librarian at the Collège Louis-le-Grand, who contended that the vast majority of texts from antiquity, including those by Cicero and Virgil and most of the texts attributed to Saint Augustine, had been forged by medieval monks.[5] By undermining the classical heritage of his own age, Hardouin struck at the secular and patristic foundations of the received historical tradition. Although his statements were officially condemned, his writings nevertheless contributed to the *crise pyrrhonienne* by offering the most extreme type of criticism for an audience enlarged by the scandal surrounding his thesis.

Finally, philosophical skeptics, such as La Mothe Le Vayer and Bayle, probed the possibility of obtaining true and certain historical knowledge, especially with respect to ancient events.[6] The essential difference between mere critics of traditional historiographical methods and historical Pyrrhonists lay in the fact that while the former attempted to discredit existing assumptions and methodologies in favor of new ones, the latter sought to challenge the very possibility of ever obtaining any certain knowledge of the past. For many philosophical skeptics, the critique of historical practices went hand in hand with their larger project of demonstrating the weakness of human understanding.

Philosophical skepticism added a new dimension to the debates and had a transformative effect on assumptions about historiography. The disputes between the so-called historical Pyrrhonists and their opponents were instrumental in reshaping history as a discipline. By doubting the very possibility of attaining a true and coherent understanding of the past and by condemning what they saw as fictitious and unreliable accounts of ancient and more recent events, these thinkers both disputed the veracity of received historical knowledge and contested established historiographical methods. In light of these criticisms, historians and antiquarian scholars faced the challenges of redefining the nature of reliable evidence and of establishing firmer methodologies of evaluating that evidence. Ultimately, the dialogical interaction between both critical and skeptical arguments, on the one hand, and anti-skeptical responses, on the other, led to a gradual reexamination of the most basic epistemological principles. These debates transformed both historical Pyrrhonism, making its claims more mitigated and reserved, and historical practice, rendering it more critical toward authorities who had been considered practically infallible.

Historians began to rely more widely on legal documents and charters and on non-textual sources, such as coins, pottery, archaeological remains, and other material objects. Scholars also began to formalize rules and procedures for establishing the relative certainty of past events. Such attempts at formalization rendered historical practice more professional and transformed the historian's role, amplifying the historian's responsibility to examine sources with greater scrutiny. Furthermore, thinkers on both sides of the debate increasingly accepted probability as a pragmatic middle ground between complete certainty and extreme Pyrrhonism. This dialogical process thus facilitated the gradual modernization of the practice of history and paved the way for it to assume a quasi-scientific status in the nineteenth century.

The debates about the methods and value of historical scholarship were most lively in the French Académie royale des inscriptions et belles-lettres, whose members published several journal issues on the possibility of obtaining firm knowledge about the history of ancient Rome.[7] In France, the debate was stimulated in part by the *Querelle des Anciens et des Modernes*. In a dispute about how exactly to approach and use ancient texts, thinkers on both sides of the issue attempted to revise the role Greek and Roman antiquity played in the learned world of the eighteenth century.[8] Echoing the Renaissance humanists, seventeenth- and eighteenth-century scholars began to scrutinize the contents of ancient texts. Increasingly, they focused less on the style of such works and more on their factual content. They also reassessed the reliability of writers and poets who had previously served as models of literary excellence and as sources of knowledge about the past.

Disputations about historical Pyrrhonism were also quite frequent in the German universities. The origin of these disputes between supporters of historical Pyrrhonism and defenders of the *fides historica* (faith in recorded history) is quite unique to the German context and can be traced to the study of the history of jurisprudence and of philosophy.[9] Following the end of the Thirty Years' War (1618–48), disputes about the historical origins of legal and political entities had a particularly high resonance, as scholars attempted to navigate a minefield of competing jurisprudential claims. Johann Eisenhart's attempt to defend historical certainty and unite the disciplines of law and history in a lecture at the University of Helmstedt in 1667 provoked a number of responses from both his contemporaries and future generations of jurists.[10] These debates were less controversial philosophically, however, since they dealt largely with the relative superiority of academic disciplines. Thus, while the French debates centered around the study of ancient history and literature and took place, as we will see, in the shadow of Bayle's and La Mothe Le Vayer's skeptical critiques, the German debates primarily examined the reliability of documentary evidence and the proper relationships between history, philosophy, and jurisprudence. Historical Pyrrhonism was thus not as controversial in the German context as it was in the French, because it was not perceived as a symptom of the larger *crise pyrrhonienne*.

A General Critique of Historical Certainty

Although the majority of the critiques of historical certainty concerned individual cases, philosophical skeptics voiced general reservations about the possibility of obtaining knowledge about the past. Bayle's examination of historical understanding is particularly interesting, because it reveals some nuanced tensions in his thinking about different types of certainty. He made a crucial distinction between historical and philosophical certainty in his *Projet et fragmens d'un dictionnaire critique*. In the preface, Bayle maintained that "historical truths could be pushed to a degree of certainty that is more indubitable" than that of geometrical truths if one considered "these two kinds of truths according to the type of certainty that is appropriate to them." The fundamental difference between historians and philosophers, Bayle argued, was that the former assumed "the full reality and objective existence" of facts outside of our understanding. In determining whether a particular prince "ruled before or after another one," historians did not need to speculate whether "something that appeared to us to exist really existed outside the mind." All they needed to do what show the "apparent reality" (*existence apparente*) of historical events by consulting testimonies and documents. Philosophers, on the other hand, needed to establish that "objects were really of such a nature outside the mind as they appeared to us." In other words, it was easier for historians to demonstrate that Caesar and Pompey really lived in ancient Rome than for philosophers to prove the existence of a circle outside the mind. According to Bayle, the avoidance of a debate about the reality of the external world made it possible to reject "historical Pyrrhonism with respect to a great number of facts." At the same time, he conceded that other details were known with less certainty. It was the historian's task, he insisted, "to show the falsity of some things, the uncertainty of many others, and the truth" of the remaining ones. According to Bayle, such demonstrations could be much more morally useful than geometrical proofs even if they remained less certain in a metaphysical sense.[11]

In other instances, Bayle appeared significantly more pessimistic about the prospects of obtaining reliable historical knowledge. In the article "Zuerius," Bayle used the example of Pierre Jurieu's sermon in which he urged his parishioners to hate their confessional enemies—a sermon Jurieu later denied giving—in order to demonstrate the difficulty of verifying just three days later what had been said in front of a crowd of twelve hundred people.[12] After discussing an extended series of arguments that attempted to establish Jurieu's guilt, Bayle explicitly opposed skeptics, who "delight in casting all facts into uncertainty," and he sought to supply posterity with arms against "future Pyrrhonians."[13] Although he seemed to be attacking Pyrrhonism, the implication of Bayle's reasoning was quite the opposite. After putting his readers through a meticulous string of arguments that sought to prove that Jurieu had actually given the sermon in question, Bayle implicitly recognized the difficulty of demonstrating such a seemingly obvious fact. Although there were a large number of witnesses, it was still impossible to verify with absolute certainty whether Jurieu had uttered the impious words. How much more difficult, the Huguenot skeptic appeared to suggest, would it be to speculate about obscure events in the distant past? By using such an extreme case, Bayle insinuated the virtual impossibility of obtaining true and certain knowledge of the past. His *Dictionnaire* provided myriad similar examples.

In his critique of the *Histoire du calvinisme* (1682), written by the Jesuit Louis Maimbourg (1610–86), Bayle suggested that the description and presentation of historical facts were sometimes as significant as their content.[14] Comparing historians to lawyers, Bayle insisted that both cleverly twisted information whenever it suited them: "There are no facts that in the hands of two able lawyers pitted against each other do not assume entirely different forms." In making judgments about past events and notable figures, historians manipulated the order of events, passed over important details, and used rhetorical devices to persuade their audience.[15] The unreliability of historical accounts rendered the knowledge of the past impossible:

> I almost never read historians with the goal of learning about things that happened in the past, but only to know what is said in each nation and in each party about what happened in the past. When I read the history of the civil wars of the last century written by our authors, I find that French Protestants were never in the wrong. But when I read about the same wars in [the accounts of] historians of the opposite side, especially if they are monks or ecclesiastics, I find myself transported to another country where I no longer recognize myself.[16]

For Bayle, such divergences in accounts were so vast that there was no possible way to reconcile them and learn what had actually happened.

The skeptic La Mothe Le Vayer offered a similar general criticism in his *Du peu de certitude qu'il y a en histoire* (1668). He proclaimed that while history contained a great number of useful ethical examples and could be instructive, neither truth nor accuracy was the discipline's essence and purpose.[17] He compared ancient histories to fables and myths in terms of their utility and argued that "suspension of belief" with respect to the contents of human history did "not stop it from being beneficial." Using examples of ancient authors such as Hesiod, Aesop, and Ovid, La Mothe Le Vayer insisted that "despite their remoteness from the truth, [the texts] do not cease to be instructive either in physics or in morals."[18] If a particular account was not entirely accurate, it could nevertheless provide readers with instructive examples of how to act in particular situations. This argument had been popular among Renaissance humanists, who argued that history was an excellent source of moral instruction because it offered ethical models.[19]

The skeptical meta-critiques of Bayle and La Mothe Le Vayer played the most significant role in perpetuating the crisis of historical consciousness in the late seventeenth century.[20] They provided epistemological foundations for explaining the increase in the detection of factual errors and uncertainties. By casting doubt upon the possibility of knowing the past, whether distant or recent, with certainty, they undermined established narratives and questioned the very significance of historical knowledge.

Walking in the Dark: The Paucity and the Unreliability of Ancient Sources

In addition to these general reservations, skeptics, scholars, and practicing historians posed several specific problems. The most basic assault upon the possibility of obtaining true and certain historical knowledge came from those who pointed to the absence or paucity of sources from antiquity and claimed that there was little evidence outside mythological narratives to establish any facts. Even the staunchest opponents of historical skepticism perceived the fundamental challenges of unearthing accurate and detailed information about ancient Rome and Greece. In a special issue of the *Mémoires* of the Académie royale des inscriptions et belles-letters, the historian Louis-Jean Lévesque de Pouilly (1691–1751) claimed that details about early Rome were entirely uncertain. He argued that since all the histories of Rome had been written at least five hundred years after the alleged founding of the city, they had relied on myth, fable, and documents that could no longer be consulted for verification.[21] Moreover, seventeenth- and eighteenth-century historians emphasized that the majority of sources on which ancient Roman historians had relied, such as ancient treatises and census tablets, had been destroyed during the siege of the city by the Gauls in the fourth century BCE.[22]

Both Lévesque de Pouilly and his ally in the debate about the reliability of ancient histories, Louis de Beaufort (1703–95), also noted that even ancient Roman historians such as Livy and Cicero had questioned the narrative of the city's founding. According to Beaufort, Livy's analysis of the tale of Romulus and Remus demonstrated that the Roman historian had dismissed as myth the fantastical notion that the two were actually raised by a she-wolf. If such notable scholars, who had had every interest in establishing the facts, doubted the veracity of Rome's alleged origins, Beaufort argued, one would not be giving in to Pyrrhonism if one shared their reservations. In fact, one would be more of a Pyrrhonian if one did not doubt the obscurity of Rome's origins and distrusted "the formal testimony of those whose authority alone can be respected and [considered] of some weight in this matter."[23] If historians who had lived significantly closer to the events in question stressed the uncertain nature of the city's first century, then early modern scholars certainly could not claim to know Rome's beginnings with certainty.

Lévesque de Pouilly and Beaufort attributed the obscurity surrounding the city's founding to the low standard of learned culture in that age. Since the first Romans had lacked a developed written culture, they had preserved their histories in myths and songs.[24] Friedrich Wilhelm Bierling, whose *Commentatio de pyrrhonismo historico* offered a new effort to reconcile skepticism and anti-skepticism, suggested that historical events were often mixed with fictional accounts because earlier cultures had preserved their histories not in a stable written record but in fables, songs, and other oral forms, which were easily alterable.[25] Antoine Anselme (1652–1737) proposed that the earliest civilizations had passed down their histories in songs because they provided the easiest way for memorizing and transmitting information.[26] Enlightenment historians tended to distrust oral accounts because they found them to be easily distortable. This corruptibility, according to many historians, accounted for the contradictions and inconsistencies in ancient history.[27]

Critics and skeptics alike claimed that even the works of the most respected Roman and Greek historians were not entirely reliable, because they had been based on the oral traditions that preceded them. The German historian Peter Friedrich Arpe (1682–1740) suggested that Herodotus's writings were not trustworthy because they contained myths and fables.[28] Lévesque de Pouilly in turn pointed to an uncanny similarity between the events described in Greek and in Roman history, proposing that later scholars had simply transposed Greek accounts onto Rome's past.[29] Such a transposition, he maintained, rendered Roman history inauthentic and unreliable.

The marquis d'Argens was similarly critical of oral traditions and mythological accounts, suggesting that the vast majority were "contrary to reason." He was particularly suspicious of founding myths, noting that "there is nothing more deceitful and false than the notions that most people have of the foundation of their state." Ancient and modern peoples alike had fabricated fantastic stories about the origins of their nations or of their religions in order to make them appear "more illustrious" to posterity. The "fabulous dynasties" of the Egyptians, the histories of "the Gods and the demi-Gods" of the Greeks, the tale of the "she-wolf that suckled Romulus and Remus," and the establishment of the kingdom of the Gauls by the son of Hector were all examples of this tendency.[30] Most of these founding myths originated in the popular imagination, but they had a very strong influence on the majority of people. In d'Argens's estimation, the structure and content of these fables resulted from "the prejudices of our youth" and from the "laziness inherent in so many persons." Children were accustomed to hearing many "false anecdotes" and "pious rhapsodies" from their parents. They came to believe and remember these vivid stories and transmitted them to their children, thereby continuing the vicious cycle of historical falsity. Because of "laziness and indolence," people failed to examine the veracity of these tales, so that they were "carried by the stream and became engulfed in error from the examples of others." Poets, painters, and orators were especially talented at perpetuating fictions and etching them in popular memory, d'Argens noted. Their vivid imaginations fabricated memorable but false stories that established traditional narratives and acquired authority over time. Consequently, even if there were some historians who "were more careful in the defense of the truth" and attempted to separate fact from fiction, there were plenty who "follow the torrent and conform themselves to popular opinion."[31]

D'Argens expanded the critique of ancient history to include not just Greece and Rome but also the rest of the world. "The history of the first ages is so obscure," he wrote, "and the little of it that has reached us is so mixed with fables that clearly contradict reason that we cannot, if we wish to make use of our natural light, admit three-quarters of the facts related therein as true." The only available information about antediluvian history came from the texts of Moses. D'Argens observed that these sources appeared to contradict Chinese and Egyptian annals that described the beginning of the world. Furthermore, d'Argens echoed La Peyrère's claim that the Bible only addressed the history of the Jews, while ignoring the Egyptians, the Ethiopians, and the Chinese, among other peoples. He went so far as to question the physical possibility of a universal flood and pointed to the conflicting "history of nations that contradicts the general inundation of the whole earth." D'Argens noted that Egyptian annals had described a flourishing empire that existed less than two centuries after the supposed universal deluge. The conflict between scripture and these sources made it difficult to establish any chronological certainty about ancient history.[32]

Indeed, factual uncertainty plagued not only ancient history but also more recent sources. La Mothe Le Vayer discussed the chronological discrepancies in accounts of the capture of Constantinople by the Ottomans, pointing to the fact that historians still could not agree whether this seminal event took place in 1453 or 1452.[33] Similarly, an anonymous analysis of Bayle's *Dictionnaire* referred to the author's article on Jacques de Beaune, baron de Semblançay (c. 1465–1527) and reinforced Bayle's position about the difficulty of establishing the nobleman's death. It suggested that such uncertainties offered "a new reason to uphold historical Pyrrhonism."[34]

Chronological inconsistencies posed a problem for more than just the verification of particular dates. They also raised questions regarding reconciliation of Western and Eastern timelines. Scholars looked beyond Greece and Rome to broaden their understanding of the ancient world. They began to compare the chronologies of Greece, Egypt, Persia, and the Assyrian kingdoms, trying to affix the ages of the most ancient realms. In attempting to apply astronomy and mathematics to history, Isaac Newton sought to correct ancient timelines, reconcile them with biblical accounts, and even predict the end of the world. His posthumously published *Chronology of Ancient Kingdoms Amended* (1728) investigated the internal consistency of ancient sequences of events, particularly the fact that the kings of early dynasties seemed to have improbably long life spans. Suggesting that all nations had wished to extend their origins further into the past, he posited that the expedition of the Argonauts had taken place nine hundred years, rather than fourteen hundred, before the birth of Christ. Newton thus concluded that the world was actually about five hundred years younger than had been assumed.[35]

Newton's work was received with mixed reviews. Even before the official publication of the full text in England, the manuscript of an abridgment made its way to France, where it was translated in 1725.[36] The Jesuit Etienne Souciet (1671–1744) issued a critique of Newton's chronology. In five separate theses, he corrected the astronomical basis of Newton's system and defended the established timeline.[37] The learned academician Nicolas Fréret (1688–1749), who had published the French version of Newton's chronology, joined Souciet in these efforts. Fréret attempted to reconcile the chronology of the most ancient civilizations as established by historical methods with Newton's chronological theories, which were based on astronomy. He claimed to have refuted Newton's hypothesis and to have explained the divergence between the Chinese and European timelines on the basis of archaeological and textual evidence.[38]

Not all responses to Newton's controversial system were negative, however. In his *Lettres philosophiques*, Voltaire praised Newton for applying his understanding of nature to the study of history but wondered whether the method would be accepted and whether "people will want to have recourse to his ideas to reform the chronology of the world."[39] In his later works, Voltaire would embrace controversial chronologies that derived from La Peyrère's *Prae-Adamitae* and argue that Adam was not in fact the first man. In the later editions of his *Dictionnaire philosophique* (1764), Voltaire even suggested that the name Adam had been borrowed by the Jews from India, which he identified as the birthplace of the first man.[40] Such speculations helped to fuel the fire of informal and formal skepticism, decentered the Judeo-Christian chronologies, and posed challenges to the historical veracity and legitimacy of the Bible.

These and many other critiques also cast doubt on the general reliability of all existing historical accounts, particularly with regard to ancient historiography. Enlightenment scholars challenged longstanding assumptions about the trustworthiness of classical authors who had long been considered important sources of information about the past. Such attacks dealt a significant blow to the epistemological status of history even if they came not from the skeptics but from humanist textual critics. Willingly or unwillingly, the latter became the intellectual fellow travelers of the Pyrrhonists in the eyes of the defenders of the *fides historica.*

In response, scholars attempted to reconstruct or to erect anew some basic foundations for true and relatively certain historical knowledge. In order to deal with the absence of documentary or archaeological evidence, the abbé Claude Sallier (1685–1761), the curator of manuscripts at the Bibliothèque royale and the Académie royale des inscriptions et belles-letters, disputed the absence of primary sources that could attest to the history of ancient Rome. He suggested that a sufficient number of primary documents were still available in the form of the annals kept by the Roman pontiffs, fragments of the acts of the senate, tablets, and peace treaties. These sources were reliable because they would have been examined by the Roman public, who could have challenged the documents had they appeared inaccurate or false. He further argued that even if modern historians did not have direct access to the primary sources from early Roman antiquity, such as treaties or ruins, they could infer the existence of those materials from descriptions of them in the accounts of many Roman historians. Citing Cicero's works on the earliest days of Rome, Sallier argued that historians had to "either admit that verified records were the sources on which this great man based his historical knowledge or maintain that he was deceived, that he ran after specious lies, and that he readily embraced the phantoms of credulity common to the men of his time."[41] Although he acknowledged the impossibility of gaining direct access to indisputable evidence, Sallier urged his readers to believe that it was reasonable to accept the majority of the facts of early Roman history based on the authority of Roman historians.[42]

Similarly, the German historian Christoph Saxius (1714–1806), who taught at the University of Utrecht, contended that the reliability of early Roman history rested firmly on the authority of authors such as Livy, whose reputation, judgment, and sincerity served as sufficient guarantees.[43] He disputed Beaufort's critique, arguing that "the certain and true writings of the history of that time are in no way lacking," and claimed that even if some of the elements related in the works of reliable ancient authors seemed fabulous or imagined, the majority of the events described had to be true because of the trustworthiness of the source.[44]

Other historians suggested that although textual evidence about antiquity might be sparse, significant discoveries could be made through the study of non-textual evidence, such as ancient ruins, statues, pottery, coins, tablets, and other materials. Writing explicitly against Bayle and La Mothe Le Vayer, the German historian Johann August Ernesti (1707–81) proposed that material evidence should be used to verify the accuracy of secondary historical accounts.[45] The abbé Anselme similarly claimed that the study of structures such as city walls, columns, and statues provided important information about the nature and progress of ancient civilizations. He maintained that in the form of such monuments, "all considerable events of the first centuries [of Rome] were preserved in the memory of men, even in places where one had no writing."[46] The remains of city walls could demonstrate the gradual growth of ancient towns, and statues and vase paintings could reveal notable historical actors.

By the time the Italian historian Scipione Maffei's (1675–1755) posthumously published *Ars critica lapidaria* appeared in 1765, the reliance on non-textual evidence had become a common practice in the study of ancient and medieval history.[47] The very formation of an institution such as the Académie royale des inscriptions et belles-lettres signaled the recognition of the need to focus on non-literary sources. Originally named the Académie royale des inscriptions et médailles, this institution was established with the purpose of recovering or composing Latin inscriptions for monuments dedicated to commemorating Louis XIV's achievements. The Crown sought to create authentic associations with the grandeur of the Roman Empire, and it needed scholars who had a vast knowledge of ancient history. Its members were thus dedicated to the study of antiquity, especially through material sources such as coins, seals, and statues. Such items would provide distinct and complementary sets of evidence that could help to confirm or expose information contained in literary sources. In an attempt to emulate Roman models, the French Crown thus sponsored and stimulated the study of antiquity.

Historians also proposed a way to deal with the apparent abundance of myths and fictional elements in ancient texts. Bierling suggested that historians could use both original and secondary accounts as evidence, without necessarily accepting all of the information contained within.[48] While advocating for a "tempered" Pyrrhonism in history, Bierling noted that no source, whether textual or material, could be taken completely at face value, and no historian, no matter how honest and reliable, could be trusted absolutely.[49] He argued that the myths in sacred history and in the Bible did not undermine the fundamental truth of the events recounted there. Indeed, Bierling suggested that such myths contained important moral lessons and could, if read critically, provide details of events with some degree of accuracy.[50]

Claude Sallier suggested that the inclusion of myths and fictional elements did not irreparably damage the reliability of ancient accounts. An attentive reader could easily disentangle events that appeared incredible and exaggerated from those that appeared realistic. Sallier implied that Roman authors sometimes inserted fables and popular beliefs into their chronicles merely to render the realistic explanations of events more obvious to the readers. Even if some ancient historians did believe in the truth of some of those myths, their texts could not be completely discredited. These fables could not "destroy the certainty of the first centuries of Rome" or make the foundations of Roman history "more suspicious or doubtful."[51] Sallier reverted to a common argument against philosophical Pyrrhonism. The presence of falsities and errors did not mean that the entire corpus of received knowledge had to be rejected as false and discarded. It was an illogical leap to conclude that because people had been mistaken about some questions—whether historical or philosophical—they had no possibility of obtaining any true and certain knowledge. Such efforts, in the minds of the defenders of the *fides historica*, overstated the amount of uncertainty in history and ignored the reality that ancient and modern historians had verified many of the supposedly disputed facts.

Sallier also countered Lévesque de Pouilly's charge about the similarity of Greek and Roman accounts. He argued that Plutarch had recognized a distinct historical tradition in Rome and that one could only reject the unique roots of Roman history if one rejected Plutarch's rightful authority. He also suggested that the stark resemblance could be attributed to the cyclical nature of history and to a common human nature: "A person observing the history of the whole world will see the theater change scenes; he will see new actors arrive and old ones leave. But this spectator will also notice that so many different scenes always bring back the same interests, that those same interests are born out of the same passions, and that those passions often engage in the same movements and produce the same effects."[52] Salier further argued that medieval and recent French histories often resembled those from antiquity but that this resemblence in no way diminished their veracity and authenticity. He not only replied to Pouilly's claim about the transposition of the Greek tradition onto Roman history but also implied that lacunae in historical knowledge could be filled by analogical reasoning. The similarity of human nature made it possible to speculate about cases in which sufficient evidence was not available.

The debates about the quality of ancient sources produced a search for rules, procedures, and practices that could remedy the difficulties posed by skeptical and critical authors. Seeking to avoid the "road to ignorance," which was paved by historical Pyrrhonists, who subjected all knowledge of antiquity to doubt, the defenders of the *fides historica* had to disentangle reliable accounts of the past from questionable ones.[53] They had to concede, however, that a significant number of ancient sources on which many historians of antiquity had relied contained fundamental problems. As a result, source criticism occupied an increasingly important position in the debates about historiography.

The Faults and Errors of Historians

Advocates of a skeptical attitude in historical investigations stressed the relative unreliability of secondary sources, whether ancient or modern, in addition to emphasizing the absence or unreliability of documentary evidence. Critics claimed that the accuracy of most historians' accounts could not always be assumed. Some blamed emotions and prejudices for corrupting historical narratives, laying particular stress on the common tendency to attribute false glory to one's own fatherland and to make fictitious claims out of enmity for other nations.[54] For example, Arpe accused Herodotus of falsifying the histories of Persia, Egypt, and other ancient civilizations in order to make it seem that the Greeks had preceded and surpassed those cultures.[55] La Mothe Le Vayer likewise noted that the Roman consul and historian Cassius Dio (c. 155–c. 235) had exaggerated the role and the accomplishments of the Athenians at the Battle of Salamis, while Polybius (c. 200–c. 118 BCE) and Philinus (d. 213 BCE) had chosen to side with Rome and Carthage, respectively, in their accounts of the Punic Wars.[56]

Similarly, Pierre Bayle suggested that all historical scholarship suffered from the problem of partisanship, with each side attempting to paint its opponents in an unfavorable light. In his critique of Maimbourg's *Histoire du calvinisme*, Bayle cited the prevalence of religious prejudice against Calvinists. In discussing the historical disputes about the Wars of Religion, Bayle claimed that he wished to withdraw himself from the debate: "[As] for myself, I wish to be a Pyrrhonian, I affirm neither one nor the other [side]."[57] In Bayle's view, it was such bias and diversity of conflicting opinions that made historical Pyrrhonism appealing to his contemporaries. He argued that the bias and prejudice of a great number of "malicious" historians "who care nothing for the truth" had made him give in to historical Pyrrhonism. Bayle did not deny the existence of an objective reality of the past, but he argued that given the partiality and unreliability of historians, one could never attain certain knowledge about it.[58]

In arguing that there was an inherent bias and prejudice in historical accounts, d'Argens echoed Bayle's emphasis on the tensions between various religious and political groups. He cited accounts of the Saint Bartholomew's Day Massacre to show how Catholic and Protestant historians offered diametrically opposite accounts of the event and of the principal participants in the violence. Indeed, historians often resembled "advocates or defenders of certain parties rather than faithful chroniclers of what had passed." Consequently, "the same facts and the same events became entirely different," because each author attempted to show that "right, reason, and truth" were on the side of his party.[59]

Chauvinism and religious prejudice were not the only alleged causes of historical bias. In some cases, scholars claimed, historians obviously had been urged or compelled to alter their accounts by their sovereigns. In his article on the Scottish antiquarian William Camden (1551–1623), Bayle noted that King James I of England and VI of Scotland (1566–1625), son of Mary Stuart (1542–87), had persuaded the historian to give an account of his mother's reign that painted her in a favorable light, supporting "historical Pyrrhonism with respect to the adventures of this Princess."[60] Beaufort similarly proposed that the vast majority of Roman histories were based on the private memoirs of notable families or on funeral orations about important public figures. Since these accounts often attempted to exaggerate the exploits of their protagonists, historians could put their trust neither in these original sources nor in secondary accounts that relied on them.[61] He argued that all histories of Rome's earliest days depended on the works of Fabius Pictor (b. 254 BCE), who had used the biased primary evidence without examining the veracity of what he retold.[62] Beaufort cited Cicero's observations about the reliability of such accounts and agreed with Bayle, who had suggested that most of Roman history had been forged: "If Mr. Bayle had had before him the words of Titus Livy and Cicero that we have cited, he would have been assured in what he reports here as a mere conjecture based on appearances. He would see that even if Rome did not learn to speak artfully and to polish her language until rather late, she never lacked people ready to disguise the truth and to embellish history with all the [possible] events that their imagination could provide."[63] Thus, neither primary nor secondary sources offered untainted and objective information.

In his treatise on the faults of historians, the Jena scholar Burkhard Gotthelf Struve (1671–1738) made a comparable critique, enumerating the reasons for which historians might willingly or unwillingly provide false accounts for posterity. He divided historians into two categories: those who erred out of ignorance and those who purposely misled their audience because of ulterior motives.[64] He listed instances in which historians had lied or had deceived readers owing to either religious or patriotic prejudice or corrupt goals, such as a desire for profit or a wish to gain favor with political authorities. Not all errors had to be attributed to vice or to underhanded purposes. Struve stated that this second group—historians who erred from ignorance—were equally responsible for the lack of certainty in history. In some cases, Struve, Bierling, and others argued, historians were simply too credulous and failed to examine the facts they were reporting with sufficient scrutiny.[65] Even the most reputable authors of antiquity were not innocent of this charge; early modern historians found mistakes, inconsistencies, and uncritical recitations of myths and fables in their works. The inability of earlier historians to distinguish between fact and fiction rendered the problem more difficult, casting doubt not only on their sincerity but also on their critical abilities.

The critiques of ancient historians eroded the influence of notable authors and posed further difficulties for scholars who sought to establish some basis for historical certainty. The arguments against historical Pyrrhonism relied on the assumption that despite the lack of original sources from antiquity, prominent ancient authors had provided reliable and nearly indisputable accounts of Greek and Roman history. By contending that no author was immune from error or prejudice, skeptics and critics undermined the traditional dependence on the authority of respected authors. In order to counter such assertions, defenders of the *fides historica* proposed procedures for evaluating the trustworthiness of historians. They also attempted to find ways to balance conflicting accounts and to resolve apparent contradictions and disagreements. Most authors conceded that blind agreement with even the most respected authorities was unbefitting a serious scholar of the past. Thus, by proposing formal rules for evaluating secondary accounts, the defenders of the *fides historica* hoped to render history more scientific and critical.

Cicero's famous dictum that a historian should tell nothing more and nothing less than the truth became almost ubiquitous in early modern disputes about historiography.[66] While evaluating their own sources for sincerity and reliability, many seventeenth- and eighteenth-century historians attempted to protect their profession from bias by demanding the same qualities from their colleagues. The Benedictine scholar Jean Mabillon (1632–1707), whose research on diplomatics and hagiography caused some stir (and earned him signal recognition) in the learned community for the force of his critical methods, stressed the importance of the historian's sincerity and love of truth. This included even situations in which the scholar's own nation, faction, or religious order might be harmed by the revelation of the truth. Equating a historian to a judge in terms of the public responsibility to seek the truth, Mabillon insisted that a good scholar "must rid himself of all sorts of affections and prejudices that are contrary to the love of truth and to sincerity." The historian had the responsibility not to distort or hide information even if it did not "appear very advantageous to the reputation of certain persons," because such information served "for the instruction and warning of posterity."[67] For Mabillon, this was an especially sensitive matter. Other members of the Benedictine order had attacked his hagiographic texts for questioning whether some of the saints had actually belonged to the order. Mabillon defended himself by arguing that his primary duty as a historian was to pursue accuracy and veracity. He maintained that if the fraternal membership of certain saints was doubtful, it was his obligation to make that fact known, since "sincerity demands that one reports certain things as certain, false things as false, and doubtful things as doubtful."[68]

Mabillon also proposed a three-layered system of authorial reliability. The most credible authors were those who lived at the time of the events they described and who either had been direct witnesses or had received testimony from direct witnesses to these happenings. The next group included those who lived very shortly after the events in question and had had the ability to confirm their veracity. Finally, scholars who lived significantly after the occurrences, including modern authors, were the least trustworthy sources, because they were far removed from the events and often merely copied what they read in earlier texts without verifying, or without having the ability to verify, the correctness of those accounts. At the same time, the mere proximity of a historian to the events he described could not, by itself, guarantee the accuracy and the veracity of what he related. One could not "accept all things blindly merely under the pretext that a contemporaneous author said them," and one had the responsibility of verifying the scholarly qualifications, prejudices, and moral rectitude of the reporter and determining "whether he is . . . contradicted by other historians of the time or by circumstances of things about which we now have some certain knowledge."[69]

Hidden Causes and Secret Motives: Interpreting the Past

The final set of problems arose from the fact that most thinkers recognized that historical writing involved not just records of facts but also attempts to explain the causes of past events and of the motivations of the various actors. While few skeptics claimed that one could completely deny the certainty of an event that was described in similar terms in multiple independent testimonies, many scholars agreed about the relative difficulty, if not outright impossibility, of providing causal explanations. First, each event could have several possible causes and pretexts, and historians had to be equipped with sound judgment to discern the most likely one. In some cases, multiple explanations could appear equally valid. Second, many motives lay hidden from the view of both contemporary witnesses and the historians describing them, leaving conjecture as the only possible recourse. In his critique of Maimbourg, Bayle argued that the diversity of equally reasonable historical explanations caused many to suspend judgment and to embrace historical Pyrrhonism.[70] Bierling, who cited Bayle's article on Camden, similarly asserted that the uncertain nature of human motivations armed Pyrrhonians with an arsenal of potential criticisms of the historical profession: "It is clear from these things that I related that the majority of the general facts reported by historians are subject to little doubt, but the circumstances and impelling reasons supply the Pyrrhonian with a great deal of material."[71]

Citing recent examples, Bierling argued that while it was certain *that* Holy Roman Emperor Charles V (1500–1558) abdicated the throne, historians had provided multiple explanations of his motivations. Some maintained that it was out of a desire for peace and rest; others attributed his abdication to his ill health; still others linked it to his son's thirst for power. Similarly, chroniclers of King Henry VIII (1491–1547) presented several possible reasons for his divorce from Catherine of Aragon (1485–1536). Catholics blamed his uncontrollable lust for Anne Boleyn (c. 1501–36). The Protestant historian and theologian Gilbert Burnet (1643–1715) maintained that Henry's conscience had not allowed him to remain married to his dead brother's wife. Others mentioned Catherine's inability to bear a male heir or the monarch's desire to become independent from Rome.[72]

Mabillon agreed that it was difficult to determine causes and motives. While there were few disagreements about facts and events, historians often diverged concerning "the intentions, the motives, and the causes of some particular events."[73] The marquis d'Argens, who likewise listed authors' ignorance of the main causes of events as a fundamental problem in historical scholarship, suggested that emotions and passions such as jealousy, ambition, love, and hatred often played a more important role than any rational motivations.[74] Motives and intentions could be concealed even from eyewitnesses, and the historical actors could be the only people who knew the true reasons for their actions. Historians did not always have access to intrigues that happened behind closed doors, and they certainly could not glance into the emotional states of historical actors.

Despite these difficulties, some scholars argued that the true value of history lay precisely in the knowledge of causes and motives. The Jesuit scholar César Vichard de Saint-Réal (1639–92) argued against mere memorization in his *De l'usage de l'histoire* (1671). He suggested that the "the true use of history does not consist in knowing many events and actions without reflecting on them at all" or in a passive memorization. "To study history," Saint-Réal insisted, was "to study the motives, the opinions, and the passions of men in order to know their drives, their turns, their deceitful actions, and . . . illusions."[75] For Saint-Réal, history served a morally didactic purpose and taught its students important ethical lessons. Unlike La Mothe Le Vayer, who shared his belief in the moral value of history, Saint-Réal maintained that the veracity of historical interpretations was crucial to understanding ethical implications correctly.

The erudite Fréret, in turn, argued against the attempted conjectures and hypotheses that filled the lacunae of our understanding of the past. Fréret suggested that such conjectures could often create even greater uncertainty, because the historians who proposed them had already picked sides and decided on narratives:

> But since such fragments often leave empty spaces between them, and since many are obscure or appear opposed to one another or to ancient histories that are known to us entirely, it is not, in general, sufficient to determine the degree of authority of the authors whose fragments one uses. One must often interpret them and add conjectures and hypotheses, which only obtain their strength from probability and from their connection to the rest of history. It is mainly on this point that the method of the scholars from the past century appears deceitful.[76]

Fréret accused scholars of using the extracts to fit their predetermined narratives. He also charged them with deploying evidence and testimonies selectively in order to lend more support to their particular interpretations.

In order to solve the potential problem of interpretation, the erudite polymath Nicolas Lenglet du Fresnoy (1674–1755), who republished Saint-Réal's treatise on the proper use of history and who penned a multivolume *Méthode pour étudier l'histoire* (1713), tried to modify the editorial role of the historian and offered some instructions to contemporary authors. He argued that Saint-Réal had rightly criticized historians for being overly moralizing and had wisely urged scholars to focus solely on narrating "exactly the main circumstances of an event" and leave moral judgments and evaluations up to the reader.[77] Lenglet du Fresnoy and Saint-Réal hoped to minimize the potential for prejudice and error and to render the study of history more engaging.

Mabillon, who had suggested the problem of interpretation as a major source of uncertainty, nevertheless contended that most interpretive differences were generally resolvable. He asserted that it was easy to know which side to take even in cases in which a divergence of opinions concerned the facts themselves, because the truth has a certain inexplicable "light" (*brilliance*) about it. After sufficient experience with historical works, one acquired the ability to distinguish trustworthy interpretations from more dubious ones.[78] One had to discriminate among various explanations based on their authors' proximity to the events and their tendency to offer sincere and impartial accounts. One also had to consider the explanations to determine which account seemed most in harmony with circumstances that were known about a particular event.[79]

Bierling's examples of multiple possible accounts led his reviewer in the *Bibliothèque germanique* to offer potential solutions that would avoid uncertainty. At times the multicausal nature of the event was in fact the best available explanation. If different explanations did not directly contradict one another, it was possible that they all played important roles, "because it is rare that men, especially great ones, do not have multiple motives for their behavior." If the hypotheses were not mutually exclusive, "the disagreement of historians about these impulses and these motives would not be favorable to Pyrrhonism, since all one needs to do is unite them."[80] Even the staunchest defenders of the *fides historica* agreed that in cases in which difficulties remained, a suspension of judgment was the only option.

All of these arguments attempted to defend traditional historical methods and to preserve the importance of authorial reliability. Other scholars confronted the claims of the Pyrrhonians by rejecting the ultimate logical conclusion of their arguments and suggesting that there were many historical facts that could not, for various reasons, be disputed. Jean Henri Samuel Formey, for example, maintained that no skeptic could doubt facts that were supported by numerous or unanimous testimonies.[81] By emphasizing indisputable events and facts, opponents of historical Pyrrhonism tried to divert attention from the weak links in the chain of historical knowledge and to establish some solid foundations on which to defend the *fides historica*.

Some scholars proposed that after ascertaining the most basic and indubitable facts, historians should establish causal and chronological connections among them. Claude Sallier, who had argued for the relative certainty of ancient Roman history, compared history to natural philosophy: "In the study of history, just as in the study of nature, one must only gather the facts." Sallier tried to apply Fontenelle's understanding of physical phenomena and experimentation to history, insisting that nearly identical methods were applicable to both disciplines. He cited the perpetual secretary of the Académie royale des sciences, who had claimed that "many separated truths, once they are great in number, offer to the mind their relationship and their mutual dependence so vividly that it seems that [even] after being violently detached from one another, they naturally seek to reunite themselves."[82]

It was precisely this interconnection among facts that was missing from the most ancient histories, according to Nicolas Fréret. Like Sallier, he claimed that the best way to increase historical certainty was by constructing a firm chain of facts that tied events together through time and established chronological and logical coherence. The greater the number of interdependent facts in such a chronological chain, he argued, the greater the likelihood that each fact was accurate on its own. However, Fréret noted, the most able historians of the preceding centuries, such as Joseph Scaliger (1540–1609), Gerardus Vossius (1577–1649), and Henry Dodwell (1641–1711), had failed to provide such a coherent chain of events for most ancient histories. It was not evident that "the histories of neighboring nations have any of the connections that should exist between the affairs of people who had common interests and a similar fortune." Fréret proposed that historians had to construct such a chain by starting with the most certain events and then descending in degrees of probability. He warned against the dangers of articulating conjectures about less certain facts.[83] Using an analogous argument about the sequences of causes and events, the Dutch historian and classical scholar Jakob Perizonius (1651–1715) noted that one necessarily had to infer the existence of the Roman Empire in the past from the existence of the Holy Roman Empire in the present.[84] By observing the effects and consequences of various historical events in the present, he claimed, one could deduce their original causes.

David Renaud Boullier, whose *Traité des vrais principes qui servent de fondement à la certitude morale* attempted to refute Bayle's Pyrrhonism, compared testimonies of witnesses in historical accounts to physical phenomena observed by natural philosophers. The simplest and most logical inference one could make upon seeing multiple effects of historical events, such as the existence of different ancient sources and monuments, was that they all derived from a common set of causes.[85] In arguing against Jean Hardouin's theory of a conspiracy by monks to forge heretical writings and attribute them to ancient and patristic authors, Boullier proposed that the actual existence of these ancient authors was a much more certain proposition: "What assures me of the truth of of all this [the authenticity of the documents that Hardouin believed forged] is that if we refuse to admit it, one must necessarily believe the most absurd thing in the world: that a few centuries before ours, there formed a great cabal of forgers who, with the plot of imposing [their conspiracy] on the whole world, forged all the books that we regard as the classics of ancient Greece and ancient Italy."[86] In Boullier's view, such a conclusion was impossible. It contradicted the principle that a correct causal explanation had to explain the observed phenomena in the most parsimonious way.

Probability, Mitigated Skepticism, and Historical Science

These debates continued over the course of the eighteenth century, gradually acquiring more sophistication. The interaction between skeptical arguments and attempts to parry them produced a limited compromise about the extent and limits of historical knowledge. First, both sides agreed that while there were some basic things about the past that could be known with almost complete certainty, the level of detail of this information varied significantly depending on the availability and the quality of sources. Consequently, even the most antiskeptical authors accepted significant constraints on what could be known with total confidence. It was the task of the historian to disentangle rumors, fictions, and fables from true and definite facts.

Thus, Lévesque de Pouilly, who had argued against the certainty of early Roman history, nevertheless suggested that one could arrive at a high degree of probability by analyzing both the internal logic of historical facts and the credibility of the authorities who reported them. Despite asserting that direct personal experience was the only absolute guarantor of complete veracity, he agreed that it would be unreasonable to doubt every event to which one was not a direct witness.[87] He urged fellow historians to take the middle road between the extremes of claiming that all history was false and fictitious, on the one hand, and believing every fact that a historian reported, on the other: "Let us reject these opposing excesses: let us recognize that in history falsities are mixed with truths but that there are marks by which we can distinguish one from the other."[88] Just as in the debates about the relationship between mind and body and in those concerning the origin of human ideas, probability and verisimilitude emerged as a constructive compromise in disputes surrounding historical certainty.

In responding to the challenge of Pyrrhonian attacks, scholars also sought to establish some basic distinctions between the levels of certainty one could attain in the physical sciences, on the one hand, and in the human sciences, on the other. Ironically, it was Huet, whose commitment to philosophical skepticism had so shocked contemporaries, who attempted to defend history against Cartesian, deist, and Pyrrhonian critiques. His *Demonstratio evangelica* offered a geometrical proof of the veracity and universal validity of scripture. Huet attempted to give history the epistemological status of mathematics—a type of undertaking that would become increasingly rare.

Just as Sallier used Fontenelle's text to compare history to natural philosophy, the anti-skeptic Boullier argued for a near equivalence between physics and history. He claimed that in both disciplines, one could determine invisible causes by observing visible effects, such as testimonies, monuments, and other remnants of the past.[89] However, other historians disputed such a connection and attempted to propose a different way of thinking about historical certainty. Both Fréret and Bierling agreed that in history, as in other human sciences, one could not obtain the level of certainty that was possible in mathematics and physics. Fréret claimed that historical demonstrations could reach only a high degree of probability and attain moral certainty—one that no rational person could doubt in good faith—but they could never command complete metaphysical certainty. The "sciences most important to man, such as ethics, politics, economics, medicine, criticism, [and] jurisprudence [were] incapable of obtaining the certainty identical to geometrical demonstrations" and could "never extend beyond great probability." However, Fréret insisted that "this probability has such force in these matters that reasonable minds would never refuse to submit to it."[90] Historians were freed from the burden of maintaining the untenable proposition that their accounts offered indubitably certain and accurate representations of the past. History, as a human science, would have its own standard of proof.

Bierling noted that the discrepancy between history and physics lay in the fact that physical phenomena were perceived directly by the senses, while historical causes and motives often lay hidden from view. Consequently, it was "unsuitable to compare historical truths to physical ones."[91] While Boullier believed that this imperceptibility could be solved by deduction, Bierling saw it as the fundamental reason for the lack of scientific certainty in history. He insisted that scholars should adopt a mild Pyrrhonist position that consisted in a careful examination of the facts, a circumspect judgment of all accounts, a meticulous weighing of the relevant evidence, and most importantly, an understanding of the limits of what could be known.[92]

Furthermore, Bierling proposed a scale of degrees of probability and divided historical facts into three classes. The first comprised what was provided either by contemporaries or by trustworthy historians and included no elements that could be held as uncertain. For instance, one had no reason to doubt that Caesar or Pompey had existed and that they had waged war against each other, just as one had no evidence to marshal against Alexander the Great's defeat of Darius. The second class comprised the knowledge of the causes and of the circumstances surrounding events in the past. Since these facts could be either hidden or disputed in divergent testimonies, one could suspend judgment about them. Lastly, the third class was made up of facts and circumstances that could not be understood without difficulty and that remained in doubt. This third class was the main reason, Bierling noted, why Pyrrhonism had a useful place in historical scholarship. Historical skeptics could always point to the multiple lacunae in historical knowledge.[93] Using this classification, Bierling was able to protect historical scholarship from extreme skepticism, while simultaneously using mitigated skepticism as a tool to obtain a more stable understanding of the past.

In light of the number of historical inaccuracies and uncertainties, an increasing number of historians advocated a mitigated Pyrrhonism in history. Skeptics and critical scholars suggested that a suspension of judgment was not only an inevitable outcome of the majority of historical investigations but also a useful means of evaluating the relative certainty of various events. The German historian Struve, who had stressed the bias, prejudice, and corruption of historians, argued that a skeptical approach in history was helpful and necessary because of the criterion of certainty on which the discipline was based. He insisted that because Pyrrhonism was useful in philosophy, then "it was certainly much more useful in history."[94] Since the *fides historica* was based on belief in the veracity of ancient testimonies and not on rational arguments, it was not as reliable as philosophical certainty. The prejudice revealed in the various debates among historians, along with conflicting witness testimonies, justified a skeptical attitude toward a great number of historical reports.[95]

Mabillon, who sought to formulate rules for establishing historical certainty, argued that there was a place for reasonable doubt in investigations of the past, since there were indeed many elements in history that were uncertain. One could not blame historians for suspending their judgment as long as this doubt was reasonable. Mabillon further asserted that if a historian, because of insufficient evidence or conflicting testimonies, could not verify the truth of the events that he was reporting, "he must, in effect, suspend his judgment until he finds the evidence to examine them."[96]

Even Sallier, who had defended the ancient records from historical Pyrrhonism, also admitted that history contained a number of uncertainties. He wrote that ancient chronicles often "disfigure the truth" by presenting embellishments and exaggerations.[97] Defining history as "an assemblage of various facts linked together by the cord of a sustained narration," Sallier concluded that the "certainty that pertains to these facts is none other than that of great probability, which depends on the manner in which an author reported them." While complete confidence in historical knowledge was unattainable, such a degree of conviction was simply unnecessary. Most skeptics asserted that a suspension of judgment about controversial questions was bound to bring about calmness of mind. For Sallier, such a result would come from the recognition that the understanding of past events could attain a high degree of probability, which "has the power to calm the anxiety of the mind and to suspend all doubts."[98]

Bierling offered one of the most nuanced defenses of applying mitigated Pyrrhonism to historical scholarship. He began by attempting to dispel the notion that Pyrrhonism amounted to a complete rejection of certainty. He explained that Pyrrho and his disciples had been significantly misinterpreted and that their goal had been merely to challenge the untenable positions of the dogmatists and force them back toward a middle ground. As noted earlier, he also saw the extreme statements of the Pyrrhonists as a *jeu d'esprit* used to ridicule the dogmatists. Having established the basis for mild skepticism, Bierling argued that since history was based on the testimonies of others, it was subject to some reasonable doubt.[99] While definitive historical truths existed, they were often inaccessible to scholars. Bierling advocated a probabilistic approach to historical studies, provided a spectrum of verisimilitude for various kinds of historical facts, and contended that a judicious suspension of judgment could actually lead to greater certainty.

While Bierling offered the most explicit explanation of such a system in his *Commentatio de pyrrhonismo historico*, a number of other philosophers and historians also began to stake out a middle way between the two perceived extremes of accepting all plausible historical accounts as true, on the one hand, and rejecting all history as false or uncertain, on the other. Perizonius, in his treatise against extreme skepticism in history, urged that one should neither claim that nothing about the past could be known nor ignore the existence of errors, inaccuracies, and obscurities.[100] The anti-skeptic Formey similarly asserted that a suspension of judgment in historical matters could not only lead to a more accurate understanding of the past but also prevent the spread of Pyrrhonism by placing realistic limits on historical knowledge. In formulating a distinction between certain facts and mere rumors, Formey embraced Bayle's claims about

overcoming historical Pyrrhonism through the elimination of popular anecdotes and the differentiation of facts from mere suppositions.[101]

Voltaire's *Encyclopédie* article "Histoire" (1765), as well as his anonymous *Le
pyrrhonisme de l'histoire* (1769), appeared significantly after the most heated
phase of the debates surrounding historical Pyrrhonism. Nevertheless, these
texts succinctly summarized the compromise between doubt and certainty that
those contests produced. Voltaire set limits to the certainty of historical knowledge by noting that "all certainty that is not mathematically demonstrable is
only high [*extrème*] probability." In order to attain such a high level of probability, a historical fact had to be verified by testimony and not contradict "the ordinary course of nature."[102] The philosophe proclaimed that he wanted "neither
excessive Pyrrhonism [*pyrrhonisme outré*] nor ridiculous credulity; . . . the main
facts could be correct, while the details are very false."[103] The historian's task
was to determine the relative veracity both of the essential matter of fact and of
the related details by consulting available evidence with rigorous scrutiny.

The compromise of accepting probability as a realistic goal for historical demonstrations mirrored similar resolutions in epistemology and natural philosophy.
Philosophers and historians no longer viewed the quest for metaphysical and
mathematical certainty—seen in texts such as Huet's *Demonstratio evangelica*—
as a tenable approach to the discipline. At the same time, the focus on degrees
of probability allowed for more fruitful investigations of the past.

Regularized Procedures and the "Professional" Historian

The epistemological compromise between the diverse skeptical and anti-
skeptical camps was not the only consequence of the debates about historical
certainty. These disputes also resulted in a gradual development of rules and
procedures for analyzing primary sources and for evaluating the reliability of
ancient and modern historians. Using these rules, scholars attempted to formalize research procedures, to create a hierarchy of reliable evidence, and to
provide the means by which conflicting testimonies could be reconciled. In this
way, historians attempted to bridge the gap between the human and the physical sciences and to render historical practice more precise, while, at the same
time, distinguishing history from other disciplines.

The erudite Fréret proposed that an ordered examination would begin with
the establishment of the most certain facts and descend to more questionable
descriptions or interpretations. By organizing historical knowledge along the
axis of certainty, Fréret hoped to construct a solid factual base. He further offered an essential rule of historical investigation by suggesting that the testimo-

nies of sources or witnesses were not fungible. One could not arbitrarily pick and choose various parts that seemed agreeable or that fit a preestablished narrative.[104] Just as a system of natural philosophy collapsed if some of its parts did not fit with the whole, so the trustworthiness of a historical account crumbled because of inconsistencies and inaccuracies. At the same time, Fréret supported the *esprit systématique* against the *esprit de système* (a distinction made later in the *Encyclopédie*),[105] suggesting that the latter forced us to accept facts without appropriate examination, while the former led us to explore, examine, compare, and critique texts in order to arrive at greater historical certainty.[106]

In addition to offering the tripartite division of historical certainty, Bierling proposed a set of rules for a productive application of skepticism to the study of the past. He argued that no historian, no matter how respected and reputed, should receive full and unquestioned confidence. Since all authors could be subject to error and prejudice, one had to look at the content of their accounts rather than simply accept their validity based on the authority of the historian. At the same time, even texts containing errors or prejudices could provide some reliable information about the past. A responsible reader needed to evaluate the historian's personal loyalties, views, and biases in order to determine which parts of his account could be trusted. Finally, Bierling also sought to refute the popular notion that a mere consensus about a particular event or the age of an oral tradition could in itself guarantee its veracity and authenticity. He urged readers to apply a critical attitude to all information.[107]

At the end of his disputation on historical certainty, the Hungarian scholar Samuel Simonides, defending a thesis at the Academy of Leipzig, offered fifteen formal guidelines for evaluating witness testimonies as well as descriptions by historians who lived significantly after the events they described:

Corollaries:

1. The task of writing history is very difficult.
2. The historian must be an honest man.
3. Those who deny all trust in history do not deserve any themselves.
4. Some historical monuments hold the public trust.
5. Historical trust is more in the fact itself than in the circumstances surrounding it.
6. A historian may often be mistaken in relating the causes of events and decisions, as the example of Tacitus shows.
7. The historical trustworthiness of an anonymous author is not always of a doubtful character.
8. A history may be wrong with respect to one thing but not in another.

COROLLARIA:

1. *Hiſtoriæ ſcribendæ provincia valde ardua eſt.*
2. *Hiſtoricum decet eſſe virum probum.*
3. *Qui omnem hiſtoriæ fidem derogant, ipſi nullam meren-tur.*
4. *Quædam hiſtorica monumenta fidem publicam habent.*
5. *Fides hiſtorica in ipſo facto evidentior eſt, quam in circum-ſtantiis facti.*
6. *Hiſtoricus in tradendis factorum & conſiliorum cauſis ſæ-pe fallere poteſt : exemplum C. Tacitus præbet.*
7. *Hiſtoriæ anonymorum ſcriptorum fides, non ſemper ſuſpecta eſt.*
8. *Hiſtoria in uno falſa, non ſtatim in altero falſa eſt.*
9. *Hiſtoria quoquo modo ſcripta delectat.*
10. *Hiſtoriæ præſtantia, non ex elegantia ſtyli ſolum æſtiman-da eſt.*
11. *Nonniſi tetrica & barbara ingenia hiſtoriæ ſtudium aver-ſantur.*
12. *Vitæ Principum & Illuſtrium Virorum non tantum, ſed quorumvis eruditorum ad hiſtoricum ſpectant.*
13. *Ut hiſtoria eccleſiaſtica ſine civili; ita hæc, ſine illa apud Chriſtianos manca eſt.*
14. *Non minor uſus hiſtoriæ in Juriſprudentia, quam in civi-li doctrina eſt.*
15. *Qui nullos in Civitate reformidant, habent, cur hiſto-riam vereantur.*

D3   VIRO

Fig. 10.1 Corollaries presented at the end of Simonides's *De bono historico*. Courtesy of Google Books.

9. History is pleasing in whatever way it is written.

10. The value of history is judged not only from the excellence of its style.

11. Only the unpolished and barbarian spirits shun the study of history.

12. The historian should consider not only lives of princes and of illustrious men but also those of any learned men.

13. Ecclesiastical history without political history is just as insufficient among the Christians as the latter without the former.

14. History is no less useful in jurisprudence than it is in the instruction of political life.

15. Those who fear no one in the state do so because they revere history.[108]

Such lists of rules became increasingly popular in eighteenth-century debates about historical certainty. By formalizing the laws of historical practice for the evaluation of sources, scholars hoped to provide history with a quasi-scientific legitimacy, while rendering it distinct from natural philosophy and other humanist disciplines.

A final, perhaps most significant outcome of these debates was a greater emphasis on the ethical standards and the quasi-professional training expected of historians. Increasingly, Enlightenment intellectuals discussed the importance of the moral character and education required to be a good and serious scholar. They stressed that historians should be sincere, exact, judicious, not overly credulous, impartial, and unprejudiced. These qualities would ensure that a historian wrote nothing more and nothing less than the truth and that he acted as both the seeker and the gatekeeper of true and certain knowledge. In an age characterized by extreme sectarian and political conflicts, this was a remarkable development.

Sincerity and the love of truth were the two most fundamental moral attributes of the historian. Mabillon maintained that while the latter characteristic ensured that a historian would endlessly seek the most accurate information about events in the past, the former guaranteed that a scholar would withhold no information and report facts to the best of his ability.[109] Lévesque de Pouilly insisted that an honest reporter should neither hide the faults committed by the side he supported nor exaggerate the misdeeds of the opposition.[110] Both admitted that historians could have emotional preferences or loyalties for particular groups but stressed that their duty was to approach the subject impartially and not let their affiliations stand in the way of the truth. Other authors emphasized professional qualifications, such as judgment, exactitude, and clarity of written expression.

The influential Jesuit René Rapin (1621–87) stressed the importance of both scholarly and moral qualifications in his *Instructions pour l'histoire* (1678). Rapin insisted that a good historian needed to possess a universal mind capable of grand ideas, impartiality, sincerity, and an ability to discern the truth from conflicting testimonies.[111] Samuel Simonides argued that historians had to be able to organize complicated series of facts, determine the causes of various events, and investigate the pertinent circumstances.[112] Mabillon, in turn, compared historians to judges, emphasizing their public responsibility of discovering and revealing the truth.[113] While Mabillon stressed the both professions' obligations to veracity, Bierling explicitly contrasted the historian to the orator, saying that the latter was much more likely to say false things or make convenient omissions in order to make his case more convincing and win praise from the audience.[114]

The case of early modern deliberations about historical knowledge confirms Richard Popkin's thesis about the dual role that skepticism played in European thought: on the one hand, it contributed to the gradual destruction of metaphysical and epistemological systems toward the end of the seventeenth century; on the other, it paved the way for the formation of new philosophical systems in the eighteenth century. The abundance of treatises that discussed ways to make history more certain signaled a deep unease among early modern scholars concerning the epistemological status of traditional humanist disciplines. The skeptical critiques of historical scholarship acted as catalysts for the revision of established assumptions and practices and ultimately contributed to the formation of a more sophisticated learned culture. All of the attempts to ensure a greater level of certainty in scholarship signaled the nascent stages of the professionalization of history as a discipline, a process that would be formally completed in the nineteenth century.

This was not, of course, the first or the only time that European scholars became self-conscious about the nature and purpose of their endeavors. Renaissance humanists had already begun to reevaluate the methods and goals of historical scholarship and had introduced new critical methods for examining ancient documents. However, one important difference between the debates about historiography among Renaissance humanists and those among scholars in the late seventeenth and early eighteenth centuries lay in the fact that participants in the latter group had to contend both with increasing biblical criticism and with the skeptics. While humanists primarily disputed the appropriate methods of scholarship, defenders of the *fides historica* had to justify the very existence of their craft. This challenge forced historians to be more explicit in articulating their methods and their assumptions.

An increasingly critical approach to ancient texts by all sides in these debates meant that insofar as historical writing was concerned, authors would be evaluated based on the accuracy of their accounts, and not just according to the style or the moral value of their texts. The factual content of ancient works would become as important as their form. The emergence of a different criterion in the evaluation of ancient authorities signaled a novel approach to classical literature. It allowed eighteenth-century historians to discover analogous errors in the works of their contemporaries and in those of their ancient predecessors, leading to a gradual refinement of historical practices. Simultaneously, it led them to perceive more clearly the wide gulf between the ancient world and their own, especially in terms of epistemological assumptions and literary practices.

Just as in the case of disputes about the origin of human ideas, the nature of the soul, the composition of matter, and the structure of the universe, the debates between the skeptics and their opponents drove scholarly discussions away from questions of metaphysical certainty and toward a practical search for the most probable version of past events. Rather than continuing ceaseless exchanges about the impossibility of entirely certain knowledge, defenders of the *fides historica* could focus on refining and sharpening the methods of source criticism. Such a compromise was profoundly useful for the discipline of history itself, since scholars could move away from attempting to disprove Pyrrhonian claims at the same time that their tactical use of Pyrrhonian critiques categorically improved their craft.

Conclusion

Skepticism and "the Enlightenment"

This book poses new questions for our understanding of the eighteenth-century intellectual culture. If we accept Dan Edelstein's definition that the Enlightenment was primarily a self-reflexive historical narrative based on the recognition by eighteenth-century thinkers that they lived in an enlightened (*éclairé*) age and that the progress of modern science, combined with a methodical application of the *esprit philosophique*, had brought mankind to an unprecedented apex of intellectual achievement, we may be surprised by the broad spectrum of thinkers who shared this view.[1] A wide variety of scholars saw themselves as taking part in intellectual activities that we consider to be crucial aspects of the Enlightenment, including many of the religious thinkers who attempted to refute philosophical skepticism. For example, David Renaud Boullier tried to articulate a standard of moral certainty and advocated for the importance of personal conviction in religious and philosophical matters. Similarly, Jean-Pierre de Crousaz sought to expel the darkness (*ténèbres*) that skepticism cast over his learned world. Laurent-Josse Le Clerc's erudite and meticulous research methods contributed to works that inspired the *Encyclopédie* project. Haller in turn conducted some of the most innovative experiments on animal physiology, proposing new ways of thinking about the composition and functions of the body. Finally, Formey was the secretary of one of Europe's major scientific academies and contributed many articles to d'Alembert and Diderot's grandiose project.

Within Jonathan Israel's taxonomy, these thinkers are considered the representatives of the so-called Moderate Enlightenment because of their attitudes about the importance of revealed religion and their collaboration with political and religious authorities. This was particularly true of the anti-skeptics at the Prussian Académie royale des sciences et belles-lettres. The institution was, after all, Frederick II's brainchild and served as a tool in his attempt to import some of the most notable philosophes from France and to deploy their ideas and rhetoric for his own purposes.[2] Furthermore, the German *Aufklärung*, much like the English and the Scottish Enlightenments, is generally seen by historians as less radical in its critique of religion than the French.[3]

However, labels such as "radical" or "moderate" should be deployed with caution. In order to understand the intellectual dynamics of the learned culture of the eighteenth century, it would be more useful to see how the actual participants in the debates perceived their own projects and the relative positions of their opponents. Formey and Haller may have been rather surprised to find themselves listed alongside Voltaire and Rousseau as members of the "Moderate Enlightenment." It is true that religiously devout scholars differentiated themselves from the irreligious, and frequently anti-religious, philosophes. This distinction was a categorical one for both sides. Belief in the truth of revealed religion was what, above all else, united the opponents of the philosophes. The attitude toward the veracity of organized religion was the major source of contention in the 1700s, creating real and sharp divisions within the intellectual community.

It is crucial to note that there was not necessarily one set of "radical" or "moderate" ideas. Apparent "radicalism" in one sphere, such as materialism in natural philosophy, did not necessarily translate to republicanism or monarchism in political questions. In theory, someone like Haller could have endorsed a materialist physiology, which some scholars associate with "radicals" like La Mettrie, Diderot, Helvetius, and D'Holbach, while remaining convinced of the truth of Christianity and its importance for the maintenance of civil society. Similarly, Diderot, who was one of the most discernible and outspoken advocates of materialism, seemed to recognize that religious faith had practical utility. He acknowledged that together, law and religion "made a pair of crutches that it was best not to take away from people who could not walk unaided."[4] The link between atheism, naturalism, and philosophical materialism, on the one hand, and radical revolutionary politics, on the other, was not an essential or a necessary one. Many of the philosophes who endorsed atheism, materialism, and skepticism and openly opposed organized religion nevertheless did not wish to suddenly overthrow the entire political and social regime. Most sought gradual reforms that would be carried out by enlightened elites. Like their orthodox adversaries, they feared the consequences of chaotic mob rule.[5]

The philosophes have been singled out as the triumphant prophets of their "enlightened" age in large part because of their opposition to revealed religion and their literary popularity during the second half of the eighteenth century. Their ideas about the composition of the physical world, their attempts to rede-

fine human nature, and their challenges to the religious and political authorities render them extremely important participants in the intellectual culture of
the period. At the same time, it is vital to remember that their mythological
status was constructed and codified during the French Revolution by those who
sought to legitimize their own policies and by critics who wished to blame them
for the violent calamities of that period. By justifying their political reforms
within the theoretical framework of ideas and rhetoric appropriated from the
philosophes, the revolutionaries could rightfully condemn their opponents as
the "enemies of human reason," just as d'Holbach had dubbed the defenders of
royal absolutism and aristocratic privilege.[6] Similarly, critics of the Revolution
described it as the inevitable outcome of a conspiratorial plot of radical philosophes who sought to overthrow the political, social, and religious fabric of
society.

Consequently, if one allows radicalism to become the definitive feature of
the Enlightenment, then one is permitting teleology to drive the analysis. One
would then have to admit that it was the Revolution "that invented the Enlightenment by attempting to root its legitimacy in a corpus of texts and founding
authors reconciled and united . . . by their preparation for rupture with the old
world," and not "the Enlightenment that produced the Revolution," as Roger
Chartier has famously claimed.[7] By establishing direct causal links between the
Revolution and a very small subset of the otherwise varied and rich corpus of
eighteenth-century ideas, one risks succumbing to hindsight bias and ex post
facto reasoning. Such explanations greatly exaggerate the importance of the so-
called Radical Enlightenment thinkers and assume that they somehow foresaw
or even intended to bring about the Revolution.

Indeed, efforts to essentialize "the Enlightenment" and to define it as a period
characterized by a set of particular political and philosophical views take away
from the richness and vibrancy of eighteenth-century learned culture. Such attempts also resulted in unproductive disputes regarding what "the Enlightenment" was really about and in persistent efforts to demonstrate that a particular
group that is not typically associated with "the Enlightenment" was actually a
part of it. By exploring the intellectual universe of the eighteenth century on its
own terms, without assumptions about where it was destined to lead, scholars
might finally abandon the intellectual crutch provided by the increasingly
meaningless phrase *the Enlightenment* and walk unaided toward previously
unexplored avenues and unexpected connections.

This investigation of the debates surrounding philosophical skepticism
and the powers of human reason provides an example of such an approach. In

attempting to defend their learned culture and its religious foundations from the challenges of Pyrrhonism, anti-skeptical thinkers of diverse religious and intellectual backgrounds formulated arguments that would become central to the growing confidence in the powers of human understanding. By undertaking refutations of their fideist contemporaries, who often embraced skepticism for religious reasons and who hoped to shield their faith from rationalist critiques, the opponents of Pyrrhonism unintentionally contributed to discourses that would expose revealed faith to such critical analyses during the course of the eighteenth century. Fideists such as Huet saw Pyrrhonian skepticism not as a tool for attacking established religious and intellectual authorities but as a refuge from what they perceived as overly ambitious attempts to prove the essential tenets of Christianity philosophically. While sharing this general goal with the Pyrrhonian Christians, their adversaries believed that whether intentionally or accidentally, skeptical critiques of the powers of human understanding enfeebled the rational foundations of revealed religion.

Unlike the philosophes, many of whom viewed rational investigations of the natural world as irreconcilable with the supernatural claims of Christianity, the anti-skeptics believed that reason and faith were not only compatible but actually mutually reinforcing. They imagined that by learning about the created universe, mankind would both improve its own physical conditions and comprehend more fully the nature of God. Much *like* the philosophes, however, the opponents of skepticism were confident about the ability of human reason to obtain a true and relatively certain understanding of the world. Unintentionally, their arguments against the "enemies of human reason," motivated by concerns for preserving the rational foundations of faith, supplied a powerful arsenal of claims for the philosophes' critiques of Christianity. Nevertheless, the religiously devout opponents of Pyrrhonism saw themselves as essential contributors to an enlightened age. Along with their irreligious interlocutors, they knew nothing about the fate that awaited their world.

The *Crise pyrrhonienne* and the Age of Practicable Reason

Richard Popkin has argued that modern philosophy emerged out of the *crise pyrrhonienne*, which destroyed the intellectual foundations of the existing order in the early eighteenth century.[8] Paul Hazard has similarly suggested that the French-speaking intellectual world of that period experienced a rapid revolutionary change in which the majority of the French went from "thinking like Bossuet" to "thinking like Voltaire."[9] The present book endeavors both to question the rapidity of the change described by Hazard and to consider previously neglected sources of the fundamental intellectual transformations that occurred during the long eighteenth century. Pyrrhonian skepticism was certainly one of the major factors that altered the confidence in the powers of human understanding and caused the deep philosophical changes that occurred over the course of this period. The challenges it posed to existing epistemological and ontological systems forced philosophers to rethink, in fundamental ways, their underlying assumptions and principles. At the same time, as we have seen, the embrace of Pyrrhonism was not always the cause, but often the result, of intense, mutually destructive debates among dogmatic philosophies that were competing in a heated contest for intellectual prominence in their learned world.

The persistence of the perceived need to disprove the general conclusions of Pyrrhonian skepticism in a variety of disciplines indicates that it was a central concern not only in metaphysical debates but also in more practical subjects, such as history and natural philosophy. The alleged proximity between philosophical skepticism and religious unbelief forced all those concerned with the rising popularity of heterodox views (such as materialism, Spinozism, and deism) to engage Pyrrhonism and prevent it from breaking open the floodgates of irreligion. In many ways, the religious apologists and the so-called orthodox thinkers, who were generally concerned with refuting Pyrrhonian skepticism, contributed some of the most essential arguments to the defense of the basic powers of human reason. This was particularly true among Protestant intellectuals, many of whom viewed the rational foundations of revealed religion as critical to demonstrating the veracity of Christianity. While Catholic apologists were concerned with the moral implications that followed from Bayle's *Dictionnaire*, many of them did not necessarily think that its skeptical claims posed a direct danger to Christianity. They believed that religious truths were guaranteed by the infallible authority of the Catholic Church and did not depend on the powers of human understanding. The Protestant *rationaux*, on the other hand, perceived the pernicious theological consequences that followed from the argument that the mind was utterly incapable of obtaining true and certain knowledge in either philosophical or religious matters. With the authority of the Church abandoned, and reason deemed weak and incapable of understanding divine truths, all means of securing an indubitable knowledge of God vanished.

In attempting to undermine Bayle's persistent influence and the proliferation of Pyrrhonian skepticism, both Catholic and Protestant authors made major contributions to eighteenth-century intellectual culture. Catholic writers who questioned the methods of Bayle's historical and critical scholarship participated in the improvement of increasingly popular dictionaries and encyclopedias, which became hallmarks of eighteenth-century erudition.[10] Similarly, Protestant opponents of skepticism continued to seek criteria of certainty that could weaken Pyrrhonian attacks, and they were successful in promoting pragmatic solutions, such as the recourse to moral certainty and probability. In many ways, the self-referential claims about the authority of reason that are so generally associated with the more radical elements of the Enlightenment and with the "Cult of Reason," which emerged during the French Revolution, were as much the brainchild of the philosophes as they were the unintended outcomes of the *rationaux* attempts to refute Pyrrhonism. It was, above all, the opponents of skepticism who had argued so vehemently to uphold the confidence in the powers of human reason throughout the first half of the eighteenth century.

In seeking to refute and to anticipate the arguments of Pyrrhonian skepticism, the "orthodox" thinkers attempted to formulate new criteria of certainty. While their main intention, in the majority of cases, was to preserve the rational foundations of revealed religion and to defend philosophical principles that were essential to Christian theology, their persistent efforts also had significant unintended consequences. In a number of important ways, the anti-skeptical case on behalf of the powers of human reason, which largely conceded the impossibility of metaphysical certainty, nevertheless articulated a practical comprise. Unable to refute the skeptics philosophically, the opponents of Pyrrhonism sought practical resolutions to their dilemma. They proposed moral certainty and probability as criteria that were both realistically attainable and sufficient for the conduct of daily life. The philosophes, whose goals differed radically from those of the religious apologists, adopted this pragmatic solution.

The dialectical interaction between the skeptics and their opponents was quite a productive one. Pyrrhonian critics played an important role in demonstrating the great number of assumptions and premises that had been taken for granted by various competing schools of philosophy. The arguments of philosophical skepticism or, in many cases, the mere anticipation of those arguments forced thinkers to reformulate their essential claims about the nature of reality and about the human ability to understand it. The looming specter of skepticism compelled apologetic thinkers to seek new strategies for defending established intellectual and religious traditions.

The influence was by no means one-directional. As Popkin and Paganini have shown convincingly, David Hume, who is considered to have been the most prominent and prolific eighteenth-century skeptic, was swayed by Crousaz's denunciation of radical Pyrrhonism and opted for a more moderate position.[11] Indeed, Boullier, Crousaz, Formey, and other anti-skeptics did not undertake their

apologetic efforts in vain. Even the philosophes, many of whom valued and frequently appropriated the critical methods of skepticism, did not believe it was
possible to embrace fully the ultimate conclusions of the Pyrrhonians. In discussing the problem of skepticism in the *Entretien entre d'Alembert et Diderot*,
the imaginary Diderot asked the fictional d'Alembert whether there was any
question on which people could remain completely undecided because the reasons for and against were equally good. The latter replied that this was not possible, invoking Jean Buridan's (1295–1358) hypothetical donkey, who died
because it could not decide whether it wanted to drink or eat. Diderot answered
as follows: "In that case, there is no such thing as a skeptic, since apart from
mathematical questions, which admit of no uncertainty, there is a for and an
against in all questions. The scales, then, are never even, and it is impossible
that they should not hang more heavily on the side we believe to have the greatest probability."[12] Articulated by one of the most controversial thinkers of the
eighteenth century, the argument encapsulated the spirit of various refutations
of Pyrrhonian skepticism throughout that period. This attitude resembled
Diderot's portrayal of Pyrrhonism in the *Encyclopédie*: it was an acceptable position in speculative matters, but it was neither useful nor applicable to practical
questions involving decisions about actions.[13] It was not a philosophical view that
applied to daily life, and it was only rarely needed in theoretical issues. Although
the philosophes admired the critical methods of thinkers such as Bayle, the rational pragmatism of Boullier, Crousaz, Formey, Mérian, and other opponents of
skepticism was much closer to the philosophes' assumptions about the powers
of human reason.

Reliance on moral certainty and probability was a common solution for thinkers who opposed extreme skepticism. On the one hand, such a turn served as an
admission that the Pyrrhonian claims about the impossibility of obtaining complete metaphysical certainty had been accurate. Unable to disprove the skeptics
completely, their opponents had to cede ground and admit that such absolute
assurance was indeed unattainable. On the other hand, the anti-skeptics did
push back against the proposition that the mind could know *nothing* with absolute
conviction by suggesting that such confidence was not necessary for philosophical or practical enquiries. Far from being excessively confident in the powers of
human understanding—as certain critics and certain panegyrists of the Enlightenment have insisted—eighteenth-century thinkers were deeply aware of the
limits of reason.

Therefore, if we are to retain the notion that the eighteenth century, and particularly its second half, was an "Age of Reason" in any conceivable way, then we

certainly have to qualify this description in a different manner. As can be seen in attempts to answer fundamental questions about the nature of the human soul and the origin of ideas, the philosophes themselves often admitted these issues to be irresolvable on a metaphysical level. In many ways, this was a strategy adopted by various thinkers who attempted to refute skepticism throughout the 1700s. Unable to answer skeptical claims in purely philosophical terms, anti-skeptical apologists demonstrated the internal inconsistency and practical inapplicability of radical Pyrrhonism. The mutual destruction of competing systems of philosophy and the continuing inability to resolve decisively the most important metaphysical questions led thinkers to turn toward the more practical aspects of philosophy, the natural sciences, and history.

The compromise on *certitude morale*, verisimilitude, and probability that emerged in epistemology, natural philosophy, and historiography also began to be applied more commonly to theological questions. Formey's *Logique des vraisemblances* famously removed the debate from the metaphysical realm, urging readers to evaluate the probability of religion in general and Christianity in particular on the basis of multiple testimonies supporting its veracity.[14] In a similar fashion, Henri-Jean-Baptiste Fabry de Moncault, comte d'Autrey (1723–77), offered a defense of Christianity entitled *Le pyrrhonien raisonnable* (1765), which was intended to appeal specifically to the philosophes and to various kinds of unbelievers (Pyrrhonians, deists, atheists, idolaters, and Jews).[15] The first part of the work presented a discourse with his Pyrrhonian friend, who ended up converting to Christianity. This friend claimed to have been attracted to the Christian religion after deciding to focus on its most basic principles and ignore obscure theological debates.[16] Following Formey's example, Autrey argued that one had to appeal to the probable nature of the essential tenets of religion rather than offer metaphysical demonstrations: "We seek verisimilitudes rather than demonstrations because verisimilitudes are ordinarily more analogous to the nature of our feeble reason; in a word, we do not allow ourselves to see whether religion can be demonstrated to a man of wit until we have rendered it probable both for the clever and the stupid alike."[17] One had to proceed gradually and systematically, Autrey explained, and expose the great verisimilitude of the essential elements of both natural religion and Christianity, until the hypothetical unbeliever slowly came to see the error of his ways. These kinds of discourses, as well as the more secular justifications of Christianity that we encountered in the first chapter, present a dramatic transformation in a learned culture that had sought metaphysical proofs for the existence of God just a generation earlier.[18]

Despite persisting metaphysical uncertainties, almost all intellectuals of the eighteenth century, independent of their philosophical or religious affiliation, really did think that human knowledge about the natural world continued to expand and that their generation did have a greater understanding of their physical surroundings than the preceding ones. This perceived progress in human knowledge was most famously articulated in the "Discours préliminaire" of the *Encyclopédie*. D'Alembert emphasized, above all, the practical importance of studying those things that were most directly related to human needs.[19] He stressed the significance of a "reasonable metaphysics" that offered principles that were "as simple as axioms" and the "same for the philosophers as for regular people." It was not *speculative* reason that d'Alembert praised, but *practicable* reason, one applied to concrete observations and calculations, not to abstract metaphysical debates. One had to restrict scientific subjects to particular enquiries and to leave aside all conjectures and speculations, which always increased the uncertainty of human knowledge.[20] This attitude encapsulated a pragmatic and practical approach to science and to philosophy. Thus, if scholars are to continue identifying the eighteenth century with the universal application of rational analysis, it may be useful to rename the Age of Reason the Age of *Practicable* Reason.

By exploring the emergence of new conceptions of rationality and the formations of new criteria of doubt and certainty, this book describes a set of dramatic transformations in eighteenth-century European intellectual culture. The debates about the powers and limits of human reason played a central role in the emergence of "epistemological modesty," as Keith Baker has termed the phenomenon. The gradual acceptance of the very strict limits to what could be known about the world transformed the content of debates in the eighteenth century. The first effect of this intellectual transformation, as Baker has argued, was a shift in the topics the public discussed. This change manifested itself in the turn away from debates about epistemology, metaphysics, and other abstract philosophical topics and toward discussions of political organization, civil society, political economy, and morality, at least as far as broad public discourse was concerned.[21] While abstract philosophy continued to thrive in universities, it became a specialized discipline rather than a central subject of public disputes, as had been the case at the end of the seventeenth century and the beginning of the eighteenth. Of course, this transformation was not precipitated just by the challenges of Pyrrhonism. The rapid increase in literacy rates resulted in a reading public that differed from that of the previous generation. The new reading public was interested in new issues and was not always concerned with the debates of the highly educated and philosophically trained intellectual community. These new readers wanted to explore practical resolutions to daily problems and not belabor matters that seemed beyond the reach of human understanding.

The second significant consequence of the emergence of epistemological modesty was the growing acceptance of religious toleration in the eighteenth century. The willingness to admit ignorance and to suspend judgment about metaphysical questions allowed for the peaceful coexistence of multiple opinions and rival truth claims. Indeed, the *Encyclopédie* article "Tolérance" (1765) based the argument for toleration on the fact that "human reason is not a precise or fixed measure" and "what seems obvious [*évident*] to one person is often obscure to another." Because ideas derived from individual experiences, and because these experiences were diverse, "it follows that no one has the right to make his perception the rule or to assert that another person must be subjugated to his opinions."[22] The emerging belief that no single person, philosophical school, or religious authority could lay exclusive claim to the knowledge of the absolute truth and to the right to enforce it on others contributed to a sense of relativism in the religious and moral spheres.[23]

The combination of intellectual confidence and epistemological modesty remains one of the most enduring legacies of eighteenth-century philosophy. The assumption that our knowledge of the world will continue to expand with each generation is almost axiomatic for all modern views about the powers and limits of human understanding. Similarly, the willingness to tolerate a multiplicity of competing philosophical, theological, political, and ethical perspectives, to suspend ultimate judgment until sufficient evidence becomes available, and to accept the possibility that one's conclusions may prove to be incorrect at some later point are all at the heart of the modern mind-set. This perspective questions the possibility of attaining any absolute truths about the world, and it places the practical needs of humanity at the center of a focused, unpresumptuous scientific enquiry.

Introduction

Epigraph: "Scepticismus debellatus, seu humanae cognitionis ratio ab imis radicibus explixacata," art. 9, *Histoire des ouvrages des savans*, February 1697, 242.

1. Richard Popkin popularized the term *crise pyrrhonienne* in reference to the early seventeenth century in the first installment of his monumental study of the history of early modern skepticism. See Popkin, *History of Scepticism: From Erasmus to Descartes*, 43–63; and Popkin, *History of Scepticism: From Savonarola to Bayle*, 144–73. In using the notion of a Pyrrhonian crisis, this book refers to the late seventeenth and early eighteenth centuries and deals, in part, with a phenomenon that the historian Paul Hazard has termed "the crisis of the European mind." See Hazard, *La crise de la conscience européenne*.

2. Baker, "Enlightenment and the Institution of Society," 117. For similar interpretations about the orientation and limits of Enlightenment conceptions of reason, see Daston, *Classical Probability in the Enlightenment*; Tonelli, " 'Weakness' of Reason in the Age of Enlightenment"; Baker, "Epistémologie et politique"; and Rasmussen, *Pragmatic Enlightenment*.

3. Huet, *Traité philosophique de la foiblesse de l'esprit humain*, 3.

4. Crousaz, *Examen du pyrrhonisme ancien et moderne*, 18.

5. Sextus Empiricus, *Les hipotiposes*, 20–85. For more on ancient Pyrrhonism, see Mates, *Skeptical Essays*; Jonathan Barnes, *Toils of Skepticism*; Burnyeat and Frede, *Original Sceptics*; and Bailey, *Sextus Empiricus and Pyrrhonean Scepticism*.

6. Sextus Empiricus, *Les hipotiposes*, 116.

7. Popkin, "New Views on the Role of Scepticism in the Enlightenment," 159.

8. For a full review of the text see "Scepticismus debellatus, seu humanae cognitionis ratio ab imis radicibus explicata," art. 9, *Histoire des ouvrages des savans*, February 1697, 240–50. For Villemandy's own account, see Villemandy, *Scepticismus debellatus*, 4–5. For a discussion of this text and of Villemandy, see Floridi, *"Cupiditas veri vivendi"*; Borghero, "Scepticism and Analysis"; and Piaia, "Histories of Philosophy in France in the Age of Descartes," 50–58.

9. Hazard, *La crise de la conscience européenne*, 5.

10. For this interpretation, see also Kors, *Atheism in France*, 3–13, 265–379.

11. Crousaz, *Examen du pyrrhonisme ancien et moderne*, dedicatory epistle to Charles François de Vintimille, [1–2].

12. "Philosophe," 509.

13. Kant, "An Answer to the Question: What is Enlightenment?," 54.

14. Baker, *Condorcet*, 129–94; Daston, *Classical Probability in the Enlightenment*; Tonelli, "Pierre-Jacques Changeux and Scepticism in the French Enlightenment,"; Tonelli, "'Weakness' of Reason in the Age of Enlightenment."

15. Hill, *Faith in the Age of Reason*; Gay, *Enlightenment: An Interpretation*, 1:21, 40; Love, *Enlightenment*; Israel, *Radical Enlightenment*, vi; Israel, *Enlightenment Contested*, 866; Blom, *Wicked Company*, xiv.

16. For an excellent account of the competing notions of certainty in the eighteenth century, see Perinetti, "Ways to Certainty."

17. Edelstein, *Enlightenment*, 1–2.

18. For excellent analyses of the history of the association between the Enlightenment and the French Revolution, see Kors, *D'Holbach's Coterie*, 301–29; Van Kley and Bradley, *Religion and Politics in Enlightenment Europe*, 2–17; McMahon, *Enemies of the Enlightenment*, 56–120; and Schmidt, "Inventing the Enlightenment."

19. For excellent summaries of the trends in Enlightenment studies, see Grote, "Review Essay"; Outram, *Enlightenment*; Edelstein, *Enlightenment*, 7–18; and Hunt and Jacob, "Enlightenment Studies."

20. Cassirer, *Philosophy of the Enlightenment*, v–vi, 7–8, 12–14.

21. Gay, *The Enlightenment: An Interpretation*, 2:ix.

22. Tonelli, "'Weakness' of Reason in the Age of Enlightenment," 223.

23. Pocock, *Barbarism and Religion*, 1–10; Pocock, "Historiography and Enlightenment."

24. Edelstein, *Enlightenment*, 12.

25. In addition to Pocock, see Porter and Teich, *Enlightenment in National Context*; and Himmelfarb, *Roads to Modernity*.

26. The most notable of these are Jacob, *Radical Enlightenment*; Israel, *Radical Enlightenment*; Israel, *Enlightenment Contested*; and Israel, *Democratic Enlightenment*. For accounts of the Counter-Enlightenment, see Everdell, *Christian Apologetics in France*; Pitassi, *Apologétique*; Masseau, *Les ennemis des philosophes*; McMahon, *Enemies of the Enlightenment*; and Albertan-Coppola, "Apologetics."

27. Lehner, "What is 'Catholic Enlightenment'?"; Lehner and Printy, *Companion to the Catholic Enlightenment in Europe*; Lehner, *Enlightened Monks*; Burson and Lehner, *Enlightenment and Catholicism in Europe*.

28. Burson, *Rise and Fall of Theological Enlightenment*.

29. Barnett, *Enlightenment and Religion*.

30. The relative compatibility between reason and religion in the Enlightenment is increasingly accepted in recent scholarship. For more, see Van Kley and Bradley, *Religion and Politics in Enlightenment Europe*; Sheehan, *Enlightenment Bible*; Sorkin, *Religious Enlightenment*; Burson, *Rise and Fall of Theological Enlightenment*; Lehner, *Enlightened Monks*; Burson and Lehner, *Enlightenment and Catholicism in Europe*; and Bulman and Ingram, *God in the Enlightenment*.

31. For an excellent examination of the historical portrayals of the Enlightenment, see Ferrone, *Enlightenment*.

32. *Enlightenment project* is a term used most commonly by scholars to refer to a supposed concrete philosophical and political program of the Enlightenment, and it is utilized both by those who endorse the program and by those who critique it. See, e.g., Habermas, "Modernity"; Liedman, *Postmodernist Critique of the Project of Enlightenment*; Wokler, "Enlightenment Project as Betrayed by Modernity"; Baker and Reill, *What's Left of the Enlightenment?*; Garrard, *Counter-Enlightenments*; and Garrard, "Enlightenment and Its Enemies."

33. Barnett, *Enlightenment and Religion*, 5.

34. Clark, "Predestination and Progress." For a similar interpretation, see Clark, " 'God' and 'The Enlightenment.' "

35. Edelstein, *Enlightenment*, 1, 16–17.

36. Ibid., 13. Edelstein cites Luhmann, *Art as a Social System*, 55.

37. Albertan-Coppola, "L'apologétique catholique française à l'âge des Lumières"; Masseau, *Les ennemis des philosophes*; McMahon, *Enemies of the Enlightenment*.

38. For more on the metaphors of light and darkness, see Roland Mortier, " 'Lumière et 'Lumières': Histoire d'une image et d'une idée au XVIIe et au XVIIIe siècle," in *Clartés et ombres du siècle des Lumières*, 13–59; Roger, "La lumière et les Lumières"; Delon, "Les Lumières"; and Spector, "Les lumières avant les Lumières."

39. *Dictionnaire de l'Académie françoise* (1694), 2:369.

40. Rochefort, *Dictionnaire général et curieux*, 621.

41. Ibid.; Richelet, *Dictionnaire françois*, 2:253.

42. Richelet, *Dictionnaire françois*, 2:253.

43. *Dictionnaire de l'Académie françoise* (1694), s.v. "Raison," 2:369.

44. *Dictionnaire de l'Académie françoise* (1762), 2:528.

45. Antoine Furetière, "Raison," in *Dictionnaire universel*, vol. 3.

46. *Dictionnaire de l'Académie françoise* (1694), 2:369.

47. For more on the plan of the work, see "Discours sur le dessein de cette logique," in Arnauld and Nicole, *La logique*, 5–26.

48. Popkin, *History of Scepticism: From Savonarola to Bayle*; Popkin, *High Road to Pyrrhonism*. For a more detailed discussion of the eighteenth century, see Popkin, "Sources of Knowledge of Sextus Empiricus in Hume's Time." Popkin also coedited a number of publications, such as Popkin and Vanderjagt, *Scepticism and Irreligion in the Seventeenth and Eighteenth Centuries*; and Popkin and Schmitt, *Scepticism from the Renaissance to the Enlightenment*.

49. See, e.g., Neto, Paganini, and Laursen, *Skepticism in the Modern Age*.

50. Popkin, *History of Scepticism: From Savonarola to Bayle*, xxiii; Popkin, "Scepticism in the Enlightenment," 14.

51. Popkin, "New Views on the Role of Scepticism in the Enlightenment."

52. See, e.g., Bernier and Charles, *Scepticisme et modernité*; and Charles and Smith, *Scepticism in the Eighteenth Century*.

53. For Israel's interpretation of Bayle and skepticism, see Israel, *Radical Enlightenment*, 331–41; and Israel, *Enlightenment Contested*, 63–93, 669–71.

54. Some typical examples are Magdelaine et al., *De l'humanisme aux Lumières*; Alan Levine, *Early Modern Skepticism and the Origins of Toleration*; Paganini, *Return of Scepticism*; and Whelan, *Anatomy of Superstition*.

Chapter 1 · *The Walking Ignorant*

1. For more on the revival of philosophical skepticism, see Popkin, introduction to *History of Scepticism: From Savonarola to Bayle*; Popkin and Schmitt, *Scepticism from the Renaissance to the Enlightenment*; Laursen, *Politics of Skepticism in the Ancients, Montaigne, Hume, and Kant*; Pierre-François Moreau, *Le retour des philosophes antiques à l'âge classique*, vol. 2; Brahami, *Le travail du scepticisme*; Neto and Popkin, *Skepticism in Renaissance and Post-Renaissance Thought*; Paganini, *Skepsis*; and Neto, Paganini, and Laursen, *Skepticism in the Modern Age*.

2. For more about Academic skepticism, see Schmitt, *Cicero Scepticus*; Neto, "Academic Scepticism in Early Modern Philosophy"; and Neto, *Academic Skepticism in Seventeenth-Century French Philosophy*.

3. Popkin, *History of Scepticism: From Savonarola to Bayle*, xvii.

4. Ibid., xvii–xviii.

5. Ibid.; Neto, "Academic Scepticism in Early Modern Philosophy," 198–99.

6. Popkin, *History of Scepticism: From Savonarola to Bayle*, xix. For more on the moral implications of Pyrrhonism, see Hiley, "Deep Challenge of Pyrrhonian Scepticism."

7. Floridi, *Sextus Empiricus*, 3–6.

8. Ibid., 25–35; Neto, "Academic Scepticism in Early Modern Philosophy," 198–99.

9. Schmitt, *Cicero Scepticus*, 73–74.

10. Kors, *Atheism in France*, 266–302.

11. For more on the French Catholic context, see R. R. Palmer, *Catholics and Unbelievers in Eighteenth-Century France*; Kors, *Atheism in France*; Northeast, *Parisian Jesuits and the Enlightenment*; Van Kley, *Religious Origins of the French Revolution*; and Burson, *Rise and Fall of Theological Enlightenment*.

12. For an excellent explanation of these theological differences, see Labrousse, *Pierre Bayle*, vol. 1; and Labrousse, *Pierre Bayle*, vol. 2.

13. Montaigne, *Essais*, 2:210–596. For more on Montaigne's "Apologie," see Popkin, *History of Scepticism: From Savonarola to Bayle*, 47–48; Vincent, "Scepticisme et conservatisme chez Montaigne"; Neto, "*Epoche* as Perfection"; and Paganini, *Skepsis*, 15–60.

14. Montaigne, *Essais*, 1:323.

15. Pierre-François Moreau, "Les arguments sceptiques dans la lecture de l'écriture sainte," 386.

16. Popkin, *History of Scepticism: From Savonarola to Bayle*, 36–38.

17. Hervet, dedicatory epistle to the cardinal of Lorraine.

18. Popkin, *History of Scepticism: From Savonarola to Bayle*, 67.

19. Ibid., 74.

20. Pierre Charron, *Les trois veritez*, 17.

21. For more on Charron, see Popkin, *History of Scepticism: From Savonarola to Bayle*, 57–61; Horowitz, "Pierre Charron's View of the Source of Wisdom"; Jean Charron, *"Wisdom" of Pierre Charron*; Gregory, *Genèse de la raison classique de Charron à Descartes*; and Neto, *Academic Skepticism in Seventeenth-Century French Philosophy*, 11–40.

22. Popkin, *History of Scepticism*, 83. See also Paganini, "'Pyrrhonisme tout pur' ou 'circoncis'?"; Giocanti, "La Mothe Le Vayer"; and Neto, *Academic Skepticism in Seventeenth-Century French Philosophy*, 67–93.

23. La Mothe Le Vayer, *Opuscule*, 8–10.

24. La Mothe Le Vayer, *Soliloques sceptiques*, 17–18.

25. La Mothe Le Vayer, *Discours pour montrer que les doutes de la philosophie sceptique sont de grand usage dans les sciences*, 74–75.

26. Ibid., 76.

27. La Mothe Le Vayer, *De la vertu des payens*, 224–25.

28. La Mothe Le Vayer, *Prose chagrine*, 309.

29. The significant historiographical debates regarding the sincerity of Bayle's explicit endorsement of Pyrrhonism and fideism are addressed in chapter 2.

30. Pierre Bayle, "Pyrrhon," remark C, in *Dictionnaire historique et critique* (1697), 2:826.

31. Pierre Bayle, "Eclaircissements," in *Dictionnaire historique et critique* (1702), 3:3140.

32. For an excellent analysis of this work, see Shelford, "Thinking Geometrically in Pierre-Daniel Huet's *Demonstratio evangelica*."

33. Huet, *Memoirs*, 2:157.

34. Pascal, *Pensées*, 48. Although he is not generally associated with Pyrrhonian skepticism, Pascal explicitly denounced all rational attempts to prove the existence of God.

35. Huet's marginal note in Pascal, *Pensées*, 48. Huet's edition of the *Pensées* (1670) is at the Bibliothèque Nationale de France, Rés. D 21375. The note is also published in Francis, *Les pensées de Pascal en France*, 382.

36. Mersenne, *La vérité des sciences contre les septiques ou pyrrhoniens*, 13–14.

37. Gassendi, *Sintagmatis philosophici*, 79–80.

38. For more on Gassendi's skepticism, see Brett, *Philosophy of Gassendi*; Rochot, "Gassendi et le *Syntagma philosophicum*"; Bloch, *La philosophie de Gassendi*; Popkin, *History of Scepticism: From Savonarola to Bayle*, 120–27; and Fisher, *Pierre Gassendi's Philosophy and Science*.

39. Popkin, *History of Scepticism: From Savonarola to Bayle*, 113–14; Neto, *Academic Skepticism in Seventeenth-Century French Philosophy*, 45–64.

40. For a seminal work on certainty and skepticism in the English context, see Shapiro, *Probability and Certainty in Seventeenth-Century England*.

41. See, e.g., Boyle, *Sceptical Chymist*; John Wilkins, *Of the Principles and Duties of Natural Religion*, 1–11; and Glanvill, "Of Scepticism and Certainty."

42. Foucher, *Dissertations sur la recherche de la vérité*, 3–4.

43. Ibid., 150, 71, 137, 93, quotations on 71 and 137. For more on Foucher, see Rabbe, *Étude philosophique sur l'abbé Simon Foucher*; Popkin, "L'abbé Foucher et le problème des qualités premières"; and Watson, *Downfall of Cartesianism*, 13–28, 40–63.

44. Popkin, *History of Scepticism: From Savonarola to Bayle*, 82.

45. For more on the *libertins érudits*, see Pintard, *Le libertinage érudit*; Charles-Daubert, *Les libertins érudits en France au XVIIe siècle*; Gregory, *Genèse de la raison classique de Charron à Descartes*; Popkin, *History of Scepticism: From Savonarola to Bayle*, 80–98; and Isabelle Moreau, *"Guérir du sot."* See also McKenna and Moreau, *Libertinage et philosophie au XVIIe siècle*.

46. La Peyrère, *Prae-Adamitae*. See also Popkin, *Isaac La Peyrère*; Almond, *Adam and Eve in Seventeenth-Century Thought*; and Grafton, *Defenders of the Text*, 204–13.

47. Simon, *Histoire critique du Vieux Testament*. For more on Simon, see Bernus, *Richard Simon et son Histoire critique du Vieux Testament*; Margival, *Essai sur Richard Simon et la critique biblique au XVIIᵉ siècle*; Steinmann, *Richard Simon et les origines de l'exégèse biblique*; and Auvray, *Richard Simon*.

48. Spinoza, *Tractatus theologico-politicus*, 15–18. For the full impact of Spinoza's critiques, see Strauss, *Spinoza's Critique of Religion*; and Israel, *Radical Enlightenment*, 230–327.

49. Spinoza, *Tractatus theologico-politicus*, 83, 33–35, 55, 175.

50. Popkin, *History of Scepticism: From Savonarola to Bayle*, 239.

51. For more on the metaphor of disease used to describe skepticism, see Matytsin, "'Curing' Pyrrhonian Doubt."

52. For an excellent article on this analogy, see Paganini, "Le scepticisme, une 'maladie' ou un remède?"

53. "Réponse à la lettre sur le progrès du pyrrhonisme," *Bibliothèque germanique* 20 (1730): 116–17.

54. Ibid., 144.

55. Ibid., 136.

56. Chartier, *Cultural Origins of the French Revolution*, 69. See also Furet and Sachs, "Growth of Literacy in France during the Eighteenth and Nineteenth Centuries."

57. Chartier, *Cultural Origins of the French Revolution*, 69.

58. Kors, *Atheism in France*, 179.

59. For an extended discussion of this trend, see Habermas, *Structural Transformation of the Public Sphere*. For recent revisions of Habermas's thesis, see Mah, "Phantasies of the Public Sphere"; and Emden and Midgley, *Beyond Habermas*.

60. Le Febvre, *Bayle en petit* (1737), 8–9.

61. Ibid., 22.

62. Joly, *Remarques critiques*, 1:ix.

63. "Les hypotyposes, ou Institutions pirrhoniennes de Sextus Empiricus en trois livres, traduites du Grec avec des notes," art. 2, *Mémoires pour l'histoire des sciences et des beaux-arts* (hereafter cited as *Mémoires de Trévoux*), January 1727, 36–37.

64. Ibid., 42–43.

65. Crousaz, *Examen du pyrrhonisme ancien et moderne*, 7, 70, preface [2], 2–3, quotations on 7 and 70.

66. Ibid., 17.

67. Ibid., 20.

68. Formey, *Pensées raisonnables*, 98.

69. Ibid., 98–99.

70. Haller, "Discours préliminaire," i.

71. Ibid.; Crousaz, *Examen du pyrrhonisme ancien et moderne*, preface [3], 1–2.

72. Bayle, "Eclaircissement sur les athées," in *Dictionnaire historique et critique* (1702), 3:3137–40.

73. Haller, "Discours préliminaire," v–xiii.

74. Ibid., xiv–xv.

75. "Réponse à la lettre sur le progrès du pyrrhonisme," *Bibliothèque germanique* 20 (1730): 116 (quotation), 117–19, 128–29.

76. From an announcement of Crousaz's forthcoming work in the *Bibliothèque germanique* 18 (1729): 99–100. Crousaz used identical terminology in his private correspondence. See Crousaz to Bignon, [1730], in Correspondance de Jean-Paul Bignon, BNF, Fonds Français 22227, fol. 37r.

77. Crousaz, *Examen du pyrrhonisme ancien et moderne*, 201.

78. Ibid., 198, 234, 344, 351.

79. Ibid., 203.

80. Ibid., 765.

81. Ibid., 209, 357, 219, 212, 231, quotations on 212 and 231.

82. Hayer and Soret, *La religion vengée*, 1:132–33.

83. Ibid., 173–74.

84. Ibid., 206–7.

85. "Réponse à la lettre sur le progrès du pyrrhonisme," *Bibliothèque germanique* 20 (1730): 137, 137–38, quotation on 137.

86. Ibid., 140–41.

87. Mérian, "Sur l'apperception de sa propre existence," 428–29.

88. Crousaz, *Examen du pyrrhonisme ancien et moderne*, preface [2], 2–3.

89. Crousaz to La Pillonière, n.d., BCUL, Fonds Crousaz, IS 2024, 2:167–68.

90. For more on this discussion, see Paganini, "Le scepticisme, une 'maladie' ou un remède?," 192–94.

91. Crousaz, *Examen du pyrrhonisme ancien et moderne*, 12.

92. Ibid. Crousaz makes similar claims on 77–78.

93. Mayer, "Crousaz," 54–55.

Chapter 2 • *Pierre Bayle:* Bête Noire *and the Elusive Skeptic*

1. Mornet, "Les enseignements des bibliothèques privés," 460–63, cited in Labrousse, "Reading Pierre Bayle in Paris," 7–8.

2. Israel, "Bayle's Double Image during the Enlightenment."

3. See, e.g., Cazes, *Pierre Bayle*; Fabre, *Les pères de la Révolution de Bayle à Condorcet*; Brunetière, *Etudes critiques sur l'histoire de la littérature française*; Dibon, *Pierre Bayle*; Labrousse, *Pierre Bayle*, vol. 1; Labrousse, *Pierre Bayle*, vol. 2; Rex, *Essays on Pierre Bayle and Religious Controversy*; Popkin, "Bayle's Sincerity"; Whelan, *Anatomy of Superstition*; and Mori, *Bayle: Philosophe*. An excellent work on the reception of Bayle in the eighteenth century is Rétat, *Le Dictionnaire de Bayle*. For more recent accounts on the trends in Bayle scholarship, see Bots, *Critique, savoir et érudition a la veille des Lumières*; Lennon, *Reading Bayle*; McKenna and Paganini, *Pierre Bayle dans la République des Lettres*; and Paganini, "Towards a 'Critical' Bayle." For an excellent overview of the recent debates, see Shank, review of *Pierre Bayle (1647–1706), le philosophe de Rotterdam*.

4. Pierre Bayle, "Spinoza," remark M, in *Dictionnaire historique et critique* (1740), 4:259.

5. Popkin, "Bayle's Sincerity."

6. The concept of "multivalent" meanings or paradigms is most powerfully articulated in Pocock, "Languages and Their Implications." Thomas Lennon discusses Bayle's "polyphonic" approach in Lennon, *Reading Bayle*, 33–41.

7. For more on the publication of the *Dictionnaire*, see Lieshout, *Making of Pierre Bayle's Dictionaire*. For more on the first project, see Vermeir, "Dustbin of the Republic of Letters."

8. Pierre Bayle to Gabriel de Naudis, 22 May 1692, in Hazard, *La crise de la conscience européenne*, 75.

9. Bayle, "Projet d'un dictionnaire critique," sec. 4.

10. Lieshout, *Making of Pierre Bayle's Dictionaire*, 72–73. For more on the changes in the genres of dictionaries and encyclopedias, see Yeo, *Encyclopaedic Visions*; Blair, *Too Much to Know*; and Hirschi, "Compiler into Genius."

11. This process is described in some detail in Lieshout, *Making of Pierre Bayle's Dictionaire*, 17–20, 104–9.

12. Pierre Bayle, preface to *Dictionnaire historique et critique* (1697), 1:1–2.

13. Ibid., 2–3.

14. Bayle, "Projet d'un dictionnaire critique," sec. 4.

15. For the best accounts of the contest between Bayle and Jurieu, see Labrousse, *Pierre Bayle*, vol. 2; and Bost, *L'affaire Bayle*.

16. Bayle identifies Jurieu in his response to the printed work. See Bayle, *Réflexions sur un imprimé*, 746. See also Kappler, *Bibliographie critique de l'œuvre imprimée de Pierre Jurieu*. For more on this episode, see Matytsin, "Fictional Letters or Real Accusations?"

17. Pierre Jurieu, preface to *Jugement du public*, 4.

18. Pierre Jurieu, "Réflexions," in *Jugement du public*, 28–29.

19. Burger, "La prohibition du *Dictionaire historique et critique*."

20. The report is discussed in detail in chapter 3.

21. "Autre extrait d'une autre Lettre du meme lieu à M . . . du 1 Mars [1697]" and "Extrait d'une lettre écrite de Londres le 28 May 1697," in Jurieu, *Jugement du public*, 19 and 25–26.

22. Jurieu, "Réflexions," 30.

23. "Extrait d'une lettre de Paris, du 10 Juin 1697," in ibid., 26.

24. "Extrait d'une lettre écrite à un des membres du synode qui c'est tenu à Berg-op-zoom," in ibid., 24–25.

25. Jurieu, "Réflexions," 33.

26. Pierre Jurieu, "Réflexion," in *Jugement du public*, 11.

27. Bayle, *Avis important*. For more on the *Avis*, see Hickson and Lennon, "Real Significance of Bayle's Authorship of the *Avis*."

28. Jurieu, "Réflexion," 13.

29. Jurieu, "Réflexions," 32.

30. Ibid.

31. "Extrait d'une lettre écrite de Londres le 28 May 1697," 25.

32. Bayle, *Réflexions sur un imprimé*, 747.

33. Ibid., 752.

34. Jurieu, *Le philosophe de Roterdam*, 108.

35. Ibid., 134–35.

36. For this interpretation of Jurieu, see Popkin, *High Road to Pyrrhonism*, 161–80; and Popkin, "Bayle's Sincerity." See also Labrousse, *Pierre Bayle*, 2:595–609; and Israel, *Radical Enlightenment*, 332–35.

37. Not all agree with this interpretation of Bayle. Mori and Israel, in particular, deny the reading of Bayle as a fideist. Michael Hickson also shows that Bayle frequently deployed Jurieu's own fideist theories against him. See, Hickson, "Theodicy and Toleration in Bayle's *Dictionary*."

38. Jurieu, *Traité de la nature et de la grace*, 244–46, 254–59.

39. Jurieu, *Le vraye système de l'église*, 280.

40. Jurieu, *L'accomplissement de prophéties*.

41. Popkin, *History of Scepticism: From Savonarola to Bayle*, 285; Labrousse, "Reading Pierre Bayle in Paris," 10.

42. For this interpretation, see Labrousse, *Pierre Bayle*, 2:293–446; Popkin, *History of Scepticism: From Savonarola to Bayle*, 285–97; and Brogi, "Bayle, Le Clerc et les 'Rationaux.'"

43. Jacques Bernard, "Réponse aux questions d'un provincial," review of Pierre Bayle's book of the same title, *Nouvelles de la République des Lettres*, January 1707, 32. For Bernard's other reactions to Bayle's defense of atheism, see Jacques Bernard, "Troisième partie de l'extrait du tome quatrième de la Réponse aux questions d'un provincial," ibid., March 1707, 256–90.

44. Jacques Bernard, "Quatrième partie de l'extrait du tome quatrième de la Réponse aux questions d'un provincial," ibid., April 1707, 441–42.

45. Bernard, "Réponse aux questions d'un provincial," 32–33.

46. Ibid., 15–16.

47. Bernard, "Troisème partie de l'extrait du tome quatrième de la Réponse aux questions d'un provincial," 281–82.

48. Ibid., 279–81. See also Romans 1:19–21 (King James Version): "Because that which may be known of God is manifest in them; for God hath shewed it unto them. For the invisible things of him from the creation of the world are clearly seen, being understood by the things that are made, even his eternal power and Godhead; so that they are without excuse: Because that, when they knew God, they glorified him not as God, neither were thankful; but became vain in their imaginations, and their foolish heart was darkened."

49. Bernard, "Quatrième partie de l'extrait du tome quatrième de la Réponse aux questions d'un provincial," 406–7.

50. Jaquelot, *Conformité de la foi avec la raison*, preface [24–33].

51. Ibid., 265–67, 271, 272–73, 290–91, quotations on 265–67 and 271.

52. Jaquelot, *Examen de la théologie de Mr. Bayle*, 78.

53. Ibid., 109–10, 117–22.

54. For more about the text, see "Eloge de M. Bayle," *Histoire des ouvrages des savans*, December 1706, 553. The "Eloge de M. Bayle" also appears in the beginning of Bayle, *Œuvres diverses de Pierre Bayle*, vol. 4.

55. For more about the significance of the work, see Hickson, "Message of Bayle's Last Title."

56. Bayle, *Entretiens de Maxime et de Thémiste*, 41–45, 111–17, quotation on 117.

57. Ibid., 118, 130–33, 137–38, 74–77.

58. Jaquelot, *Réponse aux Entretiens composés par M. Bayle*.

59. For more on the origins of the dispute, see Labrousse, *Pierre Bayle*, 1:262–65; Annie Barnes, *Jean Le Clerc*, 113–14, 127, 228, 237; Sina, "Le Dictionaire de Pierre Bayle"; and Paganini, "Bayle et les théologies philosophiques de son temps."

60. Jean Le Clerc, "Remarques sur la Réponse pour Mr. Bayle au sujet du III & X article de la Bibliothèque choisie," *Bibliothèque choisie* 10 (1706): 367–68.

61. Ibid., 371.

62. Jean Le Clerc, "Remarques sur les Entretiens postumes de Mr. Bayle, contre la Bibliothèque choisie," *Bibliothèque choisie* 12 (1707): 198–386.

63. Le Clerc's articles against Bayle appear in *Bibliothèque ancienne et moderne* 1 (1714): 204–27; 8 (1717): 219–23 and 420–32; 14 (1720): 81–91 and 383–92; 15 (1721): 176–98; 27 (1727): 320–22; and 28 (1727): 363–432.

64. Le Clerc, "Remarques sur les Entretiens postumes de Mr. Bayle," 199–201.

65. Ibid., 206.

66. "Eloge de M. Bayle," 545–56. In the eighteenth century the eulogy was attributed to Henri Basnage de Beauval, but Labrousse attributes it to Jacques Basnage in *Pierre Bayle*, 1:220.

67. "Eloge de M. Bayle," 547.

68. Ibid., 551–52.

69. "Lettre de M. Garrel à Mr. le Clerc, Docteur en medicine, & Conseiller d'Etat de la République de Genève sur la question si agitée aujourd'hui si les lumières naturelles ne sont point opposées quelquefois à ce qu'enseigne la Religion," *Histoire des ouvrages des savans*, December 1706, 543–44.

70. "Eloge de M. Bayle," 555.

71. Du Revest, *Histoire de Mr. Bayle et de ses ouvrages*; Du Revest, *Histoire de Mr. Bayle et de ses ouvrages, nouvelle édition*.

72. Du Revest, *Histoire de Mr. Bayle et de ses ouvrages*, 51.

73. "Exacte revue de l'histoire de Mr. Bayle," in ibid., 266.

74. Desmaizeaux, *Life of Mr. Bayle*. Desmaizeaux published a French version in the 1730 edition of the *Dictionnaire*. Two years later his *Vie de M. Bayle* appeared in a separate edition.

75. Desmaizeaux, *Life of Mr. Bayle*, 204–5.

76. Ibid., 206, 207–9, quotation on 209.

77. Ibid., 219.

78. Bayle, "Eclaircissement sur les athées," in *Dictionnaire historique et critique* (1702), 3:3137.

79. Labrousse, "Reading Pierre Bayle in Paris."

80. Ibid., 8; Labrousse, *Pierre Bayle*, 2:605–6.

81. Labrousse suggests that this last issue lay at the heart of the fundamental disagreement between Bayle and Jurieu.

82. The editions of 1730 and 1740 are officially counted as the fourth and fifth editions because the publishers of those editions do not count the pirated editions from Geneva (1715), Trévoux (1734), and Basel (1738). For more on the different editions, see Beuchot, "Discours préliminaire," iii–xvii; and Labrousse, *Pierre Bayle et l'instrument critique*, 183.

Chapter 3 · The Specter of Bayle Returns to Haunt France

1. Labrousse, "Reading Pierre Bayle in Paris," 15.

2. Ibid., 11.

3. Rétat, *Le Dictionnaire de Bayle*, 74; Wade, *Clandestine Organization and Diffusion of Philosophic Ideas in France*, 41–44, 50–54, 63, 124, 151.

4. Marais, *Journal et mémoires*, 2:82–83. See also Rétat, *Le Dictionnaire de Bayle*, 121–22.

5. Michel Bohm, "Epitre dédicatoire à Son Altesse Roiale Monseigneur le duc d'Orleans, régent de France," in Bayle, *Dictionnaire historique et critique* (1720).

6. Sextus Empiricus, *Sexti Empirici opera, graece et latine*.

7. Sextus Empiricus, *Les hipotiposes*.

8. Wade, *Clandestine Organization and Diffusion of Philosophic Ideas in France*, 1–10, 263–75. For more on these clandestine manuscripts, see Benitez, *La face cachée des Lumières*; McKenna and Mothu, *La philosophie clandestine à l'âge classique*; and Paganini, *Les philosophies clandestines à l'âge classique*.

9. For more on these subversive texts, see Bloch, *Le matérialisme du XVIIIᵉ siècle et la littérature clandestine*.

10. For more on ideological polarization after the 1750s in Enlightenment France, see Burson, "Crystallization of Counter-Enlightenment and Philosophe Identities"; and Burson, *Rise and Fall of Theological Enlightenment*. In his article, Burson argues that "self-conscious religious opposition to Enlightenment" was born in the 1750s, and he attributes it to tensions within the Gallican Church (960).

11. Renaudot, "Jugement de l'abbé Renaudot sur le Dictionnaire critique," 7–8.

12. Labrousse, "Reading Pierre Bayle in Paris," 11.

13. Renaudot, "Jugement de l'abbé Renaudot sur le Dictionnaire critique," 9.

14. Ibid., 6.

15. Eusèbe Renaudot to François Janiçon, 2 July 1697, in Papiers du P. Léonard, BNF, Nouvelles acquisitions françaises 7483, fol. 200Bv. Also cited in Burger, "La prohibition du *Dictionaire historique et critique*," 100.

16. "Réponse aux questions d'un provincial," art. 125, *Mémoires de Trévoux*, September 1704, 1481.

17. "Réponses aux questions d'un provincial: Tome second," art. 57, ibid., May 1706, 766–67.

18. Rétat makes this supposition in *Le Dictionnaire de Bayle*, 94n135.

19. Tournemine, *Réflexions sur l'athéisme*, 525.

20. "Mémoire sur la vie et les ouvrages de feux Mr. Bayle, envoyé de Hollande," art. 47, *Mémoires de Trévoux*, April 1707, 705.

21. Ibid.

22. See, e.g., "Examen de la théologie de Mr. Bayle," art. 112, *Mémoires de Trévoux*, September 1707, 1489–1526; and "Réponse aux Entretiens composez par Mr. Bayle," art. 106, ibid., August 1708, 1293–1305.

23. Rétat, *Le Dictionnaire de Bayle*, 95–96.

24. Laubrussel, *Traité des abus de la critique en matière de religion*, 1:xiii.

25. Ibid., 2:282–83.

26. Ibid., 328–34.

27. "Nouvelles littéraires," art. 80, *Mémoires de Trévoux*, May 1715, 930–31.

28. Bernis, *Mémoires du cardinal Bernis*, 52.

29. Rétat, *Le Dictionnaire de Bayle*, 130–31. See also Crousaz, *Examen du pyrrhonisme ancien et moderne*, 239.

30. For Le Clerc's biography, see Louis Bertrand, *Vie, écrits et correspondance littéraire de Laurent-Josse Le Clerc*.

31. Le Clerc, *Remarques sur différens articles*; Le Clerc, *Bibliothèque du Richelet*.

32. For the exchange between Marais and Le Clerc, see Louis Bertrand, *Vie, écrits et correspondance littéraire de Laurent-Josse Le Clerc*, 132–48. For a concise biography of Marais, see Lescure, "Mathieu Marais: Sa vie et ses ouvrages."

33. For more on the cultural and intellectual context of the early modern Republic of Letters, see Goldgar, *Impolite Learning*; Goodman, *Republic of Letters*; Bots and Waquet, *La République des Lettres*; and Lamy, "La République des Lettres."

34. Bouhier, *Correspondance littéraire*; Weil, *Jean Bouhier et sa correspondance*. For more on Bouhier, see Des Guerrois, *Le président Bouhier*.

35. All the letters appear in Bouhier, *Correspondance littéraire*, vol. 8. See specifically Bouhier to Marais, 5 December 1724, 43; Bouhier to Marais, 19 December 1724, 46; Bouhier to Marais, 7 January 1725, 56; Bouhier to Marais, 7 March 1725, 107; Bouhier to Marais, 14 March 1725, 114; Marais to Bouhier, 17 May 1725, 153; Bouhier to Marais, 26 June 1725, 170; and Marais to Bouhier, 29 June 1725, 175.

36. Marais to Bouhier, 22 March 1725, in ibid., 118.

37. Bouhier to Marais, 26 June 1725, in ibid., 170.

38. Marais to Bouhier, 29–30 June 1725, in ibid., 175.

39. Ibid., 177–78.

40. "Lettre de Mr. l'Abbé Le Clerc à Mr. Marais," BNF, Fonds Français 24413, pp. 2–4.

41. Ibid., 108.

42. Ibid., 112–13.

43. Le Clerc, *Remarques sur différens articles*, 136.

44. "Lettre de Mr. l'Abbé Le Clerc à Mr. Marais," 108.

45. Le Clerc, *Lettre critique sur le Dictionaire de Bayle*, v–vii.

46. "Lettre de Mr. l'Abbé Le Clerc à Mr. Marais," 140–41.

47. Bayle had argued that the former category included people who either doubted or denied the existence of God but who generally abided by the rules of society. The latter category, on the other hand, was made up of those who, while believing in the existence of God and the immortality of the soul, behaved as if there were no God. They thus tried to insincerely argue in favor of atheism in order to justify their reprehensible behavior. Bayle, *Réponse aux questions d'un provincial*, 4:164–82; Bayle, *Pensées diverses*, 392–96; Bayle, *Continuation des Pensées diverses*, 1:467–78. For secondary accounts of the distinction between practical and speculative atheists, see Kors, *Atheism in France*, 19–20, 49–50, 55–58, 256–57; Mori, " 'L'athée spéculatif' selon Bayle"; Božovič, "Philosophy of Du Marsais's *Le Philosophe*"; and Paganini, "Pierre Bayle et le statut de l'athéisme sceptique."

48. "Lettre de Mr. l'Abbé Le Clerc à Mr. Marais," 142–44.

49. Both Marais and Bouhier use the term *hypercritique*. See Bouhier to Marais, 17 July 1725, and Marais to Bouhier, 24 October 1725, in Bouhier, *Correspondance littéraire*, vol. 8, 188 and 247.

50. Marais to Bouhier, 29–30 June 1725, in ibid., 179.

51. Bouhier to Marais, 17 July 1725, in ibid., 187.

52. Marais to Le Clerc, 4 July 1725, reprinted in Louis Bertrand, *Vie, écrits et correspondance littéraire de Laurent-Josse Le Clerc*, 140–41.

53. Marais to Le Clerc, 16 November 1725, reprinted in ibid., 142–43.

54. Marais to Bouhier, 24 October 1725, in Bouhier, *Correspondance littéraire*, vol. 8, 247–48.

55. Le Clerc, *Lettre critique sur le Dictionaire de Bayle*, vii.

56. Ibid., xx.

57. "Avertissement sur cette nouvelle édition," in Bayle, *Dictionnaire historique et critique* (1734). The title page identifies this as the fifth edition, printed in Amsterdam. If the 1715 pirated Geneva edition were included in the count, this would actually be the 6th edition. The 1734 edition actually had a false imprint and was printed in Trévoux and edited by the Jesuits of the *Mémoires de Trévoux*. For more on this edition, see Beuchot, "Discours préliminaire," xv–xvi.

58. For more on the friendship between Marais and Bayle, see Lescure, "Mathieu Marais: Sa vie et ses ouvrages," 13–17.

59. Ascoli, "Quelques pages d'une correspondance inédite de M. Marais," 152–53; Rétat, *Le Dictionnaire de Bayle*, 53.

60. For a critique of Bayle that follows an identical strategy, see Le Duchat, "Remarques sur le Dictionnaire de Bayle."

61. Charles Merlin, "Véritable clef des ouvrages de S. Augustin contre les Pélagiens," in *Réfutation des critiques de Monsieur Bayle*, 2.

62. Rétat, *Le Dictionnaire de Bayle*, 187. For Merlin's accusations, see his *Réfutation des critiques de Monsieur Bayle*, 7, 85, 101.

63. Charles Merlin, "Dissertation sur la Déese Flora, par le P. Merlin, jesuite," art. 106, *Mémoires de Trévoux*, November 1735, 2206.

64. Charles Merlin, "Examen des critiques répanduës dans le Dictionnaire de M. Bayle sur divers endroits des Ecrits du même saint Docteur," in *Réfutation des critiques de Monsieur Bayle*, 27, 93 (quotation).

65. Merlin, *Apologie de David*, 1.

66. Ibid., 10, 17.

67. Ibid., 82.

68. Ibid., 118–19.

69. "Avertissement de l'imprimeur aux lecteurs," in Le Febvre, *Bayle en petit* (1737).

70. Le Febvre, *Bayle en petit* (1737), 193.

71. Ibid.

72. Crousaz, *Examen du pyrrhonisme ancien et moderne*, 12.

73. Le Febvre, *Bayle en petit* (1737), 6.

74. Ibid.

75. Ibid., 16, 22.

76. Ibid., 11, 93–94.

77. Ibid., 26.

78. Ibid., 92.

79. Ibid., 33–69, 93–94.

80. Le Febvre, *Bayle en petit* (1738).

81. Le Febvre, *Examen critique des ouvrages de Bayle*.

82. D'Aguesseau to Joly, 17 February 1747, in "Quinze lettres inédites adressées à M. l'abbé Joly par d'Aguesseau," BNF, Nouvelles acquisitions françaises 767, fols. 7r–7v.

83. D'Aguesseau to Joly, 18 June 1746, in ibid., fols. 1r–1v. Joly went on to reproduce this passage almost entirely in the preface of his *Remarques critiques*, 1:viii.

84. Beuchot, "Avant-propos," ii–iii; Beuchot, "Discours préliminaire," xxiii–xxiv.

85. Joly, *Remarques critiques*, 1:xvii–xviii, 1:l.

86. Ibid., viii.

87. Ibid., ix.

88. Ibid.

89. Ibid., x.

90. Bayle, *Historical and Critical Dictionary* (1710). The attribution of the translation is subject to some dispute. Isabel Rivers identifies Bayle's Huguenot friend Michel de la Roche as the translator. See Rivers, "Biographical Dictionaries and their Uses," 142–43. Mikko Tolonen suggests Bernard Mandeville as a possible translator in his *Mandeville and Hume*, 113–14. Elena Muceni questions this attribution; she identifies de la Roche but also finds two other people involved in the translation and doubts Mandeville's involvement. See Muceni, "Did Mandeville Translate Bayle's Dictionnaire?"

91. Rivers, "Biographical Dictionaries and their Uses," 142–43.

92. Desmaizeaux, *Mr. Bayle's Historical and Critical Dictionary*.

93. Birch, Bernard, and Lockman, *General Dictionary, Historical and Critical*, vol. 1, preface [iii]. For more on the *General Dictionary*, see Osborn, "Thomas Birch and the 'General Dictionary' "; and Rivers, "Biographical Dictionaries and their Uses," 149–52.

94. See the entries "Bayle," "Manicheans," and "Pyrrho" in Birch, Bernard, and Lockman, *General Dictionary, Historical and Critical*, 3:61–89, 7:396–402, and 8:595–602.

95. Jacques-Georges Chauffepié, preface to *Nouveau dictionnaire historique et critique*, 1:xii.

96. Jacques-Georges Chauffepié, "Manichéens," in ibid., 3:18.

97. Chauffepié, preface 1:x; Chauffepié, "Jurieu," in *Nouveau dictionnaire historique et critique*, 2:57–82.

98. Jacques-Georges Chauffepié, "Bayle," in *Nouveau dictionnaire historique et critique*, 1:155–56.

99. Mornet, "Les enseignements des bibliothèques privés," 460.

100. Marais to Bouhier, 29–30 June 1725, in Bouhier, *Correspondance littéraire*, vol. 8, 179.

101. Pappas, *Berthier's Journal de Trévoux and the Philosophes*, 21. Pappas argues that Castel was behind the journal's more aggressive reviews and editorial decisions.

102. "Essais de Theodicée, sur la bonté de Dieu, la liberté de l'homme, & l'origine du mal, par. M. Leibnitz," art. 13, *Mémoires de Trévoux*, February 1737, 206, 203–4.

103. Béat de Muralt, "Caractère de M. Bayle," art. 124, *Mémoires de Trévoux*, December 1737, 2241–42.

104. For more on this historical context, see McManners, *Church and Society in Eighteenth-Century France*; and Burson, *Rise and Fall of Theological Enlightenment*, 102–61.

Chapter 4 · Secret Skepticism

1. Lennon, "Skepticism of Huet's *Traité*," 68.

2. For a thorough explanation of this distinction, see Kors, *Atheism in France*, 114–31.

3. Ibid., 115. In the *Summa contra gentiles* 1.12, Thomas Aquinas had argued, "Quod Deum esse demonstrari non potest, sed sola fide tenetur," meaning that God's existence could not be demonstrated by natural means and could be believed by faith alone. For more on the Paduan Averroists, see Grendler, *Universities of the Italian Renaissance*, 286.

4. Transcript of the Fifth Lateran Council, 8th sess., 19 December 1513, "Condemnation of every proposition contrary to the truth of the enlightened Christian faith," http://www.intratext.com/IXT/ENG0067/_P9.HTM. See also Hefele, *Histoire des conciles d'après les documents originaux*, 8, pt. 1: 420–22.

5. René Descartes, "Epistre à Messieurs les Doyen et Docteurs de la Sacrée Faculté de Théologie de Paris," in *Méditations métaphysiques*, [3–5].

6. For this interpretation, see Kors, *Atheism in France*, 368–72.

7. Tertullian, *De carne Christi*, chap. 5, verse 4, italics added.

8. Huet, "Censure de la philosophie de M. Descartes à Mr. de Montausier," BNF, Fonds Français 14702, fol. 28v.

9. Ibid., fol. 32v. See also Huet, *Against Cartesian Philosophy*, 166.

10. Huet, "Censure de la philosophie de M. Descartes à Mr. de Montausier," fol. 32r.

11. Ibid., fol. 33r.

12. Huet, *Traité philosophique de la foiblesse de l'esprit humain*, 184–85.

13. For more on Huet and the contemporaneous debates about the relationship between faith and reason, see Northeast, *Parisian Jesuits and the Enlightenment*, 59–60.

14. Huet, *Traité philosophique de la foiblesse de l'esprit humain*, 209.

15. Ibid., 212.

16. *Alnetanae* is the place adjective for *Alnetum*, the Latin name for the Abbey Aunay in Normandy. Huet received his appointment at Aunay from the king in 1674 and retired there in 1680. In 1685, Huet moved to Soissons and then later to Avranches. The title of the work suggests that Huet believed there was some connection between his work and the time he had spent in Aunay. This would suggest that the work was conceived in the first half of the 1680s.

17. Huet, *Memoirs*, 2:202.

18. Huet, *Alnetanae quaestiones de concordia rationis et fidei*, 7, 16.

19. Ibid., 4–5.

20. Ibid., 61.

21. Ibid., 74–75.

22. Ibid., 30.

23. Christian Bartholmèss claimed in *Huet évêque d'Avranches*, 50, that the *Traité* presented the extreme conclusions that followed from the principles advanced in Huet's two preceding works (the *Censura* and the *Quaestiones*). According to April Shelford, Huet declared to Edme Pirot, a Sorbonne theologian and censor, his intention to make the *Traité* the fourth book of the *Quaestiones*. Shelford, "Faith and Glory," 453. See also Shelford, *Transforming the Republic of Letters*. The historian Germain Malbreil argued that the *Traité* was supposed to serve as the first book of the *Quaestiones*, because it would have logically paved the way for the demonstration of the superiority of faith. Malbreil, "Les droits de la raison et de la foi," 131.

24. Huet, *Memoirs*, 2:203.

25. Ibid., 204–5.

26. Shelford, "Faith and Glory," 452.

27. La Rue to Huet, n.d., in Correspondance littéraire et privée d'une partie du siècle de Louis XIV, BNF, Fonds Français 15188, pp. 329–30. I use April Shelford's translation from Shelford, "Faith and Glory," 452.

28. Shelford, "Faith and Glory," 453.

29. Pirot to Huet, 2 May 1692, in Correspondance littéraire et privée d'une partie du siècle de Louis XIV, BNF, Fonds Français 15189, fol. 37v.

30. Ibid., fol. 38v.

31. Tolmer, *Pierre-Daniel Huet*, 550–51.

32. Kors, *Atheism in France*, 370; Lennon, "Skepticism of Huet's *Traité*," 68.

33. The attribution of this review is itself, ironically, subject to scrutiny. Several sources identify du Cerceau as the author: Sommervogel, *Table méthodique des Mémoires de Trévoux*, 1:xliv; Dumas, *Histoire du Journal de Trévoux*, 90; Desautels, *Les Mémoires de Trévoux*, 184–85. Jean-Pierre Niceron, in *Mémoires pour servir à l'histoire des hommes illustres*, 10:8, claims that Castel was the sole author. Still others attribute the review to both authors: Voltaire, *Le siècle de Louis XIV*, 20:201–3; Gouraud, *Histoire du calcul des probabilités*, 46; Avenel, *Histoire de la vie et des ouvrages de Daniel Huet*, 237. Given the fact that the Jesuits of the *Mémoires de Trévoux* often collaborated on articles, it is probable that both Castel and du Cerceau contributed to the review.

34. "Traité philosophique de la foiblesse de l'esprit humain, par feu Mr. Huet, ancient Evêque d'Avranches," art. 47, *Mémoires de Trévoux*, June 1725, 989.

35. Ibid., 992–93.

36. Ibid., 994–96.

37. Ibid., 1018–19.

38. Ibid., 997.

39. Ibid., 997–98.

40. Ibid., 998.

41. Descartes, *Méditations métaphysiques*, 98–99.

42. "Traité Philosophique de la foiblesse de l'esprit humain, par feu Mr. Huet," 999.

43. Ibid., 1017–18.

44. Ibid., 1013.

45. Olivet, *Apologie*, 24.

46. Ibid., 31–33.

47. Ibid., 42.

48. Olivet and Pellisson, *Histoire de l'Académie françoise*, 2:388–90.

49. Olivet, *Apologie*, 23.

50. Jean-François Baltus, "Sentiment du R. P. Baltus Jesuite, sur le Traité de la Foiblesse de l'esprit humain," art. 4, *Bibliothèque françoise, ou Histoire littéraire de la France* 10, pt. 1 (January–May 1727): 51.

51. Ibid., 88.

52. Ibid., 98–99.

53. "Réponse à la seconde partie de l'Apologie de Monsieur l'Abbé d'Olivet, au sujet de l'article XLVII des Mémoires de Trévoux de l'année 1725," art. 10, *Mémoires de Trévoux*, February 1727, 197–225.

54. Ibid., 207.

55. Ibid., 220.

56. Ibid., 221–22.

57. Ibid., 225.

58. Ibid., 224.

59. Crousaz, *Examen du pyrrhonisme ancien et moderne*, 233.

60. For an extended discussion of the *praeambula fidei*, see Kors, *Atheism in France*, 114–20.

61. Crousaz, *Examen du pyrrhonisme ancien et moderne*, 230.

62. Ibid., 350–51.

63. Ibid., 346.

64. Huet, *Traité philosophique de la foiblesse de l'esprit humain*, 5–9. Huet argued that he did not wish to adhere to any strict philosophical system because he neither wanted to be mistaken in philosophical questions nor desired to dispute about matters in which he could reach no certainty.

65. Crousaz, *Examen du pyrrhonisme ancien et moderne*, 750.

66. Ibid., 236.

67. Ibid., 768.

68. Ibid., 750–51.

69. Ibid., 765.

70. Ibid., 757.

71. Egger, *De viribus mentis humanae disquisitio philosophica anti-huetiana*, preface [6].

Chapter 5 · A New Hope

1. For more on the various editions and translations of the text, see Floridi, *Sextus Empiricus*, 53–61; Popkin, "Samuel Sorbière's Translation of Sextus Empiricus"; and Popkin, "Curious Feature of the French Edition of Sextus Empiricus."

2. Barbier, *Dictionnaire des ouvrages anonymes et pseudonymes*, 2:54.

3. "Sexti Empirici opera, graece et latine," *Journal des savants*, 10 April 1719, 233–34.

4. "Les Œuvres de Sextus Empiricus publiées par Mr. Fabricius," *Bibliothèque ancienne et moderne* 14, pt. 1 (1720): 4–5.

5. Ibid., 5–6.

6. Ibid.

7. Ibid., 17–18.

8. Ibid., 25.

9. Ibid., 26–27.

10. Ibid., 28.

11. "Les hypotyposes ou Institutions pirrhoniennes de Sextus Empiricus en trois livres, traduites du Grec avec des notes," art. 2, *Mémoires de Trévoux*, January 1727, 37–38.

12. Ibid., 39–40.

13. Huart, preface to Sextus Empiricus, *Les hipotiposes*, [2].

14. "Les hypotyposes ou Institutions pirrhoniennes," 42–43. See chapter 1 above for the full quotation.

15. Ibid., 52.

16. Ibid., 53.

17. Ibid., 58.

18. Crousaz, *Examen du pyrrhonisme ancien et moderne*, 57–192.

19. Ibid., 70, 79, 73–74.

20. Ibid., 147.

21. Ibid., 148.

22. Bierling, *Commentatio de pyrrhonismo historico*, 2–3. Bierling cites Sextus Empiricus, *Hypotyposes*, bk. 1, chap. 1.

23. Foucher, *Dissertations sur la recherche de la vérité*, 3–4.

24. Curiously, reactions to Foucher's Academic skepticism were significantly less critical than reactions to Huet's work thirty years later. See the following reviews: "Dissertations sur la philosophie des Académiciens," *Journal des savants*, 2 February 1693, 53–55; and "Dissertations sur la recherche de la vérité," ibid., 14 December 1693, 487–89.

25. Bierling, *Commentatio de pyrrhonismo historico*, 6.

26. Ibid., 11–13, 15–17.

27. Ibid., 22.

28. Ibid., 21.

29. Ibid., 6.

30. Ibid., 5n.

31. Ibid., 24.

32. "Frederici Guilielmi Bierlingii Commentatio de Pyrrhonismo-Historico," art. 1, *Bibliothèque germanique* 10 (1725): 1–41.

33. Ibid., 1.

34. For excellent accounts of Buffier's thought, see Kathleen Sonia Wilkins, *Study of the Works of Claude Buffier*; Marcil-Lacoste, *Claude Buffier and Thomas Reid*; Burson, *Rise and Fall of Theological Enlightenment*, 47–50, 180–81; and Burson, "Claude G. Buffier and the Maturation of the Jesuit Synthesis in the Age of Enlightenment."

35. Buffier, *Traité des premières véritez*, 1:vii.

36. Ibid., 1–2, 2.

37. Ibid., 53.

38. Ibid., 71–72.

39. Ibid., 9, 10 (quotation).

40. Ibid., 13, 25 (quotation).

41. Ibid., 25–26, 77–79.

42. Ibid., 29–30.

43. Ibid., 94.

44. Ibid., 97–104.

45. Ibid., 128. The passage is paraphrased in the *Encyclopédie* article "Vraissemblance."

46. Ibid., 135–39, quotation on 136.

47. Ibid., 147–48.

48. Locke, *Essay Concerning Human Understanding*, 3.6.6, pp. 210–11.

49. See, e.g., Lee, *Anti-Scepticism*, preface [5].

50. For more on Locke's reception in France, see Yolton, *Locke and French Materialism*; and Hutchison, *Locke in France*.

51. "Extrait d'un livre anglois qui n'est pas encore publié, intitulé Essai Philosophique concernant l'Entendement, où l'on montre quelle est l'étendue de nos connois-

sances certaines, & la manière dont nous y parvenons. Communiqué par Monsieur Locke," art. 2, *Bibliothèque universelle et historique* 8 (January 1688): 49–142.

52. Locke, *Essai philosophique concernant l'entendement humain.*

53. Locke, *Abrégé de l'Essay de Monsieur Locke.*

54. On Locke's influence on Buffier, see Dagen, *L'histoire de l'esprit humain*, 77–83; Hutchison, *Locke in France*, 124–59; and Burson, *Rise and Fall of Theological Enlightenment*, 38–54.

55. Buffier, *Traité des premières véritez*, 2:253.

56. Ibid., 1:119–21.

57. Ibid., 2:257–58.

58. Burson argues in *Rise and Fall of Theological Enlightenment*, 48–49, that Buffier combined the epistemologies of Locke and Malebranche. Based on Buffier's own statements, it seems that Descartes played a role that was equal if not more important than Malebranche's in Buffier's epistemology. For Buffier's discussion of Descartes, see Claude Buffier, "Remarques sur les principes ou la métaphysique de Descartes," in Buffier, *Traité des premières véritez*, 2:238–52. For Buffier's comments about the similarities and differences between Descartes and Malebranche, see Buffier, "Observations sur la Métaphysique du Père Malbranche," in ibid., 270–75. It would also be useful to explore any affinity that Buffier may have had for both Cartesian empiricists and other occasionalists.

59. See chapter 7.

60. Aside from the extensive biographical study of Crousaz in La Harpe, *Jean-Pierre de Crousaz*, very few scholars have described his philosophy and his anti-skepticism in detail. However, in 2004 the editors of the *Revue de théologie et de philosophie* dedicated an entire issue of their journal to the discussion of Crousaz's ideas and his intellectual context. Of particular note are Mayer, "Crousaz"; and Häseler, "Succès et refus." Other detailed discussions of Crousaz's attack on Bayle can be found in Rétat, *Le Dictionnaire de Bayle*, 154–62; Häseler, "Formey et Crousaz"; Popkin, "New Views on the Role of Skepticism in the Enlightenment"; and Popkin, "Scepticism." For a discussion of Crousaz in the Dutch context, see Ruler, "Shipwreck of Belief and Eternal Bliss," 114–23.

61. La Harpe, *Jean-Pierre de Crousaz*, 9.

62. Crousaz, *Examen du pyrrhonisme ancien et moderne*, 9.

63. La Harpe, *Jean-Pierre de Crousaz*, 206–12.

64. Gibbon, *Autobiography*, 77, 89.

65. Crousaz's *New Treatise of the Art of Thinking* was an English translation of *La logique*. For a more detailed discussion of the reception of Crousaz's textbook on logic, see Häseler, "Succès et refus," 61–63.

66. Mayer, "Crousaz," 48.

67. La Harpe, *Jean-Pierre de Crousaz*, 223.

68. Crousaz, *Examen du pyrrhonisme ancien et moderne*, preface [3], 1–2.

69. Ibid., preface [3].

70. For a similar evaluation of the intellectual culture of the early eighteenth century by Pierre-Daniel Huet, see Shelford, *Transforming the Republic of Letters*, 176–78.

71. Crousaz, *Examen du pyrrhonisme ancien et moderne*, 357.

72. Ibid., 23.

73. Dan Edelstein identifies this self-reflexive and triumphalist narrative as the fundamental feature of the Enlightenment in *Enlightenment*, 2–3, 13–15.

74. Crousaz, *Examen du pyrrhonisme ancien et moderne*, 375, 65–66, 3, 63, quotations on 375 and 3.

75. Ibid., 11.

76. Ibid., 63–64, 74, 28, 771 (quotation).

77. Ibid., 764, 70.

78. Ibid., 358.

79. Ibid., 46 (quotation), 45.

80. Ibid., 761.

81. Ibid., 77.

82. Ibid., 754, 776, 765 (quotation).

83. Popkin, "Scepticism," 427. Popkin is referring to the "Apologie de monsieur Bayle, ou Lettre d'un sceptique sur l'Examen du pyrrhonisme ancien et moderne pour servir de réponse au livre de M. de Crousaz sur le pyrrhonisme," which appeared in Bayle, *Nouvelles lettres*, 195–205. This negative philosophical evaluation of Crousaz is largely shared by Mayer in "Crousaz," 54–55. Mayer dismissed the arguments of the *Examen* as *ad hominem* attacks on Bayle and on other skeptics. Similarly, Jens Häseler has suggested that the polemical style of the *Examen* led to the decline of Crousaz's reputation in Huguenot circles. Häseler, "Succès et refus," 63–66.

84. "Examen du pyrrhonisme ancien & moderne. Par Mr. De Crousaz. Second Extrait," art. 2, *Bibliothèque raisonnée des ouvrages des savans de l'Europe* 11, pt. 2 (July–September 1733): 90.

85. "Examen du pyrrhonisme ancien & moderne, par Mr. De Crousaz de l'Académie des Sciences, gouverneur de son A.S. le Prince Fréderic de Hesse-Cassel &c.," art. 52, *Mémoires de Trévoux*, May 1734, 939.

86. Other notable reviews appeared in the *Journal des savants*, May 1733, 263–67, and June 1733, 354–59; and in art. 2, *Bibliothèque françoise, ou Histoire littéraire de la France* 18, pt. 1 (1733): 55–76. They are generally sympathetic to Crousaz's project of refuting philosophical skepticism.

87. Perrenoud, *Inventaire des archives Jean-Pierre de Crousaz*, 5–8, 10, 17–18, 25–26, 31, 43, 45–46.

88. Bignon to Crousaz, 30 April 1729, BCUL, Fonds Crousaz, 6:189.

89. Bignon to Crousaz, 31 August 1731, ibid., 209.

90. Fleury to Crousaz, 31 December 1729, ibid., 193–94.

91. Fleury to Crousaz, 6 February 1742, ibid., 14, item 52, fol. 1r.

92. See, e.g., Fleury to Crousaz, 14 September 1740, ibid., 14, item 50, fol. 1v; and Freudenreich to Crousaz, 20 July 1740, ibid., 10:297.

93. Fleury to Crousaz, 22 March 1738, ibid., 6:119–20.

94. Haller to Crousaz, n.d., ibid., 14, item H, p. 5.

95. Haller to Crousaz, n.d., ibid., 10:427.

96. Formey to Crousaz, 1 April 1738, ibid., 12:173–74.

97. For more, see Häseler, "Formey et Crousaz."

98. Haller, "Discours préliminaire," i–xlviii. Haller's text was expanded and translated by Gabriel Seigneux de Correvon and published separately as *Discours sur l'irreligion, où l'on examine ses principes & ses suites funestes* in 1760.

Chapter 6 · The Berlin Compromise

1. For more on Boullier, see Yolton, *Locke and French Materialism*, 94–101, 110–35; Richard H. Popkin, "David-Renaud Boullier and Bishop Berkeley," in Popkin, *High Road to Pyrrhonism*, 355–62; Schøsler, "David-Renaud Boullier—Disciple de Locke?"; O'Neal, "L'évolution de la notion d'expérience"; O'Neal, *Changing Minds*, 71–101; Thomson, *Bodies of Thought*, 176–77; and Burson, *Rise and Fall of Theological Enlightenment*, 175.

2. Boullier, *Traité des vrais principes*, 101–5.

3. Ibid., 101.

4. Gabriel Daniel, *Voyage du monde de Descartes*, 484.

5. Boullier, *Essai philosophique sur l'âme des bêtes*, 1:85.

6. Boullier, *Traité des vrais principes*, 5, 2–3.

7. Ibid., 6, 7.

8. Ibid., 117–18, 107, 214, quotations of 117–18 and 107.

9. Ibid., 268–70.

10. Boullier, *Lettres sur les vrais principes de la religion*, 6.

11. Boullier, *Le pyrrhonisme de l'église romaine*, 40, 43, 56, 61, 76–77, 82, 86–87, 123, 162.

12. Ibid., 127.

13. Ibid., 163–64.

14. For an analysis of d'Argens's skepticism, see Correard, "Reasonable Scepticism in the French Enlightenment."

15. For details of the marquis d'Argens's early life, see Johnston, *Le marquis d'Argens*, 11–30; and Gasper, *Marquis d'Argens*, 11–85. D'Argens's autobiography is a rather insightful source that contains many intimate details about his life. See Argens, *Mémoires*.

16. Argens, *Lettres juives*.

17. Johnston, *Le marquis d'Argens*, 42–44; Schechter, *Obstinate Hebrews*, 43–44.

18. For more on the development of the history of philosophy in this period, see Piaia, "Philosophical Historiography in France from Bayle to Deslandes."

19. For more on Deslandes, see Piaia, " 'Critical' History of Philosophy and the Early Enlightenment"; and Mastrogiacomo, *Libertinage et Lumières*.

20. Saint-Aubin, *Traité de l'opinion*, 1:1–2.

21. Ibid., 10.

22. Argens, *La philosophie du bon-sens*, 4–5.

23. Ibid., 22–27, 18–19.

24. Ibid., 6–7, 31–32, 314, quotations of 6–7 and 314.

25. Ibid., 136–37, 143–44 (quotation).

26. Ibid., 165 (quotation), 166–68.

27. Ibid., 172–73.

28. Ibid., 420–21.

29. Schechter, *Obstinate Hebrews*, 43.

30. Voltaire to d'Argens, 20 December 1736, http://www.e-enlightenment.com/item /voltfrVF0880156b1c/?letters=corr&s=boyerjeanb000909&r=10. The letter is partially cited in Gasper, *Marquis d'Argens*, 102, and it also appears in Voltaire, *Les œuvres complètes de Voltaire*, ed. Besterman, 88, no. D1228.

31. Correard, "Reasonable Scepticism in the French Enlightenment," 178–85. For more on Voltaire's skepticism, see Brandão, "Voltaire et le scepticisme"; and Pujol, "Forms and Aims of Voltairean Scepticism." For more on the relationship between Voltaire and d'Argens, see Trousson, "Voltaire et le marquis d'Argens."

32. Voltaire to d'Argens, 2 October 1740, http://www.e-enlightenment.com/item /voltfrVF0910304b1c/?letters=corr&s=boyerjeanb000909&r=25. The letter also appears in *Les œuvres complètes de Voltaire*, 91, no. D2322.

33. For details on this period of d'Argens's life, see Johnston, *Le marquis d'Argens*, 64–77; and Gasper, *Marquis d'Argens*, 121–44.

34. For an erudite study of the Prussian Academy, see Bartholmèss, *Histoire philosophique de l'Académie de Prusse*. For excellent recent overviews, see Laursen, "Swiss Anti-Skeptics in Berlin"; Laursen, "Berlin Academy"; Laursen, "Tame Skeptics at the Prussian Academy"; and Lifschitz, *Language and Enlightenment*.

35. Formey, *Pensées raisonnables*, 30.

36. Ibid., 93; Diderot, *Pensées philosophiques*, 28–29.

37. Formey, *Pensées raisonnables*, 95.

38. Ibid., 98–99, 120, 113.

39. Ibid., 99, 100.

40. Ibid., 124.

41. Ibid., 121–22.

42. Ibid., 131, 128.

43. Formey to Crousaz, 25 March 1743, BCUL, Fonds Crousaz, 10:179–80.

44. Formey, *Le philosophe chrétien*, 1:vi–ix (quotations), xxii–xxiii.

45. Formey, *La logique des vraisemblances*, 4.

46. Ibid., 10.

47. Ibid., 20.

48. Correvon, "Préface de traducteur," iv–vi.

49. Ibid., iv–v.

50. Formey, "Préface de l'éditeur," 1:xiv–xv.

51. For more on Hume in the French context, see Malherbe, "Hume's Reception in France."

52. Hume, *My Own Life*, 7–8.

53. Ibid., 11–12.

54. Popkin, *High Road to Pyrrhonism*, 58. Popkin has since modified his views, and his claim has been challenged by a number of historians and philosophers. See, e.g., Charles, introduction to Charles and Smith, *Scepticism in the Eighteenth Century*.

55. Formey's five-part review appears in the *Nouvelle bibliothèque germanique, ou Histoire littéraire de l'Allemagne, de la Suisse, & des pays du Nord* 19, pt. 1 (January– March 1756): 78–109 and pt. 2 (October–December 1756): 311–32; 20, pt. 1 (January– March 1757): 57–87 and pt. 2 (April–June 1757): 268–98; 21, pt. 1 (July–September 1757): 65–81.

56. Formey, art. 7, *Nouvelle bibliothèque germanique* 19, pt. 1: 78.

57. Formey, art. 6, ibid. 19, pt. 2: 314.

58. Ibid., 315.

59. Formey, art. 3, ibid. 20, pt. 2: 283.

60. Formey, art. 6, ibid. 19, pt. 2: 317–18, 319, 321, quotations on 319 and 321.

61. Formey, art. 3, ibid. 20, pt. 2: 271.

62. Formey, "Préface de l'éditeur," xxiii.

63. Formey, art. 3, *Nouvelle bibliothèque germanique* 20, pt. 1: 70–71.

64. Formey, "Préface de l'éditeur," ii–ix. For more on the translation, see Richard H. Popkin, "The Early Critics of Hume," in *High Road to Pyrrhonism*, 208–12; and Laursen and Popkin, "Hume in the Prussian Academy."

65. Formey, "Préface de l'éditeur," viii–ix.

66. Ibid., ix–x.

67. Ibid., xiii–xiv.

68. David Hume, "Dixième essai: Sur les miracles," in *Essais philosophiques*, 2:13–74. For the English edition, see Hume, *Philosophical Essays Concerning Human Understanding*, 173–203.

69. Hume, "Dixième essai: Sur les miracles," 65–66.

70. Formey, "Préface de l'éditeur," xli–xlii.

71. Formey, art. 3, *Nouvelle bibliothèque germanique* 20, pt. 2: 284–85.

72. Ibid., 286.

73. Formey, "Préface de l'éditeur," xliii–l.

74. Ibid., xxiii.

75. Ibid., xxxviii.

76. Formey's editorial note appears in Hume, *Essais philosophiques*, 1:203–4.

77. Ibid., 204.

78. For more on Mérian, see Bartholmèss, *Histoire philosophique de l'Académie de Prusse*, 2:33–76; Laursen and Popkin, "Hume in the Prussian Academy," 156–58; and "Mérian, Jean-Bernard," in Klemme and Keuhn, *Dictionary of Eighteenth-Century German Philosophers*.

79. For an excellent philosophical analysis of Mérian's arguments, see Laursen, "Swiss Anti-Skeptics in Berlin."

80. Descartes, *Méditations métaphysiques*, 18–19.

81. Mérian, "Mémoire sur l'apperception de sa propre existence," 421. This is very similar to the argument advanced by Huet in his "Censure de la philosophie de M. Descartes à Mr. de Montausier," BNF, Fonds Français 14702, fol. 6r.

82. Mérian, "Mémoire sur l'apperception de sa propre existence," 424 (quotation), 429.

83. Ibid., 425, 426, 433–34, quotations on 426 and 433–34.

84. Buffier had made a very similar claim in his *Traité des premières véritez*, 28–29.

85. Mérian, "Mémoire sur l'apperception de sa propre existence," 434.

86. Mérian, "Réflexions philosophiques sur la ressemblance," 34.

87. Ibid., 44.

88. Mérian, "Sur le principe des indiscernables," 384.

89. For more on Beausobre, see Laursen, "Temporizing after Bayle."

90. *Arrests de la Cour de Parlement*, 29. See also Wheeler, *Biographical Dictionary of Freethinkers of All Ages and Nations*.

91. Beausobre, *Le pyrrhonisme raisonnable*, 6–7.

92. Ibid., 9, 14, 24, 28–29, 83.

93. Ibid., 57.

94. Charles, "De l'anti-pyrrhonisme au pyrrhonisme raisonnable."

95. For more on Formey's role in the Enlightenment, see Marcu, "Formey and the Enlightenment."

96. For more on Formey's contribution to the *Encyclopédie*, see ibid., 31–38; Marcu, "Un encyclopédiste oublié: Formey"; Moureau, "L'Encyclopédie d'après les correspondants de Formey"; and Donato, "Jean Henri Samuel Formey's Contribution to the Encyclopédie d'Yverdon."

97. Adams, "Formey continuateur de l'*Encyclopédie*."

98. For details, see Marcu, "Formey and the Enlightenment," 49–126.

99. For more on Haller's contributions to physiology, see Steinke, *Irritating Experiments*. For the implications of Haller's theories for La Mettrie, see 194–97.

100. Diderot, *Promenade du sceptique, ou Les allées*, 241–382.

101. Diderot, "Pyrrhonienne."

102. Ibid., 614.

103. "Vraissemblance," 482.

104. Ibid., 483–84.

105. See, e.g., Formey, *La logique des vraisemblances*; and Autrey, *Le pyrrhonien raisonnable*.

106. Crousaz, *Examen du pyrrhonisme ancien et moderne*, 378.

107. Pierre Bayle, "Zénon," in *Dictionnaire historique et critique* (1697), 2:1271–73.

Chapter 7 · *Matter over Mind*

1. For more on Cartesian dualism, see Richardson, "'Scandal' of Cartesian Interactionism"; Jolley, "Descartes and the Action of Body on Mind"; Seager, "Descartes and the Union of Mind and Body"; Almog, *What Am I?*; Baker and Morris, *Descartes' Dualism*; and Rozemond, *Descartes's Dualism*.

2. For more on the legacy of dualism and the debates about mind-body interaction in the early eighteenth century, see Watson, *Downfall of Cartesianism*. For more recent scholarship, see Burson, *Rise and Fall of Theological Enlightenment*, 33–76.

3. Descartes, *Méditations métaphysiques*, 107.

4. Descartes, *La dioptrique*, 50; Descartes to Meysonnier, 29 January 1640, in Descartes, *Œuvres de Descartes*, 3:19.

5. Descartes, *Les passions de l'âme*, 43–44.

6. Ibid., 45–46.

7. Descartes to Elisabeth, 28 June 1643, in *Œuvres de Descartes*, 3:691–92.

8. For more on this debate, see Watson, *Downfall of Cartesianism*.

9. Foucher, *La critique de la Recherche de la vérité*, 45–46.

10. Bayle, "Pyrrhon," remark B, in *Dictionnaire historique et critique* (1697), 2:824.

11. Pierre Bayle, "Zénon," remark F, in ibid., 1270.

12. Huet, *Traité philosophique de la foiblesse de l'esprit humain*, 14.

13. Ibid., 16.

14. Ibid., 15.

15. For overviews of the history of Cartesianism, see Bouillier, *Histoire de la philosophie cartésienne*, 1:538; Lennon and Easton, *Cartesian Empiricism of François Bayle*, 1; Ariew, "Cartesian Empiricism"; and Watson, *Downfall of Cartesianism*, 34. For an alternative interpretation, see Schmaltz, *Radical Cartesianism*. While Watson suggests that the empiricist Cartesians were "orthodox" followers of Descartes, Schmaltz designates them as radical.

16. See Huet, *Censura philosophia cartesianae*, 76–78.

17. Régis, *Réponse au livre qui a pour titre P. Danielis Huetii censura philosophiae cartesianae*, 147.

18. Malebranche, *Entretiens sur la métaphysique et sur la religion*, 116.

19. Ibid., 123.

20. Malebranche, *De la recherche de la vérité*, 1:321, 340.

21. Régis, *Système de philosophie*, 1:357–59.

22. Malebranche, "Réponse du P. Malebranche prestre de l'Oratoire à M. Régis," 284.

23. See, e.g., "Première réplique de M. Régis à la réponse du R. P. Malebranche," *Journal des savants*, 15 February 1694, 83–84; and "Seconde réplique de M. Régis à la réponse du R. P. Malebranche," ibid., 22 February 1694, 93–96.

24. Locke, *Essay Concerning Human Understanding*, 4.3.6, p. 270.

25. For an excellent analysis of the implications of Locke's suggestion, see Yolton, *Thinking Matter*.

26. Ibid., 17.

27. Locke, *Essay Concerning Human Understanding*, 3.6.6, pp. 210–11.

28. Voltaire, *Lettres philosophiques*, 125. For Voltaire's own English translation, see *Letters Concerning the English Nation*, 98.

29. Voltaire, *Lettres philosophiques*, 127–29.

30. For the implications of the thinking-matter hypothesis for intra-Catholic debates, see Burson, *Rise and Fall of Theological Enlightenment*, 44–45, 75–76; and Burson, "Abdication of Legitimate Heirs."

31. "Lettre du P. Tournemine de la Compagnie de Jésus, à M. de *** sur l'immatérialité de l'âme, & les sources d'incrédulité," art. 99, *Mémoires de Trévoux*, October 1735, 1915–16.

32. Ibid., 1920.

33. David Renaud Boullier, "Réflexions sur quelques principes de la philosophie de Mr. Locke, à l'occasion des lettres philosophiques de Mr. de Voltaire," *Bibliothèque françoise, ou Histoire littéraire de la France* 20, pt. 2 (1735): 200–201, 213 (quotation).

34. David Renaud Boullier, "Lettre à Mr. *** sur l'esprit philosophique de notre siècle," in *Pièces philosophiques et littéraires*, 11.

35. Ibid., 13.

36. Berkeley, *Treatise Concerning the Principles of Human Knowledge*, 49–50.

37. Ibid., 51.

38. Ibid., 58–59, 60 (quotation).

39. Ibid., preface [1–2]. For an examination of Berkeley's understanding of skepticism, see Popkin, "Berkeley and Pyrrhonism."

40. Berkeley, *Treatise Concerning the Principles of Human Knowledge*, 131.

41. Ibid., 133, 137.

42. Ibid., 133–34.

43. Ibid., 134–36.

44. Ibid., 203–4.

45. For the relationship between the Berkeley's and Malebranche's ideas, as well as Berkeley's understanding of Pyrrhonism, see Luce, *Berkeley and Malebranche*; Popkin, "Berkeley and Pyrrhonism"; Brykman, "Berkeley"; Pucelle, "Berkeley a-t-il été influencé par Malebranche?"; and McCracken, *Malebranche and British Philosophy*. For an excellent overview of various interpretations of Berkeley's thought, see Stephen H. Daniel, "How Berkeley's Works Are Interpreted."

46. Berkeley actually alludes to Malebranche in *Treatise Concerning the Principles of Human Knowledge*, 94–95.

47. Berkeley, *Three Dialogues between Hylas and Philonous*, 106–7.

48. Ibid., 166.

49. For a similar interpretation, see Popkin, "Berkeley and Pyrrhonism," 234.

50. For more on contemporary reactions to Berkeley, see Bracken, *Early Reception of Berkeley's Immaterialism*; and Menichelli, "Was Berkeley a Spinozist?" For a primary-source collection of various contemporaneous reviews, see Berman, *George Berkeley*.

51. "Three Dialogues between Hylas and Philonous," art. 14, *Journal littéraire*, May–June 1713, 156–57.

52. Ibid.

53. The original edition of this work was published as a preface to the 1713 edition of Fénelon's *Demonstration de l'existence de Dieu*. Bracken was the first to point out this new section dealing with Berkeley and immaterialism in the 1718 edition of the text in *Early Reception of Berkeley's Immaterialism*, 26.

54. Tournemine, *Réflexions sur l'athéisme*, 554. Tournemine's essay follows Fénelon's *Demonstration de l'existence de Dieu et de ses attributs* in the 1718 of Fénelon's *Œuvres philosophiques*.

55. Tournemine, *Réflexions sur l'athéisme*, 554–55.

56. Ibid., 555–57.

57. Baxter, *Enquiry into the Nature of the Human Soul*, 300–301.

58. Ibid., 311–12.

59. Ibid., 304–5.

60. Ibid., 306, n. f.

61. Ibid., 322–23.

62. Leibniz, "Sisteme nouveau de la nature et de la communication des substances," 302.

63. Ibid., 302–3.

64. Leibniz to Henri Basnage de Beauval, in "Extraits de diverses lettres," art. 14, *Histoire des ouvrages des savans*, February 1696, 274–75.

65. Leibniz, "Eclaircissement du nouveau sisteme de la communication des substances," 2 April 1696, 167–68.

66. Leibniz, "Eclaircissement du nouveau sisteme de la communication des substances," 9 April 1696, 170.

67. Crousaz, *Examen de l'Essay de Monsieur Pope sur l'homme*, 15–16.

68. Ibid., 16–17, 33–34, 23.

69. Ibid., 77–79, 82.

70. See, e.g., Crousaz to Formey, n.d., BCUL, Fonds Crousaz, 4:415–16; Crousaz to Guisi, n.d., ibid., 13, item L, p. 17; and Crousaz to Haller, n.d., ibid., 13, item A, p. 54.

71. Crousaz to Haller, n.d., ibid., 13, item A, p. 54.

72. In his *Essais de théodicée sur la bonté de Dieu*, Leibniz attempted to reconcile the existence of physical and moral evil with the simultaneous existence of an omnipotent and benevolent God. He concluded that God had indeed created the best of all possible worlds. For more on this question, see Gale, "On What God Chose"; Brown, "Leibniz's Theodicy and the Confluence of Worldly Goods"; and Rateau, *La question du mal chez Leibniz.*

73. Voltaire's character Martin in *Candide* (1759) can be perceived as the polar opposite of the Leibnizian Pangloss. The novel appears to ridicule what Voltaire sees as the logical conclusions of Leibniz's theodicy. See Barber, *Leibniz in France from Arnauld to Voltaire*; Saisselin, "Pangloss, Martin, and the Disappearing Eighteenth Century"; Starobinski, "Sur le style philosophique de Candide"; and Grieder, "Orthodox and Paradox."

74. Cuentz, *Essai d'un système nouveau*, 1:31.

75. Ibid., v–vi, viii.

76. Ibid., lxvii–lxviii, 33–38.

77. Ibid., 19, 25.

78. Ibid., 2:137–39, 142–43.

79. For more on Cuentz, see Yolton, *Locke and French Materialism*, 76–84; Thomson, *Bodies of Thought*, 168–71; and Thomson, "Un marginal de la république des sciences."

80. For more on La Mettrie and the context of his theories, see Thomson, *Materialism and Society in the Mid-Eighteenth Century*, 5–32.

81. La Mettrie, *L'homme machine*, 10.

82. La Mettrie, *Traité de l'âme*, 127.

83. For more on vitalism, see Rey, *Naissance et développement du vitalisme en France*; Thomson, "'Mechanistic Materialism' vs 'Vitalistic Materialism'?"; Williams, *Cultural History of Medical Vitalism in Enlightenment Montpellier*; Reill, *Vitalizing Nature in the Enlightenment*; Vidal, *Sciences of the Soul*; and Thomson, *Bodies of Thought*, 175–215. For more on materialism in the eighteenth century, see Thomson, *Materialism and Society in the Mid-Eighteenth Century*, 5–32; Riskin, *Science in the Age of Sensibility*; Gaukroger, *Collapse of Mechanism and the Rise of Sensibility*, 355–420; and Wolfe and Esveld, "Material Soul."

84. La Mettrie, *L'homme machine*, 16–20.

85. Ibid., 54.

86. La Mettrie, *Traité de l'âme*, 106–23, 169–81.

87. For more on materialist physiology in the eighteenth century, see Thomson, *Materialism and Society in the Mid-Eighteenth Century*, 33–77; and Steinke, *Irritating Experiments*, 49–84, 127–64.

88. La Mettrie, *Traité de l'âme*, 127.

89. Ibid., 123.

90. La Mettrie, *L'homme machine*, 54–55.

91. Ibid., 13.

92. La Mettrie, *Traité de l'âme*, 127.

93. La Mettrie, *L'homme machine*, 13–14.

94. Ibid., 14; La Mettrie, *Traité de l'âme*, 87.

95. La Mettrie, *L'homme machine*, 52–53.

96. Mornet, *Les origines intellectuelles de la Révolution française*, 60–61; Dupront, "Livre et culture dans la société française du XVIIIᵉ siècle," esp. 883; Furet, "La 'librairie' du royaume de France au 18e siècle"; Ehrard and Roger, "Deux périodiques français du 18ᵉ siècle."

97. Keith Baker similarly argues that the challenge of skepticism led to an increased focus on social questions. Baker, "Enlightenment and the Institution of Society," 114–20.

98. Formey offered an exposition of Christian Wolff's philosophy in a fictional work titled *La belle Wolffienne* (1741–53), and he advocated the use of fictions in philosophy. Formey, "Réflexions sur l'usage de la fiction dans la métaphysique," Académie des sciences, Fonds 43J, Pierre Louis Moreau de Maupertuis, item 25, fol. 1r.

99. Huet, *Traité philosophique de la foiblesse de l'esprit humain*, 3.

100. Voltaire, *Lettres philosophiques*, 133.

101. Ibid., 130–31.

102. Knight, *Geometric Spirit*, 1–2.

103. For more on Condillac's significance, see Puchesse, *Condillac*; and Hine, *Critical Study of Condillac's "Traité des systèmes,"* 1–21. For an analysis of his epistemology, see O'Neal, *Authority of Experience*, 13–60; and Charrak, *Empirisme et métaphysique*.

104. Condillac, *Essai sur l'origine des connoissances humaines*, 1:iii–vi.

105. Ibid., vi–xvi.

106. Ibid., 4–5, 7, 10.

107. Ibid., 3–4.

108. Ibid., 14–15, 17 (quotation).

109. Ibid., 13, 15, 16, 24–46, quotations on 13 and 15.

110. Ibid., xvii–xviii, 210–11. For more on Condillac's theories on language, see Sgard, *Condillac et les problèmes du langage*; Rousseau, *Connaissance et langage chez Condillac*; Aliénor Bertrand, *Condillac, l'origine du langage*; and Charrak, *Empirisme et métaphysique*, 71–93.

111. Condillac, *Essai sur l'origine des connoissances humaines*, 1:173, 177.

112. Ibid., 180.

113. Ibid., 215, 182 (quotation).

114. Ibid., 221–22, 226–27.

115. Ibid., 227–28.

116. Ibid., 229.

117. Ibid., 110.

118. Ibid., 2:256–58.

119. Ibid., 260.

120. Yvon and Diderot, "Ame," 341. For more on the article, see Crampe-Casnabet, "Les articles 'Âme' dans l'*Encyclopédie*." For more on the abbé Yvon, see Burson, "Vitalistic Materialism and Universal Histories of Philosophy"; and Burson, *The Culture of Enlightening and the Entangled Life of Abbé Claude Yvon*.

121. Lubières, "Idée," 489, 490.

122. Formey, *Pensées raisonnables*, 204.

123. Ibid., 206–7.

124. For more on the role of testimony, see Shapiro, *Probability and Certainty in Seventeenth-Century England*, 3–14, 267–72.

125. Mérian, "Sur le principe des indiscernables," 385–86.

126. For more on the waning of "rationalistic accounts of reason," see Hatfield, "Epistemology."

127. Diderot, "Métaphysique."

128. Alembert, "Discours préliminaire," ii.

129. Descartes to Elisabeth, 28 June 1643, 692.

Chapter 8 · A Matter of Debate

1. For the most explicit articulation of this claim, see Gaukroger, *Collapse of Mechanism and the Rise of Sensibility*, 3–5, 329, 336, 387–89.

2. Shank, *Newton Wars*, 35.

3. Alembert, "Discours préliminaire," xxvi–xxvii.

4. Ibid., xxxi.

5. For more on "epistemological modesty," see Baker, *Condorcet*, 87. For more on "limitations of science," see ibid., 87–95.

6. For this interpretation of Bayle, see McKenna, "L'éclaircissement sur les pyrrhoniens"; and Mori, *Bayle: Philosophe*, 13–53.

7. Israel, *Radical Enlightenment*, 338. For this interpretation, see ibid., 337–41; Israel, *Enlightenment Contested*, 267–68, 278, 669–71; and Israel, "Bayle's Double Image during the Enlightenment." For a response to Israel's rationalist interpretation, see Laursen, "Skepticism against Reason in Pierre Bayle's Theory of Toleration."

8. Israel, *Enlightenment Contested*, 278.

9. For Israel's brief discussion of Bayle's article on Zeno, see Israel, *Radical Enlightenment*, 339.

10. Todd Ryan's work on Cartesian physics mentions these paradoxes but does not go into significant detail concerning their significance. For more, see Ryan, *Pierre Bayle's Cartesian Metaphysics*, 21–22.

11. Bayle, "Pyrrhon," remark B, in *Dictionnaire historique et critique* (1697), 2:824.

12. For more on Aristotelian matter theory, see Nadler, "Doctrines of Explanation"; and Hattab, *Descartes on Forms and Mechanisms*, 2–3, 33–35.

13. For more on the relationship between Cartesianism and late Scholasticism, see Ariew, *Descartes and the Last Scholastics*; and Secada, *Cartesian Metaphysics*.

14. Descartes, *Les principes de la philosophie*, 80–81, 69–70, 75–78.

15. For an excellent study on the rediscovery of *De rerum natura*, see Ada Palmer, *Reading Lucretius in the Renaissance*.

16. For more on corpuscularianism, atomism, and Epicureanism in the seventeenth and eighteenth centuries, see Garber et al., "New Doctrines of Body and Its Powers, Place, and Space"; Lüthy, Murdoch, and Newman, *Late Medieval and Early Modern Corpuscular Matter Theories*; Gaukroger, *Descartes' System of Natural Philosophy*, 96; Gaukroger, *Emergence of a Scientific Culture*, 253–322; Wilson, *Epicureanism at the Origins of Modernity*; and Kors, *Epicureans and Atheists in France*.

17. Pierre Bayle, "Zénon," remark G, in *Dictionnaire historique et critique* (1730), 4:540.

18. Ibid.

19. Ryan, *Pierre Bayle's Cartesian Metaphysics*, 21–22.

20. Pierre Bayle, "Physiologia nove experimentalis in qua notions Aristotelis, Epicuri & Cartesii supplentur," in *Nouvelles de la République des Lettres*, December 1685, 1361. It was also printed in *Œuvres diverses de Pierre Bayle*, 1:436–37.

21. Delvolvé, *Religion, critique, et philosophie positive chez Pierre Bayle*, 349–54.

22. Pierre Bayle, "Leucippe," remark D, in *Dictionnaire historique et critique* (1730), 3:100.

23. For a polyphonic interpretation of Bayle, see Lennon, *Reading Bayle*, 28–34.

24. Bayle, "Zénon," remark G, 540.

25. Ibid., 542.

26. Ibid. Bayle quoted Arnauld and Nicole's *La logique*, pt. 4, chap. 1.

27. Bayle, "Zénon," remark H, 543.

28. Ibid., 543–44.

29. For a helpful summary of the Cartesian argument, see Argens, *La philosophie du bon-sens*, 288.

30. Bayle, "Zénon," remark I, 544.

31. Ibid.

32. Bayle, "Leucippe," remark G, 102.

33. Bayle, "Zénon," remark I, 544. For more of Bayle's view of Hartsoecker, see "Leucippe," remark G, 102.

34. Bayle, "Zénon," remark I, 545.

35. Ibid., 544.

36. Ibid., 545.

37. Bayle, "Leucippe," remark G, 102.

38. Bayle, "Zénon," remark K, 546.

39. Ibid., remark I, 545.

40. "Problème proposé aux métaphysiciens, géomètres sur l'essence de la matière," *Mercure de France*, September 1733, 1939–48.

41. Ibid., 1942–43. For Fontenelle's argument, see Fontenelle, *Eléments de la géométrie de l'infini*, 29.

42. "Problème proposé aux métaphysiciens, géomètres sur l'essence de la matière," 1943–45.

43. Saint-Aubin's two-part reply appears in *Mercure de France*, November 1733, 2393–2408, and December 1733, 2843–51. A response to his arguments is found in ibid., January 1734, 15–20 and 51–58. The original question, Saint-Aubin's letters, and some of the replies are reprinted in Saint-Aubin, *Traité de l'opinion*, 6:359–410.

44. Saint-Aubin, *Traité de l'opinion*, 6:367–69, 372 (quotation), 373–74.

45. Ibid., 374–77.

46. Ibid., 379–83, 397–98 (quotation).

47. For the classification of Cartaud de la Vilate as a Pyrrhonian, see Tonelli, "Pierre-Jacques Changeux and Scepticism in the French Enlightenment," 114. For the only detailed study of Cartaud, see Krauss, *Cartaud de la Villate*. See also Mortier, review of *Cartaud de la Villate*.

48. Cartaud de la Vilate, *Pensées critiques sur les mathématiques*, 1–2, 18–19, 33–34, 4–6, quotations on 1–2 and 4.

49. Ibid., 13, 12–14, 15, 119–20.

50. Ibid., 123, 127–40, 147–53, 161, quotations on 123 and 161.

51. Ibid., 166–68, 204–5, 296–300, 301–49, 246–66, 273–74, quotation on 168.

52. Ibid., 175, 370, 181–88, 216–22.

53. For more on these debates, see Shank, *Newton Wars*, 194–209.

54. Cartaud de la Vilate, *Pensées critiques sur les mathématiques*, 231–32 (quotation), 373.

55. Argens, *La philosophie du bon-sens*, 200–203.

56. Ibid., 262–75, 278–80, 285–87, 287–89, quotation on 285.

57. Ibid., 296, 306–7, 290, 308, quotations on 296 and 306–7.

58. Ibid., 289.

59. Ibid., 309–11.

60. Voltaire, *Lettres philosophiques*, 132.

61. Voltaire, *La métaphysique de Neuton*, 59.

62. For more on Voltaire and Newton, see Le Ru, *Voltaire newtonien*; and Shank, *Newton Wars*, 295–379.

63. Voltaire, *Éléments de la philosophie de Neuton*, 101–2.

64. Ibid., 166–70.

65. Voltaire, *La métaphysique de Neuton*, 13.

66. For Bayle's extensive analysis of Spinoza's view of substance and God, see Bayle, "Spinoza," in *Dictionnaire historique et critique* (1730), 4:253–71. For classic interpretations of Spinoza's metaphysics, see Curley, *Spinoza's Metaphysics*; and Curley, *Behind the Geometrical Method*. For recent work on the relationship between Spinoza's thought and Cartesian metaphysics, see Nadler, "Whatever Is, Is in God"; and Douglas, *Spinoza and Dutch Cartesianism*, 36–89.

67. Alembert, "Discours préliminaire," v–vi.

68. Alembert, "Corps," 261.

69. Alembert, "Matière," 189, 190.

70. Montbeillard, "Étendue," 45.

71. Alembert, "Divisibilité," 1074.

72. Montbeillard, "Étendue,", 45.

73. For the role of skepticism in the *Encyclopédie*, see Le Ru, "Le scepticisme dans l'Encyclopédie de Diderot et de d'Alembert."

74. Alembert, "Corps," 263.

Chapter 9 · *War of the Worlds*

1. For detailed accounts of these theories, see Dijksterhuis, *Mechanization of the World Picture*; Koyré, *Astronomical Revolution*; and Gaukroger, *Emergence of a Scientific Culture*, 120–26, 169–95.

2. Voltaire, *Lettres philosophiques*, 139–41.

3. Shank, *Newton Wars*, 17.

4. For more on Cartesian matter theory, see Gaukroger, *Descartes' System of Natural Philosophy*, 93–103, 130–34.

5. Descartes, *Le monde*, 49–54.

6. Gaukroger, *Descartes' System of Natural Philosophy*, 11–13.

7. Descartes, *Les principes de la philosophie*, 135.

8. Ibid., 134–38 (quotation on 138).

9. Ibid., 143–44.

10. For an excellent explanation of the Cartesian theory of *pesanteur*, see Gaukroger, *Descartes' System of Natural Philosophy*, 165–66.

11. For more on the Cartesian vortex theory, see Aiton, *Vortex Theory of Planetary Motion*, 30–85, 152–89; Clarke, *Occult Powers and Hypotheses*, 158–59, 186–87; Garber, *Descartes' Metaphysical Physics*, 227–29; and Gaukroger, *Descartes' System of Natural Philosophy*, 135–60.

12. Descartes, *Discours de la méthode*, 65.

13. Descartes, *Les principes de la philosophie*, 158.

14. For more on Descartes's methodology, see Garber, "Descartes and Experiment in the Discourse and Essays"; Larmore, "Descartes' Empirical Epistemology"; MacKenzie, "Reconfiguration of Sensory Experience"; and Sakellariadis, "Descartes's Use of Empirical Data to Test Hypotheses."

15. Descartes, *Le monde*, 3.

16. Ibid., 10–18, 32–33.

17. For an analysis of Descartes's views on the reliability of the senses and the role of hypotheses, see Clarke, "Descartes' Philosophy of Science and the Scientific Revolution."

18. For the full argument, see Gaukroger, *Descartes' System of Natural Philosophy*, 11.

19. Ibid., 95.

20. Newton, *Mathematical Principles of Natural Philosophy*, 1:19.

21. Ibid., 4–6 (quotation on 4).

22. Aiton, *Vortex Theory of Planetary Motion*, 90–99.

23. Shank, *Newton Wars*, 51–52. See also Gabbey, "Newton's Mathematical Principles of Natural Philosophy."

24. I. Bernard Cohen argues that book 1 is primarily concerned with "a mathematical construct and not with physical reality." See Cohen, *Newtonian Revolution*, 81.

25. For more the reception of Newton's theory, see Cohen, "Review of the First Edition of Newton's Principia"; Maglo, "Reception of Newton's Gravitational Theory"; Shank, *Newton Wars*, 49–65; and Belkind, "Newton's Scientific Method and the Universal Law of Gravitation."

26. "Philosophiae naturalis principia mathematica," *Journal des savants*, 2 August 1688, 153–54.

27. For analyses of the review in the *Journal des savants*, see Cohen, "Review of the First Edition of Newton's Principia," 343–48; and Shank, *Newton Wars*, 49–51.

28. For detailed analyses of Huygens's view of Newton's theory, see Maglo, "Reception of Newton's Gravitational Theory," 144–49; and Schliesser and Smith, "Huygens's 1688 Report to the Directors of the Dutch East India Company."

29. Huygens, *Discours de la cause de la pesanteur*, 125, 126.

30. Ibid., 131–33. For more on the experiment, see Aiton, *Vortex Theory of Planetary Motion*, 76–85; Clarke, *Occult Powers and Hypotheses*, 159; and Shank, *Newton Wars*, 53–55.

31. Huygens, *Discours de la cause de la pesanteur*, 159.

32. Christian Huygens to Gottfried Wilhelm Leibniz, 18 November 1690, in Huygens, *Œuvres complètes*, 9:538.

33. For this interpretation, see Maglo, "Reception of Newton's Gravitational Theory," 147. For more on the contrast between Descartes's and Newton's methodologies, see Gaukroger, *Collapse of Mechanism and the Rise of Sensibility*, 55–94.

34. Gaukroger contrasts the "horizontal" method of the Cartesians with "vertical" explanations. See also Gaukroger, *Collapse of Mechanism and the Rise of Sensibility*, 83, 153–54; and Gaukroger, "Empiricism as a Development of Experimental Natural Philosophy."

35. Gaukroger, "Empiricism as a Development of Experimental Natural Philosophy," 20.

36. Ibid., 28–33; Gaukroger, *Collapse of Mechanism and the Rise of Sensibility*, 150–86.

37. Locke, *Essay Concerning Human Understanding*, 3.6.6, pp. 210–11.

38. Cohen, "Guide to Newton's Principia," 274–80.

39. Newton, *Mathematical Principles of Natural Philosophy*, 2:387 (quotation), 184–99.

40. Ibid., 392.

41. Ibid.

42. Ibid., 390–91.

43. For more on Newton and empiricism, see the various articles in Biener and Schliesser, *Newton and Empiricism*.

44. For an analysis of Côtes's preface, see Cohen, *Introduction to Newton's "Principia,"* 227–40; and Shank, *Newton Wars*, 70–72. For more on Côtes, see Gowing, *Roger Côtes*; and Biener and Smeenk, "Cotes' Queries."

45. Côtes, "Preface of Roger Côtes," [i–iii].

46. Ibid., [iii], [v–viii], [xii], quotations on [iii], [v–vii], and [xii].

47. Ibid., [xiv–xxii], quotations on [xiv] and [xxii].

48. For more on the emergence of the Enlightenment narrative and the "making of the *philosophe*," see Shank, *Newton Wars*, 295–402; and Gaukroger, *Collapse of Mechanism and the Rise of Sensibility*, 257–89.

49. For a rich analysis of Fontenelle's *éloge*, see Shank, *Newton Wars*, 165–79. For more on Fontenelle's role at the Académie royale des sciences, see Marsak, "Bernard de Fontenelle"; Paul, *Science and Immortality*, 28–35; Mazauric, *Fontenelle et l'invention de l'histoire des sciences*; and Adkins, *Idea of the Sciences in the French Enlightenment*, 29–54.

50. Fontenelle, "Eloge de Neuton," 154, 155, 158.

51. Ibid., 157, 159, 163–64.

52. Fontenelle, *Théorie des tourbillons cartésiens*, 191–92.

53. Fontenelle, "Eloge de Neuton," 160.

54. Marsak, "Bernard de Fontenelle," 12, 23–33.

55. For more on Fontenelle and skepticism, see Peterschmitt, "'Wise Pyrrhonism' of the Académie Royale des Sciences of Paris."

56. Fontenelle, *De la connoissance de l'esprit humain*, 359 (quotation), 360–61.

57. Fontenelle, *Fragments d'un Traité de la raison humaine*, 327, 345.

58. Marsak, "Bernard de Fontenelle," 32. For Fontenelle's intellectual biography, see Niderst, *Fontenelle*.

59. Aiton, *Vortex Theory of Planetary Motion*, 209–54; Shank, *Newton Wars*, 265–86.

60. Saint-Aubin, *Traité de l'opinion*, 6:291–359.

61. Ibid., 305–6.

62. Ibid., 314–18, 321–24, 357–58, quotation on 321–22 and 358.

63. For more on Maupertuis, see Terrall, *Man Who Flattened the Earth*. The discussion of the *Discours* appears on 78–83. For another analysis of the work, see Shank, *Newton Wars*, 286–93.

64. Maupertuis, *Discours sur les différentes figures des astres*, 11.

65. Ibid., 11–13.

66. Ibid., 15–16.

67. Ibid., 16–17. It might be fruitful to compare this argument with the descriptions of the mind-body problem in several *Encyclopédie* articles cited in chapter 7.

68. Ibid., 21.

69. Ibid., 22, 32–33, 28–29, 32–33.

70. Ibid., 34, 36, 39, 45, quotations on 34, 36, and 45.

71. Shank, *Newton Wars*, 288.

72. Condorcet, *Vie de Voltaire*, 30.

73. Shank, *Newton Wars*, 295.

74. Voltaire, *Lettres philosophiques*, 151, 143, 151.

75. Ibid., 160, 161, 175–77, 179.

76. For more on the collaboration between Voltaire and Châtelet, see Wade, *Voltaire and Madame du Châtelet*. For Châtelet's biography, see Zinsser, *La dame d'esprit*. For more on Châtelet's physics, see Zinsser, "Translating Newton's 'Principia'"; Hutton, "Emilie Du Châtelet's *Institutions de physique*"; Hagengruber, "Emilie Du Châtelet between Leibniz and Newton"; and Hutton, "Between Newton and Leibniz."

77. For more on the publication history of this text, see Shank, *Newton Wars*, 369–75.

78. Voltaire, *Éléments de la philosophie de Neuton*, 213, 216.

79. For more on Voltaire's skepticism, see Brandão, "Voltaire et le scepticisme"; and Pujol, "Forms and Aims of Voltairean Scepticism."

80. Voltaire, *La métaphysique de Neuton*, 58 (quotation), 67.

81. Shank, *Newton Wars*, 458.

82. Gravesande, *Élémens de physique*, 1:iii, iv, vii.

83. Ibid., viii–x. For more on 's Gravesande's arguments, see Baker, "Enlightenment and the Institution of Society," 115–16; and Baker, *Condorcet*, 133–35.

84. Condillac, *Traité des systèmes*, 378.

85. Alembert, "Discours préliminaire," xxvi.

86. Alembert, "Attraction," 847.

87. Alembert, "Cartésianisme," 723.

88. Jourdain, *Histoire de l'Université de Paris*, 173.

89. Alembert, "Discours préliminaire," xx.

90. For more on the association between Locke and Newton, see Feingold, "Partnership in Glory"; Gaukroger, *Collapse of Mechanism and the Rise of Sensibility*, 184–86, 224–25, 263–69; and Shank, *Newton Wars*, 304, 313–15.

91. Alembert, "Discours préliminaire," xxxi.

92. Piaia, "'Critical' History of Philosophy and the Early Enlightenment," 189.

93. Voltaire, *Lettres philosophiques*, 136, 124.

94. Alembert, "Discours préliminaire," xviii.

95. Castel, *Le vrai système de physique générale de Isaac Newton*, 10.

96. Ibid., 12–13.

97. For more on the emergence of the history of philosophy as a genre, see Catana, "Concept 'System of Philosophy'"; Catana, *Historiographical Concept "System of Philosophy"*; Piaia, "'Critical' History of Philosophy and the Early Enlightenment"; and Longo, "'Critical' History of Philosophy and the Early Enlightenment."

98. Condillac, *Traité des systèmes*, 8–9, 7.

99. Ibid., 12.

100. Ibid., 15–17, 25, 21, 28–30, quotations on 15, 25, and 21.

101. Ibid., 40–42.

102. For this analysis, see Hine, *Critical Study of Condillac's "Traité des systèmes*," 20–21.

103. Condillac, *Traité des systèmes*, 354–55.

104. Ibid., 106–8, 165–66, 190, 234–42, 350, quotations on 165–66 and 190.

105. Ibid., 356–63, quotation on 358.

106. Ibid., 364–65.

107. Ibid., 365–66, 370–72, 367–68, 397–98, quotation on 372.

108. See Hine, *Critical Study of Condillac's "Traité des systèmes*," 124.

109. Condillac, *Traité des systèmes*, 387–89, 405–6, 419–23.

110. Alembert, "Discours préliminaire," xxxi.

111. Ibid.

112. For more on Leibnizianism in the Enlightenment, see Shank, *Newton Wars*, 403–79; and Gaukroger, *Collapse of Mechanism and the Rise of Sensibility*, 104–36, 283–89.

113. "Philosophe," 509.

Chapter 10 · *Historical Pyrrhonism and Its Discontents*

1. For a general discussion of early modern historiography, see Momigliano, *Essays in Ancient and Modern Historiography*; Momigliano, *Classical Foundations of Modern Historiography*; Binoche, "Le pyrrhonisme historique ou le fait mis à nu"; Burke, "Two Crises of Historical Consciousness"; Grafton, *What Was History?*; Pocock, "Historiography and Enlightenment"; and Bourgault and Sparling, *Companion to Enlightenment Historiography*. An excellent analysis of the relationship between early modern skepticism and historiography can also be found in Borghero, *La certezza e la storia*; Völkel, *"Pyrrhonismus historicus" und "fides historica"*; and Perinetti, "Philosophical Reflections on History."

2. Descartes, *Discours de la méthode*, 8.

3. Lennon, "Huet, Malebranche and the Birth of Skepticism."

4. For an excellent overview of the recent debates about the history of religion, see Levitin, "From Sacred History to the History of Religion." For more on the relationship between history and theology, see Joseph M. Levine, *Autonomy of History*.

5. Hardouin, *Chronologiae ex nummis antiquis restitutae prolusio de nummis Herodiadum*; Hardouin, *Ad censuram veterum scriptorum prolegomena*. For more on Hardouin, see Schwarzbach, "Antidocumentalist Apologetics"; Grafton, "Jean Hardouin"; and Grell, "Le vertige du pyrrhonisme."

6. La Mothe Le Vayer, *Du peu de certitude qu'il y a en histoire*; Bayle, *Critique générale de l'histoire du calvinisme de Mr. Maimbourg*; Pierre Bayle, "Zuerius," remark P, in *Dictionnaire historique et critique* (1720), 4:2933–38.

7. For more on the Académie royale des inscriptions et belles-lettres, see Barret-Kriegel, *Les historiens et la monarchie*, 169–297.

8. For more on the importance of the *Querelle*, see Edelstein, *Enlightenment*, 24–51; and Norman, *Shock of the Ancient*.

9. Reill, *German Enlightenment and the Rise of Historicism*.

10. Eisenhart's *De fide historica commentarius* was first published in 1679 and republished in 1702. See the note to the reader therein. For the most notable reply to Eisenhart, see Christian Thomasius, *Dissertationem de fide juridica*.

11. Bayle, "Projet d'un dictionnaire critique," sec. 4.

12. Popkin, *History of Scepticism: From Savonarola to Bayle*, 270; Bayle, "Zuerius," remark P, 2933–38.

13. Bayle, "Zuerius," remark P, 2938.

14. For an excellent account of Bayle's approach to historiography, see Robin, "Religious Controversy and Historical Methodology."

15. Bayle, *Critique générale de l'histoire du calvinisme de Mr. Maimbourg*, 13 (quotation), 14.

16. Ibid., 16.

17. La Mothe Le Vayer, *Du peu de certitude qu'il y a en histoire*, 6.

18. Ibid., 80–81.

19. See, e.g., Nadel, "Philosophy of History before Historicism"; Wilcox, *Development of Florentine Humanist Historiography in the Fifteenth Century*, 21–23; Fryde, *Humanism and Renaissance Historiography*, 4–8; and Grafton, *Defenders of the Text*, 25–27.

20. See Burke, "Two Crises of Historical Consciousness"; and Hazard, *La crise de la conscience européenne*, 26–35.

21. Lévesque de Pouilly, "Dissertation sur l'incertitude des quatre premières siècles de Rome," 14–15.

22. Arpe, *Pyrrho sive de dubia et incerta historiae et historicorum veterum fide argumentum*, 9; Saxius, "De incerto historiae romanorum antiquissimae, sectio II," 421. For more on the historiography of ancient Rome, see Erasmus, *Origins of Rome in Historiography*.

23. Beaufort, *Sur l'incertitude des cinq premiers siècles de l'histoire romaine*, 24.

24. Ibid., 2–8; Lévesque de Pouilly, "Dissertation sur l'incertitude des quatre premières siècles de Rome," 15–17.

25. Bierling, *Commentatio de pyrrhonismo historico*, 137–40.

26. Anselme, "Des monuments qui ont suppléé au deffaut de l'écriture," 390.

27. Mabillon, *Brèves réflexions sur quelques règles de l'histoire*, 122–26. This text existed only in manuscript form and can be found in the Bibliothèque Nationale de France, Fonds Français 17696, fol. 294r.

28. Arpe, *Pyrrho sive de dubia et incerta historiae et historicorum veterum fide argumentum*, 4–7.

29. Lévesque de Pouilly, "Dissertation sur l'incertitude des quatre premières siècles de Rome," 25–26.

30. Argens, *La philosophie du bon-sens*, 79–80.

31. Ibid., 85–92, 82, quotations on 85–86, 87–88, and 82.

32. Ibid., 39, 43–50, quotations on 39 and 45.

33. La Mothe Le Vayer, *Du peu de certitude qu'il y a en histoire*, 36–37.

34. "Remarques sur le Dictionnaire critique," BNF, Fonds Français 12433, fol. 389v.

35. Newton, *Chronology of Ancient Kingdoms Amended*, 43–48. For more on Newton's chronological research, see Buchwald and Feingold, *Newton and the Origin of Civilization*.

36. Fréret, *Abrégé de la chronologie de M. le chevalier Isaac Newton*.

37. Souciet, *Recueil des dissertations*.

38. Fréret, *Défense de la chronologie fondée sur les monumens de l'histoire ancienne*.

39. Voltaire, "Lettre XVII: Sur l'infini et sur la chronologie," in *Lettres philosophiques*, 209–10.

40. Voltaire, "Adam," in *Dictionnaire philosophique*, 2:500–501.

41. Sallier, "Discours sur les premiers monuments historiques des Romains," 35–46, quotation on 35.

42. Sallier, "Troisième discours sur la certitude de l'histoire des quatre premiers siècles de Rome," 117.

43. Saxius, "De incerto historiae romanorum antiquissimae, sectio I," 70–77.

44. Saxius, "De incerto historiae romanorum antiquissimae, sectio II," 415 (quotation), 433.

45. Ernesti, *De fide historica recte aestimanda*, 78–79.

46. Anselme, "Des monuments qui ont suppléé au deffaut de l'écriture," 396; Anselme, "Seconde dissertation sur les monuments qui ont servi de mémoires aux premiers historiens," 2 (quotation).

47. See, e.g., Anselme, "Des monuments qui ont suppléé au deffaut de l'écriture"; and Maffei, *Ars critica lapidaria*. For contemporary scholarship, see Momigliano, "Ancient History and the Antiquarian," 13–20; Haskell, *History and Its Images*; and Burke, "Two Crises of Historical Consciousness," 9.

48. Bierling, *Commentatio de pyrrhonismo historico*, 153–59.

49. Ibid., 136–37, 228–49, 251.

50. Ibid., 153–56.

51. Sallier, "Discours sur les premiers monuments historiques des Romains," 46.

52. Sallier, "Second discours sur la certitude de l'histoire des quatre premiers siècles de Rome," 54–55.

53. Eisenhart, "Lectori benevolo," in *De fide historica commentarius*, [2].

54. Arpe, *Pyrrho sive de dubia et incerta historiae et historicorum veterum fide argumentum*, 11–13.

55. Ibid., 7.
56. La Mothe Le Vayer, *Du peu de certitude qu'il y a en histoire*, 30–34.
57. Bayle, *Critique générale de l'histoire du calvinisme de Mr. Maimbourg*, 19.
58. Ibid., 27 (quotations), 34.
59. Argens, *La philosophie du bon-sens*, 63, 60–61 (quotations).
60. Bayle, *Dictionnaire historique et critique* (1702), 1:781–82.
61. Beaufort, *Sur l'incertitude des cinq premiers siècles de l'histoire romaine*, 89–100.
62. Ibid., 108.
63. Ibid., 100–101.
64. Struve, *Dissertatiuncula de vitiis historicorum*, 16.
65. See, e.g., Bierling, *Commentatio de pyrrhonismo historico*, 175; Struve, *Dissertatiuncula de vitiis historicorum*, 16–18; and Rechenberg and Brückner, *De autoritate historiae*, 13–15.
66. Cicero, *De oratores* 2.62: "Nam quis nescit primam esse historiae legem, ne quid falsi dicere audeat? Deinde ne quid veri non audeat?" The claim was repeated or quoted in several works: Bierling, *Commentatio de pyrrhonismo historico*, 291; Rechenberg and Brückner, *De autoritate historiae*, 6; Simonides, *De bono historico*, [4]; Struve, *Dissertatiuncula de vitiis historicorum*, 4; and Saxius, "De incerto historiae romanorum antiquissimae, sectio I," 56.
67. Mabillon, *Brèves réflexions sur quelques règles de l'histoire*, 111. For more on this analogy, see Ginzburg, "Checking the Evidence."
68. Mabillon, *Brèves réflexions sur quelques règles de l'histoire*, 108.
69. Ibid., 113.
70. Bayle, *Critique générale de l'histoire du calvinisme de Mr. Maimbourg*, 19.
71. Bierling, *Commentatio de pyrrhonismo historico*, 61. The citation of Bayle's article appears on ibid., 55.
72. Ibid., 37–46.
73. Mabillon, *Brèves réflexions sur quelques règles de l'histoire*, 113–14.
74. Argens, *La philosophie du bon-sens*, 72–75.
75. Saint-Réal, *De l'usage de l'histoire*, 4.
76. Fréret, "Réflexions sur l'étude des anciennes histoires," 147–48.
77. Lenglet du Fresnoy, *Méthode pour étudier l'histoire*, 2: preface [2].
78. Mabillon, *Brèves réflexions sur quelques règles de l'histoire*, 114.
79. Ibid., 113.
80. "Friderici Guilielmi Bierlingii Commentatio de Pyrrhonismo-Historico," art. 1, *Bibliothèque germanique* 10 (1725): 26.
81. Formey, *Le triomphe de l'évidence*, 1:47.
82. Sallier, "Troisième discours sur la certitude de l'histoire des quatre premiers siècles de Rome," 129.
83. Fréret, "Réflexions sur l'étude des anciennes histoires," 147 (quotation), 148.
84. Perizonius, *Oratio de fide historiarum*, 14–15.
85. Boullier, *Traité des vrais principes*, 11, 16, 66.
86. Ibid., 91.
87. Lévesque de Pouilly, "Nouveaux essais de critique sur la fidélité de l'histoire," 71–73.
88. Ibid., 71.

89. Boullier, *Traité des vrais principes*, 66.

90. Fréret, "Réflexions sur l'étude des anciennes histoires," 184–85.

91. Bierling, *Commentatio de pyrrhonismo historico*, 68–69.

92. Ibid., 7.

93. Ibid., 30–49.

94. Struve, *De pyrrhonismo historico dissertatio praeliminaris*, 6.

95. Ibid., 7–8.

96. Mabillion, *Brèves réflexions sur quelques règles de l'histoire*, 108, 118 (quotation).

97. Sallier, "Troisième discours sur la certitude de l'histoire des quatre premiers siècles de Rome," 115–16.

98. Ibid., 133–34.

99. Bierling, *Commentatio de pyrrhonismo historico*, 24–25.

100. Perizonius, *Oratio de fide historiarum*, 2–4.

101. Formey, *Le triomphe de l'évidence*, 2:50–51, 48–49.

102. Voltaire, "Histoire," 223–24.

103. Voltaire, *Le pyrrhonisme de l'histoire*, 11. For more on *Le pyrrhonisme de l'histoire*, see Pierse, "Voltaire," 160–61; and Force, "Croire ou ne pas croire." A classic text on Voltaire's approach to history is Brumfitt, *Voltaire, Historian*.

104. Fréret, "Réflexions sur l'étude des anciennes histoires," 148.

105. Alembert, "Discours préliminaire," vi.

106. Fréret, "Réflexions sur l'étude des anciennes histoires," 150–52.

107. Bierling, *Commentatio de pyrrhonismo historico*, 254–57.

108. Simonides, *De bono historico*, [27].

109. Mabillon, *Brèves réflexions sur quelques règles de l'histoire*, 107–8.

110. Lévesque de Pouilly, "Nouveaux essais de critique sur la fidélité de l'histoire," 77.

111. Rapin, *Instructions pour l'histoire*, 118–26.

112. Simonides, *De bono historico*, 9.

113. Mabillon, *Brèves réflexions sur quelques règles de l'histoire*, 104.

114. Bierling, *Commentatio de pyrrhonismo historico*, 73–74.

Conclusion

1. Edelstein, *Enlightenment*, 1–2.

2. See Sauter, "Prussian Monarchy and the Practices of Enlightenment"; and Zurbuchen, "Theorizing Enlightened Absolutism."

3. Himmelfarb, *Roads to Modernity*, 18–22; Carhart, *Science of Culture in Enlightenment Germany*, 287–96.

4. Diderot, *Jacques le fataliste et son maître*, 452.

5. Kors, *D'Holbach's Coterie*, 301–29.

6. Jonathan Israel cites this as one example of cases in which the radical ideas of Baron d'Holbach influenced the radical politics of the revolutionaries. Israel, *Democratic Enlightenment*, 809.

7. Chartier, *Cultural Origins of the French Revolution*, 5.

8. Popkin, *History of Scepticism: From Erasmus to Descartes*, 173.

9. Hazard, *La crise de la conscience européenne*, 4.

10. For the general praise of dictionaries and erudition, see Alembert, "Discours préliminaire," xxxiv.

11. Paganini, "Le scepticisme, une 'maladie' ou un remède?," 196–202; Popkin, "David Hume and the Pyrrhonian Controversy."

12. Diderot, *Entretien entre D'Alembert et Diderot*, 127.

13. Diderot, "Pyrrhonienne."

14. Formey, *La logique des vraisemblances*.

15. Autrey, *Le pyrrhonien raisonnable*, 2–3, 135.

16. Ibid., 33–34.

17. Ibid., 133–34.

18. I have written elsewhere about the changes in the tone of religious apologetics in the eighteenth century. See Matytsin, "Reason and Utility in French Religious Apologetics."

19. Alembert, "Discours préliminaire," vi.

20. Ibid., xxvii–xxviii.

21. Baker, "Enlightenment and the Institution of Society," 114–20.

22. Romily, "Tolérance," 390.

23. For more on the connection between skepticism and toleration in the Enlightenment, see Riley, "Tolerant Skepticism of Voltaire and Diderot," 259–67.

Primary Sources
Manuscript Collections
Académie des Sciences

Formey, Jean Henri Samuel. "Réflexions sur l'usage de la fiction dans la métaphysique." Fonds 43J, Pierre Louis Moreau de Maupertuis, item 25, fol. 1r.

Bibliothèque Cantonale et Universitaire de Lausanne (BCUL)

Fonds Crousaz, IS 2024.

Bibliothèque Nationale de France (BNF)

"Brèves réflexions sur quelques règles de l'histoire." Papiers de Dom Jean Mabillon. Fonds Français 17696, fols. 294r–305v.

"Copie d'une lettre de Renaudot à François Janiçon, 2 July, 1697." Papiers du P. Léonard. Nouvelles acquisitions françaises 7483, fols. 200Bv–200C.

Correspondance de Jean-Paul Bignon. Fonds Français 22226–29.

Correspondance littéraire et privée d'une partie du siècle de Louis XIV, ou recueil des lettres adressées à Huet, évêque d'Avranches. Fonds Français 15188, pp. 328–31; Fonds Français 15189, fols. 36v–39v.

Huet, Pierre-Daniel. "Censure de la philosophie de M. Descartes à Mr. de Montausier, duc et pair de France." Fonds Français 14702.

"Lettre de Mr. l'Abbé Le Clerc à M. Marais, Avocat du Parlement de Paris." Fonds Français 24413.

"Observations sur les causes dez progrez et des decadanses de la sagesse, et de la raison humaine." Fonds Français 14707.

"Quinze lettres inédites adressées à M. l'abbé Joly par d'Aguesseau, et signées de sa main. Elles sont relatives aux remarques de cet abbé sur Bayle." Nouvelles acquisitions françaises 767.

"Remarques sur le Dictionnaire critique dans lesquelles on demesle autant qu'on peut des intentions secrètes de l'auteur touchant la conformité des évènements anciens avec ceux de son temps." Fonds Français 12433.

Bibliotheken Universiteit Leiden

Fonds Prosper Marchand.

Periodicals

Bibliothèque ancienne et moderne, 1714–27

Bibliothèque choisie, 1703–13

Bibliothèque françoise, ou Histoire littéraire de la France, 1723–46

Bibliothèque germanique, 1720–41

Bibliothèque raisonnée des ouvrages des savans de l'Europe, 1728–53

Bibliothèque universelle et historique, 1686–93

Histoire des ouvrages des savans, 1687–1709

Journal des savants, 1665–1792

Journal littéraire, 1713–37

Mémoires de l'Académie royale des sciences et belles-lettres de Berlin, 1745–69

Mémoires de littérature tirez des registres de l'Académie royale des inscriptions et belles-lettres, 1719–81

Mémoires pour l'histoire des sciences et des beaux-arts (Mémoires de Trévoux), 1701–67

Mercure de France, 1724–1820

Nouvelle bibliothèque germanique, ou Histoire littéraire de l'Allemagne, de la Suisse, & des pays du Nord, 1746–59

Nouvelles de la République des Lettres, 1684–1718

Printed Works

Anselme, Antoine. "Des monuments qui ont suppléé au deffaut de l'écriture, et servi de mémoires au premiers historiens." *Mémoires de littérature tirez des registres de l'Académie royale des inscriptions et belles-lettres, depuis l'année MDCCXI jusques et compris l'année MDCCXVII* 4 (1723): 380–99.

———. "Seconde dissertation sur les monuments qui ont servi de mémoires aux premiers historiens." *Mémoires de littérature tirez des registres de l'Académie royale des inscriptions et belles-lettres, depuis l'année MDCCXVIII jusques et compris l'année MDCCXXV* 6 (1729): 1–13.

Aquinas, Thomas. *Summa contra gentiles*. 2 vols. Naples: Ursiniana, 1773.

Argens, Jean-Baptiste Boyer d'. *Lettres juives, ou Correspondance philosophique, historique et critique entre un juif voïageur en différns etats de l'Europe et ses correspondants en divers endroits*. 2d ed. 6 vols. The Hague: Paupie, 1738.

———. *Mémoires de monsieur marquis d'Argens*. London: Compagnie, 1735.

———. *La philosophie du bon-sens, ou Réflexions philosophiques sur l'incertitude des connoissances humaines*. London: Compagnie, 1737.

Arnauld, Antoine, and Pierre Nicole. *La logique, ou L'art de penser*. Paris: Savreux, 1662.

Arpe, Peter Friedrich. *Pyrrho sive de dubia et incerta historiae et historicorum veterum fide argumentum*. Kiel: Reutheri, 1716.

Arrests de la Cour de Parlement, portant condamnation de plusieurs livres & autres ouvrages imprimés: Extrait des Registres de Parlement du 23 janvier 1759. Paris: Simon, 1759.

Autrey, Henri-Jean-Baptiste Fabry de Moncault, comte d'. *Le pyrrhonien raisonnable, ou Méthode nouvelle proposée aux incrédules*. The Hague: Neaulme, 1765.

Baxter, Andrew. *An Enquiry into the Nature of the Human Soul; Wherein the Immateriality of the Soul is Evinced from the Principles of Reason and Philosophy.* London: Bettenham, 1733.

Bayle, Pierre. *Avis important aux refugiez sur leur prochain retour en France.* Amsterdam: Le Censeur, 1690.

———. *Continuation des Pensées diverses, écrites à un docteur de Sorbonne à l'occasion de la comète qui parut au mois décembre 1680, ou Réponse à plusieurs dificultez que Monsieur *** a proposées à l'auteur.* 2 vols. Rotterdam: Leers, 1705.

———. *Critique générale de l'histoire du calvinisme de Mr. Maimbourg.* Villefranche: Blanc, 1682.

———. *Dictionnaire historique et critique.* 2 vols. Rotterdam: Leers, 1697.

———. *Dictionnaire historique et critique.* 2d ed. 3 vols. Rotterdam: Leers, 1702.

———. *Dictionnaire historique et critique.* 3d ed. 4 vols. Rotterdam: Bohm, 1720.

———. *Dictionnaire historique et critique.* 4th ed. 4 vols. Amsterdam: Brunel, Wetstein, Smith, Waesberge, Humbert, Honoré, Chatelain, & Mortier, 1730.

———. *Dictionnaire historique et critique.* 5th ed. 5 vols. Amsterdam: Compagnie des Libraires, 1734.

———. *Dictionnaire historique et critique.* 5th ed. 4 vols. Amsterdam: Brunel, Humbert, Wetstein, Smith, Honoré, Chatelain, Covens, Mortier, Changuion, Catuffe, & Uytwerf, 1740.

———. *Dictionnaire historique et critique.* 11th ed. 16 vols. Paris: Desoer, 1820.

———. *Entretiens de Maxime et de Thémiste.* Amsterdam: Leers, 1707.

———. *An Historical and Critical Dictionary.* 4 vols. London: Harper, Brown, Tonson, Churchill, Horne, Goodwin, Knaplock, Taylor, Bell, Tooke, Midwinter, Lintott & Lewis, 1710.

———. *Nouvelles lettres de Mr. P. Bayle.* The Hague: Van Duren, 1739.

———. *Œuvres diverses de Pierre Bayle.* 4 vols. The Hague: Compagnie des Librairies, 1737.

———. *Pensées diverses, écrites à un docteur de Sorbonne à l'occasion de la comète qui parut au mois décembre 1680.* Rotterdam: Leers, 1683.

———. "Projet d'un dictionnaire critique." In *Projet et fragments d'un dictionnaire critique,* by Pierre Bayle. Rotterdam, Leers, 1692.

———. *Projet et fragments d'un dictionnaire critique.* Rotterdam: Leers, 1692.

———. *Réflexions sur un imprimé qui a pour titre, Jugement du Public, & particulièrement de l'Abbé Renaudot, sur le Dictionnaire critique du sieur Bayle.* In *Œuvres diverses de Pierre Bayle,* 4:746–56. The Hague: Compagnie des Libraires, 1737.

———. *Réponse aux questions d'un provincial.* 5 vols. Rotterdam: Leers, 1704–7.

Beaufort, Louis de. *Sur l'incertitude des cinq premiers siècles de l'histoire romaine.* Utrecht: Neaulme, 1738.

Beausobre, Louis Isaac de. *Le pyrrhonisme raisonnable.* Berlin: Bourdeaux, 1755.

Berkeley, George. *A Treatise Concerning the Principles of Human Knowledge. Wherein the Chief Causes of Error and Difficulty in the Sciences, with the Grounds of Scepticism, Atheism, and Irreligion, are Inquir'd Into.* Dublin: Pepyat, 1710.

———. *Three Dialogues between Hylas and Philonous. The Design of Which is Plainly to Demonstrate the Reality and Perfection of Human Knowledge, the Incorporeal Nature of the Soul, and the Immediate Providence of a Deity: In Opposition to Sceptics and Atheists*. London: James, 1713.

Bernis, François Joachim de Pierre, Cardinal de. *Mémoires du cardinal Bernis*. Ed. Philippe Bonnet. Paris: Mercure de France, 1986.

Bierling, Friedrich Wilhelm. *Commentatio de pyrrhonismo historico: Accessit propter adfinitatem argumenti de iudico historico dissertatio*. Leipzig: Foersteri, 1724.

———. *Dissertatio de pyrrhonismo historico*. Rinteln: Enax, 1707.

Birch, Thomas, John Peter Bernard, and John Lockman, eds. *A General Dictionary, Historical and Critical: In Which a New and Accurate Translation of that of the Celebrated Mr. Bayle, with the Corrections and Observations Printed in the Late Edition at Paris is Included; and Interspersed with Several Thousand Lives Never Before Published*. 10 vols. London: Bettenham, Straham, Clarke, Hatchet, Gray, Batley, Worrall, Shuckburgh, Wilcox, Millar, Osborne, Brindley, Corbet, Ward & Chandler, 1734–41.

Bouhier, Jean. *Correspondance littéraire du président Bouhier*. Ed. Henri Duranton. 14 vols. Sainte-Etienne: Université de Sainte-Etienne, 1974–88.

Boullier, David Renaud. *Essai philosophique sur l'âme des bêtes, ou l'on trouve diverses réflexions sur la nature de la liberté, sur celle de nos sensations, sur l'union de l'âme et du corps, sur l'immortalité de l'âme*. 2 vols. 2d ed. Amsterdam: Changuion, 1737.

———. *Lettres sur les vrais principes de la religion*. Amsterdam: Catuffe, 1741.

———. *Pièces philosophiques et littéraires*. N.p., 1759.

———. *Le pyrrhonisme de l'église romaine*. Amsterdam: Jolly, 1757.

———. *Traité des vrais principes qui servent de fondement à la certitude morale*. Published with *Essai philosophique sur l'âme des bêtes, ou l'on trouve diverses réflexions sur la nature de la liberté, sur celle de nos sensations, sur l'union de l'âme et du corps, sur l'immortalité de l'âme*. 2 vols. 2d ed. Amsterdam: Changuion, 1737.

Boureau-Deslandes, André-François. *Histoire critique de la philosophie*. Amsterdam: Changuion, 1737.

Boyle, Robert. *Sceptical Chymist*. London: Cadwell, 1661.

Buffier, Claude. *Traité des premières véritez, et de la source de nos jugemens, où l'on examine le sentiment des philosophes de ce temps, sur les premières notions des choses*. 2 vols in 1. Paris: La veuve Mauge, 1724.

Cartaud de la Vilate, François. *Pensées critiques sur les mathématiques*. Paris: Valleyre, 1733.

Castel, Louis-Bertrand. *Le vrai système de physique générale de Isaac Newton, exposé et analysé en parallèle avec celui de Descartes*. Paris: Simon, 1743.

Charron, Pierre. *Les trois veritez contre tous athées, idolâtres, juifs, mahumétans, hérétiques et schismatiques*. Paris: Corrozet, 1595.

Chaudon, Louis-Mayeul. *Dictionnaire anti-philosophique*. Avignon: Veuve Girard & Seguin, 1767.

Chauffepié, Jacques-Georges. *Nouveau dictionnaire historique et critique, pour servir de supplément ou de continuation au Dictionnaire historique et critique de Mr. Pierre Bayle*. 4 vols. Amsterdam: Chatelain, Uttwerf, Changuion, Wetstein, Mortier, Arkste, Merkus, & Rey, 1750–56.

Condillac, Etienne Bonnot de. *Essai sur l'origine des connoissances humaines*. 2 vols. Amsterdam: Mortier, 1746.

———. *Traité des sensations*. 2 vols. London and Paris: de Bure, 1754.

———. *Traité des systèmes*. The Hague: Neaulme, 1749.

Condorcet, Jean-Antoine-Nicolas de Caritat, marquis de. *Vie de Voltaire*. [Kiel]: Imprimerie de la société littéraire typographique, 1789.

Correvon, Gabriel Seigneux de. "Préface de traducteur." In Albrecht von Haller, *Discours sur l'irréligion, où l'on examine ses principes & ses suites funestes*, iii–xv. Trans. Gabriel Seigneux de Correvon. Lausanne: Grasset, 1760.

Côtes, Roger. "The Preface of Roger Côtes." In *The Mathematical Principles of Natural Philosophy*, by Isaac Newton, trans. Andrew Motte. London: Motte, 1729.

Crousaz, Jean-Pierre de. *Examen de l'Essay de Monsieur Pope sur l'homme*. Lausanne: Bousquet, 1737.

———. *Examen du pyrrhonisme ancien et moderne*. The Hague: de Hondt, 1733.

———. *La logique, ou Système de réflexions qui peuvent contribuer à la netteté et l'étendue de nos connaissances*. 2d ed. Amsterdam: Honoré & Châtelain, 1720.

———. *A New Treatise of the Art of Thinking, or a Compleat System of Reflections, Concerning the Conduct and the Improvement of the Mind*. London: Benjamin Hoadley, 1724.

Cuentz, Gaspard. *Essai d'un système nouveau concernant la nature des êtres spirituels, fondée en partie sur les principes du célèbre Mr. Locke, philosophe anglois, dont l'auteur fait l'apologie*. 4 vols. Neufchâtel: Imprimerie des éditeurs du Journal Helvétique, 1742.

Daniel, Gabriel. *Voyage du monde de Descartes*. Paris: Pepie, 1702.

Descartes, René. *La dioptrique*. Published with *Discours de la méthode, pour bien conduire sa raison et chercher la vérité dans les sciences*. Leiden: Maire, 1637.

———. *Discours de la méthode, pour bien conduire sa raison et chercher la vérité dans les sciences*. Leiden: Maire, 1637.

———. *Les méditations métaphysiques de René Des-Cartes touchant la premiere philosophie, dans lesquelles l'existence de Dieu, & la distinction réelle entre l'âme & le corps de l'homme, sont demonstrées*. Paris: Camusat & Le Petit, 1647.

———. *Le monde de Mr. Descartes, ou Le traité de la lumière et des autres principaux objets des sens*. Paris: Girard, 1664.

———. *Œuvres de Descartes*. Ed. Charles Adam and Paul Tannery. 12 vols. Paris: Cerf, 1897–1910.

———. *Les passions de l'âme*. Paris: Le Gras, 1649.

———. *Les principes de la philosophie*. Paris: Le Gras & Pepigne, 1651.

Desmaizeaux, Pierre. *The Life of Mr. Bayle. In a Letter to a Peer of Great Britain*. London, 1708.

———. *La vie de Mr. Bayle*. The Hague: Gosse & Neaulme, 1732.

———, ed. *Mr. Bayle's Historical and Critical Dictionary*. 2d ed. 5 vols. London: Knapton, Midwinter, Brotherton, Bettesworth, Hitch, Hazard, Tonson, Innys, Manby, Osborne, Longman, Ward, Wicksteed, Meadows, Woodward, Motte, Hinchliffe, Walthoe, Symon, Cox, Ward, Browne, Birt, Bickerton, Astley, Austen, Gilliver, Lintot, Whitridge & Willock, 1734–38.

Dictionnaire de l'Académie françoise, dédié au Roy. 2 vols. Paris: Coignard, 1694.

Dictionnaire de l'Académie françoise. 4th ed. 2 vols. Paris: Brunet, 1762.

Diderot, Denis. *Entretien entre D'Alembert et Diderot*. In *Mémoires, correspondance et ouvrages inédits de Diderot*, 4:103–29. Paris: Paulin, 1831.

———. *Jacques le fataliste et son maître.* In *Œuvres de Denis Diderot,* 5:247–477. Paris: Belin, 1819.

———. *Pensées philosophiques.* The Hague, 1746.

———. *Promenade du sceptique, ou Les allées.* In *Mémoires, correspondance et ouvrages inédits de Diderot,* 2d ed., 4:241–417. Paris: Paulin, 1834.

Diderot, Denis, and Jean-le-Rond d'Alembert, eds. *Encyclopédie, ou Dictionnaire raisonnée des sciences, des arts et des métiers.* 17 vols. Paris: Briasson, David, Le Breton & Durand, 1751–65.

Du Revest, Abbé. *Histoire de Mr. Bayle et de ses ouvrages.* Geneva: Fabri & Barrilot, 1715.

———. *Histoire de Mr. Bayle et de ses ouvrages, nouvelle édition augmentée des pièces suivantes.* Amsterdam: Desbordes, 1716.

Egger, Johannes. *De viribus mentis humanae disquisitio philosophica anti-huetiana.* Bern: Bondel, 1735.

Eisenhart, Johann. *De fide historica commentarius.* 2d ed. Helmstadt: Sustermann, 1702.

Ernesti, Johann August. *De fide historica recte aestimanda.* In *Opuscula philologica critica: Multis locis emendate et aucta,* 64–101. Leiden: Luchtmans, 1764.

Fénelon, François de Salignac de la Mothe. *Démonstration de l'existence de Dieu, tirée de la connoissance de la nature, et proportionnée à la foible intelligence des plus simples.* Paris: Estienne, 1713.

———. *Œuvres philosophiques.* Paris: Delaulne, 1718.

Fontenelle, Bernard le Bovier de. *De la connoissance de l'esprit humain.* In *Œuvres de monsieur de Fontenelle,* 9:357–64. Paris: Libraires associés, 1766.

———. *Eléments de la géométrie de l'infini.* Paris: Imprimerie royale, 1727.

———. "Eloge de Neuton." In *Histoire de l'Académie royale des sciences. Année MDCCXXVII,* 151–72. Paris: Imprimerie royale, 1729.

———. *Fragments d'un Traité de la raison humaine.* In *Œuvres de monsieur de Fontenelle,* 9:327–56. Paris: Libraires associés, 1766.

———. *Œuvres de monsieur de Fontenelle.* 11 vols. Paris: Libraires associés, 1766.

———. *Théorie des tourbillons cartésiens.* Paris: Guerin, 1752.

Formey, Jean Henri Samuel. *La belle Wolffienne.* 6 vols. The Hague: Le Vier, 1741–53.

———. *Correspondance passive de Formey: Antoine-Claude Briasson et Nicolas-Charles-Joseph Trublet; Lettres adressées à Jean-Henri-Samuel Formey (1739–1770).* Ed. Martin Frontinus, Rolf Geissler, and Jens Häseler. Paris: Champion; Geneva: Slatkine, 1996.

———. *La logique des vraisemblances.* London, 1748.

———. *Pensées raisonnables opposées aux pensées philosophiques.* Berlin: Voss, 1749.

———. *Le philosophe chrétien.* 4 vols. Leiden: Luzac, 1752–57.

———. "Préface de l'éditeur." In *Essais philosophiques sur l'entendement humain,* by David Hume, trans. Jean-Bérnard Mérian, 1:i–lxiv. Amsterdam: Schneider, 1758.

———. *Le triomphe de l'évidence.* 2 vols. Berlin: Lange, 1756.

Foucher, Simon. *La critique de la Recherche de la vérité, où l'on examine en même tems une partie des principes de M. Descartes.* Paris: Coustelier, 1675.

———. *Dissertations sur la recherche de la vérité, contenant l'histoire et les principes de la philosophie des académiciens.* Paris: Anisson, 1693.

Fréret, Nicolas. *Abrégé de la chronologie de M. le chevalier Isaac Newton, fait par lui-même et traduit sur le manuscrit anglois.* Paris: Cavelier, 1725.

————. *Défense de la chronologie fondée sur les monumens de l'histoire ancienne contre le système de M. Newton.* Paris: Durand, 1758.

————. "Réflexions sur l'étude des anciennes histoires, et sur le degré de certitude de leurs preuves." *Mémoires de littérature tirez des registres de l'Académie royale des inscriptions et belles-lettres, depuis l'année MDCCXVIII jusques et compris l'année MDCCXXV* 6 (1729): 146–89.

Furetière, Antoine. *Dictionnaire universel.* 4 vols. The Hague and Rotterdam: Leers, 1690.

Gassendi, Pierre. *Sintagmatis philosophici.* In *Petri Gassendi opera omnia in sex tomos divisa,* 1:31–90. Lyon: Anisson & Devenet, 1658.

Gauchat, Gabriel. *Lettres critiques, ou Analyse et réfutation de divers écrits modernes contre la religion.* 19 vols. Paris: Herissant, 1755–63.

Gibbon, Edward. *Autobiography.* London: Buckland & Sumner, 1846.

Glanvill, Joseph. "Of Scepticism and Certainty." In *Essays on Several Important Subjects in Philosophy and Religion.* London: Baker & Mortlock, 1676.

Gravesande, Willem Jacob van 's. *Élémens de physique démontrez mathématiquement, et confirmez par des expériences, ou Introduction à la philosophie newtonienne.* Trans. Elie de Joncourt. 2 vols. Leiden: Langerak & Verbeek, 1746.

Haller, Albrecht von. "Discours préliminaire." In *Le triomphe de l'évidence,* by Jean Henri Samuel Formey, 1:i–xlviii. Berlin: Lange, 1756.

————. *Discours sur l'irréligion, où l'on examine ses principes & ses suites funestes.* Trans. Gabriel Seigneux de Correvon. Lausanne: Grasset, 1760.

————. *Prüfung der secte die an allem zweifelt.* Göttingen: Vandenhoeck, 1751.

Hardouin, Jean. *Ad censuram veterum scriptorum prolegomena.* London: Vaillant, 1766.

————. *Chronologiae ex nummis antiquis restitutae prolusio de nummis Herodiadum.* Paris: Anisson, 1693.

Hayer, Hubert. *L'utilité temporelle de la religion chrétienne.* Paris: Desprez, 1774.

Hayer, Hubert, and Jean Soret, eds. *La religion vengée, ou Réfutation des auteurs impies, dediée à Monsieur le Dauphin.* 21 vols. Paris: Chaubert & Herissant, 1757–63.

Hervet, Gentian. Dedicatory epistle to the cardinal of Lorraine. In *Adversus mathematicos, hoc est, adversus eos qui profitentur disciplinas, opus eruditissimum, complectens universam pyrrhoniorum acutissimorum philosophorum disputandi de quibuslibet disciplinis & artibus rationem, graece nunquam, latine nunc primum editum, Gentiano Herveto Aurelio interprete,* by Sextus Empiricus [ii–iv]. Trans. Gentian Hervet. Paris: Juvenis, 1569.

Huart, Claude. Preface to *Les hipotiposes, ou Institutions pirronniennes de Sextus Empiricus, en trois livres traduites du grec, avec des notes,* by Sextus Empiricus, trans. [Claude Huart]. [Amsterdam], 1725.

Huet, Pierre-Daniel. *Against Cartesian Philosophy* = *Censura philosophiae cartesianae.* Trans. and ed. Thomas Lennon. Amherst, NY: Humanity Books, 2003.

————. *Alnetanae quaestiones de concordia rationis et fidei.* Paris: Moette, 1690.

————. *Censura philosophia cartesianae.* Paris: Horthemels, 1689.

————. *Memoirs of the Life of Peter Daniel Huet, Bishop of Avranches, Written by Himself.* Trans. John Aiken. 2 vols. London: Longman, Hurst, Reest, & Orne, 1810.

————. *Nouveaux mémoires pour servir à l'histoire du cartésianisme.* Paris, 1692.

————. *Traité philosophique de la foiblesse de l'esprit humain.* Amsterdam: Du Sauzet, 1723.

Hume, David. *Essais philosophiques sur l'entendement humain.* Trans. Jean-Bérnard Mérian. 2 vols. Amsterdam: Schneider, 1758.

———. *My Own Life.* London: Strahan & Cadell, 1777.

———. *Philosophical Essays Concerning Human Understanding.* London: Millar, 1748.

Huygens, Christiaan. *Discours de la cause de la pesanteur.* Leiden: van der AA, 1690.

———. *Œuvres complètes de Christiaan Huygens.* 22 vols. The Hague: Nijhoff, 1888–1950.

Jaquelot, Isaac. *Conformité de la foi avec la raison, ou Défense de la religion, contre les principales difficultez répandues dans le Dictionaire historique et critique de Mr. Bayle.* Amsterdam: Desbordes & Pain, 1705.

———. *Examen de la théologie de Mr. Bayle, répandue dans son Dictionnaire critique, dans ses Pensées sur les comètes, & dans ses Réponses à un provincial; où l'on défend la conformité de la foi avec la raison, contre sa Réponse.* Amsterdam: Honoré, 1706.

———. *Réponse aux Entretiens composés par M. Bayle.* Amsterdam: Honoré, 1707.

Joly, Philippe-Louis. *Remarques critiques sur le Dictionnaire de Bayle.* 2 vols. Paris: Ganeau, 1748–52.

Jurieu, Pierre. *L'accomplissement de prophéties, ou La délivrance prochaine de l'église.* Rotterdam: Acher, 1686.

———, ed. *Jugement du public et particulièrement de M. l'abbé Renaudot sur le Dictionnaire critique de Sr. Bayle.* Rotterdam: Acher, 1697.

———. *Le philosophe de Roterdam [sic] accusé, atteint et convaincu.* Amsterdam, 1706.

———. *Les soupirs de la France esclave qui aspire après la liberté.* N.p., 1689.

———. *Traité de la nature et de la grace.* Utrecht: Halma, 1688.

———. *Le vraye système de l'église & la véritable analyse de la foy.* Dordrecht: Gaspar & Goris, 1686.

Kant, Immanuel. "An Answer to the Question: What is Enlightenment?" In *Kant: Political Writings,* ed. Hans Reiss, trans. H. B. Nisbet, 54–60. Cambridge: Cambridge University Press, 1970. Originally published as "Beantwortung der Frage: Was ist Aufklärung?" *Berlinische Monatsschrift,* December 1784, 481–94.

La Mettrie, Julien d'Offray de. *L'homme machine.* In *Œuvres philosophiques,* 9–80. Berlin: Bourdeaux, 1751.

———. *Traité de l'âme.* In *Œuvres philosophiques,* 81–208. Berlin: Bourdeaux, 1751.

La Mothe Le Vayer, François de. *De la vertu des payens.* 2d ed. Paris: Coubré, 1647.

———. *Discours pour montrer que les doutes de la philosophie sceptique sont de grand usage dans les sciences.* In *Œuvres de François de La Mothe Le Vayer, conseiller d'état,* 5, pt. 2: 1–76. Dresden: Groell, 1756.

———. *Du peu de certitude qu'il y a en histoire.* Paris: Billaine, 1668.

———. *Opuscule, ou Petit traité sceptique sur cette façon de parler: N'avoir pas le sens commun.* Paris: Sommaville, 1646.

———. *Prose chagrine.* In *Œuvres de François de La Mothe Le Vayer, conseiller d'état,* 3, pt. 1: 239–386. Dresden: Groell, 1756.

———. *Soliloques sceptiques.* Paris: Billaine, 1670.

La Peyrère, Isaac de. *Prae-Adamitae, sive Exercitatio super versibus duodecimo, decimotertio, & decimoquarto, capitis quinti Epistolae D. Pauli ad Romanos: Quibis inducuntur primi homines ante Adamum conditi.* [Amsterdam: Elzevier], 1655.

Laubrussel, Ignace de. *Traité des abus de la critique en matière de religion.* 2 vols. Paris: Du Puis, 1710–11.

Le Clerc, Laurent-Josse. *Bibliothèque du Richelet, ou Abrégé de la vie des auteurs citez dans ce dictionnaire.* Lyon, 1727.

———. *Lettre critique sur le Dictionaire de Bayle.* The Hague, 1732.

———. *Remarques sur différens articles du premier volume du Dictionnaire du Moréri, de l'édition de 1718.* Orleans, 1719.

Le Duchat, Jacob. "Remarques sur le Dictionnaire de Bayle." In *Ducatiana, ou Remarques du feu M. Le Duchat,* ed. Jean Henri Samuel Formey, 1:145–217. Amsterdam: Humbert, 1738.

Lee, Henry. *Anti-Scepticism: or Notes Upon Each Chapter of Mr. Lock's Essay Concerning Humane Understanding.* London: Clavel & Harper, 1702.

Le Febvre, Jacques. *Bayle en petit, ou Anatomie de ses ouvrages.* N.p., 1737.

———. *Bayle en petit, ou Anatomie de ses ouvrages, entretiens d'un docteur avec un bibliothécaire an un abbé.* N.p., 1738.

———. *Examen critique des ouvrages de Bayle.* Amsterdam: Le Chatelain, 1747.

Leibniz, Gottfried Wilhelm. "Eclaircissement du nouveau sisteme de la communication des substances, pour servir de réponse à ce qui en a esté dit dans le Journal du 12 Septembre 1695." *Journal des savants,* 2 April 1696, 166–68.

———. "Eclaircissement du nouveau sisteme de la communication des substances, pour servir de réponse à ce qui en a esté dit dans le Journal du 12 Septembre 1695." *Journal des savants,* 9 April 1696, 169–71.

———. *Essais de théodicée sur la bonté de Dieu, la liberté de l'homme et l'origine du mal.* Amsterdam: Troyel, 1710.

———. "Sisteme nouveau de la nature et de la communication des substances, aussi-bien que de l'union qu'il y a entre l'âme & le corps." *Journal des savants,* 4 July 1695, 301–6.

Lenglet du Fresnoy, Nicolas. *Méthode pour étudier l'histoire.* 2 vols. Paris: Musier & Coustelier, 1713.

Lévesque de Pouilly, Louis-Jean. "Dissertation sur l'incertitude des quatre premières siècles de Rome." *Mémoires de littérature tirez des registres de l'Académie royale des inscriptions et belles-lettres, depuis l'année MDCCXVIII jusques et compris l'année MDCCXXV* 6 (1729): 14–29.

———. "Nouveaux essais de critique sur la fidélité de l'histoire." *Mémoires de littérature tirez des registres de l'Académie royale des inscriptions et belles-lettres, depuis l'année MDCCXVIII jusques et compris l'année MDCCXXV* 6 (1729): 71–114.

Locke, John. *Abrégé de l'Essay de Monsieur Locke, sur l'entendement humain.* Trans. and ed. Jean-Pierre Bosset. London: Watts, 1720.

———. *Essai philosophique concernant l'entendement humain, où l'on montre quelle est l'étendue de nos connoissances certaines, et la manière dont nous y parvenons.* Trans. Pierre Coste. Amsterdam: Schelte, 1700.

———. *An Essay Concerning Human Understanding.* London: Basset, 1690.

Mabillon, Jean. *Brèves réflexions sur quelques règles de l'histoire.* Ed. Blandine Barret-Kriegel. Paris: P.O.L., 1990.

Maffei, Scipione. *Ars critica lapidaria.* Lucca: Venturini, 1765.

Malebranche, Nicolas. *De la recherche de la vérité.* 4th ed. 2 vols. Amsterdam: Desbordes, 1688.

———. *Entretiens sur la métaphysique et sur la religion.* Rotterdam: Leers, 1688.

———. "Réponse du P. Malebranche prestre de l'Oratoire à M. Régis." In *Œuvres complètes*, ed. André Robinet, 17, pt. 1: 257–320. Paris: Librairie J. Vrin, 1958.

Marais, Mathieu. *Journal et mémoires de Mathieu Marais.* Ed. Adolphe Mathurin de Lescure. 4 vols. Paris: Firmin Didot, 1863–67.

Marandé, Léonard de. *Jugement des actions humaines.* Paris: Cromoisy, 1624.

Maupertuis, Pierre-Louis Moreau de. *Discours sur les différentes figures des astres.* Paris: Imprimerie royale, 1732.

Mérian, Jean-Bernard. "Mémoire sur l'apperception de sa propre existence." *Mémoires de l'Académie royale des sciences et belles-lettres: Année 1749* 5 (1751): 416–41.

———. "Réflexions philosophiques sur la ressemblance." *Mémoires de l'Académie royale des sciences et belles-lettres: Année 1751* 7 (1753): 30–56.

———. "Sur l'apperception considérée relativement aux idées, ou, sur l'existence des idées dans l'âme." *Mémoires de l'Académie royale des sciences et belles-lettres: Année 1749* 5 (1751): 441–77.

———. "Sur le principe des indiscernables." *Mémoires de l'Académie royale des sciences et belles-lettres: Année 1754* 10 (1756): 383–98.

Merlin, Charles. *Apologie de David, contre la satyre que M. Bayle a faite des actions de ce saint roy.* Paris: Chaubert, 1737.

———. *Réfutation des critiques de Monsieur Bayle sur Saint Augustin.* Paris: Rolin, 1732.

Mersenne, Marin. *La vérité des sciences contre les septiques ou pyrrhoniens.* Paris: du Bray, 1625.

Montaigne, Michel de. *Essais.* Ed. Pierre Coste. 5 vols. The Hague: Gosse & Neaulme, 1727.

Newton, Isaac. *The Chronology of Ancient Kingdoms Amended.* London: Osborn & Longman, 1728.

———. *The Mathematical Principles of Natural Philosophy.* Trans. Andrew Motte. 2 vols. London: Motte, 1729.

———. *The Principia: Mathematical Principles of Natural Philosophy.* Ed. and trans. I. Bernard Cohen and A. Whitman. Berkeley: University of California Press, 1999.

Niceron, Jean-Pierre. *Mémoires pour servir à l'histoire des hommes illustres dans la République des Lettres.* 43 vols. Paris: Briasson, 1729–45.

Olivet, Pierre-Joseph Thoulier d'. *Apologie de M. l'Abbé d'Olivet, de l'Académie françoise, en forme de commentaire sur deux articles des Mémoires de Trévoux.* Paris: Pissot, 1726.

Olivet, Pierre-Joseph Thoulier d', and Paul Pellisson. *Histoire de l'Académie françoise.* 3d ed. 2 vols. Paris: Coignard, 1743.

Pascal, Blaise. *Pensées de M. Pascal sur la religion et sur quelques autres sujets, qui ont esté trouvées après sa mort parmy ses papiers.* Paris: Desprez, 1670.

Perizonius, Jakob. *Oratio de fide historiarum contra pyrrhonismum historicum.* Leiden: Verbessei, 1702.

Rapin, René. *Instructions pour l'histoire.* Paris: Mabre-Cramoisy, 1678.

Rechenberg, Carl Otto, and Christoph Brückner. *De autoritate historiae in probandis quaestionibus iuris et facti.* Leipzig: Titus, 1709.

Régis, Pierre-Sylvain. *Réponse au livre qui a pour titre P. Danielis Huetii censura philosophiae cartesianae: Servant d'éclaircissement à toutes les parties de la philosophie, sur tout à la métaphysique*. Paris: Cusson, 1691.

———. *Système de philosophie, contenant la logique, la métaphysique, la physique et la morale*. 7 vols. Lyon: Anisson, Posuel, & Rigaud, 1691.

———. *L'usage de la raison et de la foi*. Paris: Jean Cusson, 1704.

Renaudot, Eusèbe. "Jugement de l'abbé Renaudot sur le Dictionnaire critique à monsieur le chancelier." In *Jugement du public et particulièrement de M. l'abbé Renaudot sur le Dictionnaire critique de Sr. Bayle*, ed. Pierre Jurieu, 5–11. Rotterdam: Acher, 1697.

Richelet, César-Pierre. *Dictionnaire françois*. 2 vols. Geneva: Widerhold, 1680.

Rochefort, César de. *Dictionnaire général et curieux contenant les principaux mots et les plus usitez en la langue françoise*. Lyon: Guillimin, 1685.

Saint-Aubin, Gilbert-Charles Le Gendre, marquis de. *Traité de l'opinion, ou Mémoires pour servir à l'histoire de l'esprit humain*. 2d ed. 6 vols. Paris: Briasson, 1735.

Saint-Réal, César Vichard de. *De l'usage de l'histoire*. In *Méthode pour étudier l'histoire*, by Nicolas Lenglet du Fresnoy, 2:3–101. Paris: Musier & Coustelier, 1713.

Sallier, Claude. "Discours sur les premiers monuments historiques des Romains." *Mémoires de littérature tirez des registres de l'Académie royale des inscriptions et belles-lettres, depuis l'année MDCCXVIII jusques et compris l'année MDCCXXV* 6 (1729): 30–51.

———. "Second discours sur la certitude de l'histoire des quatre premiers siècles de Rome, ou Réflexions générales sur un traité qui se trouve parmi les Œuvres Morales de Plutarque, sous ce titre Parallèles des faits Grecs et Romains." *Mémoires de littérature tirez des registres de l'Académie royale des inscriptions et belles-lettres, depuis l'année MDCCXVIII jusques et compris l'année MDCCXXV* 6 (1729): 52–70.

———. "Troisième discours sur la certitude de l'histoire des quatre premiers siècles de Rome." *Mémoires de littérature tirez des registres de l'Académie royale des inscriptions et belles-lettres, depuis l'année MDCCXVIII jusques et compris l'année MDCCXXV* 6 (1729): 115–35.

Saxius, Christoph. "De incerto historiae romanorum antiquissimae, sectio I." In *Miscellanea Lipsiensia nova*, 4, pt. 1: 40–79. Leipzig: Gleditsch, 1742.

———. "De incerto historiae romanorum antiquissimae, sectio II." In *Miscellanea Lipsiensia nova*, 2, pt. 1: 409–95. Leipzig: Gleditsch, 1743.

Sextus Empiricus. *Adversus mathematicos, hoc est, adversus eos qui profitentur disciplinas, opus eruditissimum, complectens universam pyrrhoniorum acutissimorum philosophorum disputandi de quibuslibet disciplinis & artibus rationem, graece nunquam, latine nunc primum editum, Gentiano Herveto Aurelio interprete*. Trans. Gentian Hervet. Paris: Juvenis, 1569.

———. *Les hipotiposes, ou Institutions pirroniennes de Sextus Empiricus, en trois livres traduites du grec, avec des notes*. Trans. [Claude Huart]. [Amsterdam], 1725.

———. *Sexti Empirici opera, graece et latine*. Ed. Henri Estienne, Johann Albert Fabricius, and Gentian Hervet. 2 vols. Leipzig: Gleditsch, 1718.

Simon, Richard. *Histoire critique du Vieux Testament*. Paris: Veuve Billaine, 1678.

Simonides, Samuel. *De bono historico*. Leipzig: Titius, 1695.

Souciet, Etienne. *Recueil des dissertations du Père E. Souciet de la Compagnie de Jesus. Tome II contenant: Un abregé de chronologie. Cinq dissertations contre la Chronologie de M. Newton. Une Dissertation sur une médaille singuliere d'Auguste.* Paris: Rollin, 1726.

Spinoza, Baruch. *Tractatus theologico-politicus.* Hamburg: Künrath, 1670.

Struve, Burkhard Gotthelf. *De pyrrhonismo historico dissertatio praeliminaris.* Jena: Troebert, 1721.

———. *Dissertatiuncula de vitiis historicorum, qua simul ad orationem inauguralem de meritis Germanorum in historiam et lectiones publicas invita.* Jena: Öhrling, 1705.

Tertullian. *De carne Christi.* http://www.tertullian.org/articles/evans_carn/evans_carn _03latin.htm.

Thomasius, Christian. *Dissertationem de fide juridica.* Halle an der Saale: Salfeld, 1699.

Tournemine, René-Joseph de. *Réflexions sur l'athéisme, sur la démonstration de Monseigneur de Cambray, et sur le système de Spinoza.* In *Œuvres philosophiques,* by François de Salignac de la Mothe Fénelon, 523–59. Paris: Delaulne, 1718.

Villemandy, Pierre de. *Scepticismus debellatus, seu humanae cognitionis ratio ab imis radicibus explicata; ejusdem certitudo adversus scepticos quosque veteres ac novos invicte asserta; facilis ac tuta certitudinis hujus obtinendae methodus praemonstrata.* Leiden: Boutesteyn, 1697.

Voltaire, François Marie d'Arouet. *Dictionnaire philosophique, portatif.* 6th ed. 2 vols. London, 1767.

———. *Éléments de la philosophie de Neuton, donnés par Mr. de Voltaire.* London, 1738.

———. *Letters Concerning the English Nation.* London: Davis, 1733.

———. *Lettres philosophiques.* Amsterdam: Lucas, 1734.

———. *La métaphysique de Neuton, ou Parallèle des sentimens de Neuton et de Leibnitz.* Amsterdam: Desbordes, 1740.

———. *Les œuvres complètes de Voltaire.* Ed. Theodore Besterman. 135 vols. Geneva: Institut et Musée Voltaire, 1968–77.

———. *Le pyrrhonisme de l'histoire.* In *Œuvres complètes de Voltaire,* 31:11–128. Kiel: Imprimerie de la société littéraire-typographique, 1785.

———. *Le siècle de Louis XIV.* In *Œuvres complètes de Voltaire,* vols. 20–22. Paris: Bazouge-Pigoreau, 1832.

Wilkins, John. *Of the Principles and Duties of Natural Religion.* 5th ed. London: Chiswell & Brome, 1704.

Articles in the *Encyclopédie*

Alembert, Jean-le-Rond d'. "Attraction." In *Encyclopédie, ou Dictionnaire raisonnée des sciences, des arts et des métiers,* ed. Denis Diderot and Jean-le-Rond d'Alembert, 1:846–54. Paris: Briasson, David, Le Breton & Durand, 1751.

———. "Cartésianisme." In *Encyclopédie, ou Dictionnaire raisonnée des sciences, des arts et des métiers,* ed. Denis Diderot and Jean-le-Rond d'Alembert, 2:716–26. Paris: Briasson, David, Le Breton & Durand, 1752.

———. "Corps." In *Encyclopédie, ou Dictionnaire raisonnée des sciences, des arts et des métiers,* ed. Denis Diderot and Jean-le-Rond d'Alembert, 4:261–63. Paris: Briasson, David, Le Breton & Durand, 1754.

———. "Discours préliminaire des éditeurs." In *Encyclopédie, ou Dictionnaire raisonnée des sciences, des arts et des métiers*, ed. Denis Diderot and Jean-le-Rond d'Alembert, 1:i–xlv. Paris: Briasson, David, Le Breton & Durand, 1751.

———. "Divisibilité." In *Encyclopédie, ou Dictionnaire raisonnée des sciences, des arts et des métiers*, ed. Denis Diderot and Jean-le-Rond d'Alembert, 4:1074–76. Paris: Briasson, David, Le Breton & Durand, 1754.

———. "Matière." In *Encyclopédie, ou Dictionnaire raisonnée des sciences, des arts et des métiers*, ed. Denis Diderot and Jean-le-Rond d'Alembert, 10:189–91. Paris: Briasson, David, Le Breton & Durand, 1765.

Diderot, Denis. "Métaphysique." In *Encyclopédie, ou Dictionnaire raisonnée des sciences, des arts et des métiers*, ed. Denis Diderot and Jean-le-Rond d'Alembert, 10:440. Paris: Briasson, David, Le Breton & Durand, 1765.

———. "Pyrrhonienne." In *Encyclopédie, ou Dictionnaire raisonnée des sciences, des arts et des métiers*, ed. Denis Diderot and Jean-le-Rond d'Alembert, 13:613–14. Paris: Briasson, David, Le Breton & Durand, 1765.

Lubières, Charles-Benjamin, baron de. "Idée." In *Encyclopédie, ou Dictionnaire raisonnée des sciences, des arts et des métiers*, ed. Denis Diderot and Jean-le-Rond d'Alembert, 8:489–94. Paris: Briasson, David, Le Breton & Durand, 1765.

Montbeillard, Philibert Guéneau de. "Étendue." In *Encyclopédie, ou Dictionnaire raisonnée des sciences, des arts et des métiers*, ed. Denis Diderot and Jean-le-Rond d'Alembert, 6:43–47. Paris: Briasson, David, Le Breton & Durand, 1756.

"Philosophe." In *Encyclopédie, ou Dictionnaire raisonnée des sciences, des arts et des métiers*, ed. Denis Diderot and Jean-le-Rond d'Alembert, 12:509–11. Paris: Briasson, David, Le Breton & Durand, 1765.

Romily, Jean-Edme. "Tolérance." In *Encyclopédie, ou Dictionnaire raisonnée des sciences, des arts et des métiers*, ed. Denis Diderot and Jean-le-Rond d'Alembert, 16:390–95. Paris: Briasson, David, Le Breton & Durand, 1765.

Voltaire, François Marie d'Arouet. "Histoire." In *Encyclopédie, ou Dictionnaire raisonnée des sciences, des arts et des métiers*, ed. Denis Diderot and Jean-le-Rond d'Alembert, 8:220–30. Paris: Briasson, David, Le Breton & Durand, 1765.

"Vraissemblance." In *Encyclopédie, ou Dictionnaire raisonnée des sciences, des arts et des métiers*, ed. Denis Diderot and Jean-le-Rond d'Alembert, 17:482–86. Paris: Briasson, David, Le Breton & Durand, 1765.

Yvon, Claude, and Denis Diderot. "Ame." In *Encyclopédie, ou Dictionnaire raisonnée des sciences, des arts et des métiers*, ed. Denis Diderot and Jean-le-Rond d'Alembert, 1:327–43. Paris: Briasson, David, Le Breton & Durand, 1751.

Secondary Works

Adams, David J. "Formey continuateur de l'*Encyclopédie*." *Recherches sur Diderot et sur l'Encyclopédie* 13 (1992): 117–29.

Adkins, G. Matthew. *The Idea of the Sciences in the French Enlightenment: A Reinterpretation*. Newark: University of Delaware Press, 2014.

Aiton, Eric J. *The Vortex Theory of Planetary Motion*. New York: American Elsevier, 1972.

Åkerman, Susanna. "The Answer to Scepticism of Queen Christina's Academy (1656)." In *Anticipations of the Enlightenment in England, France, and Germany*, ed. Alan

Charles Kors and Paul J. Korshin, 92–101. Philadelphia: University of Pennsylvania Press, 1987.

Albertan-Coppola, Sylviane. "Apologetics." In *Encyclopedia of the Enlightenment*, ed. Alan Charles Kors, 1:58–63. Oxford: Oxford University Press, 2003.

———. "L'apologétique catholique française à l'âge des Lumières." *Revue de l'histoire des religions* 205, no. 2 (1988): 151–80.

Almog, Joseph. *What Am I? Descartes and the Mind-Body Problem.* Oxford: Oxford University Press, 2001.

Almond, Philip C. *Adam and Eve in Seventeenth-Century Thought.* Cambridge: Cambridge University Press, 1999.

Ariew, Roger. "Cartesian Empiricism." *Revue roumaine de philosophie* 50 (2006): 71–84.

———. *Descartes and the Last Scholastics.* Ithaca, NY: Cornell University Press, 1999.

Ascoli, Georges. "Quelques pages d'une correspondance inédite de M. Marais." *Revue du XVIIIᵉ siècle* 1, no. 2 (1913): 150–74.

Auvray, Paul. *Richard Simon, 1638–1712: Étude bio-bibliographique avec des textes inédits.* Paris: Presses Universitaires de France, 1974.

Avenel, Joseph d'. *Histoire de la vie et des ouvrages de Daniel Huet, évêque d'Avranches.* Mortain: Lebel, 1853.

Bailey, Alan. *Sextus Empiricus and Pyrrhonean Scepticism.* Oxford: Clarendon, 2002.

Baker, Gordon, and Katherine Morris. *Descartes' Dualism.* New York: Routledge, 1996.

Baker, Keith Michael. *Condorcet: From Natural Philosophy to Social Mathematics.* Chicago: University of Chicago Press, 1975.

———. "Enlightenment and the Institution of Society: Notes for a Conceptual History." In *Main Trends in Cultural History: Ten Essays*, ed. Willem Melching and Wyger Velema, 95–120. Amsterdam: Rodopi, 1994.

———. "Epistémologie et politique: Pourquoi l'Encyclopédie est-elle une dictionnaire?" In *L'Encyclopédie: Du réseau au livre et du livre au réseau*, ed. Robert Morrissey and Philippe Roger, 51–58. Paris: Champion, 2001.

Baker, Keith Michael, and Peter Hans Reill, eds. *What's Left of the Enlightenment? A Postmodern Question.* Stanford, CA: Stanford University Press, 2001.

Barber, William H. *Leibniz in France from Arnauld to Voltaire: A Study of the French Reaction to Leibnizianism.* Oxford: Oxford University Press, 1955.

Barbier, Antoine-Alexandre. *Dictionnaire des ouvrages anonymes et pseudonymes composés, traduits ou publiés en français et en latin, avec les noms des auteurs, traducteurs et éditeurs.* 2d ed. 4 vols. Paris: Barrois, 1822–27.

Barnes, Annie. *Jean Le Clerc (1657–1736) et la République des Lettres.* Paris: Droz, 1938.

Barnes, Jonathan. *The Toils of Skepticism.* Cambridge: Cambridge University Press, 1990.

Barnett, S. J. *The Enlightenment and Religion: The Myths of Modernity.* Manchester: Manchester University Press, 2003.

Barret-Kriegel, Blandine. *Les historiens et la monarchie.* Vol. 3, *Les académies de l'histoire.* Paris: Presses Universitaires de France, 1988.

Bartholmèss, Christian. *Histoire philosophique de l'Académie de Prusse, depuis Leibniz jusqu'à Schelling, particulièrement sous Frédéric-le-Grand.* 2 vols. Paris: Ducloux, 1850–51.

———. *Huet évêque d'Avranches ou le scepticisme théologique.* Paris: Franck, 1850.

Belgioioso, Giulia. "Arnauld's Posthumous Defense of the 'Philosophie Humaine' against Heretics and Sceptics." In *The Return of Scepticism: From Hobbes and Descartes to Bayle*, ed. Gianni Paganini, 167–96. Dordrecht: Kluwer Academic, 2003.

Belkind, Ori. "Newton's Scientific Method and the Universal Law of Gravitation." In *Interpreting Newton: Critical Essays*, ed. Andre Janiak and Eric Schliesser, 138–68. Cambridge: Cambridge University Press, 2012.

Benitez, Miguel. *La face cachée des Lumières: Recherches sur les manuscrits philosophiques clandestins de l'âge classique*. Paris: Universitas; Oxford: Voltaire Foundation, 1996.

Berman, David, ed. *George Berkeley: Eighteenth-Century Responses*. New York: Garland, 1989.

Bernier, Marc André, and Sébastien Charles, eds. *Scepticisme et modernité*. Saint-Etienne: Université de Saint-Etienne, 2005.

Bernus, Auguste. *Richard Simon et son Histoire critique du Vieux Testament: La critique biblique au siècle de Louis XIV*. Lausanne: Bridel, 1869.

Bertrand, Aliénor, ed. *Condillac: L'origine du langage*. Paris: Presses Universitaires de France, 2002.

Bertrand, Louis. *Vie, écrits et correspondance littéraire de Laurent-Josse Le Clerc*. Paris: Techener & Vic, 1878.

Beuchot, Adrien-Jean-Quentin. "Avant-propos." In *Dictionnaire historique et critique*, by Pierre Bayle, 1:i–vi. 11th ed. Paris: Désoer, 1820.

———. "Discours préliminaire de la onzième édition du Dictionnaire de Bayle." In *Dictionnaire historique et critique*, by Pierre Bayle, 1:i–xxx. 11th ed. Paris: Désoer, 1820.

Biener, Zvi, and Eric Schliesser, eds. *Newton and Empiricism*. Oxford: Oxford University Press, 2014.

Biener, Zvi, and Chris Smeenk. "Cotes' Queries: Newton's Empiricism and Conceptions of Matter." In *Interpreting Newton: Critical Essays*, ed. Andre Janiak and Eric Schliesser, 105–37. Cambridge: Cambridge University Press, 2012.

Binoche, Bertrand. "Le pyrrhonisme historique ou le fait mis à nu." In *Popularité de la philosophie*, ed. Philippe Beck and Denis Thouard, 41–51. Paris: ENS, 1995.

Blair, Ann. *Too Much to Know: Managing Scholarly Information before the Modern Age*. New Haven, CT: Yale University Press, 2010.

Bloch, Olivier René, ed. *Le matérialisme du XVIIIᵉ siècle et la littérature clandestine*. Paris: Librairie Philosophique J. Vrin, 1982.

———. *La philosophie de Gassendi: Nominalisme, matérialisme, métaphysique*. The Hague: Nijhoff, 1971.

Blom, Philipp. *A Wicked Company: The Forgotten Radicalism of the European Enlightenment*. New York: Basic Books, 2010.

Borghero, Carlo. *La certezza e la storia: Cartesianismo pirronismo e la conoscenza storica*. Milan: Angeli, 1983.

———. "Scepticism and Analysis: Villemandy as a Critic of Descartes." In *The Return of Scepticism: From Hobbes and Descartes to Bayle*, ed. Gianni Paganini, 213–29. Dordrecht: Kluwer Academic, 2003.

Bost, Hubert. *L'affaire Bayle: La bataille entre Pierre Bayle et Pierre Jurieu devant le consistoire de l'église wallonne de Rotterdam*. Saint-Étienne: Institut Claude Longeon, 2006.

Bots, Hans, ed. *Critique, savoir et érudition a la veille des Lumières: Le Dictionaire historique et critique de Pierre Bayle, 1647–1706 = Critical Spirit, Wisdom, and Erudition on the Eve of the Enlightenment: The Dictionnaire historique et critique of Pierre Bayle, 1647–1706.* Amsterdam: APA–Holland University Press, 1998.

Bots, Hans, and Françoise Waquet. *La République des Lettres.* Paris: Belin, 1997.

Bouillier, Francisque Cyrille. *Histoire de la philosophie cartésienne.* 3d ed. 2 vols. Paris: Delagrave, 1868.

Bourgault, Sophie, and Robert Sparling, eds. *A Companion to Enlightenment Historiography.* Leiden: Brill, 2003.

Božovič, Miran. "The Philosophy of Du Marsais's *Le Philosophe.*" *Filozofski vestnik* 39, no. 2 (2008): 61–76.

Bracken, Harry. *The Early Reception of Berkeley's Immaterialism, 1710–1733.* The Hague: Nijhoff, 1965.

Brahami, Frédéric. *Le travail du scepticisme: Montaigne, Bayle, Hume.* Paris: Presses Universitaires de France, 2001.

Brandão, Rodrigo. "Voltaire et le scepticisme." *Philosophiques* 35, no. 1 (2008): 261–74.

Brett, George S. *The Philosophy of Gassendi.* London: Macmillan, 1908.

Brockliss, Laurence W. B. "Aristotle, Descartes and the New Science: Natural Philosophy at the University of Paris, 1600–1740." *Annals of Science* 38, no. 1 (1981): 33–69.

———. *French Higher Education in the Seventeenth and Eighteenth Centuries: A Cultural History.* Oxford: Clarendon, 1987.

———. "The Moment of No Return: The University of Paris and the Death of Aristotelianism." *Science and Education* 15, nos. 2–4 (2006): 259–78.

———. "Philosophy Teaching in France, 1600–1740." *History of Universities* 1 (1981): 131–68.

Brogi, Stefano. "Bayle, Le Clerc et les 'Rationaux.'" In *Pierre Bayle dans la République des Lettres: Philosophie, religion, critique,* ed. Antony McKenna and Gianni Paganini, 211–30. Paris: Champion, 2004.

Brown, Gregory. "Leibniz's Theodicy and the Confluence of Worldly Goods." *Journal of the History of Philosophy* 26, no. 4 (1988): 571–79.

Brumfitt, J. H. *Voltaire, Historian.* London: Oxford University Press, 1958.

Brunetière, Ferdinand. *Etudes critiques sur l'histoire de la littérature française.* 4th ed. 5th ser. Paris: Hachette, 1926.

Brykman, Geneviève. "Berkeley: Sa lecture de Malebranche à travers le *Dictionnaire* de Bayle." *Revue internationale de philosophie* 114 (1975): 496–514.

Buchwald, Jed Z., and Mordechai Feingold. *Newton and the Origin of Civilization.* Princeton, NJ: Princeton University Press, 2012.

Bulman, William J., and Robert G. Ingram, eds. *God in the Enlightenment.* Oxford: Oxford University Press, 2016.

Bunge, Wiep van, and Hans Bots, eds. *Pierre Bayle (1647–1706), le philosophe de Rotterdam: Philosophy, Religion and Reception; Selected Papers of the Tercentenary Conference Held at Rotterdam, 7–8 December 2006.* Leiden: Brill, 2008.

Burger, Pierre-François. "La prohibition du *Dictionaire historique et critique* de Pierre Bayle par l'abbé Renaudot (1648–1720)." In *Critique, savoir et érudition a la veille des Lumières: Le Dictionaire historique et critique de Pierre Bayle, 1647–1706 = Critical Spirit, Wisdom, and Erudition on the Eve of the Enlightenment: The Dictionnaire historique et critique of Pierre Bayle, 1647–1706*, ed. Hans Bots, 81–107. Amsterdam: APA–Holland University Press, 1998.

Burke, Peter. "Two Crises of Historical Consciousness." *Storia della Storiographia* 33 (1998): 3–16.

Burnyeat, Miles, and Michael Frede, eds. *The Original Sceptics: A Controversy.* Indianapolis: Hackett, 1998.

Burson, Jeffrey D. "Abdication of Legitimate Heirs: The Use and Abuse of Locke in the Jesuit *Journal de Trévoux* and the Origins of Counter-Enlightenment, 1737–1767." *Studies on Voltaire and the Eighteenth Century* 7 (2005): 297–327.

———. "Claude G. Buffier and the Maturation of the Jesuit Synthesis in the Age of Enlightenment." *Intellectual History Review* 21, no. 4 (2011): 449–72.

———. *The Culture of Enlightening and the Entangled Life of Abbé Claude Yvon.* Notre Dame: University of Notre Dame Press, forthcoming.

———. "The Crystallization of Counter-Enlightenment and Philosophe Identities: Theological Controversy and Catholic Enlightenment in Pre-Revolutionary France." *Church History* 77, no. 4 (2008): 955–1002.

———. *The Rise and Fall of Theological Enlightenment: Jean-Martin de Prades and Ideological Polarization in Eighteenth-Century France.* Notre Dame: University of Notre Dame Press, 2010.

———. "Vitalistic Materialism and Universal Histories of Philosophy in the Contributions of Abbé Claude Yvon to the *Encyclopédie.*" *Historical Reflections* 40, no. 2 (2014): 7–33.

Burson, Jeffrey D., and Ulrich L. Lehrer, eds. *Enlightenment and Catholicism in Europe: A Transnational History.* Notre Dame: University of Notre Dame Press, 2014.

Carhart, Michael. *The Science of Culture in Enlightenment Germany.* Cambridge, MA: Harvard University Press, 2007.

Cassirer, Ernst. *The Philosophy of the Enlightenment.* Princeton, NJ: Princeton University Press, 1951.

Catana, Leo. "The Concept 'System of Philosophy': The Case of Jacob Brucker's Historiography of Philosophy." *History and Theory* 44, no. 1 (2005): 72–90.

———. *The Historiographical Concept "System of Philosophy": Its Origin, Nature, Influence and Legitimacy.* Leiden: Brill, 2008.

Cazes, Albert. *Pierre Bayle.* Paris: Dujarric, 1905.

Charles, Sébastien. "De l'anti-pyrrhonisme au pyrrhonisme raisonnable: Réflexions sur le scepticisme des Lumières." In *Libre pensée et littérature clandestine. Partie II: Scepticisme et anti-scepticisme au siècle des Lumières*, ed. Sébastien Charles and Gianni Paganini, 289–99. Paris: Champion, 2015.

———. Introduction to *Scepticism in the Eighteenth Century: Enlightenment, Lumières, Aufklärung*, ed. Sébastien Charles and Plínio Junqueira Smith, 1–19. Dordrecht: Springer, 2013.

Charles, Sébastien, and Plinio Junqueira Smith, eds. *Scepticism in the Eighteenth Century: Enlightenment, Lumières, Aufklärung.* Dordrecht: Springer, 2013.

Charles-Daubert, Françoise. *Les libertins érudits en France au XVIIe siècle.* Paris: Presses Universitaires de France, 1998.

Charrak, André. *Empirisme et métaphysique: L'essai sur l'origine des connaissances humaines de Condillac.* Paris: Vrin, 2003.

Charron, Jean. *The "Wisdom" of Pierre Charron: An Original and Orthodox Code of Morality*. Chapel Hill: University of North Carolina Press, 1961.

Chartier, Roger. *The Cultural Origins of the French Revolution*. Trans. Lydia Cochrane. Durham, NC: Duke University Press, 1991.

Clark, Jonathan. "'God' and 'The Enlightenment': The Divine Attributes and the Question of Categories in British Discourse." In *God in the Enlightenment*, ed. William J. Bulman and Robert G. Ingram, 215–35. Oxford: Oxford University Press, 2016.

———. "Predestination and Progress: Or, Did the Enlightenment Fail?" *Albion: A Quarterly Journal Concerned with British Studies* 35, no. 4 (2003): 559–89.

Clarke, Desmond. "Descartes' Philosophy of Science and the Scientific Revolution." In *The Cambridge Companion to Descartes*, ed. John Cottingham, 258–85. Cambridge: Cambridge University Press, 2012.

———. *Occult Powers and Hypotheses: Cartesian Natural Philosophy under Louis XVI*. New York: Oxford University Press, 1989.

Cohen, I. Bernard. "A Guide to Newton's Principia." In *The Principia: Mathematical Principles of Natural Philosophy*, by Isaac Newton, ed. and trans. I. Bernard Cohen and A. Whitman, 1–370. Berkeley: University of California Press, 1999.

———. *Introduction to Newton's "Principia."* Cambridge: Cambridge University Press, 1971.

———. *The Newtonian Revolution: With Illustrations of the Transformation of Scientific Ideas*. Cambridge: Cambridge University Press, 1980.

———. "The Review of the First Edition of Newton's Principia in the *Acta Eruditorum*, with Notes on the Other Reviews." In *The Investigation of Difficult Things: Essays on Newton and the History of the Exact Sciences*, ed. P. M. Hartman and Alan E. Shapiro, 323–53. Cambridge: Cambridge University Press, 1992.

Correard, Nicolas. "Reasonable Scepticism in the French Enlightenment: Some Connections between Jean-Baptiste Boyer d'Argens, Louis de Beausobre, and Voltaire." In *Scepticism in the Eighteenth Century: Enlightenment, Lumières, Aufklärung*, ed. Sébastien Charles and Plínio Junqueira Smith, 173–88. Dordrecht: Springer, 2013.

Crampe-Casnabet, Michèle. "Les articles 'Âme' dans l'*Encyclopédie*." *Recherches sur Diderot et sur l'Encyclopédie* 25 (1998): 91–99.

Curley, Edwin M. *Behind the Geometrical Method: A Reading of Spinoza's Ethics*. Princeton, NJ: Princeton University Press, 1988.

———. *Spinoza's Metaphysics: An Essay in Interpretation*. Cambridge, MA: Harvard University Press, 1969.

Dagen, Jean. *L'histoire de l'esprit humain dans la pensée française de Fontenelle à Condorcet*. Paris: Klincksieck, 1977.

Daniel, Stephen H. "How Berkeley's Works Are Interpreted." In *George Berkeley: Religion and Science in the Age of Enlightenment*, ed. Silvia Parigi, 3–40. Dordrecht: Springer, 2010.

Daston, Lorraine. *Classical Probability in the Enlightenment*. Princeton, NJ: Princeton University Press, 1988.

Delon, Michel. "Les Lumières: Travail d'une métaphore." *Studies on Voltaire and the Eighteenth Century* 152 (1976): 527–41.

Delvolvé, Jean. *Religion, critique, et philosophie positive chez Pierre Bayle*. New York: Burt Franklin, 1971.

Desautels, Alfred. *Les Mémoires de Trévoux et le mouvement des idées au XVIIIe siècle, 1701–1734*. Rome: Institutum Historicum, 1956.

Des Guerrois, Charles. *Le président Bouhier, sa vie, ses ouvrages, et sa bibliothèque*. Paris: Ledoyen, 1855.

Dibon, Paul. *Pierre Bayle, le philosophe de Rotterdam*. Paris: Vrin, 1959.

Dijksterhuis, E. J. *The Mechanization of the World Picture*. Oxford: Oxford University Press, 1969.

Donato, Clorinda. "Jean Henri Samuel Formey's Contribution to the Encyclopédie d'Yverdon." In *Schweizer im Berlin des 18. Jahrhunderts*, ed. Martin Fontius and Helmut Holzhey, 87–98. Berlin: Akademie Verlag, 1996.

Douglas, Alexander X. *Spinoza and Dutch Cartesianism*. Oxford: Oxford University Press, 2015.

Dumas, Gustave. *Histoire du Journal de Trévoux, depuis 1701 jusqu'en 1762*. Paris: Boivin, 1936.

Dupront, Alphonse. "Livre et culture dans la société française du XVIIIe siècle (réflexions sur une enquête)." *Annales* 20, no. 5 (1965): 867–98.

Edelstein, Dan. *The Enlightenment: A Genealogy*. Chicago: University of Chicago Press, 2010.

———. *The Terror of Natural Right: Republicanism, the Cult of Nature, and the French Revolution*. Chicago: University of Chicago Press, 2009.

Ehrard, Jean, and Jacques Roger. "Deux périodiques français du 18e siècle: 'Le Journal des savants' et 'les Mémoires de Trévoux.'" In *Livre et société dans la France du XVIIIe siècle*, ed. Geneviève Bollème, Jean Ehrard, François Furet, Daniel Roche, Jacques Roger, 1:3–59. Paris: Mouton, 1965.

Emden, Christian J., and David R. Midgley, eds. *Beyond Habermas: Democracy, Knowledge, and the Public Sphere*. New York: Berghahn Books, 2013.

Erasmus, Hendrik Johannes. *The Origins of Rome in Historiography from Petrarch to Perizonius*. Assen: Van Gorcum, 1962.

Everdell, William R. *Christian Apologetics in France, 1730–1790: The Roots of Romantic Religion*. New York: Edwin Mellen, 1987.

Fabre, Joseph. *Les pères de la Révolution de Bayle à Condorcet*. Paris: Alcan, 1910.

Feingold, Mordechai. *The Mathematicians' Apprenticeship: Science, Universities and Society in England, 1560–1640*. Cambridge: Cambridge University Press, 1984.

———. "Partnership in Glory: Newton and Locke through the Enlightenment and Beyond." In *Newton's Scientific and Philosophical Legacy*, ed. Paul B. Scheurer and G. Debrock, 291–308. Dordrecht: Kluwer Academic, 1988.

Ferrone, Vincenzo. *The Enlightenment: History of an Idea*. Trans. Elisabetta Tarantino. Princeton, NJ: Princeton University Press, 2015.

Fisher, Saul. *Pierre Gassendi's Philosophy and Science: Atomism for Empiricists*. Leiden: Brill, 2005.

Floridi, Luciano. "*Cupiditas veri vivendi*: Pierre de Villemandy's Dogmatic vs. Cicero's Sceptical Interpretation of 'Man's Desire to Know.'" *British Journal for the History of Philosophy* 3, no. 1 (1995): 29–56.

———. *Sextus Empiricus: The Transmission and Recovery of Pyrrhonism*. Oxford: Oxford University Press, 2002.

Force, Pierre. "Croire ou ne pas croire: Voltaire et le pyrrhonisme de l'histoire." In *Érudition et fiction: Troisième rencontre internationale Paul-Zumthor, Montréal, 13–15 octobre 2011*, ed. Éric Méchoulan, 57–70. Paris: Classiques Garnier, 2014.

Francis, Raymond. *Les pensées de Pascal en France de 1842 à 1942*. Paris: Librairie Nizet, 1959.

Fryde, Edmund B. *Humanism and Renaissance Historiography*. London: Continuum International, 1983.

Furet, François. "La 'librairie' du royaume de France au 18e siècle." In *Livre et société dans la France du XVIIIᵉ siècle*, ed. Geneviève Bollème, Jean Ehrard, François Furet, Daniel Roche, Jacques Roger, 1:3–32. Paris: Mouton, 1965.

Furet, François, and Wladimir Sachs. "The Growth of Literacy in France during the Eighteenth and Nineteenth Centuries." *Historical Methods Newsletter* 7, no. 3 (1974): 145–46.

Gabbey, Alan. "Newton's Mathematical Principles of Natural Philosophy: A Treatise on 'Mechanics'?" In *The Investigation of Difficult Things: Essays on Newton and the History of the Exact Sciences*, ed. P. M. Hartman and Alan E. Shapiro, 305–22. Cambridge: Cambridge University Press, 1992.

Gale, George. "On What God Chose: Perfection and God's Freedom." *Studia Leibnitiana* 8 (1976): 69–87.

Garber, Daniel. "Descartes and Experiment in the *Discourse* and *Essays*." In *Essays on the Philosophy and Science of René Descartes*, ed. Stephen Voss, 288–310. New York: Oxford University Press, 1993.

———. *Descartes' Metaphysical Physics*. Chicago: University of Chicago Press, 1992.

Garber, Daniel, John Henry, Lynn Joy, and Alan Gabbey. "New Doctrines of Body and Its Powers, Place, and Space." In *The Cambridge History of Seventeenth-Century Philosophy*, ed. Daniel Garber and Michael Ayers, 553–623. Cambridge: Cambridge University Press, 1998.

Garrard, Graeme. *Counter-Enlightenments: From the Eighteenth Century to the Present*. New York: Routledge, 2006.

———. "The Enlightenment and Its Enemies." *American Behavioral Scientist* 49, no. 5 (2006): 664–80.

Gascoigne, John. "A Reappraisal of the Role of the Universities in the Scientific Revolution." In *Reappraisals of the Scientific Revolution*, ed. David C. Lindberg and Robert S. Westman, 207–60. Cambridge: Cambridge University Press, 1990.

Gasper, Julia. *The Marquis d'Argens: A Philosophical Life*. Plymouth, UK: Lexington Books, 2014.

Gaukroger, Stephen. *The Collapse of Mechanism and the Rise of Sensibility: Science and the Shaping of Modernity*. Oxford: Oxford University Press, 2010.

———. *Descartes' System of Natural Philosophy*. Cambridge: Cambridge University Press, 2002.

———. *The Emergence of a Scientific Culture: Science and the Shaping of Modernity, 1210–1685*. Oxford: Oxford University Press, 2006.

———. "Empiricism as a Development of Experimental Natural Philosophy." In *Newton and Empiricism*, ed. Zvi Biener and Eric Schliesser, 15–38. Oxford: Oxford University Press, 2014.

Gay, Peter. *The Enlightenment: An Interpretation*. Vol. 1, *The Rise of Modern Paganism*. New York: Knopf, 1966.

———. *The Enlightenment: An Interpretation*. Vol. 2, *The Science of Freedom*. New York: Knopf, 1969.

Ginzburg, Carlo. "Checking the Evidence: The Judge and the Historian." *Critical Inquiry* 18, no. 1 (1991): 79–92.

Giocanti, Sylvia. "La Mothe Le Vayer: Modes de diversion sceptique." In *Libertinage et philosophie au XVIIe siècle*, ed. Antony McKenna and Pierre-François Moreau, 2:32–48. Saint-Etienne: Université de Saint-Etienne, 1997.

Goldgar, Anne. *Impolite Learning: Conduct and Community in the Republic of Letters*. New Haven, CT: Yale University Press, 1995.

Goodman, Dena. *The Republic of Letters: The Cultural History of the French Enlightenment*. Ithaca, NY: Cornell University Press, 1996.

Gouraud, Charles. *Histoire du calcul des probabilités depuis ses origines jusqu'à nos jours*. Paris: Duraud, 1848.

Gowing, Ronald. *Roger Côtes: Natural Philosopher*. Cambridge: Cambridge University Press, 1983.

Grafton, Anthony. *Defenders of the Text: The Traditions of Scholarship in an Age of Science, 1450–1800*. Cambridge, MA: Harvard University Press, 1991.

———. "Jean Hardouin: The Antiquary as Pariah." *Journal of the Warburg and Courtauld Institutes* 62 (1999): 241–67.

———. *What Was History? The Art of History in Early Modern Europe*. Cambridge: Cambridge University Press, 2007.

Gregory, Tullio. *Genèse de la raison classique de Charron à Descartes*. Paris: Presses Universitaires de France, 2000.

Grell, Chantal. "Le vertige du pyrrhonisme: Hardouin face à l'histoire." In *The Return of Scepticism: From Hobbes and Descartes to Bayle*, ed. Gianni Paganini, 363–74. Dordrecht: Kluwer Academic, 2003.

Grendler, Paul Friedrich. *The Universities of the Italian Renaissance*. Baltimore: Johns Hopkins University Press, 2004.

Grieder, Josephine. "Orthodox and Paradox: The Structure of Candide." *French Review* 57, no. 4 (1984): 485–92.

Grote, Simon. "Review Essay: Religion and Enlightenment." *Journal of the History of Ideas* 75, no. 1 (2014): 137–60.

Habermas, Jürgen. "Modernity: An Unfinished Project." In *Habermas and the Unfinished Project of Modernity: Critical Essays on the Philosophical Discourse of Modernity*, ed. Maurizio Passerin d'Entrèves and Seyla Benhabib, 38–55. Cambridge, MA: MIT Press, 1997.

———. *The Structural Transformation of the Public Sphere: An Inquiry into a Category of Bourgeois Society*. Trans. Thomas Burger. Cambridge, MA: MIT Press, 1989.

Hagengruber, Ruth. "Emilie Du Châtelet between Leibniz and Newton: The Transformation of Metaphysics." In *Emilie Du Châtelet between Leibniz and Newton*, ed. Ruth Hagengruber, 1–59. Dordrecht: Springer, 2012.

Häseler, Jens. "Formey et Crousaz, ou comment fallait-il combattre le scepticisme?" In *The Return of Scepticism: From Hobbes and Descartes to Bayle*, ed. Gianni Paganini, 449–61. Dordrecht: Kluwer Academic, 2003.

———. "Succès et refus des positions de Crousaz dans le refuge Huguenot." *Revue de théologie et de philosophie* 136, no. 1 (2004): 57–66.

Haskell, Francis. *History and Its Images: Art and the Interpretation of the Past.* New Haven, CT: Yale University Press, 1993.

Hatfield, Gary. "Epistemology." In *Encyclopedia of the Enlightenment*, ed. Alan Charles Kors, 2:10–20. Oxford: Oxford University Press, 2003.

Hattab, Helen. *Descartes on Forms and Mechanisms.* Cambridge: Cambridge University Press, 2009.

Hazard, Paul. *La crise de la conscience européenne, 1680–1715.* Paris: Boivin, 1935.

Hefele, Karl Joseph, ed. *Histoire des conciles d'après les documents originaux.* Trans. Henri Leclercq. 11 vols. Paris: Letouzey et Ané, 1907–52.

Hickson, Michael W. "The Message of Bayle's Last Title: Providence and Toleration in the *Entretiens de Maxime et de Thémiste*." *Journal of the History of Ideas* 74, no. 4 (2010): 547–67.

———. "Theodicy and Toleration in Bayle's *Dictionary*." *Journal of the History of Philosophy* 51, no. 1 (2013): 49–73.

Hickson, Michael W., and Thomas Lennon. "The Real Significance of Bayle's Authorship of the *Avis*." *British Journal for the History of Philosophy* 17, no. 1 (2009): 191–205.

Hiley, David R. "The Deep Challenge of Pyrrhonian Scepticism." *Journal of the History of Philosophy* 25, no. 2 (1987): 185–213.

Hill, Jonathan. *Faith in the Age of Reason: The Enlightenment from Galileo to Kant.* Oxford: Lion Books, 2004.

Himmelfarb, Gertrude. *The Roads to Modernity: The British, French, and American Enlightenments.* New York: Knopf, 2004.

Hine, Ellen McNiven. *A Critical Study of Condillac's "Traité des systèmes."* The Hague: Nijhoff, 1979.

Hirschi, Caspar. "Compiler into Genius: The Transformation of Dictionary Writers in Eighteenth Century France and England." In *Scholars in Action: The Practice of Knowledge and the Figure of the Savant in the 18th Century*, ed. André Holenstein, Hubert Steinke, and Martin Stuber, 1:145–72. Leiden: Brill, 2013.

Horkheimer, Max, and Theodor Adorno. *Dialectic of Enlightenment.* Trans. John Cumming. New York: Herder & Herder, 1972.

Horowitz, Maryanne Cline. "Pierre Charron's View of the Source of Wisdom." *Journal of the History of Philosophy* 9 (1971): 443–57.

Hunt, Lynn. *Inventing Human Rights: A History.* New York: Norton, 2007.

Hunt, Lynn, and Margaret Jacob. "Enlightenment Studies." In *Encyclopedia of the Enlightenment*, ed. Alan Charles Kors, 1:418–30. Oxford: Oxford University Press, 2003.

Hutchison, Ross. *Locke in France, 1688–1734.* Oxford: Voltaire Foundation, 1991.

Hutton, Sarah. "Between Newton and Leibniz: Emilie Du Châtelet and Samuel Clarke." In *Emilie Du Châtelet between Leibniz and Newton*, ed. Ruth Hagengruber, 77–95. Dordrecht: Springer, 2012.

———. "Emilie Du Châtelet's *Institutions de physique* as a Document in the History of French Newtonianism." *Studies in the History and Philosophy of Science* 35 (2004): 515–31.

Israel, Jonathan. "Bayle's Double Image during the Enlightenment." In *Pierre Bayle (1647–1706), le philosophe de Rotterdam: Philosophy, Religion and Reception; Selected Papers of the Tercentenary Conference Held at Rotterdam, 7–8 December 2006*, ed. Wiep van Bunge and Hans Bots, 135–51. Leiden: Brill, 2008.

———. *Democratic Enlightenment: Philosophy, Revolution, and Human Rights 1750–1790*. Oxford: Oxford University Press, 2011.

———. *Enlightenment Contested: Philosophy, Modernity, and the Emancipation of Man, 1670–1752*. Oxford: Oxford University Press, 2006.

———. *Radical Enlightenment: Philosophy and the Making of Modernity, 1650–1750*. Oxford: Oxford University Press, 2001.

Jacob, Margaret. *Radical Enlightenment: Pantheists, Freemasons and Republicans*. London: Allen & Unwin, 1981.

Jenkinson, Sally. "Bayle and Hume on Monarchy, Scepticism, and Forms of Government." In *Monarchisms in the Age of Enlightenment: Liberty, Patriotism, and the Common Good*, ed. Hans Blom, John Christian Laursen, and Luisa Simonutti, 66–77. Toronto: University of Toronto Press, 2007.

Johnston, Elsie. *Le marquis d'Argens: Sa vie et ses œuvres*. Geneva: Slatkine, 1971.

Jolley, Nicholas. "Descartes and the Action of Body on Mind." *Studia Leibnitiana* 19, no. 1 (1987): 41–53.

Jourdain, Charles Marie. *Histoire de l'Université de Paris, au XVIIᵉ au XVIIIᵉ siècle*. Paris: Hachete, 1862.

Kappler, Emile. *Bibliographie critique de l'œuvre imprimée de Pierre Jurieu, 1637–1713*. Paris: Champion, 2002.

Klemme, Heiner, and Manfred Keuhn, eds. *The Dictionary of Eighteenth-Century German Philosophers*. http://www.oxfordreference.com/view/10.1093/acref/9780199797097.001.0001/acref-9780199797097-e-0367.

Knight, Isabel F. *The Geometric Spirit: The Abbé de Condillac and the French Enlightenment*. New Haven, CT: Yale University Press, 1968.

Kors, Alan Charles. *Atheism in France*. Vol. 1, *The Orthodox Sources of Disbelief, 1650–1729*. Princeton, NJ: Princeton University Press, 1991.

———. *D'Holbach's Coterie: An Enlightenment in Paris*. Princeton, NJ: Princeton University Press, 1976.

———. *Epicureans and Atheists in France, 1650–1729*. Cambridge: Cambridge University Press, 2016.

———. *Naturalism and Unbelief in France, 1650–1729*. Cambridge: Cambridge University Press, 2016.

Kors, Alan Charles, and Paul J. Korshin, eds. *Anticipations of the Enlightenment in England, France, and Germany*. Philadelphia: University of Pennsylvania Press, 1987.

Koyré, Alexandre. *The Astronomical Revolution: Copernicus, Kepler, Borelli*. Trans. R. E. W. Maddison. Paris: Hermann, 1973.

Krauss, Werner. *Cartaud de la Villate: Ein Beitrag zur Entstehung des geschichtlichen Weltbildes in der französischen Frühaufklärung*. 2 vols. Berlin: Akademie Verlag, 1960.

Labrousse, Elisabeth. *Bayle*. Trans. Denys Potts. Oxford: Oxford University Press, 1983.

———. *Pierre Bayle*. Vol. 1, *Du pays de Foix à la cité d'Erasme*. The Hague: Nijhoff, 1963.

———. *Pierre Bayle*. Vol. 2, *Hétérodoxie et rigorisme*. The Hague: Nijhoff, 1964.

———. *Pierre Bayle et l'instrument critique*. Paris: Seghers, 1965.

———. "Reading Pierre Bayle in Paris." In *Anticipations of the Enlightenment in England, France, and Germany*, ed. Alan Charles Kors and Paul J. Korshin, 7–16. Philadelphia: University of Pennsylvania Press, 1987.

La Harpe, Jacqueline Ellen Violette de. *Jean-Pierre de Crousaz (1663–1750) et le conflit des idées au siècle des lumières*. Berkeley: University of California Press, 1955.

Lamy, Jérôme. "La République des Lettres et la structuration des savoirs à l'époque moderne." *Littératures* 67 (2012): 91–106.

Larmore, Charles. "Descartes' Empirical Epistemology." In *Descartes: Philosophy, Mathematics and Physics*, ed. Stephen Gaukroger, 6–22. Sussex: Harvester, 1980.

Laursen, John Christian. "The Berlin Academy." In *The Columbia History of Western Philosophy*, ed. Richard H. Popkin, 490–94. New York: Columbia University Press, 1999.

———. *The Politics of Skepticism in the Ancients, Montaigne, Hume, and Kant*. Leiden: Brill, 1992.

———. "Skepticism against Reason in Pierre Bayle's Theory of Toleration." In *Pyrrhonism in Ancient, Modern, and Contemporary Philosophy*, ed. Diego E. Machuca, 131–44. Dordrecht: Springer, 2001.

———. "Swiss Anti-Skeptics in Berlin." In *Schweizer im Berlin des 18. Jahrhunderts*, ed. Martin Fontius and Helmut Holzhey, 261–81. Berlin: Akademie Verlag, 1996.

———. "Tame Skeptics at the Prussian Academy." In *Libertinage et philosophie au XVIIᵉ siècle*, ed. Antony McKenna and Pierre-François Moreau, 12:221–30. Saint-Etienne: Université de Saint-Etienne, 2010.

———. "Temporizing after Bayle: Isaac de Beausobre and the Manicheans." In *The Berlin Refuge, 1680–1780: Learning and Science in European Context*, ed. Sandra Richter, Martin Mulsow, and Lutz Danneberg, 89–110. Leiden: Brill, 2003.

Laursen, John Christian, and Richard Popkin. "Hume in the Prussian Academy: Jean-Bernard Mérian's 'On the Phenomenalism of David Hume.'" *Hume Studies* 23, no. 1 (1997): 153–91.

Lehner, Ulrich L. *Enlightened Monks: The German Benedictines, 1740–1803*. Oxford: Oxford University Press, 2011.

———. "What is 'Catholic Enlightenment'?" *History Compass* 8, no. 2 (2010): 166–78.

Lehner, Ulrich L., and Michael Printy, eds. *A Companion to the Catholic Enlightenment in Europe*. Leiden: Brill, 2010.

Lennon, Thomas M. "Did Bayle Read Saint-Evremond?" *Journal of the History of Ideas* 63, no. 2 (2002): 225–37.

———. "Huet, Malebranche and the Birth of Skepticism." In *The Return of Scepticism: From Hobbes and Descartes to Bayle*, ed. Gianni Paganini, 149–65. Dordrecht: Kluwer Academic, 2003.

———. *Reading Bayle*. Toronto: University of Toronto Press, 1999.

———. "A Rejoinder to Mori." *Journal of the History of Ideas* 65, no. 2 (2004): 335–41.

———. "The Skepticism of Huet's *Traité philosophique de la foiblesse de l'esprit Humain*." In *Scepticisme et modernité*, ed. Marc André Bernier and Sébastien Charles, 65–75. Saint-Etienne: Université de Saint-Etienne, 2005.

Lennon, Thomas M., and Patricia Easton. *The Cartesian Empiricism of François Bayle*. New York: Garland, 1992.

Le Ru, Veronique. "Le scepticisme dans l'Encyclopédie de Diderot et de d'Alembert." *Revue de métaphysique et de morale* 65 (2010): 75–92.

———. *Voltaire newtonien: Le combat d'un philosophe pour la science.* Paris: Vuidbet, 2005.

Lescure, Adolphe Mathurin de. "Mathieu Marais: Sa vie et ses ouvrages." In *Journal et mémoires de Mathieu Marais*, ed. Adolphe Mathurin de Lescure, 1:1–102. Paris: Firmin Didot, 1864.

Levine, Alan, ed. *Early Modern Skepticism and the Origins of Toleration.* Lanham, MD: Lexington Books, 1999.

Levine, Joseph M. *The Autonomy of History: Truth and Method from Erasmus to Gibbon.* Chicago: University of Chicago Press, 1999.

Levitin, Dmitri. "From Sacred History to the History of Religion: Paganism, Judaism, and Christianity in European Historiography from Reformation to 'Enlightenment.'" *Historical Journal* 55, no. 4, (2012): 1117–60.

Liedman, Sven-Eric, ed. *The Postmodernist Critique of the Project of Enlightenment.* Amsterdam: Rodopi, 1997.

Lieshout, H. H. M. van. *The Making of Pierre Bayle's Dictionaire historique et critique.* Trans. Lynne Richards. Amsterdam: APA–Holland University Press, 2001.

Lifschitz, Avi. *Language and Enlightenment: The Berlin Debates of the Eighteenth Century.* Oxford: Oxford University Press, 2012.

Longo, Mario. "A 'Critical' History of Philosophy and the Early Enlightenment: Johann Jacob Brucker." In *Models of the History of Philosophy*, vol. 2, *From the Cartesian Age to Brucker*, ed. Gregorio Piaia and Giovanni Santinello, 477–577. Dordrecht: Springer, 2011.

Love, Ronald. *The Enlightenment.* London: Greenwood, 2008.

Luce, Arthur Aston. *Berkeley and Malebranche: A Study in the Origins of Berkeley's Thought.* London: Oxford University Press, 1934.

Luhmann, Niklas. *Art as a Social System.* Trans. Eva Knodt. Stanford, CA: Stanford University Press, 2000.

Lüthy, Christoph, John E. Murdoch, and William R. Newman, eds. *Late Medieval and Early Modern Corpuscular Matter Theories.* Leiden: Brill, 2001.

MacKenzie, Ann Wilbur. "The Reconfiguration of Sensory Experience." In *Reason, Will, and Sensation: Studies in Descartes's Metaphysics*, ed. John Cottingham, 251–72. Oxford: Clarendon, 1994.

Magdelaine, Michelle, Maria-Cristina Pitassi, Ruth Whelan, and Antony McKenna, eds. *De l'humanisme aux Lumières, Bayle et le protestantisme: Mélanges en l'honneur d'Elisabeth Labrousse.* Paris: Universitas, 1996.

Maglo, Koffi. "The Reception of Newton's Gravitational Theory by Huygens, Varignon, and Maupertuis: How Normal Science May Be Revolutionary." *Perspectives on Science* 11, no. 2 (2003): 135–69.

Mah, Harold. "Phantasies of the Public Sphere: Rethinking the Habermas of Historians." *Journal of Modern History* 72, no. 1 (2000): 153–82.

Malbreil, Germain. "Les droits de la raison et de la foi, la dissociation de la raison, la métamorphose de la foi, selon Pierre-Daniel Huet." *Dix-Septième Siècle* 37, no. 2 (1985): 119–34.

Malherbe, Michel. "Hume's Reception in France." In *Receptions of David Hume in Europe*, ed. Peter Jones, 43–97. London: Continuum, 2005.

Marcil-Lacoste, Louise. *Claude Buffier and Thomas Reid: Two Common Sense Philosophers*. Kingston: McGill-Queen's University Press, 1982.

Marcu, Eva D. "Un encyclopédiste oublié: Formey." *Revue d'histoire littéraire de la France* 53 (1953): 298–305.

———. "Formey and the Enlightenment." PhD diss., Columbia University, 1952.

Margival, Henri. *Essai sur Richard Simon et la critique biblique au XVIIᵉ siècle*. Paris: Maillet, 1900.

Marsak, Leonard M. "Bernard de Fontenelle: The Idea of Science in the French Enlightenment." *Transactions of the American Philosophical Society* 49, no. 7 (1959): 1–64.

Masseau, Didier. *Les ennemis des philosophes: L'antiphilosophie au temps des lumières*. Paris: Albin Michel, 2000.

Mastrogiacomo, Elisabetta. *Libertinage et Lumières: André-François Boureau-Deslandes*. Paris: Champion, 2015.

Mates, Benson. *Skeptical Essays*. Chicago: University of Chicago Press, 1981.

Matytsin, Anton M. "'Curing' Pyrrhonian Doubt: Anti-Skeptical Rhetoric in the Early 18th Century." *Societate si politica / Society and Politics* 6, no. 1 (2012): 66–79.

———. "Fictional Letters or Real Accusations? Anonymous Correspondence in the Bayle-Jurieu Controversy." *Societate si politica / Society and Politics* 7, no. 2 (2013): 178–90.

———. "Reason and Utility in French Religious Apologetics." In *God in the Enlightenment*, ed. William J. Bulman and Robert G. Ingram, 63–82. Oxford: Oxford University Press, 2016.

Mayer, Jonathan. "Crousaz: Critique éclairée, mais peu éclairante, du scepticisme au XVIIIᵉ siècle." *Revue de théologie et de philosophie* 136, no. 1 (2004): 47–55.

Mazauric, Simone. *Fontenelle et l'invention de l'histoire des sciences à l'aube des Lumières*. Paris: Fayard, 2007.

McCracken, Charles. *Malebranche and British Philosophy*. Oxford: Clarendon, 1983.

McKenna, Antony. "L'éclaircissement sur les pyrrhoniens." In *Critique, savoir et érudition a la veille des Lumières: Le Dictionaire historique et critique de Pierre Bayle, 1647–1706 = Critical Spirit, Wisdom, and Erudition on the Eve of the Enlightenment: The Dictionnaire historique et critique of Pierre Bayle, 1647–1706*, ed. Hans Bots, 297–320. Amsterdam: APA–Holland University Press, 1998.

McKenna, Antony, and Pierre-François Moreau, eds. *Libertinage et philosophie au XVIIᵉ siècle*. 13 vols. to date. Saint-Etienne: Université de Saint-Etienne, 1996–.

McKenna, Antony, and Alain Mothu, eds. *La philosophie clandestine à l'âge classique*. Paris: Voltaire Foundation, 1997.

McKenna, Antony, and Gianni Paganini, eds. *Pierre Bayle dans la République des Lettres: Philosophie, religion, critique*. Paris: Champion, 2004.

McMahon, Darrin. *Enemies of the Enlightenment: The French Counter-Enlightenment and the Making of Modernity*. Oxford: Oxford University Press, 2001.

McManners, John. *Church and Society in Eighteenth-Century France*. Oxford: Clarendon, 1998.

Menichelli, Caterina. "Was Berkeley a Spinozist? A Historiographical Answer (1718–1751)." In *George Berkeley: Religion and Science in the Age of Enlightenment*, ed. Silvia Parigi, 171–88. Dordrecht: Springer, 2010.

Momigliano, Arnaldo. "Ancient History and the Antiquarian." In *Studies in Historiography*, 1–39. London: Weidenfeld & Nicolson, 1966.

———. *The Classical Foundations of Modern Historiography*. Berkeley: University of California Press, 1990.

———. *Essays in Ancient and Modern Historiography*. Oxford: Blackwell, 1977.

Monod, Albert. *De Pascal à Chateaubriand: Les défenseurs français du christianisme de 1670 à 1802*. Geneva: Slatkine Reprints, 1970.

Moreau, Isabelle. *"Guérir du sot": Les stratégies d'écriture des libertins à l'âge classique*. Paris: Champion, 2007.

Moreau, Pierre-François. "Les arguments sceptiques dans la lecture de l'écriture sainte." In *Le retour des philosophes antiques à l'âge classique*, vol. 2, *Le scepticisme au XVIᵉ et au XVIIᵉ siècle*, ed. Pierre-François Moreau, 382–90. Paris: Michel, 2001.

———, ed. *Le retour des philosophes antiques à l'âge classique*. Vol. 2, *Le scepticisme au XVIᵉ et au XVIIᵉ siècle*. Paris: Michel, 2001.

Mori, Gianluca. " 'L'athée spéculatif' selon Bayle: Permanence et développements d'une idée." In *De l'humanisme aux Lumières, Bayle et le protestantisme: Mélanges en l'honneur d'Elisabeth Labrousse*, ed. Michelle Magdelaine, Maria-Cristina Pitassi, Ruth Whelan, and Antony McKenna, 595–609. Paris: Universitas, 1996.

———. "Athéisme et philosophie chez Bayle." In *Pierre Bayle dans la République des Lettres: Philosophie, religion, critique*, ed. Antony McKenna and Gianni Paganini, 181–211. Paris: Champion, 2004.

———. *Bayle: Philosophe*. Paris: Champion, 1999.

———. "Bayle, Saint-Evremond, and Fideism: A Reply to Thomas M. Lennon." *Journal of the History of Ideas* 65, no. 2 (2004): 323–34.

———. "A Short Reply." *Journal of the History of Ideas* 65, no. 2 (2004): 343–44.

Mornet, Daniel. "Les enseignements des bibliothèques privés, 1750–1780." *Revue d'histoire littéraire de la France* 17 (1910): 449–96.

———. *Les origines intellectuelles de la Révolution française, 1715–1787*. 3d ed. Paris: Armand Colin, 1938.

Mortier, Roland. *Clartés et ombres du siècle des Lumières*. Geneva: Droz, 1969.

———. Review of *Cartaud de la Villate: Ein Beitrag zur Entstehung des geschichtlichen Weltbildes in der französischen Frühaufklärung*, by Werner Krauss. *Revue belge de philologie et d'histoire* 41, no. 2 (1963): 544–46.

Moureau, François. "L'Encyclopédie d'après les correspondants de Formey." *Recherches sur Diderot et sur l'Encyclopédie* 3 (1987): 125–45.

Muceni, Elena. "Did Mandeville Translate Bayle's Dictionnaire? A Hypothesis under Scrutiny." In *Libertinage et philosophie au XVIIᵉ siècle*, ed. Antony McKenna and Pierre-François Moreau, vol. 14 (forthcoming).

Munck, Thomas. *The Enlightenment: A Comparative Social History, 1721–1794*. London: Arnold, 2000.

Nadel, George. "The Philosophy of History before Historicism." *History and Theory* 3 (1963): 291–315.

Nadler, Steven. "Doctrines of Explanation in Late Scholasticism and in the Mechanical Philosophy." In *The Cambridge History of Seventeenth-Century Philosophy*, ed. Daniel Garber and Michael Ayers, 513–52. Cambridge: Cambridge University Press, 1998.

———. "'Whatever Is, Is in God': Substance and Things in Spinoza's Metaphysics." In *Interpreting Spinoza*, ed. Charles Huenemann, 53–70. Cambridge: Cambridge University Press, 2008.

Neto, José Raimundo Maia. "Academic Scepticism in Early Modern Philosophy." *Journal of the History of Ideas* 58, no. 2 (1997): 199–220.

———. *Academic Skepticism in Seventeenth-Century French Philosophy: The Charronian Legacy, 1601–1662*. Dordrecht: Springer, 2014.

———. "*Epoche* as Perfection: Montaigne's View of Ancient Skepticism." In *Skepticism in Renaissance and Post-Renaissance Thought*, ed. José Raimundo Maia Neto and Richard H. Popkin, 13–42. Amherst, NY: Humanity Books, 2004.

Neto, José Raimundo Maia, Gianni Paganini, and John Christian Laursen, eds. *Skepticism in the Modern Age: Building on the Work of Richard Popkin*. Leiden: Brill, 2009.

Neto, José Raimundo Maia, and Richard H. Popkin, eds. *Skepticism in Renaissance and Post-Renaissance Thought*. Amherst, NY: Humanity Books, 2004.

Niderst, Alain. *Fontenelle*. Paris: Plon, 1991.

Norman, Larry. *The Shock of the Ancient: Literature and History in Early Modern France*. Chicago: University of Chicago Press, 2011.

Northeast, Catherine M. *The Parisian Jesuits and the Enlightenment, 1701–1762*. Oxford: Voltaire Foundation, 1991.

O'Neal, John C. *The Authority of Experience: Sensationist Theory in the French Enlightenment*. University Park: Penn State University Press, 1996.

———. *Changing Minds: The Shifting Perception of Culture in Eighteenth-Century France*. Newark: University of Delaware Press, 2002.

———. "L'évolution de la notion d'expérience chez Boullier et Condillac sur la question de l'âme des bêtes." *Recherches sur Diderot et sur l'Encyclopédie* 29 (2000): 149–75.

Osborn, James Marshal. "Thomas Birch and the 'General Dictionary,' 1734–1741." *Modern Philology* 36, no. 1 (1938): 25–46.

Outram, Dorinda. *The Enlightenment*. 3d ed. Cambridge: Cambridge University Press, 2013.

Paganini, Gianni. "Bayle et les théologies philosophiques de son temps." In *Pierre Bayle (1647–1706), le Philosophe de Rotterdam: Philosophy, Religion and Reception; Selected Papers of the Tercentenary Conference Held at Rotterdam, 7–8 December 2006*, ed. Wiep van Bunge and Hans Bots, 103–20. Leiden: Brill, 2008.

———. *Les philosophies clandestines à l'âge classique*. Paris: Presses Universitaires de France, 2005.

———. "Pierre Bayle et le statut de l'athéisme sceptique." *Kriterion* 50, no. 120 (2009): 391–406.

———. "'Pyrrhonisme tout pur' ou 'circoncis'? La dynamique du scepticisme chez La Mothe Le Vayer." In *Libertinage et philosophie au XVIIe siècle*, ed. Antony McKenna and Pierre-François Moreau, 2:7–31. Saint-Etienne: Université de Saint-Etienne, 1997.

————, ed. *The Return of Scepticism: From Hobbes and Descartes to Bayle*. Dordrecht: Kluwer Academic, 2003.

————. "Le scepticisme, une 'maladie' ou un remède? Bayle, Crousaz, Hume." In *Libertinage et philosophie au XVIIᵉ siècle*, ed. Antony McKenna and Pierre-François Moreau, 12:191–206. Saint-Etienne: Université de Saint-Etienne, 2010.

————. *Skepsis: Le débat des modernes sur le scepticisme; Montaigne, Le Vayer, Campanella, Hobbes, Descartes, Bayle*. Paris: Vrin, 2008.

————. "Towards a 'Critical' Bayle: Three Recent Studies." *Eighteenth-Century Studies* 37, no. 3 (2004): 510–20.

Palmer, Ada. *Reading Lucretius in the Renaissance*. Cambridge, MA: Harvard University Press, 2014.

Palmer, R. R. *Catholics and Unbelievers in Eighteenth-Century France*. Princeton, NJ: Princeton University Press, 1939.

Pappas, John N. *Berthier's Journal de Trévoux and the Philosophes*. Geneva: Institut et Musée Voltaire, 1957.

Paul, Charles B. *Science and Immortality: The "Éloges" of the Paris Academy of Sciences (1699–1791)*. Berkeley: University of California Press, 1980.

Perinetti, Dario. "Philosophical Reflections on History." In *The Cambridge History of Eighteenth-Century Philosophy*, ed. Knud Haakonssen, 2:1107–40. Cambridge: Cambridge University Press, 2006.

————. "The Ways to Certainty." In *The Routledge Companion to Eighteenth Century Philosophy*, ed. Aaron Garrett, 265–93. London: Routledge, 2014.

Perrenoud, Marianne. *Inventaire des archives Jean-Pierre de Crousaz, 1663–1750*. Lausanne: Bibliothèque Cantonale et Universitaire, 1969.

Peterschmitt, Luc. "The 'Wise Pyrrhonism' of the Académie Royale des Sciences of Paris: Natural Light and Obscurity of Nature According to Fontenelle." In *Scepticism in the Eighteenth Century: Enlightenment, Lumières, Aufklärung*, ed. Sébastien Charles and Plínio Junqueira Smith, 77–91. Dordrecht: Springer, 2013.

Piaia, Gregorio. "A 'Critical' History of Philosophy and the Early Enlightenment: André-François Boureau-Deslandes." In *Models of the History of Philosophy*, vol. 2, *From the Cartesian Age to Brucker*, ed. Gregorio Piaia and Giovanni Santinello, 177–211. Dordrecht: Springer, 2011.

————. "The Histories of Philosophy in France in the Age of Descartes." In *Models of the History of Philosophy*, vol. 2, *From the Cartesian Age to Brucker*, ed. Gregorio Piaia and Giovanni Santinello, 3–91. Dordrecht: Springer, 2011.

————. "Philosophical Historiography in France from Bayle to Deslandes." In *Models of the History of Philosophy*, vol. 2, *From the Cartesian Age to Brucker*, ed. Gregorio Piaia and Giovanni Santinello, 166–75. Dordrecht: Springer, 2011.

Piaia, Giorgio, and Giovanni Santinello, eds. *Models of the History of Philosophy*. Vol. 2, *From Cartesian Age to Brucker*. Dordrecht: Springer, 2011.

Pierse, Siofra. "Voltaire: Polemical Possibilities of History." In *A Companion to Enlightenment Historiography*, ed. Sophie Bourgault and Robert Alan Sparling, 153–87. Leiden: Brill, 2003.

Pintard, René. *Le libertinage érudit dans la première moitié du XVIIᵉ siècle*. Paris: Boivin, 1943.

Pitassi, Maria-Cristina, ed. *Apologétique, 1680–1740: Sauvetage ou naufrage de la théologie? Actes du colloque tenu à Genève en juin 1990 sous les auspices de l'Institut d'histoire de la Réformation.* Geneva: Labor et Fides, 1991.

Pocock, J. G. A. *Barbarism and Religion.* Vol. 1, *Enlightenments of Edward Gibbon.* Cambridge: Cambridge University Press, 1999.

———. "Historiography and Enlightenment: A View of Their History." *Modern Intellectual History* 5, no. 1 (2008): 83–96.

———. "Languages and Their implications." In *Politics, Language, and Time: Essays on Political Thought and History,* 3–41. New York: Atheneum, 1971.

Popkin, Richard H. "L'abbé Foucher et le problème des qualités premières." *Bulletin de la société d'étude du XVIIᵉ siècle* 33 (1957): 633–47.

———. "Bayle's Sincerity." *New York Review of Books,* 12 October 1967. http://www.readability.com/articles/ioopfqdq.

———. "Berkeley and Pyrrhonism." *Review of Metaphysics* 5 (1951): 223–46.

———. "A Curious Feature of the French Edition of Sextus Empiricus." *Philological Quarterly* 35 (1956): 350–52.

———. "David Hume and the Pyrrhonian Controversy." *Review of Metaphysics* 6, no. 1 (1952): 65–81.

———. *The High Road to Pyrrhonism.* Ed. Richard A. Watson and James E. Force. San Diego: Austin Hill, 1980.

———. *The History of Scepticism: From Erasmus to Descartes.* Rev. ed. Assen: Van Gorcum, 1964.

———. *The History of Scepticism: From Savonarola to Bayle.* Oxford: Oxford University Press, 2003.

———. *Isaac La Peyrère (1596–1676): His Life, Work and Influence.* Leiden: Brill, 1987.

———. "New Views on the Role of Skepticism in the Enlightenment." In *Scepticism in the Enlightenment,* ed. Richard H. Popkin, Ezequiel de Olaso, and Giorgio Tonelli, 157–72. Dordrecht: Kluwer Academic, 1997. Originally published in *Modern Language Quarterly* 53, no. 3 (1992): 279–97.

———. "Samuel Sorbière's Translation of Sextus Empiricus." *Journal of the History of Ideas* 14, no. 4 (1953): 617–21.

———. "Scepticism." In *The Cambridge History of Eighteenth-Century Philosophy,* ed. Knud Haakonssen, 1:426–51. Cambridge: Cambridge University Press, 2006.

———. "Scepticism in the Enlightenment." In *Scepticism in the Enlightenment,* ed. Richard H. Popkin, Ezequiel de Olaso, and Giorgio Tonelli, 1–16. Dordrecht: Kluwer Academic, 1997. Originally published in *Studies on Voltaire and the Eighteenth Century* 26 (1963): 1321–35.

———. "Sources of Knowledge of Sextus Empiricus in Hume's Time." *Journal of the History of Ideas* 54, no. 1 (1993): 137–41.

Popkin, Richard H., Ezequiel de Olaso, and Giorgio Tonelli, eds. *Scepticism in the Enlightenment.* Dordrecht: Kluwer Academic, 1997.

Popkin, Richard H., and Charles B. Schmitt. *Scepticism from the Renaissance to the Enlightenment.* Wiesbaden: Kommission bei Otto Harrassowitz, 1987.

Popkin, Richard H., and Arie Johan Vanderjagt, eds. *Scepticism and Irreligion in the Seventeenth and Eighteenth Centuries.* Leiden: Brill, 1993.

Porter, Roy, and Mikuláš Teich, eds. *The Enlightenment in National Context*. Cambridge: Cambridge University Press, 1981.

Pucelle, Jean. "Berkeley a-t-il été influencé par Malebranche?" *Les études philosophiques* 4, no. 1 (1979): 19–38.

Puchesse, Gustave Baguenault de. *Condillac: Sa vie, sa philosophie, son influence*. Paris: Plon, 1910.

Pujol, Stéphane. "Forms and Aims of Voltairean Scepticism." In *Skepticism in the Eighteenth Century: Enlightenment, Lumières, Aufklärung*, ed. Sébastien Charles and Plínio Junqueira Smith, 189–204. Dordrecht: Springer, 2013.

Rabbe, Félix. *Étude philosophique sur l'abbé Simon Foucher*. Paris: Didier, 1867.

Rasmussen, Dennis C. *The Pragmatic Enlightenment: Recovering the Liberalism of Hume, Smith, Montesquieu, and Voltaire*. Cambridge: Cambridge University Press, 2014.

Rateau, Paul. *La question du mal chez Leibniz: Fondements et élaboration de la théodicée*. Paris: Champion, 2008.

Reill, Peter Hanns. *The German Enlightenment and the Rise of Historicism*. Berkeley: University of California Press, 1975.

———. *Vitalizing Nature in the Enlightenment*. Berkeley: University of California Press, 2005.

Rétat, Pierre. *Le Dictionnaire de Bayle et la lutte philosophique au XVIIIe siècle*. Paris: Société d'Edition "Les Belles Lettres," 1971.

Rex, Walter E. *Essays on Pierre Bayle and Religious Controversy*. The Hague: Nijhoff, 1965.

Rey, Roselyne. *Naissance et développement du vitalisme en France de la deuxième moitié du siècle à la fin du Premier Empire*. Oxford: Voltaire Foundation, 2000.

Richardson, Robert C. "The 'Scandal' of Cartesian Interactionism." *Mind* 91, no. 361 (1982): 20–37.

Riley, Patrick. "The Tolerant Skepticism of Voltaire and Diderot: Against Leibnizian Optimism and 'Wise Charity.'" In *Early Modern Skepticism and the Origins of Toleration*, ed. Alan Levine, 249–70. Lanham, MD: Lexington Books, 1999.

Riskin, Jessica. *Science in the Age of Sensibility: The Sentimental Empiricists of the French Enlightenment*. Chicago: University of Chicago Press, 2002.

Rivers, Isabel. "Biographical Dictionaries and their Uses from Bayle to Chalmers." In *Books and Their Readers in Eighteenth-Century England: New Essays*, ed. Isabel Rivers, 135–69. London: Continuum, 2003.

Robin, Jeffrey Bruce. "Religious Controversy and Historical Methodology in Pierre Bayle's *Critique générale*." MA thesis, University of Ottawa, 1994.

Rochot, Bernard. "Gassendi et le *Syntagma philosophicum*." *Revue de Synthèse* 67 (1950): 67–79.

Roger, Jacques. "La lumière et les Lumières." *Cahiers de l'Association internationale des études françaises* 20 (1968): 167–77.

Rousseau, Nicolas. *Connaissance et langage chez Condillac*. Geneva: Droz, 1986.

Rozemond, Marleen. *Descartes's Dualism*. Cambridge, MA: Harvard University Press, 1998.

Ruler, Han van. "The Shipwreck of Belief and Eternal Bliss: Philosophy and Religion in Later Dutch Cartesianism." In *The Early Enlightenment in the Dutch Republic, 1650–1750*, ed. Wiep van Bunge, 109–36. Leiden: Brill, 2003.

Ryan, Todd. *Pierre Bayle's Cartesian Metaphysics: Rediscovering Early Modern Philosophy.* New York: Routledge, 2009.

Saisselin, Remy G. "Pangloss, Martin, and the Disappearing Eighteenth Century." *Comparative Literature Studies* 2, no. 2 (1965): 161–70.

Sakellariadis, Spyros. "Descartes's Use of Empirical Data to Test Hypotheses." *Isis* 73, no. 1 (1982): 68–76.

Sauter, Michael. "The Prussian Monarchy and the Practices of Enlightenment." In *Monarchisms in the Age of Enlightenment: Liberty, Patriotism, and the Common Good,* ed. Hans Blom, John Christian Laursen, and Luisa Simonutti, 217–39. Toronto: University of Toronto Press, 2007.

Schechter, Ronald. *Obstinate Hebrews: Representations of Jews in France, 1715–1815.* Berkeley: University of California Press, 2003.

Schliesser, Eric, and George E. Smith. "Huygens's 1688 Report to the Directors of the Dutch East India Company on the Measurement of Longitude at Sea and the Evidence It Offered Against Universal Gravity." *Archive for the History of the Exact Sciences* (forthcoming).

Schmaltz, Tad M. *Radical Cartesianism: The French Reception of Descartes.* Cambridge: Cambridge University Press, 2002.

Schmidt, James. "Inventing the Enlightenment: Anti-Jacobins, British Hegelians, and the *Oxford English Dictionary.*" *Journal of the History of Ideas* 64, no. 3 (2003): 421–43.

Schmitt, Charles B. *Cicero Scepticus: A Study of the Influence of the Academica in the Renaissance.* The Hague: Nijhoff, 1972.

Schøsler, Jørn. "David-Renaud Boullier—Disciple de Locke? Quelques remarques sur la question de la matière pensante." *Studies on Voltaire and the Eighteenth Century* 323 (1994): 271–77.

Schwarzbach, Bertram Eugene. "Antidocumentalist Apologetics: Hardouin and Yeshayahu Leibowitz." *Revue de théologie et de philosophie* 115 (1983): 373–90.

Seager, William E. "Descartes and the Union of Mind and Body." *History of Philosophy Quarterly* 5, no. 2 (1988): 119–32.

Secada, Jorge. *Cartesian Metaphysics: The Scholastic Origins of Modern Philosophy.* Cambridge: Cambridge University Press, 2000.

Sgard, Jean, ed. *Condillac et les problèmes du langage.* Geneva: Slatkine, 1982.

Shank, J. B. *The Newton Wars and the Beginning of the French Enlightenment.* Chicago: University of Chicago Press, 2008.

———. Review of *Pierre Bayle (1647–1706), le philosophe de Rotterdam: Philosophy, Religion, and Reception; Selected Papers of the Tercentenary Conference Held at Rotterdam, 7–8 December 2006,* ed. Wiep van Bunge and Hans Bots. *H-France Review* 11 (2011): 1–14.

Shapiro, Barbara J. *Probability and Certainty in Seventeenth-Century England: A Study of the Relationships between Natural Science, Religion, History, Law, and Literature.* Princeton, NJ: Princeton University Press, 1983.

Sheehan, Jonathan. *The Enlightenment Bible: Translation, Scholarship, Culture.* Princeton, NJ: Princeton University Press, 2005.

Shelford, April. "Faith and Glory: Pierre-Daniel Huet and the Making of the *Demonstratio evangelica* (1679)." PhD diss., Princeton University, 1997.

————. "Thinking Geometrically in Pierre-Daniel Huet's *Demonstratio evangelica*." *Journal of the History of Ideas* 64, no. 4 (2002): 599–617.

————. *Transforming the Republic of Letters: Pierre-Daniel Huet and European Intellectual Life, 1650–1720*. Rochester, NY: University of Rochester Press, 2007.

Sina, Mario. "Le Dictionaire de Pierre Bayle à travers la correspondance de Jean Le Clerc." In *Critique, savoir et érudition a la veille des Lumières: Le Dictionaire historique et critique de Pierre Bayle, 1647–1706 = Critical Spirit, Wisdom, and Erudition on the Eve of the Enlightenment: The Dictionnaire historique et critique of Pierre Bayle, 1647–1706*, ed. Hans Bots, 217–33. Amsterdam: APA–Holland University Press, 1998.

Sommervogel, Carlos. *Table méthodique des Mémoires de Trévoux (1701–1775)*. 2 vols. Paris: Durand, 1864.

Sorkin, David. *The Religious Enlightenment: Protestants, Jews, and Catholics from London to Vienna*. Princeton, NJ: Princeton University Press, 2008.

Spector, Céline. "Les lumières avant les Lumières: Tribunal de la raison et opinion publique." In *Les Lumières, un héritage et une mission: Hommage à Jean Mondot*, ed. Nicole Pelletier and Gilbert Merlio, 53–66. Bordeaux: Presses Universitaires de Bordeaux, 2012.

Starobinski, Jean. "Sur le style philosophique de Candide." *Comparative Literature* 28, no. 3 (1976): 193–200.

Steinke, Hubert. *Irritating Experiments: Haller's Concept and the European Controversy on Irritability and Sensitivity, 1750–1790*. New York: Rodopi, 2005.

Steinmann, Jean. *Richard Simon et les origines de l'exégèse biblique*. Paris: Desclée de Brouwer, 1960.

Strauss, Leo. *Spinoza's Critique of Religion*. Trans. E. M. Sinclair. New York: Schocken Books, 1982.

Terrall, Mary. *The Man Who Flattened the Earth: Maupertuis and the Sciences in the Enlightenment*. Chicago: University of Chicago Press, 2002.

Thomson, Ann. *Bodies of Thought: Science, Religion, and the Soul in the Early Enlightenment*. Oxford: Oxford University Press, 2008.

————. "Un marginal de la république des sciences: Caspar Cuenz." *Dix-huitième siècle* 40, no. 1 (2008): 29–42.

————. *Materialism and Society in the Mid-Eighteenth Century: La Mettrie's "Discours Préliminaire."* Geneva: Droz, 1981.

————. " 'Mechanistic Materialism' vs 'Vitalistic Materialism'?" *La Lettre de la Maison française d'Oxford* 14 (2001): 22–36.

————. "Qu'est-ce qu'un manuscrit clandestin?" In *Le matérialisme du XVIIIᵉ siècle et la littérature clandestine*, ed. Olivier Bloch, 13–16. Paris: Vrin, 1982.

Tolmer, Léon. *Pierre-Daniel Huet (1630–1721), humaniste, physicien*. Bayeux: Colas, 1949.

Tolonen, Mikko. *Mandeville and Hume: Anatomists of Civil Society*. Oxford: Voltaire Foundation, 2013.

Tonelli, Giorgio. "Pierre-Jacques Changeux and Scepticism in the French Enlightenment." *Studia Leibnitiana* 6 (1974): 106–26.

————. "The 'Weakness' of Reason in the Age of Enlightenment." *Diderot Studies* 14 (1971): 217–44. Reprinted in *Scepticism in the Enlightenment*, ed. Richard H. Popkin, Ezequiel de Olaso, and Giorgio Tonelli, 35–50. Dordrecht: Kluwer Academic, 1997.

Trousson, Raymond. "Voltaire et le marquis d'Argens." *Studi francesi* 10 (1966): 226–39.

Van Kley, Dale. *The Religious Origins of the French Revolution: From Calvin to the Civil Constitution, 1560–1791.* New Haven, CT: Yale University Press, 1996.

Van Kley, Dale, and James Bradley, eds. *Religion and Politics in Enlightenment Europe.* Notre Dame, IN: University of Notre Dame Press, 2001.

Vermeir, Koen. "The Dustbin of the Republic of Letters: Pierre Bayle's '*Dictionaire*' as an Encyclopedic Palimpsest of Errors." *Journal of Early Modern Studies* 1, no. 1 (2012): 109–49.

Vidal, Fernando. *The Sciences of the Soul: The Early Modern Origins of Psychology.* Trans. Saskia Brown. Chicago: University of Chicago Press, 2011.

Vincent, Hubert. "Scepticisme et conservatisme chez Montaigne, ou qu'est-ce qu'une politique sceptique." In *Le retour des philosophes antiques à l'âge classique,* vol. 2, *Le scepticisme au XVIᵉ et au XVIIᵉ siècle,* ed. Pierre-François Moreau, 132–63. Paris: Michel, 2001.

Völkel, Markus. *"Pyrrhonismus historicus" und "fides historica": Die Entwicklung der deutschen historischen Methodologie unter dem Gesichtspunkt der historischen Skepsis.* Frankfurt: Lang, 1987.

Wade, Ira. *The Clandestine Organization and Diffusion of Philosophic Ideas in France from 1700 to 1750.* Princeton, NJ: Princeton University Press, 1938.

———. *Voltaire and Madame du Châtelet: An Essay on the Intellectual Activity at Cirey.* Princeton, NJ: Princeton University Press, 1941.

Wall, Ernestine van der. "Orthodoxy and Scepticism in the Early Dutch Enlighten-ment." In *Scepticism and Irreligion in the Seventeenth and Eighteenth Centuries,* ed. Richard H. Popkin and Arie Johan Vanderjagt, 121–41. Leiden: Brill, 1993.

Wallace, William A. *Galileo and His Sources: The Heritage of the Collegio Romano in Galileo's Science.* Princeton, NJ: Princeton University Press, 1984.

Watson, Richard A. *The Downfall of Cartesianism: A Study of Epistemological Issues in Late Seventeenth-Century Cartesianism.* The Hague: Nijhoff, 1966.

Watson, Richard A., and Marjorie Grene. *Malebranche's First and Last Critics.* Edwardsville: Southern Illinois University Press, 1995.

Weil, Françoise. *Jean Bouhier et sa correspondance.* Paris: Université Paris-Sorbonne, 1975.

Wheeler, Joseph M. *A Biographical Dictionary of Freethinkers of All Ages and Nations.* London: Progressive, 1889.

Whelan, Ruth. *The Anatomy of Superstition: A Study of the Historical Theory and Practice of Pierre Bayle.* Oxford: Voltaire Foundation, 1989.

Wilcox, Donald. *The Development of Florentine Humanist Historiography in the Fifteenth Century.* Cambridge, MA: Harvard University Press, 1969.

Wilkins, Kathleen Sonia. *A Study of the Works of Claude Buffier.* Geneva: Institut et Musée Voltaire, 1969.

Williams, Elizabeth A. *A Cultural History of Medical Vitalism in Enlightenment Montpellier.* Aldershot: Asgathe, 2003.

Wilson, Catherine. *Epicureanism at the Origins of Modernity.* Oxford: Oxford University Press, 2008.

Wokler, Robert. "The Enlightenment Project as Betrayed by Modernity." *History of European Ideas* 24, nos. 4–5 (1998): 301–13.

Wolfe, Charles T., and Michaela van Esveld. "The Material Soul: Strategies for Naturalizing the Soul in an Early Modern Epicurean Context." In *Conjunctions of Mind, Soul and Body from Plato to the Enlightenment*, ed. Danijela Kambaskovic, 371–421. Dordrecht: Springer, 2014.

Yeo, Richard R. *Encyclopaedic Visions: Scientific Dictionaries and Enlightenment Culture*. Cambridge: Cambridge University Press, 2001.

Yolton, John W. *Locke and French Materialism*. Oxford: Clarendon, 1991.

———. *Thinking Matter: Materialism in Eighteenth-Century Britain*. Minneapolis: University of Minnesota Press, 1983.

Zinsser, Judith P. *La dame d'esprit: A Biography of Madame de Châtelet*. New York: Viking, 2007.

———. "Translating Newton's 'Principia': The Marquise du Châtelet's Revision and Additions for a French Audience." *Notes and Records for the Royal Society of London* 55, no. 2 (2001): 227–45.

Zurbuchen, Simone. "Theorizing Enlightened Absolutism: The Swiss Republican Origins of Prussian Monarchism." In *Monarchisms in the Age of Enlightenment: Liberty, Patriotism, and the Common Good*, ed. Hans Blom, John Christian Laursen, and Luisa Simonutti, 240–66. Toronto: University of Toronto Press, 2007.

Page numbers in *italics* refer to figures.